Sergeant L
& His Regin.

Sergeant Lamb & His Regiments

A Recollection and History of the American War of Independence with the 9th Foot & Royal Welsh Fuzileers

An Original and Authentic Journal of Occurrences During the Late American War, from its Commencement to the Year 1783

Roger Lamb

A Brief History of Lamb's Regiments During the American War of Independence

Richard Cannon

LEONAUR

Sergeant Lamb & His Regiments
A Recollection and History of the American War of Independence with the 9th Foot &
Royal Welsh Fuzileers
An Original and Authentic Journal of Occurrences During the Late American War,
from its Commencement to the Year 1783
By Roger Lamb
A Brief History of Lamb's Regiments During the American War of Independence
By Richard Cannon

FIRST EDITION IN THIS FORM

First published in the titles
An Original and Authentic Journal of Occurrences During the Late American War,
from its Commencement to the Year 1783
and
Extracts from *The Ninth, or the East Norfolk, Regiment of Foot*
and
The History of the Twenty-Third Regiment or Royal Welsh Fusiliers

Leonaur is an imprint of Oakpast Ltd
Copyright in this form © 2023 Oakpast Ltd

ISBN: 978-1-915234-96-4 (hardcover)
ISBN: 978-1-915234-97-1 (softcover)

http://www.leonaur.com

Publisher's Notes

Contents

Preface

For many years past I have felt a strong desire to give to the public, a summary and impartial view of that momentous and interesting subject—the rise, progress, and consummation of the late American War.

From my own personal knowledge of many of the events that are herein related, and from a diligent research into many respectable authorities, I entertain a good hope, that, my *Journal* of occurrences will not be unacceptable to the judicious reader.

There are few probably to whom this work will be more interesting than to those who have borne a part in the events which are here, recorded, and whose recollection of the important transactions noticed in this volume, the author has no doubt will bear full accordance to the truth of his testimony.

It may be thought rather strange, that a work of this kind should be announced to the public so long after the occurrences took place. But I beg leave to mention, that I have not seen any impartial detail of the more minute, but no less important occurrences of the war, which, as secret springs, actuated the public movements, and which were never any further disclosed to the world, but as comprised in the general result.

The only attempt of the kind which I have seen, was a work published in America, and written by a member of Congress, but which I found to be exceedingly partial, both in its statement of facts, and views of the merits of the question to be decided.

The present work being edited at so late a period, will have this advantage, that all party views having now subsided, the author has no motive to influence his publication, but that of being an impartial annalist, relating facts which have come within his own knowledge, and which will remain as a faithful record of those transactions, unbiassed by prejudice, for the information of the future historian.

The impartial eye of posterity, will read the work, and form their opinion, unmoved by any political considerations, and having no other sensations than those arising from the feeling of regret.

R. Lamb.

October, 1809.

CHAPTER 1

General Gage Fortifies Boston Neck

As the rise and establishment of the American Republic, has given a new face to the western world, a summary view of the occurrences that led to the independence of that country, (before I enter upon my *Journal*,) will no doubt be pleasing to the reader.

The mother country, in planting her colonies in North America, had endowed them with every privilege enjoyed by her subjects at home. She left them at full liberty to govern themselves by whatever laws the wisdom of their own Provincial assemblies might think expedient, and empowered them to pursue their respective interests, but claimed the exclusive benefit of their trade, and their allegiance to the same sovereign.

The Americans, on the other hand, cherished the most tender veneration for the mother country. The name of an Englishman gave them an idea of everything that was great and estimable in human nature, and they considered the rest of mankind as barbarians, compared with the people from whom they were descended. The colonists had often experienced the protection of Britons, and witnessed their valour: as the contest (*viz*. the war of 1757, 1758, and 1759), with France had been begun on their account, they considered themselves bound to assist their protectors with zeal and fidelity.

By a succession of the most brilliant victories by sea and land, Great Britain effectually subdued the united powers of France and Spain, and acquired possession of a vast extent of territory in both the Indies. The peace of Paris, in 1763, terminated a war which exalted her to the zenith of military glory. By this treaty she remained sole mistress of North America, and her Colonies were relieved from the fear of their ambitious French neighbours.

Such was the state of the British Colonies at the conclusion of a war, in which they had been more than conquerors. Indeed, the cession of Canada had placed them in a state of perfect security from the French, and the Indians were too contemptible an enemy to excite much apprehension.

The colonies had for ages been accustomed to look to the mother country for aid against the French, from a consciousness of their inability to contend alone against that powerful nation. Protection on the one side, naturally implied obedience on the other; and her colonies continued to view Great Britain with an eye of filial reverence, while the menaces of an ambitious neighbour kept them in awe. But when the cession of the French territory in America to the British crown removed a formidable and ambitious rival from the western hemisphere, the colonists began to view their situation in another light, and to cherish ideas of their future greatness.

Their flourishing condition at this period was remarkable. Their trade had prospered in the midst of all the difficulties and distresses of a war in which they were so immediately concerned. Their population, continued on the increase, notwithstanding the ravages and depredations that had been so fiercely carried on by the French, and the native Indians in their alliance. They had many spirited and active individuals of all denominations. They were flushed with the uncommon prosperity that attended them in their commercial affairs and military transactions. Hence, they were ready for all kind of undertakings, and saw no limits to their hopes and expectations.

As they entertained the highest opinion of their valour and importance, and of the immense benefit that Great Britain derived from its connexion with them, their notions were adequately high in their own favour. They deemed themselves entitled to every kindness and indulgence which the mother country could bestow.

Although their pretensions did not amount to a perfect equality of advantages and privileges in matters of commerce, yet in those of government they thought themselves fully competent to the task of conducting their domestic concerns with little or no interference from abroad. Though willing to admit the supremacy of Great Britain, they viewed it with a suspicious eye, and with a marked desire and intent speedily to give it limitations.

The French, who have for many ages been the professed and natural enemies of Britain, had long viewed, with equal envy and apprehension, the flourishing state of the colonies in North America. No doubt at present subsists, that they began immediately after the peace of Paris to carry into execution the scheme they had formed for the separation of the British colonies from the mother country, conscious that, whilst a good understanding subsisted between Great Britain and her colonies the superiority must henceforth remain for ever on the side of Britain. It was only by their disunion that France could hope to regain the station and consequence she had formerly possessed in Europe.

The first step taken by France to secure this object was to employ her secret emissaries in spreading dissatisfaction among the British colonists; and the effects produced by her machinations were precisely such as she had intended and expected. The disposition of the inhabitants of North America began gradually to alter from that warmth of attachment to the mother country which had so particularly characterised them. They began to view her rather in the light of a sovereign than that of a parent, and to examine with a scrupulous nicety, the nature of those ties that rendered them parts of her empire.

The national debt of Great Britain had been much increased by the late war; a multitude of new taxes were levied at home, and as the quarrel originated on account of the colonies, and as they derived the principal advantages from the peace of 1763, it was thought equitable that they should contribute to the common exigencies.

In March 1764, a bill was passed in the British Parliament, laying heavy duties on all articles imported into the colonies from the French and other islands of the West Indies, and ordering those duties to be paid in specie into the exchequer of Great Britain. In the same session another bill was passed, to restrain the currency of paper money in the colonies.

These acts of the English legislature excited the surprise and displeasure of the North Americans. They sent warm and energetic remonstrances to the mother country, and laid every argument. before the ministry that ingenuity could suggest, but in vain. As they had hitherto furnished their contingent in men and money, by the authority of their representatives in the colonial assemblies, they asserted, that not being represented in the British Parliament, it could have no right to tax them. Finding, however, that all their arguments were ineffectual to remove their grievances, they formed associations to prevent the use of British manufactures, till they should obtain redress.

The animosity of the colonists was further increased by the advice which they received in 1765, that an act was passed in the British Parliament, to establish stamp duties in America, similar to those in Great Britain.

The General Assembly of Virginia was the first that openly declared against the right of Britain to lay taxes on America. Of this assembly Washington was a member. He most zealously opposed what he considered an encroachment on the liberties of his countrymen. Upon reading the resolutions which were then passed in that assembly, the boldness and novelty affected one of the members to such a degree, that he cried out, "Treason!" "Treason!"

These Resolutions were nevertheless well received by the people, and immediately forwarded to the other provinces. They circulated extensively, and gave a spring to all the discontented. Till they appeared, most were of opinion, that the act would be quietly adopted. Murmurs indeed were common, but they seemed to be such as would die away. The countenance of so respectable a colony as Virginia, confirmed the wavering, and emboldened the timid. Opposition to the stamp act, from that period, assumed a bolder face, and the flame spread from breast to breast, till the conflagration became general. In the meantime, the minds of the Americans underwent a total transformation. Instead of their late peaceable and steady attachment to the British nation, they were daily advancing to the opposite extreme.

A new mode of displaying resentment against the friends of the stamp act began in Massachusetts, and was followed by other colonies. About this time a few gentlemen hung out on the limb of a large tree towards the entrance of Boston, two effigies, one designed for the stamp master and the other for a jack boot, with a head and horns peeping out at the top. Great numbers both from town and country came to see them. A spirit of enthusiasm was diffused among the spectators. In the evening the whole was cut down and carried in procession, shouting "Liberty and property for ever: no stamps."

They next pulled down a new building lately erected by Mr. Oliver, chief justice of the province; they then went to his house, before which they beheaded his effigy, and at the same time broke his windows. Eleven days after similar violence was repeated. The mob attacked the house of Mr. William Story, deputy register of the court of admiralty, broke his windows, forced into his dwelling house, destroyed the books and files belonging to the said court, and ruined a great part of his furniture.

They next proceeded to the house of Benjamin Hallowel, comptroller of the customs, where they repeated similar excesses, and drank and destroyed his liquors. They afterwards proceeded to the house of the governor, Mr. Hutchinson, and soon demolished it. They carried off his plate, furniture, and apparel, scattered or destroyed letters and other curious and useful papers, which for thirty years he had been collecting.

Similar disturbances broke out in the adjacent colonies nearly about the same time. On the 27th August, 1765, the people of Newport, in Rhode Island, exhibited three effigies, intended for Messieurs Howard, Moffat, and Johnson, in a cart, with halters about their necks, and after hanging them on a gallows for some time, cut them down, and burnt them amidst the acclamations of thousands. On the day following, the people collected at the house of Mr, Martin Howard, a lawyer, who had written in defence of the right of parliament to tax the Americans, and demolished everything that belonged to it. They proceeded to Dr. Moffat's, who in conversation had supported the same right, and made a similar devastation of his property.

In Connecticut they exhibited effigies in sundry places, and afterwards committed them to the flames.

In New York, the stamp master having resigned, the stamp papers were taken into Fort George, by Lieutenant-Governor Colden. The people disliking his political sentiments, broke open his stable, took out his coach, and carried it in triumph through the principal streets to the gallows. On one end of this they suspended the effigy of the lieutenant governor, having in his right hand a stamped bill of lading, and in the other a figure of the devil. After some time, they carried the apparatus to the gate of the fort, and from thence to the bowling green, under the muzzles of the guns and burned the whole amid the acclamations of many thousands. They went thence to Major James's house, stripped it of every article, and consumed the whole, because he was a friend to the stamp act.

The next evening the mob reassembled, and insisted on the lieutenant governor delivering the stamped papers into their hands, and threatened in case of a refusal to take them by force. After some negotiation, it was agreed that they should be delivered to the corporation, and they were deposited in the city hall. Ten boxes of the same, which came by another conveyance, were burned.

When the ship which brought the stamp papers to Philadelphia, first appeared round Gloucester Point, all the vessels in the harbour hoisted their colours half-mast high; the bells were rung muffled till evening, and every countenance added to the appearance of sincere mourning.

About two months before this, the expediency of calling a continental congress, to be composed of deputies from each of the provinces, had occurred to the people of Massachusetts. The assembly of that province passed a resolution in favour of that measure, and fixed on New York as the place, and the second Tuesday of October as the time for holding the same. Soon after they sent circular letters to the speakers of the several assemblies, requesting their concurrence. This was the first Congress held in North America.

While a variety of methods were adopted to oppose the stamp act, the first of November on which it was to commence its operation approached. This in Boston was ushered in by a funeral tolling of bells. Many shops and stores were shut. The effigies of several persons were carried about the streets in public derision, and then torn in pieces by the enraged populace.

On the same day at Portsmouth, in New Hampshire, the morning was ushered in with tolling all the bells in the town. In the course of the day, notice was given to the people to attend a funeral. A coffin neatly ornamented, and inscribed with the word "Liberty," in large letters, was carried to the grave. The funeral procession began from the state house, attended with two unbraced drums, while the inhabitants who followed the coffin were in motion, minute guns were fired and continued till the coffin arrived at the place of interment: an oration in favour of the deceased was then pronounced.

It was scarcely ended before the coffin was taken up, it having been perceived that some remains of life were left, at which the inscription was immediately altered to "Liberty revived." The bells immediately exchanged their melancholy for a joyful sound, and satisfaction appeared in every countenance. In Maryland the effigy of the stamp master, on one side of which was written, "Tyranny," on the other "Oppression," and across the breast, "D—n my country, I'll get money," was carried through the streets, from the goal to the whipping post, and from thence to the pillory. After suffering many indignities, it was first hanged and then burned.

In consequence of a petition from the new formed Congress to the king and both houses of parliament, the stamp act was repealed; to the universal joy of the colonists, and the general satisfaction of the English, whose manufactures had suffered a considerable depression in consequence of the American associations against their importation.

★★★★★★★★★★

In the course of the debate, Lord Chatham rose and with an animation which no art or study can imitate, spontaneously flowing from the consciousness of great talents, delivered his opinion on the present

14

situation of affairs in America; concluding with these words, "Let affection be the only bond of coercion. The system of policy I would earnestly exhort Great Britain to adopt, in relation to America, is happily expressed in the words of a favourite poet:

Be to her faults a little blind,
Be to her virtues very kind;
Let all her ways be unconfin'd,
And clap your padlock on her mind.—Prior.

Upon the whole, I will beg leave to tell the house in a few words, what is really my opinion. It is, that the stamp act be repealed, *absolutely, totally,* and *immediately.*"

★★★★★★★★★★

But the parliament by repealing the stamp act, did not relinquish the ideas of their right to tax the colonies, and the bill for laying a duty on tea, paper, painters' colours and glass, was passed, and sent to America in 1768. This act occasioned new discontents in the colonies, especially at Boston; and though parliament thought proper in 1770 to take off those duties, except three pence a pound on tea, yet even this trifling impost, kept alive the jealousy of the colonists, who denied the supremacy of the British legislature. The troops quartered in Boston were another cause of offence to the inhabitants, and on all occasions, they manifested an inclination to quarrel with men whom they considered inimical to their liberties.

Reciprocal insults soured the tempers, and mutual injuries embittered the minds of the opposite parties; besides some fiery spirits who thought it an indignity to have troops quartered among them, were constantly exciting the town's people to quarrel with the soldiers.

★★★★★★★★★★

Lord Chatham's state of health during the two preceding sessions, had precluded him from making any considerable parliamentary exertions, and he had rarely attended the house on any occasion, but, finding himself at this period somewhat relieved from the pressure of his complaint, he took the opportunity on the third reading of the bill, for quartering soldiers in America, to lay before the house and the public, his thoughts on it, and on American affairs in general, in a speech worthy of his distinguished talents and illustrious reputation.

"If My Lords, we take a transient view of those motives which induced the ancestors of our fellow subjects in America, to leave their native country, to encounter the innumerable difficulties of the unexplored regions of the western world, our astonishment at the present conduct of their descendants will naturally subside. There was no corner of the globe to which they would not have fled, rather than to submit to the slavish and tyrannical spirit which prevailed at that period in their native country; and viewing them in their originally forlorn, and now flourishing state, they may be cited as illustrious instances to shew what great exertions mankind will naturally make, when left to the free exercise of their own powers. Notwithstanding my intention to give my hearty negative to the question now before you, I condemn, My Lords, in the severest manner, the turbulent and unwarrantable conduct of the Americans in some instances, particularly in the late riots of Boston."

And in the conclusion of his speech, he said:

"Pass then, My Lords, instead of these harsh and severe edicts, an amnesty over their errors; by measures of lenity and affection allure them to their duty; act the part of a generous and forgiving parent. A period may arrive when this parent may stand in need of every assistance she can receive from a grateful and affectionate offspring. The welfare of this country, My Lords, has ever been my greatest joy, and under all the vicissitudes of my life, has afforded me the most pleasing consolation. Should the all disposing hand of Providence prevent me from contributing my poor and feeble aid in the day of her distress, my prayers shall be ever for her prosperity:—Length of days be in her right hand, and in her left hand, riches and honour! May her ways be ways of pleasantness, and all her paths be peace!"

★★★★★★★★★★

In the beginning of March 1770, a quarrel between the military and the townsmen of Boston took place, more serious than any of those which had preceded it. A private of the 29th Regiment, passing early on a Saturday morning along a public rope walk, was provoked by insulting words to engage a party of his comrades to attack the rope makers. The battle being indecisive, it was determined to fight it out on the Monday following. The populace being in the interim fully apprised of the intended encounter, assembled in great numbers, armed with clubs and other weapons, at the time appointed; the bells also ringing an alarm, and violent clamours of "town-born, turn out," being heard in all parts of the city.

The mob directed its course to Murray's Barracks, and dared the soldiery, by very offensive language, to combat, at the same time pelting them with snowballs, covering stones: at length retiring from the barracks, the populace were addressed in the street, by "a tall large man, in a red cloak and a white wig;" and after listening for some minutes to his harangue with great attention, they exclaimed with shouts and huzzas "for the main guard!" for which they immediately began their route in different divisions. Captain Preston, the officer on duty, on the appearance of the frantic multitude, who with oaths and execrations pressed in upon the soldiers, advancing to the very points of the bayonets, endeavoured by every effort to restrain the soldiers from violence.

But a party of the most furious of the populace, in sailors' habits, struck the guns down with their clubs, and a blow was aimed by one of them at Captain Preston. On which a confused noise of "fire!" was heard, and seven pieces were discharged, seven persons were killed and wounded. The town was immediately in commotion and nothing but the timely retreat of the troops, and the expostulation of the governor prevented the people from proceeding to open hostilities.

A few days after the whole province of Massachusetts rose in arms, and the soldiers were obliged to retire to Castle William for protection. On the removal of the troops, the ferment began to subside. Captain Preston, who commanded the main guard, with the seven soldiers who fired, were committed to jail; but after a full and fair trial, were, by a verdict worthy of the highest praise, honourably acquitted: two only excepted, who were found guilty of man slaughter.

Mr. Quincy and Mr. J. Adams, (afterwards member of the American Congress), counsel for the prisoners, who were themselves warm partisans of America, exerted their utmost ability in their defence. One of these gentlemen, addressing the jury said:—

> We must steel ourselves against prepossessions, which contaminate the fountain of justice. To your candour and impartiality, I submit the prisoners and their cause. The law, in all vicissitudes of government, fluctuations of passion, or flights of enthusiasm, will preserve a steady undeviating course. To use the words of a patriot, a hero, a martyr to liberty, Algernon Sidney, 'tis *mens sine affectu;* without regard to persons it commands that which is good, and it punishes that which is evil; it is deaf, inexorable, inflexible. On the one hand, it is exorable to the cries and lamentations of the prisoners; on the other, it is deaf, deaf as an adder, to the clamours of the populace.

During the session of the Massachusetts assembly, in the summer of 1773, a discovery was made which added fresh fuel to the flame long since kindled in that province. The celebrated Dr. Franklin, deputy post master general of America, and agent of the house of representatives in Boston, had by some unknown means when in London, acquired possession of certain letters, written in confidence, by Governor Hutchinson, and Lieutenant Governor Oliver, to some of their friends and correspondents in England, in which they expressed themselves very freely on the situation of affairs in America, and their sentiments were such as might reasonably be expected from their local situation: they saw that eloquent orators, were successfully employed to preserve the remembrance of every disagreeable occurrence which had happened between the soldiers and the inhabitants.

In those inflammatory addresses, the blessings of liberty; the horrors of slavery; the dangers of a standing army; the rights of the colonies; and a variety of such topics were presented to the public view, under the most pleasing and alarming forms: these addresses administered fuel to the fire already kindled, and kept it burning with an incessant fame.

★★★★★★★★★★

These extravagant and exaggerated addresses are a most striking evidence of that diseased and dangerous state of the public mind, which could prompt these effusions of enthusiastic zeal, by which a resentment, scarcely short of phrenzy, was excited throughout America. All seemed to feel the influence of "the madding hour."

★★★★★★★★★★

The governor and lieutenant governor were men very respectable in their private character, and viewing these transactions passing before them, in their zeal for the re-establishment of order and tranquillity, they recommended that government should adopt more vigorous measures in support of its authority, which they beheld every day more and more disregarded.

Those letters were, by a licence which cannot be justified, even though prompted by motives the most patriotic, transmitted by Dr. Franklin to his friends at Boston, upon whom they made an impression much easier to conceive than to describe.

The assembly of Boston, thrown into a violent flame by the reading of those letters, unanimously resolved to petition the king to remove General Hutchinson and the Lieutenant Governor Oliver, for ever from the government of the province.

The petition being transmitted to the agent of the assembly, Dr. Franklin, was by him delivered to Lord Dartmouth: and on its being presented to the king, His Majesty signified his pleasure that it should be laid before him in council. Dr. Franklin was summoned in his official capacity as agent of the province in support of the petition,

Mr. Wedderburn, afterwards Lord Loughborough, and Chancellor of Great Britain, appearing as council for the defendants. Mr. Wedderburn said:—

Dr. Franklin, stands in the light of the *first mover* and *prime conductor* of this whole contrivance against His Majesty's two governors: and having by the help of his own special confidents and party leaders, first made the assembly *his* agent, in carrying on his own secret designs, he now appears before Your Lordships to give the finishing stroke to the work of his own hands. How these letters came into the possession of anyone but the right owners, is a mystery for Dr. Franklin to explain. Your Lordships know the train of mischiefs which followed the concealment.

★★★★★★★★★★

In consequence of the transmission of these letters, a duel was fought between Mr. Wheatly, brother to the correspondent of the two governors, and his friend Mr. Temple, who mutually suspected each other of being accessary to the communication of them, and in this rencounter Mr. Wheatly was dangerously wounded.

★★★★★★★★★★

After they had been left for five months to have their full operation, at length comes out a letter, which it is impossible to read without horror, expressive of the coolest and most deliberate malevolence. My Lords, what poetic fiction only had penned for the breast of a cruel African, Dr. Franklin has realised and transcribed from his own—His, too, is the language of a *Zanga*.

——*Know then 'twas I,*
I forged the letter, I disposed the picture:
I hated, I despised, and I destroy.

And he now appears before Your Lordships, wrapped up in impenetrable secrecy, to support a charge against His Majesty's governor and lieutenant governor, and expects that your lordships should advise punishing them on account of certain letters which he will not produce, and which he dares not tell how he obtained. These are the lessons taught in Dr. Franklin's school of politics. With regard to his constituents, the factious leaders at Boston, who make this complaint against their governors, if the relating of their evil doings be criminal, and tending to alienate His Majesty's affections, must not the doing of them be more so? Yet now they ask that His Majesty will gratify and reward them for doing these things, and that he will punish the governors for relating them, because they are so very bad, that it cannot but offend His Majesty to hear of them.

★★★★★★★★★★

Dr. Franklin was one of the first who employed his pen in the cause of America. Two pieces of his had about this time attracted a large share of public attention, and had an extensive influence in America. The one purported to be an edict from the King of Prussia, for taxing the inhabitants of Great Britain, as descendants of emigrants from his dominions. The other was entitled *Rules for Reducing a Great Empire to a Small One*. In both of these he endeavoured to expose the claims of Great Britain, and the proceedings of the British ministry with the severity of pungent satire. These publications had a tendency of inflaming the Americans more and more against the mother country.

★★★★★★★★★★

The disputes between Great Britain and her colonies had now existed above ten years, with intervals of tranquillity. The reservation of the duty on tea, the stationing a standing army in Massachusetts, the continuance of a board of commissioners in Boston, and the appointing the governors and judges of the province independent of the people, were the causes of that irritation which pervaded all ranks of the community.

The American controversy was now recommenced, in consequence of tea being sent to the colonies by the East India company. The Americans took measures to prevent the landing of the tea. A universal spirit of opposition animated the colonists from New Hampshire to Georgia; and the province of Massachusetts distinguished itself by the most violent and decisive proceedings. Three ships from England, freighted with tea, lay in the harbour of Boston; and the townsmen resolved to destroy it rather than suffer it to be landed. For this purpose, a number of men disguised like Mohawk Indians, on the 18th December 1773, entered the ships, and threw overboard three hundred and forty-two chests of tea, being the whole of their cargoes.

The British Government finding themselves everywhere insulted and despised, resolved to enforce their authority, and as Boston had been the principal scene of outrage, it was determined to punish that town in an exemplary manner. On the 25th of March 1774, an act was passed, called the Boston Port Bill, "to discontinue the landing and discharging, lading and shipping, of goods, wares, and merchandizes, at the town of Boston or within the harbour."

The news of the bill was received by the Bostonians with the most extravagant tokens of resentment, and during the ferment the new Governor, General Gage, arrived from England. This gentleman had been appointed on account of his being an officer of reputation, and a man esteemed by the Americans, among whom he had resided many years.

The first official act of his government was the removal of the assembly to Salem, a town seventeen miles distant from Boston.

Virginia again took the lead in a public avowal of its sentiments, and recommended to the colonies to appoint a Congress of delegates, to deliberate on the critical state of their affairs.

Meanwhile the Bostonians were not inactive. They framed an agreement, which they called a solemn *league* and *covenant,* by which the subscribers engaged in the most sacred manner, to discontinue all commercial intercourse with Great Britain till the late obnoxious acts were repealed, and the colony of Massachusetts restored to its chartered rights. Resolutions of a similar nature were entered into by the other provinces, and when General Gage attempted to counteract the covenant by a proclamation, the Americans retorted by insisting that the law allowed subjects to associate, in order to obtain redress of their grievances.

Within little more than a month after the news of the Boston Port Bill reached America, it was communicated from state to state; and a flame of discontent was kindled in almost every breast, through the widely extended provinces.

His Majesty's armed schooner, the *Gaspee,* having been stationed in Rhode Island to prevent the smuggling, for which that place was notorious, the vigilance of the officer who commanded that vessel, so enraged the people, that they boarded her at midnight, to the number of two hundred armed men, and after wounding him, and forcing him and his people to go on shore, concluded this daring exploit by burning the schooner. Though a reward of five hundred pounds, together with a pardon, if claimed by an accomplice, was offered by a proclamation for the discovering and apprehending any of the persons concerned in the atrocious act, no effectual discovery could be made.

In the month of September 1774, the General Congress of all the colonies met at Philadelphia. That body consisted of fifty-one delegates, chosen by the representatives of each province.

On the meeting of this Congress, they chose Peyton Randolph their president, and Charles Thompson their secretary. The first act of Congress was their approbation of the conduct of the Bostonians, and an exhortation to them to persevere in their opposition to government till the restoration of their charter. They avowed their allegiance to His Majesty, and drew up a petition in which they entreated him to grant them peace, liberty, and safety. After several resolutions tending to recommend unanimity to the provinces, and after having resolved that another Congress should meet in Philadelphia, on the 10th of May following, if their grievances should not be redressed, they recommended to the people the speedy nomination of new delegates, and then separated.

To relieve the distresses of the people of Boston, liberal collections were made throughout the colonies, and forwarded for the supply of their immediate distresses. Domestic manufactures were encouraged, that the wants of the inhabitants from the non-importation act might be diminished, and the greatest zeal was discovered by a large majority of the people, to comply with the determinations of the new made Congress.

The terms Whigs and Tories, for want of a better, were now introduced in America, as the distinguishing names of parties. By the former were meant those who were for making a common cause with Boston, and supporting the colonies in their oppositions to the claims of the British Government. By the latter, those who condemned the turbulent and unwarrantable conduct of their countrymen, particularly in the late riots of Boston.

Meanwhile reinforcements of British troops arrived in Boston, which increased the general disaffection to such a degree, that the people were ready to rise at a moment's warning. From inconsiderable causes love was changed into suspicion, that gradually ripened into ill will, and soon ended in hostility. The Americans now began seriously to prepare for war, embodied and trained their militia. The sound of drums and fifes everywhere saluted the ear. Parents and children, husbands and lovers, the young and the old, were possessed of the same martial spirit.

Nothing was to be seen or heard of, but the purchasing of arms and ammunition, casting of balls, and the making of all those preparations, which testify the most immediate danger and determined resistance; and to render themselves independent of foreigners for the supply of military stores, they erected mills and manufactures for gunpowder, both in Philadelphia and Virginia.

These hostile preparations which were daily made through the province, induced General Gage to fortify that neck of land which joins Boston to the mainland at Roxbury.

He also seized upon the powder which was lodged in the arsenals at Cambridge and Charlestown. This excited a most violent and universal ferment; several thousands of people assembled at Cambridge, and it was with difficulty they were restrained from marching directly to Boston, to demand a delivery of the powder, with a resolution in case of a refusal to attack the British troops.

The people thus assembled, proceeded to Lieutenant-Governor Oliver's house, and to the houses of several of the new counsellors, and obliged them to resign, and to declare that they would no more act under the laws lately enacted. In less than twenty-four hours there were upwards of thirty thousand men in arms, who marched towards Boston. Other risings of the people took place in different parts of the country, and their violence was such, that in a short time the new counsellors, the commissioners of the customs, and all who had taken an active part in favour of Great Britain, were obliged to screen themselves in Boston. Even in Boston itself the company of cadets, consisting wholly of gentlemen who used to attend the governor, disbanded themselves, and returned the standard he had, (as was the custom,) presented them with on his accession the government.

This was occasioned by his having deprived the celebrated John Hancock, afterwards president of the Congress, of his commission as colonel of the cadets.

About this time a meeting was held of the principal inhabitants of the towns adjacent to Boston. The purport of this, was publicly to renounce all obedience to the late acts of parliament, and to form an engagement to indemnify such as should be prosecuted on that account. All ranks and degrees of men were exhorted to learn the use of arms, and the receivers of the public revenues were ordered not to deliver it into the treasury, but retain it in their own hands, till the constitution should be restored, or a Provincial Congress dispose of it otherwise,

The awful moment now approached which was to involve Great Britain and her colonies in all the horrors of a civil war. In February, 1775, the Provincial Congress of Massachusetts met at Cambridge, several military institutions for the protection of the province were established, among the most remarkable of which was that of the *minute* men, A number of the most active and expert of the New England militia were selected, who were to be under obligations to turn out at a minute's warning, from which perpetual vigilance they derived their title. Jedediah Pribble, Artemus Ward, and Seth Pomeroy, were elected general officers to command those minute men, in case they should be called out to action.

Matters had now proceeded so far, that every idea of reconciliation with Great Britain was lost. The Americans, therefore, without ceremony, began to seize on the military stores and ammunition belonging to government. They first commenced at New Port, in Rhode Island, where the inhabitants carried off forty pieces of cannon, appointed for the protection of that place; and on being asked the reason of this proceeding, they replied that the people had seized them lest they should be made use of against themselves. After this, the assembly met, and resolved that ammunition and warlike stores should be purchased with the public money.

CHAPTER 2

Battle of Bunker's Hill

General Gage having been informed that a large quantity of military stores were collected at Concord, about twenty miles from Boston, sent a detachment to that place, under the command of Colonel Smith and Major Pitcairn; the general wished to prevent hostilities by depriving the Americans of the means necessary for carrying on war. With this view he determined to destroy the stores, which he knew were collected for the support of a Provincial army. Wishing to accomplish this without bloodshed, he took every precaution to effect it by surprise, and without alarming the country.

On the 18th of April, 1775, at eleven o'clock at night, the flank companies embarked at the common, landed at Phipps's farm, and proceeded with the utmost silence; every person they met was secured, in order to prevent the country from being alarmed; but notwithstanding these precautions, they soon found, by the continual firing of guns and ringing of bells, that they were discovered by the minute men. About five o'clock the next morning the British troops had reached Lexington, fifteen miles from Boston: here the militia and minute men were assembled on the green in order to oppose the British troops. Major Pitcairn, who commanded the advance guard, rode forward, and called out to them to disperse, but they still continued in a body.

At this moment some shots were fired at the British troops, from a house in that neighbourhood. The advance guard, finding they were fired upon, returned the fire, and three or four of the militia were killed on the green. The troops then proceeded to Concord, where they destroyed the stores, and engaged in a skirmish with the Provincials, in which many were killed on both sides.

In the return of the British troops from Concord to Lexington, a space of six miles, they were pursued with the utmost fury by the

Americans, who fired at them from behind stone walls, high enough to cover the assailants from the fire of men who were marching with the greatest expedition. At Lexington, the British troops were joined by a detachment under Lord Percy, with two field pieces. As the cannon were managed with the greatest skill and activity, they awed the Americans, and kept them at a greater distance, but they continued a constant, though irregular and scattered fire. The close firing from behind the walls, by good marksmen, galled the British troops very much.

A little after sunset the Royal Army reached Bunker's Hill, worn down with excessive fatigue, having marched that day near forty miles. On the next day they crossed Charlestown Ferry, and returned to Boston. The British had sixty-five killed, and one hundred and eighty wounded. Among the latter were Colonel Smith and several other British officers. The Americans had fifty killed and thirty-eight wounded.

By the nearest calculation that can be made, there were from one thousand eight hundred to two thousand troops on this service, being about half the force that was then stationed at Boston. The event sufficiently showed how ill-informed those were who had so often asserted at home, that a regiment or two could force their way through any part of the continent, and that the very sight of a grenadier's cap, would be sufficient to put an American Army to flight.

This affair at Lexington animated the courage of the Americans to the highest degree, insomuch that in a few days their army amounted to twenty thousand men. This formidable body of troops were joined by a corps from Connecticut, under General Putnam, a veteran officer. The Americans now completely blockaded the town of Boston, which however was so strongly fortified by General Gage, that they did not venture to attack it. Meanwhile Congress met at Philadelphia, on the 10th of May, 1775, and John Hancock was unanimously elected president.

★★★★★★★★★★

This gentleman was born in the province of Massachusetts Bay, in which he enjoyed a very considerable fortune. From the first disturbance in America about the Stamp Act, he took a very active part in defence of what he considered to be the rights and liberties of his native country. Most of the addresses sent from America to England, originated from his pen. He was then in his thirty-eighth year, and was married to one of the most beautiful and accomplished ladies in America, who brought him a very considerable addition to his paternal fortune.

★★★★★★★★★★

About the latter end of May, reinforcements of British troops from England arrived at Boston, under the command of Generals Howe, Burgoyne, and Clinton, whose services in the preceding war had gained them great reputation. The town of Boston stands on a peninsula, divided from Charlestown, by a river about the breadth of the Thames, at London bridge. Eastward of Charlestown, there is an eminence called Bunker's Hill, which commands the whole town of Boston.

In the night of the 16th of June, the Americans took possession of this place, and worked with such diligence and silence, that before the dawn they had nearly completed a redoubt and strong entrenchment, which extended half a mile. When they were discovered by the British troops, they were plied with an incessant cannonade from the ships and floating batteries, besides the cannon that could reach the place from Boston.

The Americans however continued their work, which they completed about noon, when a considerable body of infantry, consisting of one battalion of marines, ten companies of grenadiers, as many of light infantry, and the 5th, 38th, 43rd, 47th, and 52nd Battalions, with proper artillery, amounting in the whole to two thousand men, were landed at the foot of Bunker's Hill, under the command of Major-General Howe, and Brigadier-General Pigot, the former being appointed to attack the lines, and the latter the redoubt.

The British troops ascended the bill with the greatest intrepidity, but on their approach to the entrenchments, they were received with a discharge of cannon and musketry, that poured down a full half hour upon them like a torrent. The execution it did was terrible, insomuch, that some of the oldest officers and soldiers, declared it was the hottest service they had ever seen. General Howe, whose fortitude was remarkable on this trying occasion, stood for a few moments almost alone, the greatest part of the officers and soldiers, who stood near his person, being either killed or wounded. His coolness, firmness, and presence of mind, on this occasion cannot be too much applauded. It fully answered all the ideas, so generally entertained of the courage of his family.

★★★★★★★★★★

About seventeen years before this, General Howe's brother was killed before the French lines at Ticonderoga. This gallant officer, Colonel Howe, from the moment he landed in America, had conformed, and made his regiment conform to the kind of service which the country required. He did not suffer any under his command to encumber

27

themselves with superfluous baggage; he himself set the example and shared like a common soldier. The first to encounter danger, to endure hunger, to support fatigue. Rigid in his discipline, but easy in his manners, his officers and soldiers readily obeyed the commander, because they loved the man. General Abercrombie under whose command he acted, in writing his dispatches to government, says:

"But this success cost us very dear, not as to the loss of numbers, for we had only two officers killed, but as to consequence, His Lordship (Colonel Howe) being the first man that fell; and as he was very deservedly, universally beloved and respected throughout the whole army, it is easy to conceive the grief and consternation his untimely fall occasioned; for my part, I cannot help owning that I feel it most heavily, and lament him as sincerely."

Soon after the news of Lord Howe's death arrived in England, the following advertisement appeared in the public papers:

To the Gentlemen, Clergy, Freeholders, &c. of the Town and County of Nottingham.

As Lord Howe is now absent upon the public service, and, lieutenant-Colonel Howe is with his regiment at Louisbourg, it rests upon me to beg the favour of your votes and interest, that Lieutenant-Colonel Howe may supply the place of his late brother, as your representative in parliament.

Permit me, therefore, to implore the protection of every one of you, as the mother of him whose life has been lost in the service of his country.

Albemarle-street,   Charlotte Howe."
September 14, 1758.

An application worthy of a Roman matron.

★★★★★★★★★★

While these operations were going off at the breastwork and redoubt, the British light infantry, commanded by General Pigot, was engaged with the Americans on the left, in order that they might take their line in flank.

Though they exhibited the most undaunted courage, they met with an opposition which called for its greatest exertions. The Americans here reserved their fire till the British troops were near, and then poured it upon the light infantry, with such an incessant stream, and in so true a direction, as mowed down their ranks, and threw our troops into disorder. At this critical moment General Clinton, who arrived from Boston during the engagement, by a happy manoeuvre rallied the troops almost instantaneously, and brought them again to the charge: the works were now attacked with such fury, that the

Americans were driven beyond the Neck that leads to Charlestown.

The British troops having been annoyed by the enemy from the houses of that town, set it on fire, and in a short time the whole, consisting of about five hundred buildings, chiefly of wood, was in one great blaze. The lofty steeple of the meeting-house formed a pyramid of fire, above the rest, and struck the astonished eyes of numerous beholders with a magnificent but dreadful spectacle; thousands both within and without Boston were anxious spectators of this awful scene. In the town of Boston, the heights of every kind were covered with citizens, and such of the British troops as were not on duty.

It was greatly dreaded by the Americans that the British troops would push the advantage they had gained, and march immediately to their headquarters at Cambridge. The immediate advance of the king's troops into Cambridge, would, undoubtedly, at this critical period, have been productive of various and important advantages. The appearance of the royal forces, after such a contest would have animated their friends, discouraged their enemies, and continued, the confusion, and dispersion of the American Army. But they advanced no farther than Bunker's Hill. There they threw up works for their own security. The Provincials did the same, on Prospect Hill, in front of them. Both were guarding against an attack, and both were in a bad condition to receive one.

In this short engagement the carnage was very great, in proportion to the number of troops. The loss of the British Army amounted in killed and wounded to one thousand and fifty-four, including eighty-nine officers. The Battle of Quebec, in 1759, which gave Great Britain the province of Canada, was not so destructive to British officers as the Battle of Bunker's Hill. That the officer's suffered so much, must be imputed to their being aimed at. The generality of the Americans were good marksmen; the whole of their previous military knowledge had been derived from hunting, and the ordinary amusements of sportsmen. The dexterity which by long habit they had acquired in hitting beasts, birds, and marks, was fatally applied to the destruction of our officers. From their fall much confusion was expected; they were, therefore, particularly singled out.

Among those who were more generally regretted upon this occasion were Lieutenant-Colonel Abercrombie, and Major Pitcairn of the marines, Majors Williams and Spendlove, the last of whom died of his wounds sometime after the action. These brave officers sealed their lives with such distinguished honour as to render their loss the more sensibly felt. There was scarcely a single officer who had not some opportunity of signalising himself; the generals and field officers used the most extraordinary exertions.

According to the American account their loss did not exceed five hundred men, beside all their cannon.

This disparity of numbers may be accounted for, by their having fought behind entrenchments, which sheltered them from the fire of the British troops, and whence their marksmen could take aim with precision.

Our troops justly claimed this dear bought victory. The spirited conduct of the British officers merited and obtained great applause. On the American side, they particularly regretted the death of General Warren. Considering, however, that this was the first time they had been in actual service, it must be owned that they behaved with great resolution and bravery, and by no means merited the appellation of *cowards,* with which they were so often branded in England.

****

The following letter was written by a British soldier to his wife in England, the day after this memorable battle:

"Yesterday we had a bloody and obstinate fight, in which many were killed, and numbers wounded. I have received two balls, one in my groin, and the other near the breast. I am now so weak with the loss of blood, that I can hardly dictate these few lines, as the last tribute of my unchangeable love to you. The surgeons inform me, that three hours will be the utmost I can survive. Alas, too true was the dire presage that brooded in my mind, that we should never meet again on this side an awful eternity,

"During our passage from England to America, I gave myself up to read the bible, as it was the only book I was possessed of. The Almighty Parent of mankind was pleased to draw my heart to him, by the sweet attraction of his grace; and at the same time to enlighten my mind. There was in our regiment a corporal, whose name was Pierce, a pious man; I inquired after him, and we soon contracted a strong friendship. He was pleased to explain to me the amazing love of God, in giving his son Jesus Christ to bleed and die for mankind. He condescended to unfold to me the mystery of salvation by faith, the nature of the new birth, and the great necessity of holiness of heart and life. In short, he became my spiritual father and, under God, to him I owe all the good I am acquainted with.

"Soon after we landed, God was pleased to speak peace to my soul. Oh, the bliss, the unutterable joy that I then felt through the blood of the Lamb! How did I long to tell all the world what Jesus had done

30

for me! But how did I long, yea, burn, to have you to taste and know the love of God in Christ Jesus! I would have given all the world to have been with you, to have informed you of the pearl of great price. As we shall never meet more in this vale of tears, let me impose this last, this dying obligation upon you; and if ever I was dear to you, let me beg of you not to neglect the last advice of your departing husband.

"It is, that you give yourself up to God, read the Bible, and good books, and be often found among them who inquire after salvation. And the Lord shall guide you in his ways. O endeavour to bring up the dear little ones in the fear of God. Never fix your heart upon the vain and unsubstantial things of the world. Heaven and the love of God are the only things that demand our hearts, or at least are worthy of engrossing then.

"And you, my dear infants, though you have not the perfect knowledge of your worthless father, I beg of you to meet, me in the realms of bliss. The God that blessed Jacob and Joseph shall bless you. Seek him and he will be found of you; call upon him, and he will hear and bless you. What has the world but sin and sorrow. The rich are oppressed with wealth; and the poor are groaning for the want of that which the others are burdened with. The men in power are afflicted with holding the reins, and guiding the helm; and the governed are oppressed with imaginary evils.

"The life of a soldier is blood and cruelty, and that of a sailor, is filled with dangers and deaths. A city life is full of confusion and strife; and that of the country is loaded with toil and labour. But the evil of all evils, flows from our own sinful nature. Wherever we are, we may be happy; we have the key to bliss in our own breasts. The world itself never get made any one happy: God is the bliss and solace of a reasonable soul; and God is everywhere, and we have everywhere access to him. Learn then, my dear children, when you grow up, to seek your permanent happiness in God, through a crucified Redeemer.

"My dear wife, should the spirits of the departed have any knowledge of things here below, and at the same time, any intercourse with them, (though unseen,) how shall I rejoice to be thy guardian angel, to attend you, and smile to see you combat sin, conquer the world, and subdue the flesh. How shall I smile to meet you on the bright frontiers of heaven. These hands shall weave for you, the wreath triumphant! I first shall hail you welcome to your native mansions! I first shall guide you to the celestial city, and introduce you among the jubilant throng, who tread the streets of the New Jerusalem. I first will lead you to the sacred throne of our God, where we will together bow, transported at the feet of the ever-adorable Jesus. Then, then, will we strike our melodious harps of gold, in the most exalted strains of harmony and love. Then shall our love be consummated, refined and eternalised!

"The world recedes, it disappears
Heaven opens on my eyes, my ears
With sounds seraphic ring:
Lend, lend your wings, I mount, I fly!
Oh! Grave where is thy victory?
Oh Death! where is thy sting?"

"More would I say, but life ebbs out apace, my tongue ceases to perform its office; bright angels stand round the gory turf on which I lie, ready to escort me to the arms of my Jesus; bending saints reveal my shining crown, and beckon me away: yea, methinks, my Jesus bids me come. *Adieu! Adieu!* Dear Love.

"John Randon."

★★★★★★★★★★

During these transactions at Boston, Congress continued to act with all the vigour which its constituents had expected. They resolved on the establishment of an army, and a large paper currency for its support; and they nominated a general to the supreme command of their forces. Washington was by their unanimous vote appointed commander in chief.

I hope it will not be esteemed an unnecessary digression, to give some account of the life of this celebrated man.

In the year 1657, his grandfather together with several relatives, emigrated from England to America, and settled in the colony of Virginia, where by unremitting industry, they became opulent and respectable, and gave their name to the parish of Washington, in Westmoreland County. George Washington was born in Chotank, in the above-mentioned county, on the 11th February 1732. He received a private education, was initiated in the elements of religion, morality, and science, by a private tutor.

In the tenth year of his age, he lost his father, who died in 1742, and the patrimonial estate devolved to an elder brother. This young gentleman had been an officer in the colonial troops, sent on the expedition against Carthagena. On his return, he called the family mansion Mount Vernon, in honour of the British admiral of that name, and destined his brother George to serve in the navy.

Accordingly, in his fifteenth year, young Washington was entered as midshipman on board a British frigate, stationed on the coast of Virginia; he prepared to embark with all the alacrity of youth, but his nautical career was stopped by the interposition of maternal love. Ever obedient to an affectionate mother, young Washington relinquished his desire of going to sea; the energies of his mind were to be exerted on a more stable element.

He remained at home during four subsequent years, employed in useful and elegant studies with a pleasing alternation of business; and in the delightful fields and groves of Mount Vernon, he gradually attained a knowledge of agriculture. Rural avocations appear to have been his delight, at this early period of life; yet he afterwards convinced the world, that martial ardour animates the breast of the husbandman.

In the year 1751, he was appointed Adjutant General of the Virginia Militia; and in consequence of the death of his brother, the family mansion of Mount Vernon, together with a large estate, came into his possession. At this time the extensive boundaries and increasing population of the colony, made it expedient to form the militia corps into three divisions, and Washington in his twentieth year was appointed major. He attended to his duty as an officer, with exemplary propriety and vigilance; was indefatigable in the discipline of the troops; and generally beloved, both by the officers and privates, for his mildness and generosity.

In the year 1753, the encroachments of the French upon the western boundaries of the British colonies, excited a general alarm in Virginia, insomuch that Governor Dinwiddie deputed Washington to ascertain the truth of those rumours; he was also empowered to enter into a treaty with the Indians, and to remonstrate with the French, on the injustice of their proceedings. The distance, to the French settlement was more than four hundred miles, and one half of the rout led through a wilderness, inhabited only by Indians. He, nevertheless, set out in an uncommonly severe season, attended only by one companion. From Winchester he proceeded on foot, with his provisions on his back.

When he arrived and delivered his message, the French *commandant* refused to comply, and claimed the country as belonging to the king, his master, and declared that he should continue to seize, and send as prisoners to Canada, every Englishman that should attempt to trade on the Ohio, or any of its branches.

Before Major Washington returned, the Virginians had sent out workmen and materials to erect a fort at the conflux of the Ohio, and Monongahela. While they were engaged in this work, the French came upon them, drove them out of the country, and erected a regular fortification on the same spot. These spirited proceedings overset the schemes of the Ohio company, but its members, both in England and America, were too powerful to brook the disappointment.

It was therefore resolved to instruct the colonies to oppose with arms the encroachments of the French, on the frontiers of Virginia. It was now necessary to increase the military establishment; and early in the spring, 1754, a new regiment was raised, of which Professor Fry, of the college, was appointed Colonel, and Washington, Lieutenant Colonel. Mr. Fry died soon after the regiment was embodied, and was succeeded by Washington, who paid unremitting attention to the discipline of this new corps. He established magazines of provisions and ammunition, and opened the roads to the frontiers in order to pre-occupy that important post, at the confluence of the Monongahela and Allegany Rivers.

His regiment was to have been reinforced by a detachment of regulars, from the southern colonies, and a corps of Provincials from North Carolina and Maryland; but impelled by the urgency of the occasion, he proceeded without the expected succours in the month of May. When he ascended the Laurel Hills, fifty miles distant from the place of destination, his scouts brought him intelligence that the enemy were in possession of the posts, and soon afterwards his troops were attacked by a detachment of the French, and after a severe conflict defeated, and compelled to lay down their arms.

The conduct of Washington on this occasion was censurable; he ought to have waited for the necessary reinforcements, a junction with whom would probably have crowned his enterprise with success. His inexperience, and the active ardour of a youthful mind, may afford some palliation of his imprudence; but his rashness in this instance was so different from his subsequent prudence, that probably this inauspicious commencement of his military career was the origin of the circumspection which afterwards marked his conduct in a successful defensive war.

In the summer of 1754, the French having built several forts within the boundaries of the British settlements, an army of veterans was sent from France to support those unjustifiable encroachments. In the following year, General Braddock was sent to America, at the head of two veteran regiments from Ireland, to reduce the forts on the Ohio. On his arrival, he was joined by the independent and Provincial corps of America; but when the army was ready to march, the want of waggons for the conveyance of stores, had almost proved an insurmountable obstacle to the expedition.

In this emergency, an active American stepped forward, and removed the difficulty; this was the celebrated Benjamin Franklin, he exerted his influence so effectually with his countrymen, that in a short time he collected one hundred and fifty waggons, which proved an ample supply for the army.

As in consequence of a military regulation, "no officer, who did not derive his commission from the king, could command one who did," Washington resigned; but emulous to defend his country with distinguished zeal, he voluntarily served under General Braddock, as an extra *aide-de-camp.* That general marched against Fort du Quesne; but soon after he crossed the River Monongahela, the van division of his army was attacked by an ambuscade of French and Indians, and totally defeated. The thickness of the woods prevented both the European and Provincial troops from being able to defend themselves with effect; they could neither keep their ranks, nor charge the enemy with the bayonet, while the Indians, who were expert at bush fighting, and were widely scattered, fired on them from behind the trees, where they were concealed, and took a fatal aim. Washington had cautioned General Braddock in vain; his violent desire of conquest had made him deaf to the voice of prudence; he saw his error when too late, and bravely perished in his endeavours to save the division from destruction.

The gallant, but unfortunate general, had four horses shot under him before he fell, and almost every officer whom duty obliged to be on horseback, was either killed or wounded, except Washington. Amid this carnage, Washington, with great presence of mind, rallied the troops, and at the head of a corps of grenadiers, covered the retreat of the division, and secured their passage over the ford of Monongahela.

Anxious for the preservation of the army, and unmindful of the fatigues he had undergone, during a sultry day in July, in which he had scarcely a moment of rest, he hastened to concert measures with Colonel Dunbar, who commanded the rear division, which had not been engaged. Neither the wilderness, through which he was obliged to pass, the innumerable dangers that surrounded him in his progress, nor his exhausted state, could prevent him from pursuing the line of his duty. He travelled during the night accompanied by two guides, and reached the British camp in safety. Thus, his perseverance and wisdom saved the residue of his troops. Colonel Dunbar assumed the chief command, and with considerable difficulty effected a retreat, but was obliged to destroy his baggage, to prevent it from falling into the hands of the enemy.

Soon after this transaction, the regulation of rank, which had been considered as a grievance by the colonial officers, was changed in consequence of a spirited remonstrance from Washington; and the Governor of Virginia, rewarded the services of this brave officer, by appointing him to the command of all the troops of the colony.

The natural energy of his mind was now called into action; and his thoughts were continually employed in forming new plans for the protection of the frontiers. In the year 1757, Washington was in Fort Edward, under the command of General Webb, when Monsieur Montcalm, the French general, advanced to take Fort William Henry, on Lake George. Washington having heard of the intended attack, and being apprehensive that Lieutenant-Colonel Monro, who commanded at Fort William Henry, would not be strong enough to resist the French, eagerly interceded with his general to be sent with his regiment to the assistance of Monro, but his services were rejected, and the unfortunate commander forced to make the best terms he could with the French general, who afterwards in violation of the treaty that had been made, permitted the Indian savages to fall upon them, and strip them of everything of value. The following detail of the massacre of the English troops at Fort William Henry is thus related by Mr. Carver, then a captain in one of the Provincial regiments.

> General Webb, who commanded the English Army in North America, which was then encamped at Fort Edward, having intelligence that the French troops under M. Montcalm were making some movements towards Fort William Henry, he detached a corps of about fifteen hundred men, consisting of English and Provincials, to strengthen the garrison.

In this party the relator went as a volunteer among the latter.

> The apprehensions of the English general were not without foundation; for the day after their arrival, they saw Lake George, to which it lies contiguous, covered with an immense number of boats; and in a few hours they found their lines attacked by the French general, who had just landed with eleven thousand regulars and Canadians, and two thousand Indians. Colonel Monro, a brave officer, commanded in the fort, and had no more than two thousand three hundred men.
>
> With these he made a gallant defence, and probably would have been able at last to preserve the fort, had he been properly sup-

36

ported, and permitted to continue his efforts. On every summons to surrender sent by the French general, who offered the most reasonable terms, his answer repeatedly was, that he yet found himself in a condition to repel the most vigorous attacks his besiegers were able to make; and if he thought his present force insufficient, he could soon be supplied with a greater number from the adjacent army.

But the colonel having acquainted General Webb with his situation, and desired he would send him some fresh troops, the general dispatched a messenger to him with a letter, wherein he informed him that it was not in his power to assist him, and therefore gave him orders to surrender up the fort on the best terms he could procure. This packet fell into the hands of the French general, who immediately sent a flag of truce, desiring a conference with the governor.

They accordingly met, attended only by a small guard, in the centre between the lines. When Montcalm told the colonel that he was come in person to demand possession of the fort, as it belonged to the king his master, the colonel replied, that he knew not how that could be; nor should he surrender it up whilst it was in his power to defend it. The French general rejoined, at the same time delivering the packet into the colonel's hand, 'By this authority do I make the requisition.' The governor had no sooner read the contents of it, and was convinced that such were the orders of the commander in chief, and not to be disobeyed, than he hung his head in silence, and reluctantly entered into a negotiation.

In consideration of the gallant defence the garrison had made, they were to be permitted to march out with all the honours of war, to be allowed covered waggons to transport their baggage to Fort Edward, and a guard: to protect them from the fury of the savages.

The morning after the capitulation was signed, as soon as day broke, the whole garrison, now consisting of about two thousand men, besides women and children, were drawn up within the lines, and on the point of marching off, when a great number of the Indians gathered about, and began to plunder. The British troops at first were in hopes that this was their only view, and suffered them to proceed without opposition. Indeed, it was not in their power to make any, had they been so inclined, for though they were permitted to carry off their arms, yet they were not allowed a single round of ammunition. In these hopes, however, they were disappointed, for presently some of them began to attack the sick and wounded, when such as were not able to crawl into the ranks, notwithstanding they endeavoured to avert the fury of their enemies, by their shrieks and groans, were soon dispatched.

Here the English were fully in expectation that the disturbance would have concluded, and their little army began to move, but in a short time they saw the front division driven back, and discovered that they were entirely encircled by the savages; they expected every moment that the guard, which the French, by the articles of capitulation had agreed to allow them, would have arrived, and put an end to their apprehensions, but none appeared. The Indians now began to strip every one, without exception, of their arms and clothes, and those who made the least resistance felt the weight of their tomahawks.

Captain Carver happened to be in the rear division, but it was not long before he shared the fate of his companions. Three or four of the savages laid hold of him, and whilst some held their weapons over his head, the others soon disrobed him of his coat, waistcoat, hat, and buckles, omitting not to take from him what money he had in his pocket. As this was transacted close by the passage that led from the lines on to the plain, near which a French sentinel was posted, he ran to him and claimed his protection; but he only called him an English dog, and thrust him with violence back again into the midst of the Indians.

He now endeavoured to join a body of his own troops that were crowded together at some distance; but innumerable were the blows that were made at him, with different weapons as he passed on; luckily, however, the savages were so close together, that they could not strike at him without endangering each other; notwithstanding which, one of them found means to make a thrust at him with a spear, which grazed his side, and from another he received a wound, with the same kind of weapon, in his ankle. At length he gained the spot where his countrymen stood, and forced himself into the midst of them. But before he got thus far out of the hands of the Indians, the collar and wristbands of his shirt were all that remained of it, and his flesh was torn and scratched in many places by their savage gripes.

By this time the war hoop was given, and the Indians began to murder those that were nearest to them without distinction. It is not in the power of words to give any tolerable idea of the horrid scene that now ensued; men, women, and children, were dispatched in the most wanton and cruel manner, and immediately scalped. Many of these savages drank the blood of their victims, as it flowed warm from the fatal wound.

The English now perceived, though too late to avail them, that they were to expect no relief from the French; and that, contrary to the agreement they had so lately signed, to allow a sufficient force to protect them from these insults, they tacitly permitted them; for Captain Carver could plainly perceive the French officers walking about at some distance, discoursing together with apparent unconcern. An unprejudiced observer would be apt to conclude, that a body of ten thousand Christian troops, most Christian troops! had it in their power to prevent the massacre from becoming so general. But whatever was the cause from which it proceeded the consequences of it were dreadful, and not to be paralleled in modern history.

As the circle in which Captain Carver stood enclosed, by this time was much thinned, and death seemed to be approaching with hasty strides, it was proposed by some of the most resolute to make one vigorous effort, and endeavour to force their way through the savages, the only probable method of preserving their lives that now remained. This, however desperate, was resolved on, and about twenty of them sprung at once into the midst of them.

In a moment they were all separated, and what was the fate of Captain Carver's companions he could not learn till some months after, when he found that only six or seven of them effected their design. Intent only on his hazardous situation, he endeavoured to make his way through his savage enemies, in the best manner possible. And he has often been since astonished, when he has recollected with what composure he took, as he did, every necessary step for his preservation. Some he overturned, being at that time young and athletic, and others he passed by, dexterously avoiding their weapons; till at last two very stout chiefs, as he could distinguish by their dress, whose strength he could not resist, laid hold of him by each arm, and began to force him through the crowd.

He now resigned himself to his fate, not doubting but that they intended to dispatch him, and then to satiate their vengeance with his blood, as he found they were hurrying him towards a retired swamp, that lay at some distance. But before they had got many yards, an English gentleman of some distinction, as he could discover by his breeches, the only covering he had on, which were of fine scarlet velvet, rushed close by them. One of the Indians instantly relinquished his hold, and springing on this new object, endeavoured to seize him as his prey; but the gentleman being strong, threw him on the ground, and would probably have got away, had not he who held Captain Carver's other arm, quitted him to assist his brother.

Captain Carver seized the opportunity, and hastened away to join another party of English troops, that were yet unbroken, and stood in a body at some distance. But before he had taken many steps, he hastily cast his eye towards the gentleman, and saw the Indian's tomahawk gash into his back, and heard him utter his last groan; this added both to his speed and desperation. He had left this shocking scene but a few yards, when a fine boy about twelve years of age, that had hitherto escaped, came up to him, and begged that he would let him lay hold of him, so that he might stand some chance of getting out of the hands of the savages. Captain Carver told him that he would give him every assistance in his power, and to this purpose bid him lay hold; but in a few moments he was torn from his side, and by his shrieks he judged was soon made an end of. He could not help forgetting his own cares for a minute, to lament the fate of so young a sufferer; but it was utterly impossible for him to take any methods to prevent it.

He now got into the midst of his friends, but they were unable to afford each other any succour. As this was the division that had advanced the furthest from the fort, he thought there might be a possibility (though but a very bare one,) of his forcing a way through the outer ranks of the Indians, and getting to a neighbouring wood, which he perceived at some distance. He still encouraged to hope by the almost miraculous preservation he had already experienced. Nor were his hopes in vain, or the efforts he made ineffectual. Suffice it to say, that he reached the wood, but by the time he had penetrated a little way into it, his breath was so exhausted that he threw himself into a brake, and lay for some minutes apparently at the last gasp.

At length he recovered the power of respiration, but his apprehensions returned with all their former force, when he saw several savages pass by, probably in pursuit of him, at no very great distance. In this situation he knew not whether it was better to proceed, or endeavour to conceal himself where he lay, till night came on; fearing, however, that they would return the same way, he thought it most prudent to get farther from the dreadful scene of his past distresses. Accordingly, striking into another part of the wood, he hastened on as fast as the briars and the loss of one of his shoes would permit him; and after a slow progress of some hours, gained a hill that overlooked the plain which he had just left, from whence he could discern that the bloody storm still raged with unabated fury.

After passing three days without sustenance, and enduring the severity of the cold dews for three nights, he at length reached Fort Edward, when with proper care his body soon recovered its wonted strength, and his mind as far as the recollection of the late melancholy events would permit, its usual composure. It was computed that fifteen hundred persons were killed, or made prisoners by these savages, during this fatal day. Many of the latter were carried off by them, and never returned. A few through favourable accidents found their way back to their native country, after having experienced a long and severe captivity.

The brave Colonel Monro had hastened away soon after the confusion began, to the French camp, to endeavour to procure the guard agreed by the stipulation; but his application proving ineffectual, he remained there till General Webb sent a party of troops to demand and protect him back to Fort Edward. But these unhappy occurrences, which would probably have been prevented, had the colonel been left to pursue his own plans, together with the loss of so many brave fellows, murdered in cold blood, to whose valour he had been so lately a witness, made such an impression on his mind that he did not long survive. He died in about three months, of a broken heart, and with truth it might be said, that he was an honour to his country.

It is very remarkable, that very few of those different tribes of Indians that shared in this slaughter, ever lived to return home. The smallpox, by means of their communication with the Europeans, found its way amongst them, and made an equal havoc, to what they themselves had done. The methods they pursued on the first attack of that malignant disorder, to abate the fever attending it, rendered it fatal. Whilst their blood was in a state of fermentation, and nature was striving to throw out the peccant matter, they checked her operations, by plunging into the water; the consequence was, that they died by hundreds. The few that survived were transformed by it into hideous objects, and bore to the grave deep indented marks of this much dreaded disease. Monsieur Montcalm fell soon after, on the plains of Quebec. That the unprovoked cruelties of this commander were not approved of by the generality of his countrymen, we have since been convinced of by many proofs. One only, however, which was received from a person who was witness to it, shall at present be given. A Canadian merchant of some consideration, having heard of the surrender of the English Fort, celebrated the fortunate event with great rejoicings and hospitality, according to the custom of that country; but no sooner did the news of the massacre which ensued reach his ears, than he put an immediate stop to his festivity, and exclaimed in the severest terms against their inhuman permission, declaring at the same time, that those who had connived at it, had thereby drawn down on that part of their king's dominions the vengeance of heaven. To this he added, that he much feared that the total loss of them, would deservedly be the consequence. How truly this prediction has been verified we all know.

★★★★★★★★★★★

I was at this place in the year 1777, and many of the inhabitants recollected the dreadful circumstances which are here detailed; it is remarkable that the pond near to which the massacre was committed, is called the *Bloody Pond* to this day, R. L.

★★★★★★★★★★

In the year 1758, Washington commanded the van brigade of the army, under General Forbes, and distinguished himself by the capture of Fort du Quesne. During this successful campaign, he acquired a perfect knowledge of tactics. His frequent skirmishes with the French and Indians, in the woody regions along the frontiers, taught him vigilance and circumspection, and roused that spirit of enterprise which is ever ready to seize the crisis that leads to victory. The troops under his command were gradually inured in that most difficult kind of warfare, bush fighting, while the activity of the French, and ferocity of the Indians were overcome by his superior valour. After the enemy had been defeated in several battles, and compelled to retreat far beyond the colonial boundaries, General Forbes left a sufficient garrison in the different forts which he had captured along the banks of the Ohio, and returned with the army into winter quarters.

In the course of this decisive campaign, which restored the tranquillity and security of the middle colonies, Washington had suffered many hardships, which impaired his health. He was afflicted with an inveterate pulmonary complaint, and extremely debilitated, insomuch that in the spring of 1759, he resigned his commission, and retired to Mount Vernon.

By a due attention to regiment, in the salubrious bowers of his family retreat, he gradually recovered from his indisposition. In the year 1761, love invaded his retirement. The object of his choice was an amiable young widow, whose maiden name was Dandridge. She was descended from a reputable family, and two of her brothers were officers in the British Navy. This lady was the widow of Colonel Custis, who had left her sole executrix to his extensive possessions, and guardian to his two children.

The union of Washington with this accomplished woman (Mrs. Washington was born, 1732 and she died 1802), was productive of their mutual felicity; and as he incessantly pursued agricultural improvements, his taste embellished and enriched the fertile fields of Mount Vernon. Meanwhile, he was appointed a magistrate, a member of the assembly of the state, and a judge of the court. These honourable avocations kept the powers of his mind in a state of activity; he attended to his civil duties with exemplary propriety; and gave a convincing proof, that the simplicity of the farmer is homogeneal with the more dignified views of the senator.

CHAPTER 3

General Gage Sails for England

The moment now approached in which Washington was to relinquish those honourable civil avocations, and one of the most remarkable events recorded in history, obliged him to act a conspicuous part on the great theatre of the world.

Congress voted him as ample a salary as was in their power to bestow, but he generously declined all pecuniary emoluments. His reply to the president of Congress, on his nomination to the supreme command of the army, was in the following words:

Mr. President, though I am truly sensible of the high honour done me in this appointment, yet I feel great distress from a consciousness that my abilities and military experience may not be equal to the extensive and important trust; however, as the Congress desire it, I will enter upon the momentous duty, and exert every power I possess in their service, and in support of the glorious cause. I beg they will accept my most cordial thanks for this distinguished testimony of their approbation.

But least some unlucky event should happen, unfavourable to my reputation, I beg it may be remembered by every gentleman in the room, that I this day declare with the utmost sincerity, I do not think myself equal to the command I am honoured with.

As to pay, sir, I beg leave to assure the Congress, that as no pecuniary consideration could have tempted me to accept this arduous employment, at the expense of my domestic case and happiness, I do not wish to make any profit from it. I will keep an exact account of my expenses; those I doubt not, they will discharge, and this is all I desire.

The appointment of Washington was attended with other promotions, namely, four major-generals, one adjutant-general, and eight brigadier-generals.

1st. Major-General Artemus Ward.
2nd.   "   "   Charles Lee.
3rd.   "   "   Philip Schuyler.
4th.   "   "   Israel Putnam. (See note following).
Adjutant-General Horatio Gates.
The eight brigadiers were,

1st.   Seth Pomeroy.
2nd.   Richard Montgomery.
3rd.   David Wooster.
4th.   William Heath.
5th.   Joseph Spencer.
6th.   John Thomas.
7th.   John Sullivan.
8th.   Nathaniel Green.

★★★★★★★★★★

Note:—General Putnam, who had served with reputation under Lord Amherst, at the head of the Connecticut troops, during the last war, had long since retired to a remote farm, which he cultivated with his own hands; and when the intelligence of his appointment was notified to him, he was found like another Cincinatus, in a leathern frock and apron, occupied amongst his labourers, in fencing in his land. Without a moment's hesitation, within eighteen hours he repaired to the headquarters at Cambridge, which was little short of one hundred English miles distant.

The following anecdote is related from the life of the general by Colonel Humphries:

Soon after Mr. Putnam removed to Connecticut, the wolves, very numerous, broke into his sheep fold, and killed seventy fine sheep and goats, besides wounding many lambs and kids. This havoc was committed by a she wolf, which, with her annual whelps, had for several years infested the vicinity. The young were commonly destroyed by the vigilance of the hunters, but the old one was too sagacious to come within reach of gunshot; upon being closely pursued, she would generally fly to the western woods, and return the next winter, with another litter of whelps. This wolf, at length became such an intolerable nuisance, that Mr. Putnam entered into a combination with five of his neighbours, to hunt alternately until they could destroy her.

Two, by rotation, were to be constantly in pursuit. It was known, that having lost the toes from one of her feet, by a steel trap, she made one track shorter than another. By this vestige, the pursuers recognised, in a light snow, the rout of this pernicious animal. Having followed her to Connecticut River, and found she had turned back in a direct course towards Pomfret, they immediately returned, and by ten the next morning the blood hounds had driven her into a den, about three miles distant from the house of Mr. Putnam; the people soon collected with dogs, guns, straw, fire, and sulphur, to attack the common enemy. With this apparatus several unsuccessful efforts were made to force her from the den. The hounds came back badly wounded, and refused to return. The smoke of blazing straw had no effect. Nor did the fumes of burnt brimstone, with which the cavern was filled, compel her to quit the retirement.

Wearied with such fruitless attempts, which had brought the time to ten o'clock at night, Mr. Putnam tried once more to make his dog enter, but in vain; he proposed to his negro man to go down into the cavern, and shoot the wolf; the negro declined the hazardous service. Then it was, that his master angry at his disappointment, and declaring that he was ashamed to have a coward in his family, resolved himself to destroy the ferocious beast, lest she should escape through some unknown fissure of the rock.

His neighbours strongly remonstrated against the perilous enterprise: but he knowing that wild animals were intimidated by fire, and having provided several strips of birch bark, the only combustible material which he could obtain, that would afford light in this deep and darksome cave, he prepared for his descent. Having accordingly divested himself of his coat and waistcoat, and having a long rope fastened round his legs, by which he might be pulled back, at a concerted signal, he entered head foremost, with the blazing torch in his hand.

The aperture of the den, on the east side of a very high ledge of rocks, is about two feet square; from thence it descends obliquely fifteen feet, then running horizontally about ten more, it ascends gradually sixteen feet towards its termination. The sides of this subterraneous cavity are composed of smooth and solid rocks, which seem to have been divided from each other by an earthquake. The top and bottom are also of stone, and the entrance, in winter, being covered with ice, is exceedingly slippery: It is in no place high enough for a man to raise himself upright: nor in any part more than three feet in width.

Having groped his passage to the horizontal part of the den, the most terrifying darkness appeared in front of the dim circle of light afforded by his torch. It was silent as the house of death. None but monsters of the desert had ever before explored this solitary mansion of horror. He cautiously proceeding onward, came to the ascent, which he slowly mounted on his hands and knees, until he discovered the glaring eye-balls of the wolf, who was sitting at the extremity of the cavern. Startled at the sight of fire, she gnashed her teeth, and gave a sullen growl.

As soon as he had made the necessary discovery, he kicked the rope as a signal for pulling him out. The people, at the mouth of the den, who had listened with painful anxiety, hearing the growling of the wolf, and supposing their friend to be in the most imminent danger, drew him forth with such celerity, that his shirt was stripped over his head, and his skin severely lacerated. After he had adjusted his clothes, and loaded his gun with nine buck-shot, holding a torch in one hand, and the musket in the other, he descended a second time. When he drew nearer than before, the wolf, assuming a still more fierce and terrible appearance, howling, rolling her eyes, snapping her teeth, and dropping her head between her legs, was evidently in the attitude, and on the point of springing at him.

At the critical instant he levelled and fired at her head. Stunned with the shock, and suffocated with the smoke, he immediately found himself drawn out of the cave. But having refreshed himself, and permitted the smoke to dissipate, he went down the third time. Once more he came within sight of the wolf, who appearing very passive, he applied the torch to her nose; and perceiving her dead, he took hold of her ears, and then kicking the rope (still tied round his legs) the people above, with no small exultation, dragged them both out together.

★★★★★★★★★★

On the following day a special commission was presented to Washington, by Congress. At the same time, they resolved unanimously, "that they would maintain and assist him, and adhere to him with their lives and fortunes, in the cause of American Liberty." Instructions were also given him for his government, by which, after reciting various particulars, he was directed "to destroy or make prisoners all persons who now are, or who hereafter shall appear in arms against the good people of the colonies:" but the whole was summed up by authorising him "to order and dispose of the army under his command as might be most advantageous for obtaining the end for which it had been raised, making it his special care in discharge of the great trust committed to him, that the liberties of America received no detriment."

About the same time twelve companies of riflemen were ordered to be raised in Pennsylvania, Maryland, and Virginia. The men to the amount of one thousand four hundred and thirty, were raised and forwarded with great expedition, to the American headquarters at Cambridge.

In the beginning of July 1775, General Washington set out for the camp at Cambridge, in order to assume the command of the army.

On his way thither he was treated with every demonstration of respect, escorted by detachments of gentlemen, who had formed volunteer associations, and was honoured with public addresses of congratulation, from the Provincial Congress of New York and Massachusetts.

Our troops at this time were entrenched on Bunker's Hill, and defended by three floating batteries, in Mystic River and a twenty-gun ship below the ferry, between Boston and Charlestown. The Americans were entrenched on Winter Hill, Prospect Hill, and Roxbury, with communications by small posts over an extent of ten miles; there were also parties in several towns along the sea coast. General Ward commanded the right wing at Roxbury, General Lee the left on Prospect Hill, and the centre was commanded by General Washington.

As the American soldiers had repaired to the camp in their ordinary clothing, the hunting shirt was adopted for the sake of uniformity. At the same time, the inhabitants were recommended not to fire a gun at beast, bird, or mark, in order that they might husband their stock of powder and ball for the purpose of destroying the British troops.

The military spirit was now so high and general, that war and its preparations occupied the hands and the minds of all orders of people, throughout the provinces. Persons of fortune and family, who were not appointed officers, entered cheerfully as private men, and served with alacrity in the ranks.

The provinces of Georgia, Maryland and Pennsylvania, having now acceded to the confederacy, it from this time assumed the title of *The Thirteen United Colonies.*

In September General Gage sailed for England, and the command of the British Army devolved on General Howe. Meanwhile, the army under Washington continued the blockade of Boston so closely, as to prevent all intercourse between that town and the country.

The British troops at Boston endured the tedious blockade, with their characteristic fortitude, and suffered many inconveniences from want of necessaries of every kind.

Washington exerted his skill and activity in order to compel the British Army, either to surrender or evacuate Boston before any succours could arrive from England. On the 2nd of March 1776, he opened a battery on the west side of the town, and bombarded it. This attack was supported by a tremendous cannonade, and on the 5th another battery was opened on the eastern shore. The garrison sustained this dreadful bombardment with the greatest fortitude; it lasted fourteen days without intermission; when General Howe finding the place no longer tenable, determined, if possible, to drive the enemy from their works.

Preparations were therefore made for a most vigorous attack, on a hill called Dorchester Neck, which the Americans had fortified in such a manner, as would in all probability have rendered the enterprise next to desperate. No difficulties, however, were sufficient to damp the spirit of the general; and everything was in readiness, when a sudden storm prevented this intended exertion of British valour. Next day, upon a more close inspection of the works they were to attack, it was thought advisable to desist from the enterprise altogether. The fortifications were very strong, and extremely well provided with artillery, and besides other implements of destruction upwards of one hundred hogsheads of stones were provided to roll down upon our army as they came up; which, as the ascent was extremely steep, must have done prodigious execution.

On the 17th of March 1776, General Howe finding the town of Boston no longer tenable, resolved to embark for Halifax, and the voyage thither was both short and prosperous.

The evacuation of Boston was not interrupted by the Americans, lest our troops should set it on fire.

Thus was the long-contested town of Boston at length given up, the colony of Massachusetts's Bay, for the present freed from war, and left at liberty to adopt every measure which could tend to its future strength and security. The estates and effects of those Loyalists, or Tories, as they were then called, who accompanied General Howe, to Halifax, were ordered to be sold, and the produce applied to the public service. Some who ventured to stay behind, were brought to trial as public enemies, and betrayers of their country; and the estates of such as were found guilty, were confiscated in the same manner. But nothing occupied so much at present the minds of the people of Boston, or had so much attention paid to it, by the province in general, as the putting of that town into a formidable state of defence. Some French engineers were employed to superintend the works, and every inhabitant dedicated two days in the week to their construction,

As Washington was uncertain of the destination of the fleet and army, which had left Boston, and as New York lay exposed to any sudden attack, he detached several of his best Regiments, under General Lee, for the defence of that city.

On the 7th of June, 1776, the motion for declaring the colonies free and independent, was now moved in Congress, by Richard Henry Lee, of Virginia. When the time of taking the subject under consideration arrived, much ingenuity and eloquence were displayed on both sides of the question. The debates were continued for some time, and with great animation. In these, John Adams, and John Dickinson took leading and opposite parts. The former began one of his speeches, by an invocation of the god of eloquence, to assist him in defending the claims, and enforcing the duty of his countrymen.

He strongly urged the immediate dissolution of the political connexion of the colonies with Great Britain: from the voice of the people; from the necessity of the measure, in order to attain foreign assistance; from a regard to consistency; and from the prospects of glory and happiness, which opened beyond the war, to a free and independent people. Mr. Dickinson replied to this speech. (Author of a series of letters signed a Pennsylvania Farmer). He began by observing that the member from Massachusetts (Mr. Adams,) had introduced his defence of the declaration of independence, by invoking a heathen god, but that he should begin his objections to it, by solemnly invoking the Governor of the universe, so to influence the minds of the members of Congress, that if the proposed measure was for the benefit of America, nothing which he should say against it, might make the least impression.

He then urged that the present time was improper for the declaration of independence; that the war might be conducted with equal vigour without it; that it would divide the Americans, and unite the people of Great Britain against them. He then proposed that some assurance should be obtained of assistance from a foreign power, before they renounced their connexion with Great Britain, and that the declaration of independence should be the condition to be offered for this assistance. He likewise stated the disputes that existed between several of the colonies, and proposed that some measures for the settlement of them should be determined upon, before they lost sight of that tribunal, which had hitherto been the umpire of all their differences.

The fatal day at length arrived which must be deeply regretted by every true friend to the British Empire, when *thirteen English colonies in America, declared themselves Free and Independent States;* abjured all allegiance to the British crown, and renounced all political connexion with the mother country.

On this day, the 4th of July 1776, the Congress published a manifesto stating a list of grievances, which, notwithstanding their repetitions, had remained unredressed; for these reasons they determined on a final separation from the mother country, and to hold the people of Great Britain as the rest of mankind, "enemies in war, in peace friends." Part of this Declaration of Independence was as follows:

We hold these truths to be self-evident, that all men are created equal; that they are endowed by the Creator, with certain unalienable rights; that among these are life, liberty, and the pursuit of happiness, (at this time some of the members of Congress were holding slaves, how specious, yet how palpably inconsistent these declarations from such a people!); that to secure these rights, governments are instituted among men, deriving their just powers from the consent of the governed; that whenever any form of government becomes destructive of these ends, it is the right of the people to alter or to abolish it, and to institute a new government, laying its foundation on such principles, and organising its powers in such form, as to them shall seem most likely to effect their safety and happiness.

It concluded in this manner:

We, the representatives of the United States of America, in General Congress assembled, appealing to the Supreme Judge of the world for the rectitude of our intentions, do, in the name, and by the authority of the good people of these colonies, solemnly publish and declare, that the united colonies are, and of right ought to be, free and, independent states, and that they are absolved from all allegiance to the British Crown; and that all the political connexion between them and the state of Great Britain, is, and ought to be, totally dissolved; and that, as free and independent states, they have full power to levy war, conclude peace, contract alliances, establish commerce, and to do all other acts and things which independent states may of right do. And for the support of this declaration, with a firm reliance on the protection of Divine Providence, we mutually pledge to each other, our lives, our fortunes and our sacred honour.

Many even of the friends of America were astonished at this bold act of Congress, in breaking of all subordination to the parent state. They said:

Great Britain, has founded colonies at great expense, has incurred a load of debt by wars on their account, has protected their commerce, and raised them to all the consequence they possess, and now in the insolence of adult years, rather than pay their proportion of the common expenses of government, they ungratefully renounce all connexion with the nurse of their youth, and the protectress of their riper years.

This solemn renunciation of allegiance to Great Britain was followed by the greatest preparations for war throughout the United States.

Great Britain in the meantime was resolved to open the campaign with such a powerful force, as would look down all opposition, and effectuate submission, without bloodshed; to the accomplishment of this end three principal objects were to be carried into execution. The first was the relief of Quebec, and the recovery of Canada, which was also included a subsequent invasion of the north western frontiers of the adjacent provinces. As the four provinces of New England had originally begun the confederacy against Britain, and were still considered the most active in the continuation of it: it was thought, that any impression made upon them would contribute in an effectual manner to the reduction of all the rest. For this purpose, an army of four thousand chosen British troops, and three thousand Germans, was ordered for Canada, to accomplish the above purposes.

★★★★★★★★★★

Treaties had been lately entered into between His Majesty the Landgrave of Hesse Cassel, the Duke of Brunswick, and the Hereditary Prince of Hesse Cassel for the hiring of different bodies of their troops for the American service, amounting in the whole to seventeen thousand three hundred men. The conditions of these treaties were, that the troops were to enter into pay before they began to march; and that the levy money was to be paid at the rate of seven pounds ten shillings per man.

★★★★★★★★★★

The second object was the making a strong impression on the southern colonies, which it was hoped, would at least have succeeded so far as to the recovery of one of them. The execution of this object was committed to General Sir Henry Clinton, and Admiral Sir Peter Parker. They had two thousand eight hundred land forces, which they hoped, with the co-operation of the shipping would be fully sufficient.

The third and principal point of attack, and on which the greatest hopes of success were founded, to take New York, with a force sufficient to keep possession of Hudson's River, and form a line of communication with the Royal Army in Canada. The command of this force, consisting of thirteen thousand Hessians and Waldeckers, and seventeen thousand British troops, was given to General Sir William Howe, and his brother Admiral Lord Howe. The Congress in one of her public declarations said: "America, is amazed to find the name of *Howe* in the catalogue of her enemies—she loved his brother;" referring to the gallant nobleman, Lord Howe, who so gloriously fell in the defence of the colonies, in the former war at Ticonderoga.

The admiral and general, in addition to their military powers, were appointed commissioners for restoring peace to the colonies. This force was truly formidable, and such as no part of the new world had ever seen before. Nor was it, perhaps, ever exceeded by any army in Europe, of an equal number, whether considered with respect to the excellency of the troops, the abundant provision of all manner of military stores and warlike materials, or the goodness and number of artillery of all sorts with which it was provided. It was besides supported by a very numerous fleet, particularly well adapted to the nature of the service.

In the meantime, Washington took every precaution for defensive operations, by erecting forts, and stationing troops in different places, at the most vulnerable points. The nature of the country was peculiarly favourable to defence, and presented many natural barriers of bills and mountains, intersected by rivers, and interspersed with trees, rocks, and precipices; several defiles, skirted by impenetrable woods, and majestic rivers, flowing with impetuous currents, which seemed to bid defiance to the invader.

The following is a correct list of the stations of the British regiments, which were ordered to act against the Americans in the beginning of the year 1776.

STATIONED IN BOSTON.

17th	Dragoons..Preston's.		43d	Foot.....Cary's.
4th	Foot.........Hodgson's.		44th	do........Abercrombie's.
5th	do............Percy's.		45th	do.......Haviland's.
10th	do............Sandford's.		47th	do.......Carleton's.
22d	do............Gage's.		49th	do.......Maitland's.
23d	do............Howe's.		52d	do.......Clavering's.
35th	do............F. H.Campbell's.		63d	do......T. Grant's,
38th	do............Pigot's.		64th	do.......Pomeroy's.
40th	do............Hamilton's,		65th	do.......Urmston's at Boston and Halifax.

53

ROYAL ARTILLERY IN BOSTON.

Five Companies, each

1 Captain,	1 First Lieutenant
1 Captain Lieutenant,	3 Second Lieutenants,
3 Serjeants,	12 Gunners,
3 Corporals,	1 Fife,
6 Bombardiers,	2 Drums,

48 Matrosses.*

IN QUEBEC, AND OTHER PARTS OF CANADA.

7th Foot.........Bertie's.   8th Foot.....Armstrong's, at
the upper posts, Niagara, Detroit, &c.

26th do..........Lord W. Gordon's. M'Clean's, now raising in
Canada.

ROYAL ARTILLERY.

1 Company at Quebec.   1 Company at Montreal.

IN NEWFOUNDLAND.

1 Invalid Company, do.

AT ST. AUGUSTINE.

1 Company do.

14th Foot........Cunningham's, partly at St. Augustine's, partly
with lord Dunmore, in Virginia, and partly in Halifax.

ON THEIR PASSAGE FROM IRELAND TO BOSTON.

17th Foot.........Monckton's.   46th Foot....Vaughan's,
27th do............Massey's.   55th do........James Grant's.

READY TO SAIL FROM CORK TO AMERICA.

15th Foot...........Cavan's.   42d Foot.....Lord Murray's.
33d do.............Cornwallis's. 54th do........Frederick's.
37th do.............Coote's.   57th do........Irwin's.

ORDERED FOR BOSTON.

16th Dragoons......Burgoyne's.—One thousand of the king's
guards to be drafted from the three regiments, and commanded by colonel Matthews. Marines intended to be made up two
thousand.

29th Foot..........Evelyn's, destined for Quebec, and to sail so
as to arrive there as early as the navigation of the river
St. Lawrence will admit.

* When the British troops evacuated Boston on the 17th of March 1776,
they did not exceed seven thousand effective men.

54

9th Foot..........Ligonier's.	34th Foot.....Lord Cavendish's.
20th do............Parker's.	53d do.........Elphinstone's.
24th do............Taylor's.	62d do.........Jones's.

The Highland battalions, viz. lord John Murray's and Fraser's, were to consist of one thousand each.

The marching regiments for the American service were to consist of twelve companies, of fifty-six effective rank and file each company. Two companies of each battalion were to remain in Great Britain and Ireland for the purpose of recruiting.

Sometime before this, orders were issued from the war office that any person who should enlist as a soldier in any of His Majesty's marching regiments of foot should be entitled either to his discharge, at the expiration of three years, or at the end of the war, at the option of His Majesty.

CHAPTER 4

The Author's Journal Commences

On the 3rd of April, 1776, I embarked with the 9th Regiment of Foot, in which I was then a non-commissioned officer, at the Cove of Cork, on board the *Friendship*, transport, and on the 8th sailed with the fleet for Quebec.

April 20th. Our ship sailing at the rate of five miles an hour, a soldier whose name was Brooks, leaped off the forecastle into the ocean; the vessel in a moment made her way over him, and he arose at her stern. He immediately with all his might, swam from the ship. The men who were upon the deck alarmed the captain and officers, who had just sat down to dinner; the ship was ordered to be put about, and the boat hoisted out, and manned, the unfortunate man was soon overtaken, and it was with difficulty that the sailors could force him into the boat. When he was brought back, he was ordered between decks, and a sentinel placed over him; the next morning he was in a high fever, and continued very bad the remainder of the voyage. The fear of punishment was the cause of this desperate action, as the day before he had stolen a shirt from one of his messmates' knapsacks.

30th. The fleet sailing at the rate of six miles an hour: a sergeant had an altercation with his wife while they were sitting at breakfast, in consequence of which he got up in a rage, leaped overboard and was seen no more.

May 3rd. The wind strong at N.W. and running at the rate of seven miles an hour, one of the recruits standing on the forecastle was so provoked by his comrades, that in a fit of rage he jumped overboard, uttering at the same time dreadful curses upon them. He was. swallowed up by the great deep in a moment!

14th. Sailing over the banks of Newfoundland, we passed by several islands of ice, which came floating down from the River St. Lawrence.

15th. This morning we had a view of the mountains of New-foundland, covered with snow; however, as we had been forty days at sea without seeing any land, this dreary island was very pleasant to our sight.

19th. This day we entered the noble bay of St. Lawrence, between Cape de Retz, on the island of Newfoundland and Cape Breton, (our fleet all in sight,) and after doubling Cape Rosieres, we entered the river, which is in this place about ninety miles in breadth; here the sea was very boisterous. On the south side lies the Bay of Gaspie. Below this bay is a steep rock, which is called the Bored Island, from an opening in its middle, through which a ship may pass with her sails up. At a league's distance from the Bored Island, lies the island Bonaventure; and at a league's distance from that, the Island Miscon, which has an excellent harbour, and is eight leagues in circumference. A spring of fresh water spouts up to a considerable height in the offing, not far from this island.

20th. Early this morning the island Anticosti presented itself to our sight, the current setting strongly in upon it, rendered our navigation extremely dangerous, especially as the island is lined with breakers. This island is narrow, and lies in the middle of the river, it extends about forty leagues from N. E. to S. W. Our French pilot represented it as absolutely good for nothing; its coasts, however, are said to be well stored with fish.

21st. This evening after passing the island of Anticosti, our navigation became more tolerable, but still the fleet used great precaution.

22nd. The weather remarkably cold this day, but the wind fair, which soon brought us in sight of the Mounts Notre Dame and Lewis; here we saw for the first time, a number of neat French plantations, In the evening we sailed by Trinity Point, which we endeavoured to avoid with great care, and before dark we had a view of the Paps of Montani, so called from the appearance of the mountain, situated about two leagues from the shore. The land in this neighbourhood was represented to be not only unprofitable, but frightful, being covered with rocks, sands, and impenetrable thickets. On the other side the river, lies the shoal of Maniconague, which is the most dangerous in this river.

23rd. Our navigation was now very slow, the shores appeared uncomfortable, and uninhabited; in the evening we doubled a bay, called Tadoussac, on the south side of this bay lies Red Island, which is a dangerous rock of that colour, whose surface is equal with the water, and often proves fatal to shipping. Here the River St. Lawrence is not above three leagues wide; and the lands at each side lofty and thickly covered with trees.

26th. This day we sailed by the island of Caudres, which appeared to be very well inhabited and cultivated; churches, crucifixes, and images, were now to be seen almost everywhere: here the passage of the river is dangerous without a fair wind, in particular there is a whirlpool, which we carefully guarded against. Next appeared in our view, the Bay of St. Paul, where the plantations on the north shore begin; they consist of valuable woods of pine trees, among which are red pines, which are esteemed very beautiful. The village of St. Paul's is situated in a vale, and has a very romantic appearance from the river.

27th. Early this morning we had a view of a very high promontory, which we were informed terminates a chain of mountains, that reach near five hundred leagues to the westward. This promontory is called Cape Torment. A number of islands now presented themselves to our view, among which is that of Orleans, which forms a most beautiful prospect, a clear open country, with villages, and churches innumerable, and being all whitewashed on the outside, gave them a neat, elegant appearance, from our ships. This island is about fourteen leagues in circumference; it produces excellent wheat and fine fruits, and forms two channels, of which the south is the most navigable. Here the water becomes fit to drink; for it is brackish at Cape Torment, though it is a hundred and ten leagues from the sea.

From the island of Orleans, the river grows so narrow, that before Quebec it is not a mile over. The Point Levy, which juts out beyond the isle of Orleans, entirely hides the south channel of the river, as the Isle of Orleans does that on the north; so that from thence to the port of Quebec appears like a large bason, or bay, land locked on all sides, and capable of containing one hundred ships of the line, at four hundred and twenty miles distance from the sea.

In the River St. Lawrence, are sea wolves, sea cows, porpoises, the *chaourasou*, turtles, lobsters, sea plaice, salmon, trout, with a variety of other fish. The sea wolf, so called from its howling, is an amphibious creature; his head resembles that of a dog; he has four very short legs, of which the fore ones have nails, but the hind ones terminate in fins. The largest are said to weigh two thousand pounds, and are of different colours. Their flesh is good eating, but the profit of it lies in its oil, which is proper for burning, and currying leather. Their skins make excellent covering for trunks, and though not so fine as Morocco leather, they preserve their freshness better, and are less liable to crack. The shoes and boots made of these skins do not admit water, and when properly tanned make excellent and lasting covers for seats.

The sea cow, is larger than the sea wolf, but resembles it in figure. It is as white as snow, and has two teeth of the thickness and length of a man's arm, that, when grown, look like horns, and are very fine ivory, as well as its other teeth. It seldom happens that they are caught in the water, but they are taken on shore by the following stratagem. The inhabitants of Arcadia, tie a bull to a stake, fixed on the shore, in the depth of about two feet water; they then beat, and otherwise torment him, by twisting his tail, until they make him roar; which as soon as these animals hear, they make towards the shore, and when they get into shallow water, they crawl to the bull, and are taken with little difficulty. The Arcadians as well as the Indians eat some parts of this animal, and what they dislike they boil with its fat, to an oily or greasy substance, with which they save or cure the skins of other animals for leather.

Some of the porpoises of the River St. Lawrence, are said to yield a hogshead of oil, and of their skins are made waistcoats, which are exceeding strong, and musket proof.

The *chaourasou* is an armed fish, resembling a pike but is covered with scales, that are proof against a dagger; some of them are above five feet long, and about the thickness of a man's thigh: this fish is said even to catch and devour birds; in order to, which, he conceals himself among the canes, or reeds, in such a manner, that nothing is to be seen besides his weapon, which he holds, raised perpendicularly above the surface of the water: the birds which come to take rest, imagining the weapon to be only a withered reed, make no scruple of perching upon it; but they are no sooner alighted, than the fish opens his throat, and so suddenly makes at his prey, that it rarely escapes.

29th. Our fleet now arrived at Quebec, which is the capital of the province of Canada, and an Episcopal See. It is situated at the confluence of the Rivers St. Lawrence and St. Charles, or the little river. It is built on a rock, partly, of marble, and partly of slate. The haven which lies opposite the town, is safe and commodious, and about five fathoms deep. Before the city was taken by our troops, in the year 1759, it is said to have made a very fine appearance. Among the principal edifices, were the episcopal palace; the cathedral; the fort or citadel, which was the residence of the governor; the house and church of the Recollets; the church of the Ursuline nuns, in which is the tomb of Monsieur Montcalm, who commanded the French, and was killed at the Battle of Quebec, in which also fell that young hero, Wolfe, who commanded the English; the sumptuous college of Jesuits; the *intendant's* house, the king's magazines, &c. &c.

This city is divided into the upper and lower, and was well fortified, when Wolfe laid siege to it. The fort or citadel stands on the brink of the rock, and is a fine work: a pretty large esplanade, and a gentle declivity, the whole making a very fine platform, lies between the fort and the summit of Cape Diamond. About half a mile towards the county, lies the Hospital General, which is the finest house in all Canada.

★★★★★★★★★★

To this house the French general, Marquis Montcalm was carried after he was wounded, at the taking of Quebec, in the year 1759. It is said that when his wound was dressed, and he settled in bed, the surgeons who attended him were desired to acquaint him ingeniously with their sentiments of him, and being told that his wound was mortal, he calmly replied, "I am glad of it." His excellency then demanded, "whether he could survive it long, and how long?" He was told "about twelve hours, or perhaps less."

"So much the better," rejoined the general; "I am happy I shall not live to see the surrender of Quebec." He then ordered his secretary into the room, to settle his private affairs, which as soon as they were dispatched, he dismissed him. He was visited by Monsieur de Ramsey, the French king's lieutenant, and by other principal officers, who desired to receive his excellency's commands, with the farther measures to be pursued for the defence of Quebec.

To this, the *marquis* made the following answer; "I'll neither give orders, nor interfere any farther: I have much business that must be attended to, of greater moment than your ruined garrison, and this wretched country: my time is very short, therefore pray leave me; I wish you all comfort, and to be happily extricated from your present perplexities." He then called for his chaplain, who with the bishop of the colony, remained with him till he expired. Sometime before this great man departed, he paid the British Army this compliment.

"Since it was my misfortune to be discomfited and mortally wound-

ed, it is great consolation to me to be vanquished by so brave and generous an army; if I could survive this wound, I would engage to beat
three times the number of such forces as I commanded this morning,
with a third of their number of British troops."

CHAPTER 5

Ticonderoga and Crown Point Taken by the Americans

Our army was now informed of the military operations of the Americans in Canada last winter, with a particular account of the siege of Quebec. It seems that it had early occurred to the Americans, that if the sword decided the controversy between Great Britain and them, the possession of Ticonderoga would be essential to the security of their states; this fort situated on a promontory, formed at the junction of the waters of Lake George and Lake Champlain, is the key of all communication between New York and Canada.

A scheme was planned by the Americans, for obtaining possession of this valuable post. Having provided a sufficient quantity of powder and ball, they set off for Bennington, to obtain the co-operation of Colonel Allen of that place. Two hundred and seventy men, mostly of that hardy people, who are called Green Mountain Boys, were speedily collected at Castleton, which was fixed on as the place of rendezvous. At this place Colonel Arnold joined them. He had been early chosen a captain of a volunteer company, by the inhabitants of New Haven, among whom he resided.

As soon as he received news of the Lexington skirmish, he marched off for the vicinity of Boston. Immediately after his arrival, be waited on the Massachusetts' committee of safety, and informed them, that there were at Ticonderoga many pieces of cannon, and a great quantity of military stores; that the fort was in a ruinous condition, and garrisoned only by forty men. They appointed him colonel, and commissioned him to raise four hundred men, and attack Ticonderoga. On the 9th May, 1775, Allen and Arnold crossed over with their troops, and landed near the garrison. They contended for some time, who should lead on the attack, and it was at last agreed that they should both go in together, at the head of their troops. They advanced and entered the fort at the dawning of day.

A British sentinel fired his piece at them, and then retreated through the covered way to the parade. The Americans followed, and immediately drew up. The commander was called upon to surrender the fort. He asked by what authority? Allen replied, "I demand it in the name of the Great Jehovah, and the continental Congress." The fort, with its stores, and forty-eight prisoners, immediately fell into the hands of the Americans. A strong party was sent off to take possession of Crown Point, where a sergeant and twelve men performed garrison duty. This was also effected.

The next object that drew the attention of the Americans, was to obtain the command of Lake Champlain; but to accomplish this, it was necessary for them to get possession of a sloop of war, lying at St. John's, in the northern extremity of the lake, For the purpose of capturing this sloop, it was agreed to man and arm a schooner, lying at South Bay, that Arnold should command her, and that Allen should bring forward some *batteaux* on the same expedition. A favourable wind carried the schooner ahead of the *batteaux*, and Arnold got immediate possession of the sloop by surprise.

The wind again favouring him, he returned with his prize to Ticonderoga, and rejoined Allen. The latter soon went home, and the former with a number of men, agreed to stay there in garrison. In this rapid manner the possession of Ticonderoga, and the command of Lake Champlain was obtained. Intelligence of these events was in a few days communicated to Congress, which met for the first time, at ten o'clock, on the same day, in the morning of which Ticonderoga was taken. They rejoiced in the spirit of enterprise displayed by their countrymen, and ordered the cannon and stores to be removed from Ticonderoga to Lake George.

At the same time, Congress endeavoured to bring over the Indians to their side, for which purpose they resolved to appoint commissioners to explain to them the grounds of their dispute with Britain, and cultivate their friendship by treaties and presents; to which end they determined to purchase and distribute among them a suitable assortment of goods, to the amount of forty thousand pounds sterling. They likewise sent the following speech to them:

Brothers, *Sachems*, and Warriors! We, the delegates from the twelve United Provinces, now sitting in General Congress, at

Philadelphia, send their talk to you, our brothers.

Brothers and friends, now attend! When our fathers crossed the great water, and came over to this land, the King of England gave them a talk, assuring them, that they and their children should be his children; and that if they would leave their native country, and make settlements, and live here, and buy, and sell, and trade with their brethren beyond the water, they should still keep hold of the same covenant chain, and enjoy peace; and it was covenanted, that the fields, houses, goods, and possessions, which our fathers should acquire, should remain to them, as their own, and be their children's for ever, and at their sole disposal.

Brothers and friends, open a kind ear! We will now tell you of the quarrel between the counsellors of King George, and the inhabitants of the colonies of America.

Many of his counsellors have persuaded him to break the covenant chain, and not to send us any more good talks. They have prevailed upon him to enter into a covenant against us; and have torn asunder, and cast behind their back, the good old covenant, which their ancestors and ours entered into, and took strong hold of. They now tell us they will put their hands into our pockets without asking, as though it were their own; and at their pleasure they will take from us our charters, or written civil constitution, which we love as our lives; also, our plantations, our houses and goods, whenever they please, without asking our leave. They will tell us that our vessels may go to that or this island in the sea, but to this or that particular island we shall not trade anymore; and in case of our non-compliance with these new orders, they shut up our harbours.

Brothers, we live on the same ground with you; the same island is our common birth place; we desire to sit down under the same tree of peace with you; let us water its roots, and cherish its growth, till the large leaves and branches shall extend to the setting sun, and reach the skies. If anything disagreeable should ever fall out between us, the twelve United Colonies, and you, the six Nations, to wound our peace, let us immediately seek measures for healing the breach. From the present situation of our affairs, we judge it expedient to kindle up a small fire at Albany, where we may hear each other's voice, and disclose our minds fully to one another.

Arnold having begun his military career with a series of successes, was urged by his natural impetuosity to project more extensive operations. He wrote a letter to Congress, strongly urging an expedition into Canada, in order to reduce the whole province.

Sir Guy Carleton, the king's governor, in Canada, no sooner heard that the Americans had surprised Ticonderoga and Crown Point, and obtained the command of Lake Champlain, than he planned a scheme for their recovery. Having only a few regular troops under his command, he ordered Colonel Johnson to hold a conference with the Indians, and try to counteract the views of Congress, by endeavouring to engage them to take up the hatchet.

★★★★★★★★★★

This gentleman was son to the famous Sir William Johnson, who had so greatly distinguished himself in America, in the war of 1755. The following anecdote is related of Sir William: Soon after he had been appointed superintendent of Indian affairs in America, he wrote to England for some suits of clothes, richly laced. When they arrived, Hendrick, chief of the Mahawk Nation was present, and particularly admired them. In a few days Hendrick called on Sir William, and acquainted him that he had a dream. On Sir William inquiring what it was, he told him he had dreamed that he had given him one of those fine suits which he had lately received. Sir William took the hint, and immediately presented him with one of the richest suits. Hendrick, highly pleased with the generosity of Sir William, retired. Sir William sometime after this, happening to be in company with Hendrick, told him also that he had a dream. Hendrick being very solicitous to know what it was, Sir William informed him, that he had dreamed that he, (Hendrick,) had made him a present of a particular tract of land, (the most valuable on the Mahawk River,) of about five thousand acres. Hendrick presented him with the land immediately, with this shrewd remark. "Now, Sir William, I will never dream with you again, for you dream too hard for me."

★★★★★★★★★★

In order to gain their co-operation, he invited them to feast on a Bostonian, and to drink his blood. This, in the Indian style, meant no more, than to partake of a roasted ox and a pipe of wine, at a public entertainment, which was given on design to influence them to co-operate with the British troops. The American patriots, affected to understand it in its literal sense. It furnished in their mode of explication, a convenient handle for operating on the passions of the people, though at the same time, it was well known that if we had not employed them, they would most certainly have acted against us.

The Americans were now determined to make a vigorous attack upon Canada. Their success at Ticonderoga and Crown Point, had already paved the way for this bold enterprise, and had broken down the fences which guarded the entrance into that province. They were also sensible they had already gone such lengths as could only be vindicated by arms; and that if a certain degree of success did not attend their resistance, they would be at the mercy of an irritated government.

Montgomery, an enterprising man, having been appointed a brigadier general, flew to the new formed Congress. He said:

> Gentlemen, if you will give me six thousand men, and proper provisions for the business, I'll set off in the winter, march to Quebec, scale the walls, take General Carleton by surprise, make his soldiers prisoners, take all Canada, and then we shall make better terms with the British Parliament.

The Congress agreed to his proposals. He crossed Lake Champlain, and made as much haste as the difficulty of the way would allow. His first step was to gain over the Indians whom General Carleton had employed, and this in a great measure he accomplished; after which, on receiving the full number of troops appointed for the expedition, he determined to lay siege to St. John's. In this he was facilitated by the reduction of Chamblee, a small fort in the neighbourhood, where he found a large supply of powder.

While Montgomery was prosecuting the siege, the governor General Carleton, collected a party of Canadians and Indians, intending to proceed to the garrison of Fort St. John's, and to attack the besiegers; but Colonel Warner, with a large party of green mountain boys, and a four pounder, prevented the execution of the design. The governor's party was suffered to come near the shore, but was then fired upon with such effect, as to make them retire, after sustaining some loss.

The failure of General Carleton to relieve the garrison, was a sufficient recompense to the Americans for that of Colonel Allen, which had happened sometime before. The success which had attended this gentleman against Crown Point and Ticonderoga, had emboldened him to make a similar attempt on Montreal; but being attacked by the militia of the place, supported by a detachment of regulars, he was entirely defeated, taken prisoner, and sent to England.

An account of General Carleton's repulse being communicated to the garrison of St. John's, Major Preston, the commanding officer, seeing no hope of any relief, consented to surrender the fort. They received honourable terms of capitulation, and were treated with the greatest humanity by the Americans.

General Montgomery next took measures to prevent the British shipping from passing down the river from Montreal to Quebec. This he accomplished so effectually, that the whole were taken. The town itself was obliged to surrender at discretion, and it was with the utmost difficulty that General Carleton escaped in an open boat, under cover of a dark night.

Montreal stands on an island in the River St. Lawrence, which is ten leagues in length, and almost four in breadth, at the foot of a mountain which gives name to it, about half a league from the south shore. The whole island is a most delightful spot, and produces everything that can administer to the convenience of life. The town is of an oblong form, well peopled, and surrounded by a wall.

The streets are well laid out, and the houses built in a very handsome manner. It is divided into two parts, the upper and the lower; in the last the merchants and men of business generally reside. The upper town, however, contains the principal buildings, such as the palace of the governor, the houses of the chief officers, the convent of the Recollets, the Jesuits church and seminary, the free school, and the parish church. The governor's palace is a large fine building. Besides a general hospital, the neighbourhood of the city contains many elegant villas; and most of the vegetables of Europe grow in it. All the banks of the river from thence to Quebec, which is one hundred and eighty miles, is like one continued village, adorned with fine plantations, and gentlemen's seats at proper distances.

No further obstacle now remained in the way of the Americans to the capital, except what arose from the nature of the country, and these indeed were very considerable. Nothing, however, could damp the ardour of the Provincials, notwithstanding it was now the middle of November, and the depth of winter was at hand.

About the same time Canada was invaded in the usual march from New York, a considerable detachment from the American Army at Cambridge, was conducted into that province, by a new and, unexpected passage. Arnold who conducted this bold undertaking, thereby acquired the name of the American Hannibal. He was detached with a thousand men from Cambridge to penetrate into Canada, by ascending the River Kennibec and descending by the Chaundiere to the River St. Lawrence. Great were the difficulties the Americans had to encounter so long, in marching three hundred miles through an uninhabited country. In ascending the Kennibec, they were constantly obliged to work upwards, against an impetuous current. They were often compelled by cataracts or other impediments, to land and haul their *batteaux* up rapid streams and over falls of rivers.

Nor was their march by land more eligible than this passage by water. They had deep swamps, thick woods, difficult mountains, and craggy precipices alternately to encounter. At some place, they had to cut their way for miles together, through forests so thick that their progress was only four or five miles a day. They, however, proceeded with unabated fortitude and constancy. Provisions grew at length so scarce, that some of the men eat their dogs, cartouche boxes, breeches, shoes, &c. At one time when they were a hundred miles from any habitation or prospect of a supply, their whole store was divided, which yielded four pints of four for each man. On the last morning before their arrival, at their destination, after they had baked and eaten the remainder of their provisions, they had thirty miles to travel before they could expect any further supply.

The men bore up under these complicated distresses, with the greatest fortitude. They gloried in the hope of completing a march which would rival the fame of similar expeditions, undertaken by the heroes of antiquity. Having spent thirty-one days in traversing a hideous wilderness, without ever seeing anything human, they at length reached the inhabited parts of Canada. The Canadians were struck with amazement, when they saw this armed force emerging from the wilderness, it had never entered their conception that it was possible for human beings to traverse such immense wilds.

The most pointed instructions had been given to this corps to conciliate the affections of the Canadians. It was particularly enjoined upon them, is the son of Lord Chatham, (later Lord Chatham, and Master of the Ordnance), then an officer in one of the British regiments in that province, should fall into their hands, to treat him with all possible attention, in return for the great exertions of his father, in behalf of American liberty.

The city of Quebec was at this time in a state of great weakness, but Sir Guy Carleton at this time arrived from Montreal; his presence was itself a garrison, he was a man of ten thousand eyes, and was not to be taken unawares. The confidence reposed in his talents, inspired the garrison to make the most determined resistance. He issued a proclamation, in which he set forth, "that all persons liable to do military duty, and residing in Quebec, who refused to arm in conjunction with the Royal Army, should in four days quit Quebec, with their families, and withdraw themselves from the limits of the district, by the 1st of December, on pain of being treated afterwards as spies or rebels."

All who were unwilling to cooperate with the British Army, being thus disposed of, the remaining inhabitants, though unused to arms, became in a little time so far acquainted with them, as to be very useful in defending the town. They supported fatigues, and submitted to command, with a patience and cheerfulness, that could not be exceeded by men familiarized to the hardships and subordinations of a military life.

On the 1st of December, General Montgomery joined Arnold upon the Heights of Abraham before Quebec, and notwithstanding the extreme severity of the season in this inclement climate, he immediately began erecting his batteries, which by a perfect novelty in military science, being composed of snow and water, soon became solid ice. But finding his artillery make little impression, he determined on a general assault.

★★★★★★★★★★

During the siege, a woman from the American camp stole into Quebec, with letters addressed to the principal merchants, advising them to an immediate submission, and promising great indulgence in case of their compliance. Enclosed was a letter to General Carleton, with a summons to deliver up the town. The messenger was sent to prison for a few days, and then drummed out.

★★★★★★★★★★

Early in the morning, on the 31st of December, 1775, during a snow storm the attack was made by two divisions, in two different quarters of the town. These divisions were commanded by Colonel Arnold, and the general in person. Montgomery's division proceeded to make the attack, by the way of Cape Diamond, while Arnold's division attacked the suburbs of St. Rue. On the first onset, Montgomery led on his men with undaunted resolution; he was attended with a number of carpenters with saws, in order to cut down the pickets, he even pulled some of them down with his own hands, and entered with his *aide-de-camp*, Mr. M'Pherson, and two more American officers at the head of his division; here they were received with a heavy fire of musketry.

Montgomery, with his officers and a number of men were killed, and the remainder of the division falling into immediate disorder, were repulsed with much slaughter. On the other side Colonel Arnold forced the first barrier, which consisted of thirty men, but before he could attempt the second, a reinforcement of the garrison, in consequence of the defeat of Montgomery in the opposite quarter, was collected against him; here Arnold received a dangerous wound in the leg, by a musket ball, and was compelled to retire to the camp. To add to their embarrassment, they lost the help of one of their companies, which was quartered on the north side of the River St. Charles, by their not having notice of the attack in due time, which in endeavouring to join the main body, were surprized by a party of our men, under the command of Captain Laws, who made a sortie through Palace Gate, and most of them were, made prisoners.

The Americans near the second barrier took possession of some houses, but as our troops which sallied out of Palace Gate, came upon their rear, and their numbers being greatly lessened by being killed and wounded, they were obliged to retreat to the barrier which they had but a little before taken, here they maintained their ground until ten o'clock in the morning, when, after a brave resistance, they were obliged to lay down their arms.

The loss which the garrison sustained was but small in comparison. One lieutenant of the navy, and six rank and file killed, and thirteen rank and file wounded; but the loss of the Americans was very considerable; seven officers were killed and six wounded, upwards of six hundred officers and men were taken prisoners. Montgomery was shot through both his thighs and his head. When his body was taken up, his features were not in the least distorted, but his countenance appeared regular, placid, and serene; an elegant coffin was prepared, and he was interred with all military and funeral honours.

★★★★★★★★★★

In General Montgomery's *Memoirs* written sometime after his death, by Dr. Smith, of Philadelphia, a celebrated American partisan, speaking on this subject, he says:

"O thou swift winged messenger of destruction, how didst thou triumph in that moment! the stroke that severed Montgomery from his army, deprived them of more than a member. It reached the vitals, and struck the whole body with a temporary death. As when the forked lightening, darting through the forest, amidst the black tempests of night, rends some towering oak, and lays its honours in the dust, the inferior trees which it had long sheltered from the storm, stand mournful around. So stood the astonished bands, over their fallen chieftain! nor over him alone, but over others, in their prime of glory, prostrate by his side.

"Such examples of magnanimity filled even adversaries with veneration and esteem. Forgetting the foes in the heroes, they gathered up their breathless remains, and committed them to kindred dust; with pious hands, 'and funeral honours meet;' So may your own remains, and particularly thine, O Carleton, be honoured, should it ever be your fate to fall in hostile fields! or if, amid the various chances of war, your lot should be among the prisoners and the wounded, may you be distinguished with an ample return of that benevolence which you have shewn to others! such offices of humanity, softening the savage scenes of war, will entitle you to an honour which all the pride of conquest cannot bestow."

★★★★★★★★★★

He was tall and slender, well limbed, of a genteel, easy, graceful and manly address; to the courage of the soldier, he added the military skill of the general, and had the voluntary love, esteem, and confidence of the American troops, who greatly lamented him. In the afternoon, the American officers were confined in the seminary, and well accommodated with bedding, &c. they were treated with the greatest politeness and generosity by the British officers; the privates were confined in the Recollets, or Jesuits college, and well used.

★★★★★★★★★★

Major Meig, who succeeded Arnold in the command after he was wounded, in writing upon this subject, says, "I dined this day with Captain Law, whom in the morning I made prisoner; but in a few hours after I was in my turn made prisoner also. Captain Law treated me with the greatest politeness and generosity."

★★★★★★★★★★

Montgomery's knee buckles, and his *aide-de-camp's* gold brooch, with several other valuable articles found with the dead officers, were all restored to the Americans, which were highly gratifying to them.

"British soldiers in the moment of victory, will have mercy on a prostrate foe, as the brave and generous cannot be cruel."

General Montgomery received a liberal education in Ireland, his native country. In the year 1753 he had obtained the rank of captain in the 17th Regiment of Foot, and stood full in the way of higher preferment; having borne a share in all our American wars, and the reduction of Canada, in the year 1759; as soon as peace was restored, he took leave of the army, and having soon connected himself by marriage with an antient and honourable family in the province of New York, he chose a delightful retirement upon the banks of Hudson's

River, where he continued until appointed by the American Congress a brigadier general.

Colonel Arnold with the shattered remains of his troops, retreated three miles from the city where he had the temerity to encamp. Early in the spring, the *Isis*, of fifty-four guns, accompanied by the *Surprise* frigate, and the *Martin* sloop, on board of which was part of the 29th Foot, forced their passage through the ice, before the navigation of the River St. Lawrence was deemed practicable.

Governor Carleton was too great a proficient in the art of war, to delay seizing the advantages which the consternation of the besiegers and the arrival of this reinforcement afforded. He marched out at their head to attack the Americans. On his approach he found everything in confusion: the late besiegers abandoning their artillery and military stores, had in great precipitation retreated. In this manner, at the expiration of five months, the mixed siege and blockade of Quebec was raised. The fortitude and perseverance of the garrison reflected honour on both officers and privates.

The reputation acquired by General Carleton in his military character, for bravely and judiciously defending the province committed to his care, was exceeded by the superior applause, merited from his exercise of the virtues of humanity and generosity. Among the numerous sick in the American hospitals, several incapable of being moved were left behind. The victorious general proved himself worthy of success by his treatment of these unfortunate men: he not only fed and clothed them, but permitted them when recovered to return home. Apprehending that fear might make some conceal themselves in the woods, rather than by applying for a relief, make themselves known, he removed their doubts by the following proclamation:

Whereas I am informed, that many of His Majesty's deluded subjects, of the neighbouring provinces, labouring under wounds and divers disorders, are dispersed in the adjacent woods and parishes, and in great danger of perishing for want of proper assistance, all captains and other officers of militia are hereby commanded to make diligent search for all such distressed persons, and afford them all necessary relief, and convey them to the general hospital, where proper care shall be taken of them: all reasonable expenses which may be incurred in complying with this order, shall be paid by the receiver-general. And lest a consciousness of past offences should deter such miserable wretches from receiving that assistance which their distressed situation may require; I hereby make known to them, that as soon as their health is restored, they shall have free liberty to return to their respective provinces.

A rich Frenchman, who commanded a regiment of Canadians under Montgomery, and who joined him in Montreal, was likewise taken prisoner. A few weeks after General Carleton ordered the Frenchman to make his appearance upon the parade of the castle. He was brought there under a file of soldiers; General Carleton was walking at the top of the parade. As soon as the man was brought in, he waved his hat for the soldiers to retire and shut the gates. An interview must now take place; let the reader imagine what the Frenchman felt: he expected to be hanged like a dog, or sent over to England to be tried by the English judges.

Up to the general he must come, for he could not expect that the general would run towards him. He summoned his courage, and walked with a slow dignified step up to the parade towards the general. As soon as he came up, he expected nothing but frowns and the most stinging reproaches, as he was one of the king's subjects in the governor's jurisdiction.

The general stopped and looked at him with a mixture of dignity and condescension, and said, "Sir, when did you hear from your family?"

"General," replied the other, "I have not heard from them these three months." (The general knew that very well, for he had intercepted all his letters.)

"Sir, said he, which way do you chuse to go home, by land or water? If you chuse to go by water, you shall have my barge: if you chuse to go by land you shall ride in my coach."

The man was struck with amazement, fell down at his feet, and clasping the governor's knees, burst into a violent exclamation; "O general, you are too good! you are too good!" The general raised him from the ground, sent him home with honour and joy to his family, with such gratitude in his heart as never forsook him. He continued a faithful subject as long as he lived.

After this gentleman was gone home to Montreal, General Carleton sent for the American prisoners, in small companies, and addressed them with such sweetness and good humour, as was sufficient to melt every heart:

My lads, why did you come to disturb an honest man in his government, that never did any harm to you in his life? I never invaded your property, nor sent a single soldier to distress you. Come, my boys, you are in a very distressing situation, and not able to go home with any comfort; I must provide you with shoes, stockings, and good warm waistcoats. I must give you some good victuals to carry you home. Take care, my lads, that you do not come here again, lest I should not treat you so kindly.

This humane line of conduct was more injurious to the views of the leaders in the American councils, than any severity that could be used against them.

In General Carleton's dispatches to government, particular mention is made of Lieutenant-Colonel M'Clean, and his newly raised regiment of Scotch emigrants, for their indefatigable zeal in the king's service, during the siege. Also, Captain Hamilton of His Majesty's ship, the *Lizard*, with the officers and seamen, who were formed into a battalion on shore, discharged their duty with alacrity and spirit. Major Caldwell who commanded the militia likewise, proved himself an active and diligent officer.

CHAPTER 6

Lord Dunmore Sails with the Fleet

Quebec being thus freed from danger, it is now necessary to take a transient view of the state of affairs, at this period in some of the southern provinces. Lord Dunmore, the Governor of Virginia, was involved in disputes similar to those which had taken place in other colonies; these disputes arose to such violence, that His Lordship was obliged to take refuge on board the *Fowey* ship of war, into which he attempted to transfer the sittings of the assembly; requisition which the legislative body absolutely refused to comply with. His Lordship being thus divested of his authority, carried on a sort of predatory war against the province.

In order to protect the loyalists who now began to flock to the royal standard, His Lordship constructed a fort near Norfolk, a maritime town of some consequence: this fort he furnished with artillery. The Americans also fortified themselves within cannon shot of the same place, with a narrow causeway in their front. In this state both parties continued quiet for some days. Lord Dunmore now formed a design of surprising the enemy in their entrenchments; this was undertaken before daylight, on the 9th of December, 1775.

Captain Fordyce, at the head of the Grenadiers of the 14th Regiment of Foot, amounting to sixty men, passed the causeway, and boldly marched up to the American entrenchments, with fixed bayonets, and with a coolness and intrepidity which first excited the astonishment, and afterwards the praise of their enemies. They were exposed without cover to the fire of the Provincials in front, and enfiladed by another part of their works. The brave Captain Fordyce with several of his men fell, the lieutenant and others were taken, and all the survivors of this valiant grenadier company, whether prisoners or not, were wounded. Captain Fordyce was interred with every military honour, by the victors; the English prisoners treated with kindness, but the

Americans who had joined the king's standard experienced the greatest cruelties.

A short time before this, a scheme of importance was formed by Major Connolly, a Pennsylvanian of an intrepid and aspiring disposition, and attached to the cause of Britain. The first step of his plan was to enter into a league with the Ohio Indians. This he communicated to Lord Dunmore, and it received his approbation. Upon which, Connolly set out, and actually succeeded in his design. On his return he was dispatched to General Gage at Boston, from whom he received a colonel's commission, and set out in order to accomplish the remainder of his scheme.

The plan in general was to proceed to Fort Detroit, where Captain Lord of the Royal Irish was to meet him with two companies, and a field piece. Connolly was to raise a regiment, with as many Indians and partisans as he could; to enable him to do this, he had power to promise every person that entered into the service, three hundred acres of land, when the troubles were over, and what other pecuniary rewards he might think proper; was to appoint and commission all the officers under him, which commissions were to be confirmed by Lord Dunmore. With this force he was to penetrate through the country, in order to cut off the communication between the southern and northern colonies, destroy Fort Pit, and Fort Fincastle, and meet Lord Dunmore on the 10th of April following, at Alexandria. Connolly's companions were Lieutenant Cameron and Dr. Smith.

On their road through Maryland, they were all three taken, cast into prison, and closely confined. On searching their portmanteaus, a copy of Connolly's plan was found. The Congress immediately published the following speech, from Lord Dunmore to White Eyes, a famous Indian warrior, which they said was found in the colonel's custody:

Brother, captain White Eyes, I am glad to hear your good speeches, sent to me by Major Connolly, and you may be assured I shall put the one end of the belt which you have sent me, into the hands of our great king, who will be glad to hear from his brothers, the Delawares, and will take a strong hold of it. You may rest satisfied, that our foolish young men shall never be permitted to take your lands, but on the contrary, the great king will protect you, and preserve you in the possession of them. Our young people in the country have been very foolish, and done many impudent things, for which they must soon be sorry, and of which I make no doubt, they have acquainted you; but I must desire you not to listen to them, as they would be willing that you should act equally foolish with themselves. But rather let what you hear, pass in at one ear, and out at the other, so that it may make no impression on your heart, until you hear from me fully, which shall be as soon as I can give farther information, who am your friend and brother.

Captain White Eyes will please to acquaint the Corn Stalk with these my sentiments also, as well as the chiefs of the Mingors, and the other six nations, Your sincere friend, and elder brother, Dunmore.

The Americans never lost an opportunity of magnifying every circumstance which would in anywise tend to the promotion of their own cause, while at the same time, they covered in obscurity the very motives and views with which they themselves used to accomplish their ends. Some months before this, the inhabitants of Virginia had endeavoured to gain the Indians over to their side, in order to assist them against the loyalists in that state. This well-known narrative is given by an American partisan. It begins as follows:

We may challenge the whole orations of Demosthenes and Cicero, and of any more eminent orator, if Europe has furnished more eminent, to produce a single passage superior to the speech of Logan, a Mingo chief, to Lord Dunmore, when Governor of the State of Virginia. The story is as follows; of which and of the speech, the authenticity is unquestionable. In the spring of the year 1774, a robbery and murder were committed on an inhabitant of the frontiers of Virginia, by two Indians of the Shawanee tribe; the neighbouring whites, according to their custom, (they were under the necessity in their defence to resist force by force), undertook to punish this outrage in a summary way.

★★★★★★★★★★

The inhabitant, one of the Loyalists. Undoubtedly these Indians were instigated to take up the hatchet by the Americans against their brethren, and for what cause? Why, because they adhered to the British Government.

★★★★★★★★★★

Colonel Cresap, infamous for the many murders he had committed on this much injured people, collected a party, and proceeded down the Kanhaway in quest of vengeance. Unfortunately, a canoe of women and children with one man only, was seen coming from the opposite shore, unarmed and unsuspecting any hostile attack from the whites. Cresap and his party concealed themselves on the bank of the river, and the moment the canoe reached the shore, singled out their objects, and at one fire killed every person in it. This happened to be the family of Logan, who had long been distinguished as a friend of the whites. This unworthy return provoked his vengeance.

He accordingly signalised himself in the war which ensued. In the autumn of the same year, a decisive battle was fought at the mouth of the great Kanhaway, between the collected forces of the Shawanees, Mingoes, and Delawares, and a detachment of the Virginia militia. (Under the command of Lord Dunmore.) The Indians were defeated, and sued for peace. Logan, however, disdained to be seen among the suppliants, but lest the sincerity of a treaty should be distrusted, from which, so distinguished a chief absented himself, he sent by a messenger the following speech, to be delivered to Lord Dunmore:

"I appeal to any white man to say if ever he entered Logan's cabin hungry, and he gave him not meat; if he ever came cold and naked, and he clothed him not. During the course of the last long and bloody war, Logan remained idle in his cabin, an advocate for peace. Such was my love for the whites, that my countrymen pointed as they passed, and said, *Logan is the friend of white men.* I had even thought to have lived with you, but for the injuries of one man. Colonel Cresap, the last spring, in cold blood, and unprovoked, murdered all the relations of Logan, not sparing even my women and children.

"There runs not a drop of my blood in the veins of any living creature. This called on me for revenge. I have sought it; I have killed many; I have fully glutted my vengeance. For my country, I rejoice at the beams of peace; but I do not harbour a thought that mine is the joy of fear. Logan never felt fear. He will not turn on his heel to save his life. Who is there to mourn for Logan? Not one."

Lord Dunmore retreated from Norfolk, and that place was taken possession of by the Provincials, who treated the Loyalists that had remained there, with great severity, at the same time that they greatly distressed those onboard Lord Dunmore's fleet, by refusing to supply them with any necessaries. Nor was this all; the vicinity of the shipping was so near, as to afford the riflemen an opportunity of aiming at the people on board, and exercising the cruel occupation of killing them, in which they did not fail every day to employ themselves. These proceedings at last drew a remonstrance from His Lordship; in which he insisted that the fleet should be furnished with necessaries, and that the soldiers should desist from the cruel treatment above mentioned; but both these requests being denied, a resolution was taken to set fire to the town.

After giving the inhabitants proper warning, a party landed, under, cover of a ship of war, and set fire to that part which lay nearest to the shore; but the flames were observed at the same time to break forth in every other quarter, and the whole town was reduced to ashes. This universal destruction, by which a loss of more than three hundred thousand pounds was incurred, is said to have been occasioned by order of the Congress itself, that the loyalists might find no refuge there for the future. The Americans after this transaction, burned and destroyed the houses and plantations within reach of the guns of the ships of war, and obliged the inhabitants to remove with their cattle, provisions, and portable effects, further into the country.

The heat of the season, and the numbers crowded together in Lord Dunmore's fleet, produced a pestilential fever, which made great havoc, especially among the negroes. At last, finding themselves in the utmost hazard of perishing, by famine as well as disease, they set fire to the least valuable of their vessels, reserving only about fifty for themselves, in which they bid a final *adieu* to Virginia, some sailing to Florida, some to Bermuda, and the rest to the West Indies.

In South Carolina, the Provincials had a more formidable enemy to contend with. A squadron whose object was the reduction of Charlestown, had been fitted out in December, 1775, but by reason of unfavourable weather, did not reach Cape Fear, in North Carolina, till the month of May, 1776; and here it met with further obstacles till the end of the month. Thus, the Americans, always noted for their alertness in raising fortifications, had time to strengthen those of Charlestown, in such a manner as rendered it exceedingly difficult to be attacked. The British squadron consisted of two fifty-gun ships, four of thirty guns, two of twenty; an armed schooner, and a bomb-ketch, all under the command of Sir Peter Parker; the land forces were commanded by General Clinton, Lord Cornwallis, and Brigadier-General Vaughan.

It was now determined to try the event of an attack on the city of Charlestown, the capital of South Carolina. The Americans had erected works on Sullivan's Island, mounted with thirty pieces of cannon, in a very advantageous situation, for annoying ships in their approach to the town. The militia of the province were also collected in great numbers for the defence of the metropolis, aided by several continental regiments, and the whole commanded by General Lee.

On the 28th of June, the *Bristol* and *Experiment*, each of fifty guns, supported by several smaller vessels, had with some difficulty crossed the bar, and advanced to the attack of the fort on Sullivan's Island, constructed entirely of palmetto, a soft and spongy wood, in which a ball entering is buried, and makes no extended fracture. Though an attack on this fort was practical from the sea, it was very difficult to obtain a co-operation of the land forces.

This was attempted by landing them on an island adjacent to Sullivan's Island, on the east, from which it is separated by a narrow creek. Opposite to this creek the Americans had posted a strong body of troops, with cannon and entrenchments, while General Lee was posted on the main land, with a bridge of boats between that and Sullivan's Island; so that he could at pleasure send reinforcements to the troops in the fort on Sullivan's Island.

The attack commenced early in the morning by a bomb-ketch, which began to throw shells into the fort, and about mid-day the two fifty-gunships came up and began a severe fire.

Three other frigates were ordered to take their station, between Charlestown and the fort, in order to enfilade the batteries, and cut off the communication with the main land; but, through the ignorance of the pilots, they all stuck fast; and though two of them were disentangled, they were found to be totally unfit for service: the third was burnt, that she might not fall into the hands of the enemy

The attack was therefore confined to five armed ships and a bomb-ketch, between whom and the fort a dreadful fire ensued. The *Bristol* suffered exceedingly. The springs on her cable being shot away, she was for some time exposed to the enemy's fire. As the Americans poured in great quantities of red-hot balls, she was twice in flames. The brave Captain Morris after receiving five wounds, was obliged to go between decks, to have his arm amputated. After undergoing this operation, he insisted to be carried on the quarter deck to resume his command; here he received another wound, but still refused to quit his station; at last, he received a red-hot ball in his belly, which put an end to his life.

A few moments before he died, one of the officers asked him if he had any directions to give with respect to his family, to which he heroically answered, "None, I leave them to the providence of God, and the generosity of my country." His Majesty on receiving an account of this affair, sent the captain's widow a handsome present, and settled a pension on her and her children.

Of all the officers and seamen who stood on the quarter deck of the *Bristol*, not one escaped without a wound, excepting Sir Peter Parker alone, though he received several contusions during the action, yet he modestly says in his dispatches they were not worth mentioning. Indeed, his intrepidity and presence of mind during the action was very remarkable. The engagement lasted till darkness put an end to it.

During the height of the attack, the Provincial batteries remained for some time silent, so that it was concluded that they had been abandoned, but this was found to proceed only from want of powder, for as soon as a supply of this article was obtained, the firing was resumed as brisk as before. During the whole of this desperate engagement, it was found impossible for the land forces to give any assistance to the fleet. The enemy's works were found to be much stronger than they had been imagined, and the depth of water effectually prevented them from making any attempt. Captain Scott of the *Experiment*, and Lord William Campbell, late governor of the colony, who now with great gallantry served as a volunteer on board the fleet, were also dangerously wounded, with more than two hundred of as brave men as ever the British Navy produced, of the crews of these two ships only.

Particular mention was made of the bravery of Lieutenants Caulfield, Molloy, and Nugent, of the *Bristol*. Every man, that was engaged did his duty. The *Experiment* and *Bristol* were so much damaged, that it was thought they could not be got over the bar; however, this was at last accomplished by a very great exertion of naval skill, to the surprise of the Americans, who had expected to make them both prizes. On the American side the loss was judged to be very considerable, as most of their troops were dismounted, and reinforcements had poured into the fort during the whole time of the action.

During this attack General Lee exposed himself to great danger; as the balls whistled about, he observed one of his *aide-de-camps* shrink every now and then, and by the motion of his body seemed to evade the shot.

"Death sir," cried Lee," what do you mean, do you doge? Do you know that the King of Prussia lost above a hundred *aide-de-camps* in one campaign?"

"So, I understand, sir," replied the officer, so but I did not think you could spare so many."

A short *memoir* of this gentleman may not be unnecessary.

He was born in Chester, in the year 1726; his father, a man of considerable property in that county, was in the year 1745 appointed Colonel of the 44th Regiment of Foot.

As Charles was an only son, his father bestowed upon him a very liberal education, and in the year 1745 he obtained a commission for him in his own regiment, in which he continued till the year 1760, passing through the ranks of ensign, lieutenant, and captain.

During this time Charles Lee was present at several actions, the first of which was at the defeat of General Braddock, at Monongahela; after this he was at the attack of the lines of Ticonderoga, in 1758, where he was shot through the body. The next year he was with General Prideaux at the reduction of Niagara, and in the year 1760 was at the conquest of Canada, with General Amherst.

The campaign being ended, Captain Lee obtained leave to return to England, where, in the year 1761, he was appointed major in the 103rd Regiment, which, on the breaking out of the Spanish war, was sent to Portugal, under the command of Lord Loudon. In Portugal, as well as in America, Major Lee behaved with distinguished bravery; and General Burgoyne, under whose immediate direction he was, bore testimony of his firmness in executing the orders he received to surprise the Spanish camp, which he did with a bravery and intrepidy that settled his character as a distinguished officer.

At the peace of 1763, Major Lee's corps was disbanded, and he, unwilling to remain inactive, obtained leave to enter into the service of the King of Poland, by whom he was greatly caressed; he afterwards went as a volunteer in the war between Russia and the Ottoman Porte.

In the year 1772, he returned to England, and in the month of May, in that year, he was honoured with the rank of lieutenant-colonel, after which he went to America, to visit a numerous set of friends he had in that country.

Whether he had at that time entertained any intention of intermeddling in the dispute between Great Britain and the colonies, we cannot pretend to decide: but as soon as the colonies began to raise forces, he immediately resigned his half pay, and with the greatest alacrity accepted the post of Major-General in their armies.

In person General Lee was five feet eight inches high, slender in his make, but able to endure the greatest hardships, little caring what he eat or drank, or on what he slept. His actions have shewn him to be brave, active, and determined; this may be seen by the following circumstance. At the time General Clinton sailed from Boston, Lee, at the head of a strong detachment from the American Army before that place, immediately set out to secure New York from the attempt which it was supposed the British troops would have made upon that city.

Having succeeded in that object, General Clinton could not but be surprised at his arrival in Virginia, to find Lee in possession, and in the same state of preparation in which he had left him at New York. Upon his departure for Cape Fear, Lee again traversed the continent with the utmost expedition to secure North Carolina: and at length upon the further progress of the fleet and army to the southward, Lee again proceeded with equal celerity to the defence of Charlestown.

General Lee was a studious man, and of intense application, not only in his profession as a soldier, but even that of a lawyer. As he visited most of the courts of Europe, he acquired a perfect knowledge of their languages. He spoke the Indian language as well as English, and as he passed great part of the former war among the Indians, they had a particular friendship for him.

His resentment against the British Government was very strong, but for what cause it is not conjectured; however, it is well known that he was of an ardent, fiery disposition, of which the following letter is a specimen; the reader will observe that this letter was written to a gentleman in Maryland, in the beginning of the year 1776, some months before any reinforcements arrived from England to America. (Maryland was one of the last states which yielded to the declaration of independence to the British crown.)

This modern Achilles says:

I know not, in the whole course of my life, I ever read anything which so much moved my pity and indignation as the late declaration of the convention of Maryland. They declare, they shall esteem separation from Great Britain as the last of misfortunes. What! when an attempt has been made to rob you and your posterity of your birth-rights; when your fields have been laid waste, your towns have been burnt, and your citizens butchered (see note end of chapter); it when your property is seized and confiscated in all parts of the world; when an inexorable tyrant, an abandoned parliament, and a corrupt, pusillanimous people, have formed a hellish league to rob you of everything men hold most dear; is it possible there should be creatures, who march on two legs, and call themselves human, who can be so destitute of sentiment, courage, and feeling, as sobbingly to protest, they should consider separation from these butchers and robbers as the last of misfortunes?

"Oh, I could brain you with your ladies' fans."
★★★★★★★★★★

When!—Where! At this very time seven thousand British troops were shut up in Boston, surrounded by an innumerable host of Americans: Canada at the same time overrun by another army of Americans and Indians.

Surely one cannot help being astonished at the virulence with which Mr. Lee speaks, on the present occasion, against his country, which had loaded him and his family with honours,

Describe Achilles, as Achilles was,
Impatient—rash—inexorable—proud—
Scorning all judges, and all law but arms.

CHAPTER 7

Author's Journal Continued

It is now high time to take notice of the military operations of the British forces to which I was attached in Canada. It has been already mentioned that Colonel Arnold raised the siege of Quebec and retreated with the greatest precipitation towards Three Rivers.

On the 29th June, 1776, having accomplished our voyage to Quebec, General Carleton found himself at the head of twelve thousand regular troops, among whom were those of Brunswick. With this force we set out for Three Rivers, where we expected that Arnold would have made a stand, but he had fled to Sorel, a place one hundred and fifty miles distant from Quebec, where he was at last met by the reinforcements, ordered by Congress, under the command of General Thomas; who was appointed by that body, commander in chief in Canada, in the room of Montgomery. A few days after he arrived at the American encampment, he was seized with the smallpox, and died, having forbidden his men to inoculate, he conformed to his own rule, and refused to avail himself of that precaution. On his death the command at first devolved on Arnold, and afterwards on General Sullivan.

In the meantime, our troops proceeded with all expedition from Quebec to Three Rivers, which place was appointed the general rendezvous of the army. In our passage up the River St. Lawrence, our eyes were entertained with beautiful landscapes, the banks being in many places very bold and steep, and shaded with lofty trees, and in others crowded with villages, the air became so mild and temperate, that we thought ourselves transported into another climate.

June 5th our regiment was ordered to land, and to press forward with all expedition.

6th, Arrived at Three Rivers. This town lies halfway between Quebec and Montreal, and about thirty leagues from each; it has its name from Three Rivers which join their current above a quarter of a mile below the village, and fall into the great one, St. Lawrence. It is much resorted to by the several tribes of Indians who come down those rivers, and trade with the inhabitants in various kind of furs. The country about it is fertile in corn, fruits, &c.

For the sake of many of my readers who perhaps have never read the following anecdote, which is related of an Algonquin woman, I shall take the liberty of relating it in this part of my journal.

That nation being at war with the Iroquois, she happened to be taken prisoner and was carried to one of the villages belonging to them. Here she was stripped naked, and her hands and feet bound with ropes, in one of their cabins. In this condition she remained ten days, the savages sleeping round her every night. The eleventh night, while they were asleep, she found means to disengage one of her hands, after which she immediately freed herself from the ropes, and went to the door. Though she had now an opportunity of escaping unperceived, her revengeful temper, could not let slip so favourable an opportunity of killing one of her enemies. The attempt was manifestly at the hazard of her own life; yet, snatching up a hatchet, she killed the savage that lay next her; and springing out of the cabin, concealed herself in a hollow tree which she had observed the day before.

The groans of the dying person soon alarmed the other savages, and the young ones immediately set out in pursuit of her. Perceiving from her tree, that they all directed their course one way, and that none of the savages were near her, she left her sanctuary, and flying by an opposite direction, ran into a forest without being perceived. The second day after this her footsteps were discovered, and they pursued her with such expedition that the third day she discovered her enemies at her heels; upon this she threw herself into a pond of water, and diving among some reeds and bulrushes, she could just breathe above water without being perceived.

Her pursuers after making the most diligent search, were forced to return. For thirty-five days this woman held on her course, through woods and deserts, without any other sustenance than roots and wild berries. When she came to the River St. Lawrence, she made with her own hands a kind of wicker raft on which she crossed. As she went by the French for Three Rivers, without well knowing where she was, she perceived a canoe full of savages, and fearing they might be. Iroquois, ran again into the woods, where she remained till sunset. Continuing her course, soon after she saw Three Rivers, and was then discovered by a party whom she knew to be Hurons, a nation in alliance with the Algonquins; she then squatted down behind a bush, calling out to them, that she was not in a condition to be seen, because she was naked. They immediately threw her a blanket, and then conducted her to the fort, where she recounted her story.

June 8th. At three o'clock this morning our drums beat to arms, and we soon marched out of the village to meet our foe.

This being the first skirmish I ever was engaged in, it really appeared to me to be a very serious matter, especially when the bullets came whistling by our ears. In order to encourage the young soldiers amongst us, sone of the veterans who had been well used to this kind of work, said, "there is no danger if you hear the sound of the bullet, which is fired against you, you are safe, and after the first charge all your fears will be done away." These remarks I found to be perfectly true many a time afterwards. The cannon from the ships in the river, and the field pieces on land, began now to roar; many of the unfortunate Americans were killed and wounded.

> *Present we heard the battle's loud alarm,*
> *The hideous cannon with continued roar,*
> *Proclaims approaching death and wide spread harm:*
> *Confusion echoes from the martial shore.*

Surely war, whether offensive or defensive, is a picture idea of desolation!

This was a very bold enterprise indeed of the Americans to attack our troops.

Two thousand of them crossed over from Sorel in fifty boats, landed at the Point du Lai, before daylight, with an intention to surprise us at Three Rivers. General Fraser, who commanded the British van, was not to be taken by surprise. The Americans soon found that they were greatly mistaken in their intelligence concerning our position:

When they discovered their mistake, they were greatly alarmed, particularly when they found that Brigadier-General Nesbit, who had landed the troops from the transports, had got behind them. After some time, they gave up offensive measures, and retreated to the woods. Our troops still pushed forward in hopes of taking their boats and cutting off their retreat; two boats only were taken, the rest escaped. The number of the Americans killed and wounded were considerable; about two hundred surrendered, or were taken prisoners in the woods. Generals Thompson and Irwin, who commanded this party, with several other American officers were among the prisoners: few of the British fell on this day.

9th. Ordered on board our transports with all expedition; the wind springing up fair, the fleet sailed towards Sorel.

11th. Our ship grounded on a sand bank, just in the middle of the River St. Lawrence; here we remained fast near two hours, and then drifted; we received no damage, and soon regained our station.

14th. Landed at Sorel, here we heard that the Americans had retreated, only two hours before. All the fires in their encampment were burning.

15th. Our troops began to march in three columns, under the command of General Burgoyne, who led the pursuit.

16th. Continued our march day and night, expecting every hour to come up with them. However, in all their haste, they took care to set on fire their *batteaux*, ships, military stores, &c. It must be confessed that their distresses at this time were very great. A British Army close on their rear, and threatening them with destruction; their men obliged to drag their loaded *batteaux* up the rapids by mere strength, often to their middle in water. They were likewise encumbered with great numbers labouring under that dreadful disease, the small pox, which is so fatal in America, It was said that two regiments at one time had not a single man in health, another had only six, and a fourth only forty, and two more were nearly in the same condition,

While the Americans were retreating, they were daily annoyed by the remonstrances of the inhabitants of Canada, who had either joined or befriended them. Many of the Canadians had taken a decided part in their favour, rendered them essential services, and thereby incurred the heavy penalties annexed to the crime of supporting rebellion. These, though Congress had assured them but a few months before, "that they would never abandon them to the fury of their common enemies," were, from the necessity of the case, left exposed to the resentment of their rulers. The retreating army recommended them to cast themselves on the mercy of that government, against which they had offended.

★★★★★★★★★★

They did indeed receive mercy, for I never saw any of them either imprisoned or otherwise punished by our government, for their joining the Americans at that time, and I was in Canada for twelve months after this.

★★★★★★★★★★

18th. Took possession of the redoubts at St. John's, and found all the buildings in flames, all the craft and large boats the enemy could not drag up the rapids of Chamblee, with some provisions, were also burnt: twenty-two pieces of cannon were left behind, and several other marks appeared of great precipitation and fright, in the retreat of the enemy.

26th. We heard that the Americans had retreated across Lake Champlain to Crown Point. We could not for want of boats urge our pursuit any farther.

September 30th. We have been very busy these three months past in constructing a fleet, in order to face the enemy on water. The spirit of our troops has risen in proportion to the difficulties which they had to encounter. A fleet is now prepared. The ship *Inflexible*, mounting eighteen twelve-pounders is ready to sail; three weeks ago, her keel was laid. Two schooners, one of fourteen and another of twelve six-pounders. A flat bottom *radeau*, carrying six twenty-four pounders, and six twelve-pounders, besides howitzers. A *gondola*, with seven nine-pounders. Twenty smaller vessels, with brass field pieces, from nine to twenty-four pounders. A number of long boats. A great number of *batteaux*, destined for the transportation of the army, have been in three months little less than created.

October 1st. Our little squadron was put under the command of Captain Pringle, and is now ready to sail.

Upon the 11th, our squadron came up with the American fleet, commanded by Arnold; they were at anchor under the island Valicour, and seemed a strong line, extending from the island to the west side of the continent. The wind was so unfavourable, that the ship *Inflexible*, and some other vessels of force, could not be brought to action.

Orders were now given to anchor, in a line as near as possible to the American fleet, that their retreat might be cut off. This was frustrated by the extreme obscurity of the night, and in the morning the American fleet had got a considerable distance from our ships up the lake.

13th. Eleven sail of the Americans was seen making off to Crown Point, when after a chase of seven hours, Captain Pringle, on board of the *Maria*, of fourteen six pounders, having the armed vessels, *Carleton* and *Inflexible*, a small distance a-stern, came up with the enemy, the rest of the fleet almost out of sight. The action began at twelve o'clock, and lasted two hours. The *Washington* galley struck during the action, and sometime after, Arnold in the *Congress* galley, and five *gondolas*, ran on shore and blew up the vessels.

In this perilous enterprise he paid attention to a point of honour. He did not quit his own galley till she was in flames, lest our sailors should board her, and strike her flag. The killed and wounded in our fleet did not amount to forty. General Carleton was on board the *Maria* during the action, and praised in the highest terms the conduct of the officers and men of the corps of artillery who served the gun boats, and who sustained for many hours the whole fire of the enemy's fleet, (the matrosses who served in the gunboats were drafts from the Irish Artillery in Chapelizod), the rest of the vessels not being able to work up near enough to join effectually in the engagement.

The Americans hearing of the defeat of their naval force, set fire to all the buildings and houses in and near Crown Point, and retired to Ticonderoga.

The result of this sea fight, though unfortunate for the Americans, raised the reputation of Arnold higher than ever in addition to the fame of a brave soldier, he acquired that of an able naval officer. Waterburg, the second in command, and brigadier general in the American Army, was taken. Out of fifteen American armed vessels which engaged our fleet in the morning, three only escaped; the rest were taken, burnt and destroyed.

General Carleton landed at Crown Point, and took possession of the ground from which the Americans had retreated, and was there joined by our army. He sent out several reconnoitring parties, and pushed forward a strong detachment on both sides of the lake, which approached near to Ticonderoga. Some of our vessels came within cannon shot of the American works at that place. But the strength of that garrison, and the season of the year restrained us from making any attempt, at that time, on Ticonderoga.

31st. Our army embarked on board of the *batteaux*, and on the 2nd of November landed at St. John's, in Canada.

Such was the termination of the northern campaign in 1776. After the death of Montgomery, evacuations of posts, defeats, and retreats, had almost interruptedly been the portion of the Americans.

The winter quarters of the British Army was in the following order:

Royal Artillery, commanded by General Phillips,	General Hospital, Montreal.
Van Brigade, commanded by gen. Frazer, grenadiers, light Infantry and 24th regiment,	At LePrairie, Longeuil, &c. extending on the south side of the river St. Lawrence to St. Curs.

First Brigade commanded by brigadier general Powel.

9th regiment..........................Isle Jesus.
47th do.† ....St. Luce, Recollet, St. Geneviere and St. Lawrent.
53d.......................................Chamblee.

Second Brigade, commanded by brigadier general Hamilton.

20th regiment.........................Isle au Noix.
21st do...............................St. John's.
34th do...............................Quebec.
62d do................................Point Levy, opposite to Quebec.

German troops commanded by generals Reidesel and Speicht, were quartered from Bertheier to Three Rivers, and forty miles below Three Rivers, on the road to Quebec.

Maclean's Royal Highlanders, emigrants, quartered at Chinage Bonne, and River du China.

Sir John Johnson's regiment, called the New Yorker's, quartered at Lachine, La Point Clare, and St. Ann.

8th regiment................................Upper Posts, Niagara, Detroit, &c.

† Lieutenant colonel Nesbit died about this time, at Quebec, he was a brave, humane officer, and greatly beloved by the brigade which he commanded.

The Isle of Jesus where the 9th Regiment was quartered, lies in the neighbourhood of Montreal, and is about eight leagues in length, and two in breadth; here as in other parts of Canada, the forests present a most beautiful appearance, and contain a great variety of trees, among which are pine, fir, cedar, oak, maple, ash, walnut, beech, elm, and poplar. The Indians hollow the red elm into canoes, of which, made out of one piece, will contain twenty persons. About November, the bears and wild cats take up their habitations in the hollow elms, and remain there till April.

Here are also found cherry trees, plumb trees, the vinegar tree, the fruit of which, being infused in water, produces vinegar; and an aquatic plant, called *atoca*, the fruit of which may be made into a confection; the white thorn, the cotton tree, on the top of which grow several tufts of flowers, which when shaken in the morning, before the dew falls off, produces honey that may be boiled up into sugar, the seed being a pod, containing a very fine kind of cotton: the sun plant, which resembles a marigold, and grows to the height of seven or eight feet; Turkey corn, French beans, gourds, melons, *capillaire*, and the hop plant.

Canada is said to be inhabited by two hundred thousand French, who live in affluence. They have full liberty to hunt, fish, fell timber for fuel, or building, and to sow and plant as much land as they can cultivate. Their greatest hardship is the winter cold, which is here so excessive from December to April, that the greatest rivers are frozen over, and the snow lies commonly two or three feet deep on the ground, though it extends no farther north than 48° of latitude.

The forests of Canada are also well stocked with birds. They contain two kinds of eagles, the largest of which have a white head and neck, and prey upon hares and rabbits, which they carry up to their nests: but the others are grey, and prey on birds and fishes. The partridges are grey, red, and black, with long tails, which they spread out as a fan, like a turkey cock, and make a very beautiful appearance. The chief Canadian bird of melody, is the white bird, which is very handsome, and remarkable for announcing the return of spring.

The fly bird is thought to be the most beautiful of any in nature; with all his plumage, he is no larger than a cock chaffer, and he makes a noise with his wings, like the humming of a large fly: his legs are like two needles, and from his bill, which is of the same thickness, a small sting proceeds, with which he pierces the flowers, and thereby nourishes himself with the sap.

The female has nothing striking in its appearance; but the male is a perfect beauty, having on its head a small tuft of the most beautiful black, his breast red, his belly white, his back, wings and tail green, like that of a rosebush: specks of gold scattered all over the plumage, add greatly to its beauty; and an imperceptible down produces the most delightful shadings that can be imagined. Rattlesnakes are found here, some of them as thick as a man's leg: when he moves his body, which is covered with rows of scales, his tail rattles, whence he has his name: his bite is mortal, but an herb grows wherever this reptile is found in this country, called the rattle snake's plant, which is an infallible antidote to the poison of his bite, by chewing it and applying it in the nature of a plaster to the wound. The rattle snake seldom bite passengers, unless he is provoked or trod upon: the Indians, however, pursue them and greatly prize their flesh, which they eat.

There is a carnivorous animal here called the *carcajou*, of the cat kind, having a very long tail; its body is about two feet in length. It is said that this animal, winding himself about a tree, will dart from thence upon the elk, twist his strong tail round his body, and cut his throat in a moment. Wolves are scarce in Canada, but they afford the finest furs in all the country; their flesh is white and good to eat, and they pursue their prey to the tops of the largest trees. There are three sort of squirrels here; that called the flying squirrel will leap forty paces and more, from one tree to another. This little animal is easily tamed, and is very lively.

The Canadian porcupine is less than a middling dog; when roasted, he eats full as well as a sucking pig. There are two sort of bears here, one a reddish and the other of a black colour, but the former is the most dangerous. Some of the rivers breed a kind of crocodile, that differs but little from those of the Nile. The meadow grounds, in Canada, which are well watered, yield excellent grass, and breed vast numbers of great and small cattle; their horses are small, but very active; where the arable land is well manured, it produces rich crops, tobacco in particular, thrives exceedingly.

The lakes are both large and numerous, Lake Superior, or the Upper Lake, which is situated the farthest north, is reckoned one hundred leagues in length, and seventy where broadest. Indeed, the whole country abounds with large lakes and rivers; so that here a man may wander one thousand miles on the banks of the finest lakes and rivers in the world, without meeting with a human creature.

Chapter 8

General Lee Taken

It has been already observed, that the command of the force which was designed to act against New York was given to Admiral Lord Howe, and his brother Sir William; officers, who as well for their personal character, as their known bravery, stood high in the confidence of the British Nation.

The admiral and general in addition to their military powers, were appointed commissioners for restoring peace to the colonies, and so desirous was the general to effect his favourite purpose of pacification, that he lay a considerable time before New York, without attempting to commence hostilities, until he should be joined by his brother, whom he expected daily from England, with an enlargement of their powers as commissioners for restoring peace to the colonies. On the 12th July, 1776, Lord Howe reached Staten Island, the headquarters of the general, and immediately sent on shore by a flag to Amboy, a circular letter, addressed to the governors of the different colonies, acquainting them with his appointment as commissioner in conjunction with the general, together with a declaration to the inhabitants.

Copies of these papers were sent by General Washington to Congress, who immediately published them in all the newspapers, that every one, as they said, might see the insidiousness of the British ministry, and that they had nothing to trust to besides the exertion of their own valour.

The admiral and general unwilling to proceed to coercive measures, and anxious to effect their favourite purpose of pacification, deputed Colonel Paterson, the adjutant-general, with a message to General Washington, stating that the commissioners were invested with powers of reconciliation, and that they would derive the greatest pleasure from effecting an accommodation, and wished this visit to be considered as the first advance towards that desirable object.

The following conversation, (published by order of Congress), passed at the interview between General Washington and Colonel Paterson:

After usual compliments, in which, as well as through the whole conversation, Colonel Paterson addressed General Washington by the title of excellency, Colonel Paterson entered upon the business by saying, that General Howe much regretted the difficulties which had arisen, respecting the address of the letters to General Washington, that the address was deemed consistent with propriety, and founded upon precedents of the like nature, by ambassadors and plenipotentiaries, where disputes of difficulties of rank had arisen; that General Washington might recollect he had last summer addressed a letter to General Howe, "To the honourable William Howe, esquire;" that Lord Howe and General Howe did not mean to derogate from the respect or rank of General Washington; for they held his person and character in the highest esteem; that the direction, with the addition of &c. &c. &c. implied everything that ought to follow.

★★★★★★★★★★

A few days before this interview General Howe sent a letter, directed "To George Washington, esquire," which he refused to receive, as not being addressed to him in his official capacity. In his letter to Congress on the subject, he wrote as follows: "I would not on any occasion sacrifice essentials to *punctilio*, but in this instance, I deemed it a duty to my country and appointment, to insist on that respect, which in any other than a public view, I would willingly have waved." Congress applauded his conduct in a public resolution, and at the same time directed, that no letter or message" should be received on any occasion whatever, from the enemy, by the commander in chief, or others, the commanders of the American Army, but such as were directed to them in the character they severally sustained.

★★★★★★★★★★

He then produced a letter, which he did not directly offer to General Washington, but observed that it was the same letter which had been sent, and laid it on the table, with the superscription, "To George Washington, &c. &c. &c." The general declined the letter, and said, that a letter directed to a person in a public character should have some description or indication of it, otherwise it would appear a mere private letter; that it was true, &c. &c. &c. implied everything, and they also implied anything; that the letter to General Howe alluded to, was an answer to one received, under a like address from him, which the

95

officer on duty having taken, he did not think proper to return, but answered it in the same mode of address; that he should absolutely decline any letter directed to him as a private person, when it related to his public station.

Colonel Paterson then said, that General Howe would not urge his delicacy any farther, and repeated his assertions, that no failure of respect was intended. He then said he would endeavour as well as he could to recollect General Howe's sentiments on the letter, and the resolution of Congress sent him a few days before, respecting the treatment of our prisoners in Canada; and added that the affairs of that province were in another department not subject to the control of General Howe, but that he and General Howe utterly disapproved of every infringement of the rights of humanity.

Colonel Paterson then took a paper out of his pocket, and after looking it over, said he had expressed nearly the same words. General Washington then said, that he had also forwarded a copy of the resolves to General Burgoyne, to which Colonel Paterson replied, he did not doubt but a proper attention would be paid to them, and that he (General Washington) was sensible that cruelty was not the characteristic of the British Nation. Colonel Paterson then proceeded to say he had it in charge to mention the case of General Prescot, who they were informed was treated with such rigour, that under his age and infirmities fatal consequences might be apprehended.

General Washington replied, that General Prescot's treatment had not fallen under his notice, that he had treated all persons under his particular direction with kindness, and made their situation as easy and comfortable as possible; that he did not know where General Prescot was, but believed his treatment was different from their information. General Washington then mentioned the case of Colonel Allen, and the officers who had been confined in Boston jail.

As to the first, Colonel Paterson answered, that General Howe had no knowledge of it, but by information from General Washington, and that the Canada company was not under his direction or control; but as to the other prisoners at Boston, whenever the state of the army at that place admitted it, they were treated with humanity, and even indulgence: he asserted this upon his honour, and should be happy in an opportunity to prove it.

General Washington then observed, that the conduct of several of the officers would well have warranted a different treatment from what they had received; some having refused to give any parole, and others having broken it when given, by escaping or endeavouring so to do. Colonel Paterson answered, that as to the first, they misunderstood the matter very much, and seemed to have mistaken the line of propriety exceedingly; and as to the latter, General Howe utterly disapproved, and condemned their conduct. That, if a remonstrance was made, such violations of good faith would be severely punished; but that he hoped General Washington was too just to draw public inference from the misbehaviour of some private individuals; that bad men were to be found in every class and society.

And such behaviour was considered as a dishonour to the British Army. Colonel Paterson then proceeded to say, that the goodness and benevolence of the king had induced him to appoint Lord Howe and General Howe his commissioners to accommodate this unhappy dispute; that they had great powers, and would derive the greatest pleasure from effecting an accommodation, and that he, (Colonel Paterson,) wished to have this visit considered, as making the first advances to this desirable object. General Washington replied, he was not invested with any powers on this subject, by those from whom he derived his authority. But from what had appeared or transpired on this head, Lord Howe and General Howe were only to grant pardons; that those who had committed no fault, wanted no pardon; that the Americans were only defending what they deemed their indisputable right.

Colonel Paterson said, that would open a very wide field for argument. He expressed his apprehensions, that an adherence to forms was likely to obstruct business of the greatest moment and concern. He then observed that a proposal had been made of exchanging Governor Skene for Mr. Lovell; that he now had authority to accede to that proposal. General Washington replied, that the proposition had been made by the direction of Congress, and having been then rejected, he could not now renew the business, or give any answer, till he had previously communicated with them.

Colonel Paterson was treated with the greatest attention and politeness during the whole business, and expressed strong acknowledgements that the usual ceremony of blinding his eyes had been dispensed with. At the breaking up of the conference, General Washington strongly invited him to partake of a small collation provided for him, which he politely declined, alleging his late breakfast, and an impatience to return to General Howe, though he had not executed his commission so amply as he wished. Finding he did not purpose staying, he was introduced to the general officers, after which he took his leave, and was safely conducted to his own boat, which waited for him, about four miles distant from the city.

While the two royal commissioners, Admiral and General Howe were endeavouring in their civil capacity, to effect a reunion between Great Britain and the Colonies, in order to avert the calamities of war, Congress seemed more determined in opposition, and ridiculed the power with which the commissioners were invested "of granting general and particular pardons to all those, who, though they had deviated from their allegiance, were willing to return to their duty." Their general answer to this was "that they who had committed no fault, wanted no pardon," and immediately entered into a resolution:

That the good people of the United States may be informed of the plan of the commissioners, and what the terms, with which the insidious court of Great Britain had endeavoured to amuse and disarm them, and that the few who still remained suspended by a hope, founded either in the justice or moderation of their late king, might now at length be convinced that the valour alone of their country was to save its liberties.

This was immediately followed by another resolution in order to detach the Germans who had entered into the service of Britain; it was penned in these words:

Resolved, that these states will receive all such foreigners who shall leave the Armies of His Britannic Majesty in America, and shall choose to become members of any of these States, and they shall be protected in the free exercise of their respective religions, and be invested with the rights, privileges, and immunities of natives, as established by the laws of these States; and moreover, that this Congress will provide for every such person, fifty acres of unappropriated lands, in some of these States to be held by him and his heirs as absolute property.

An attack upon Long Island being determined on by our commanders, the fleet covered the descent of the army, which effected a landing with forty pieces of cannon, in two hours and a half, near a town called Utrecht, on the south-western extremity of the Island, without any opposition, on the twenty-second of August, 1776. General Putnam, with a large body of troops, lay encamped and strongly fortified at Brooklyn: a range of hills were between the armies, the principal pass of which was at a village called Flat Bush. Large detachments of the American Army occupied the hills and passes. The right of the British Army was commanded by General Clinton, Lord Percy and Lord Cornwallis; the centre, composed of Hessians, under General Heister, took post at Flat Bush, and the left, under General Grant, near the shore.

About nine in the evening of the 26th, the van of the army, consisting of the light infantry, grenadiers, and light-horse, marched to the right in order to seize a pass near the village of Jamaica. General Clinton being arrived within half a mile of the pass about two hours before daybreak, settled his disposition for the attack. One of his patrols falling in with a patrol composed of American officers, took them all. The way being thus open, the whole army descended into the level country which led to the American lines at Brooklyn.

At half past eight o'clock on the morning of the 27th, the attack was commenced by the light infantry and light dragoons, upon large bodies of the Americans, who retreated towards their camp. Here they were met by the Hessians and exposed to the fire of two parties; Generals Heister and Grant in their front, and General Clinton in their rear; they were immediately thrown into the utmost confusion; and in their effort to retreat back to the lines at Brooklyn, great numbers were killed and taken prisoners, among the latter Major-General Sullivan, Brigadier-General Lord Sterling, Brigadier-General Udell, ten field officers, eighteen captains, forty-three lieutenants, eleven ensigns, one adjutant, three surgeons, two volunteers, and one thousand and six rank and file.

★★★★★★★★★★

The following account of Lord Sterling was given about this time in the English publications:

"His father, Mr. Alexander, (for that was his real name) went to America many years ago, where he acquired a considerable estate. Upon the death of Lord Sterling, a Scotch peer, whose name was Alexander, either the late or present. Mr. Alexander came over to England and laid claim to the title. When the cause was tried by the House of Lords and the claim rejected, the Lords forbade him to assume the title on pain of being led round Westminster-Hall labelled as an impostor; but ever since, by the courtesy of his countrymen, he has been distinguished by the title of Lord Sterling. The first Lord Sterling obtained a grant of Long Island, and was the first that settled it with British inhabitants. He died in 1640."

★★★★★★★★★★

Washington had crossed over from New York in the height of the engagement: "when he saw the disposition of the two armies, it is said that he wrung his hands and cried out "Good God! what brave fellows I must this day lose:" but he came too late to retrieve the fortune of the day. He had the mortification to see some of his best troops killed or taken without being able to afford them any assistance, but he used his utmost exertions to save those that remained by a well conducted retreat.

The victory was complete; the Americans lost upwards of three thousand men, including near eleven hundred taken prisoners, with thirty-two pieces of cannon. Among the Americans who fell, a regiment from Maryland was particularly regretted. It consisted wholly of young men of the best families in that province. They behaved with the most admirable heroism, were every man killed or wounded, and thus perished in the bloom of youth.

A member of Congress (Dr. Ramsay), in his account of this engagement, says:

The British troops displayed great valour throughout the whole day; the variety of the ground occasioned a succession of engagements, pursuits and slaughter, which lasted for many hours; British discipline, in every instance, triumphed over the native valour of raw troops, who had never been in action, and whose officers were unacquainted with the stratagems of war.

The British Army had to lament the following officers and men killed and wounded:

KILLED.
Lieut. Col. Grant   10th Regiment,
Captain Sir A. Murray   17th   do.
Captain Nelson   52nd   do.
Captain Logan, 2nd Regiment Marines,
Second Lieut. Lovell, Royal Artillery,
3 sergeants,
53 rank and file.

WOUNDED.
Lieut. Col. Monckton   45th Regiment,
Captain Grove   23rd do.
Captain Brown   44th do.
Captain Kennedy   do. do.
Lieut. Morgan   17th do.

Lieut. Crammond	42nd *do.*
Lieut. Mair	43rd *do.*
Lieut. Wier	*do. do.*
Lieut. Brown	44th *do.*
Lieut. Addison	52nd *do.*

Lieut. Nugent, 1st Regiment Marines,
11 sergeants,
3 drummers,
231 rank and file.

After this defeat Washington did not think it expedient to risk another battle against the British Army. Conformable to this opinion, dispositions were made for an immediate retreat. In the beginning of the night of the 29th of August, in the most profound silence, he conveyed his troops on board of boats, crossed the East River, more than a mile wide, and landed them in the city of New York, on the opposite shore.

Soon after this retreat the first Division of the British Army, commanded by General Clinton, being covered by a few ships of war, proceeded up the East River to Kepps' Bay, about three miles north of New York, where they landed without opposition.

The Americans now abandoned the city of New York, and a brigade of the British troops took possession of it.

After the Americans had evacuated New York, they took up a strong position on the north of that Island, which is near sixteen miles long, and in some parts not more than two miles in breadth. Here they fortified the strong pass of Kingsbridge, by which their communication with the continent was kept open.

General Howe formed a plan of cutting off Washington's communication with the eastern country, and enclosing him so as to compel a general engagement on the island. On the twelfth of October, the guards, light infantry, together with Colonel Donop's corps of Hessian grenadiers and *chasseurs*, marched from the advanced posts on New York Island, and embarking in boats at Turtle Bay, passed up the East River through Hell-gate, entered the sound and landed on Frog's Neck in Westchester County. About this time General Lee arrived from South Carolina, and in a council of war which was held immediately after his arrival at the American encampment, strongly urged the American commanders to quit the Island of New York immediately.

He also urged the expediency of evacuating Fort Washington at the same time. In this last motion he was opposed by General Green, who maintained that the possession of that important post would prevent a large body of the enemy from joining their main force, and in conjunction with Fort Lee, would be of essential service to the Americans in covering their transportation of provisions and stores up the North River. He likewise said, that at the very worst the garrison could be brought off at any time by boats from the Jersey side of the river. Greene's plan was adopted, and Fort Washington was garrisoned with three thousand men for its defence.

In the meantime, the British troops crossed at Frog's Neck, and found the bridge which joined it to the main land broken down by the Americans, who had thrown up some works on the opposite side. Our troops having now been reinforced, embarked again in boats and landed at Pelham's Manor, and advanced towards New Rochelle; on their march they were annoyed by a party of Americans, under the command of General Lee, who had posted themselves behind stone walls on the line of march.

Our troops now gained the road which leads from Connecticut to Kingsbridge. The Americans apprehending their communication to the eastward would be cut off, moved from their camp at Kingsbridge, and extended their left to the White Plains, a chain of stony hills so called. On the 21st of October, the British troops took possession of the heights of New Rochelle. On the 25th our army marched in two columns, and took a position with the Brunx River in front. The Americans at the same time assembled their main force at White Plains behind entrenchments, where they seemed determined to make a stand. A general action was hourly expected.

On the 28th in the morning our army advanced to attack the enemy, who seeing our troops in motion, a body of eight thousand came out of their lines and posted themselves on the top of a very steep hill, above the ford.

The second brigade, commanded by General Leslie, consisting of the 5th, 28th, 35th, and 49th Regiments, with a battalion of Hessians, and a party of light dragoons, marched down and crossed the ford, though much annoyed by grape shot, ascended the hill with the greatest intrepidity, attacked and routed the body of the Americans that were posted there, driving them to their entrenchments. General Howe, on the morning of the 1st of November, prepared to attack them but General Washington in the meantime, quitted his entrenchments, crossed the North River, and took post in the neighbourhood of Fort Lee, having previously set fire to the huts and barracks which they had built for their winter quarters.

The Americans having retreated, General Howe finding they avoided a general action, and that the nature of the country did not admit of their being forced to it, was determined on the reduction of Fort Washington. This was the only post the Americans held on New York Island, almost opposite Fort Lee from which it was separated by the North River. Everything being prepared for attacking Fort Washington, a general assault was determined on. On the 16th of November four attacks were made at the same time in the following order: the first, on the north side, was led on by General Knyphausen, with two columns of Hessians. The second, on the east, led by brigadier General Mathews, at the head of the light infantry, and a battalion of the King's Guards; this column was supported by Lord Cornwallis, with the British grenadiers and 33rd Regiment.

★★★★★★★★★★,

The fate of the gallant officer, General Mathews, some years after this was truly lamentable.

In the beginning of the year 1783, General Mathews landed with a small army under his command, on the coast of Malabar, in the East Indies, in order to relieve the Carnatic, which was at that time suffering under the ravages of Hyder Ally's formidable, victorious army. After General Mathews had taken several important fortresses, his little army was obliged to surrender prisoners to Tippoo Saib, who in direct breach of the capitulation, treated them with a degree of inhumanity, which chills the blood even to think of. Seventeen British officers were compelled to swallow poison by his order, and all miserably perished in prison. General Mathews himself did not expire by the poison, but horrid to relate, had his head wrung from his body, by order of that tiger-hearted monster Tippoo Saib.

★★★★★★★★★★

The third was under the direction of Lieutenant-Colonel Sterling, with the 42nd Regiment; and the fourth was commanded by Lord Percy. The columns under General Knyphausen when advancing to the fort, had to pass through a thick wood which was occupied by a large body of riflemen, and suffered very much from their well-directed fire. In the meantime, a body of British light infantry advanced against a party of the Americans, who were annoying them from behind rocks and trees, and obliged them to disperse. This made way for the landing of the rest of the troops without opposition. Lord Percy carried an advanced work on his side, and Lieutenant-Colonel

Sterling forced his way up a steep height, and took one hundred and seventy prisoners.

Their outworks being carried, the Americans retreated from their lines and crowded into the fort; Colonel Rahl, who led the right column of General Knyphausen's attack, pushed forward and lodged his column within one hundred yards of the fort, where he was soon after joined by the left column. Two thousand seven hundred Americans who were in the fort surrendered. Shortly after Fort Washington had thus fallen, Lord Cornwallis, with a considerable force, passed over the North River in order to attack Fort Lee, and make a further impression in the Jerseys. The garrison, consisting of two thousand men, were saved by an immediate evacuation, at the expense of their artillery and stores.

General Washington now retreated to New Ark, having abundant reason from the posture of affairs, to count on the necessity of a farther retreat. He asked Colonel Reed "Should we retreat to the back parts of Pennsylvania, will the Pennsylvanians support us?"

The colonel replied, "If the lower counties are subdued and give up, the back counties will do the same."

The general replied, "we must retire to Augusta County, in Virginia, numbers will be obliged to repair to us for safety, and we must try what we can do in carrying on a predatory war, and if overpowered, we must cross the Allegany mountains." (Dr. Ramsay's *American Revolution.*)

The reduction of Fort Washington, the evacuation of Fort Lee, and the diminution of the American Army, by the departure of those whose time of service had expired, encouraged the British forces, notwithstanding the severity of the winter, and the badness of the roads, to pursue the retreating American Army.

Lord Cornwallis led the van of the British Army, and was close in the rear of General Washington, as he retreated successively to New Ark, Brunswick, Princeton, Trenton, and the Pennsylvanian side of the Delaware

The pursuit was urged with so much rapidity, that the rear of the American Army pulling down bridges, was often, within sight and gunshot of the van of the British building them up.

During the retreat of the Americans, General Lee was taken prisoner at Baskenridge. He had been ordered to join General Washington with his division, but those orders were not obeyed. He continued to hang upon the rear of the advancing army. Colonel Harcourt having received intelligence of his careless situation, being attended only by a small guard, and at a distance from his troops, immediately formed a plan of surprising him, which he effected with great address, and he was safely carried prisoner to the British camp. The Americans had reposed extravagant confidence in his military talents.

To have lost such an idol of the state at any time would have been distressing, but it was an aggravation of the misfortune to lose him under such circumstances, which favoured an opinion, that despairing of the American cause, he suffered himself to be taken prisoner. Congress soon after interceded for his enlargement, and offered to give six British field officers in exchange for him, but this was at that time refused, as it was said that General Lee being a deserter from the king's service, did not come under the denomination of a prisoner of war: retaliation was then threatened by the Americans. To stop the effusion of innocent blood, the British commander gave him up.

How different was the conduct of the American leaders, in respect of Major André, which shall hereafter be related.

During these successes in the Jerseys, General Clinton, with two brigades of British, and two of Hessian troops, accompanied by a squadron of ships of war, under the command of Sir Peter Parker, were sent to make an attempt on Rhode Island, and became masters of it without losing a man: at the same time, they blocked up commodore Hopkins' squadron, and a number of privateers at Providence.

Hitherto the British troops had succeeded in every object since their landing at Staten Island. The American soldiers being greatly dispirited by repeated defeats, claimed their discharge; twelve months was the time of their engagement, at the expiration of that period numbers of them returned home, in consequence of which General Washington found his army greatly decreased.

Congress exerted themselves to retrieve their losses, and to recruit their army. They altered their mode of enlisting men, and ordered a new army to be levied, of which the soldiers should be bound to serve three years, or during the continuance of the war. Twenty dollars were allowed to every soldier, besides an allotment of lands at the end of the war to all that survived, and to the families of those who should lose their lives in the service of their country. These promises of Congress were accompanied with vigorous exertions. Pennsylvania, in this crisis of danger, raised a powerful militia; the merchant, the farmer, the tradesman, and the labourer, flocked to General Washington's standard.

The British Army now occupied a chain of towns and villages

through the Jerseys, even to the vicinity of Philadelphia.

A strong detachment of Hessians lay at Trenton, another at Bordenton, and a third at Burlington; these towns are on the opposite bank of the Delaware, and the latter is within twenty miles of Philadelphia.

On the evening of the 25th of December, General Washington, by a masterly enterprise, recrossed the Delaware, marched his troops in two divisions to Trenton, drove in the Hessian out posts, and attacked the main body, who were thrown into confusion, after Colonel Rahl their commanding officer was mortally wounded.

Finding they were now surrounded by the Americans, twenty-three officers and eight hundred and eighty-eight men, laid down their arms and surrendered prisoners of war; between thirty and forty were killed and wounded.

After this enterprise, Washington crossed the Delaware, and returned with the prisoners to Philadelphia; he then repassed that river, and took possession of Trenton.

Several detachments of our troops now assembled at Princeton, where they were joined by a strong detachment from Brunswick, commanded by Lord Cornwallis; who immediately marched to Trenton, and attacked the Americans on the 2nd of January, 1777. At four o'clock in the afternoon, the advanced guard of the Americans were compelled to retreat, but our troops were checked by some field pieces which were posted on the opposite bank.

Thus, two armies, on whom the success or failure of the American Revolution depended, were crowded into the village of Trenton, and only separated by a creek in many places fordable. The British troops lay on their arms that night in order to be in readiness to make another attack next morning. Meanwhile Washington silently withdrew his troops, leaving fires burning in his camp and the usual patrols for the purpose of deception; favoured by the obscurity of night, and after a circuitous march, he reached Princeton early in the morning.

On their approach to Princeton, the centre of the Americans were charged by the 17th, 40th, and 55th Regiments under the command of Colonel Mawhood with such intrepidity, that they were compelled to give way in disorder. In this emergency, Washington rode forward; he placed himself between his flying troops and the British, with his horse's head fronting the latter. The Americans encouraged by his exhortations and example, rallied and attacked the British in turn, and although Washington was for some moments between two fires, he escaped without a wound.

During this contest, the British troops displayed the most invincible valour. One of the three regiments commanded by colonel Mawhood, undismayed by the superiority of the Americans, in point of numbers, charged with the bayonet, forced their way through a column of the enemy, and marched forward to Maidenhead. The other two regiments, though they suffered severely, retired in good order and retreated to Brunswick.

The British Army now evacuated Trenton and Princeton, and retreated to New Brunswick. General Washington immediately stationed troops in all these important places which he had thus regained.

The American headquarters were at Morristown and General Putnam was directed to take post at Princeton.

This campaign was closed with few advantages to the British arms, except the possession of New York.

We shall now turn our attention to the affairs of the Northern Army.

CHAPTER 9

Northern Army Opens the Campaign

In the beginning of June, 1777, the Northern Army, which consisted of four thousand British troops, and three thousand Germans, marched from their winter quarters, in the different parts of Canada, and encamped on the western side of Lake Champlain. Here they were joined by some Canadians, and the army was put under the command of General Burgoyne. The soldiers were in a high state of discipline, and had been kept in their winter quarters with the greatest care, in order to prepare them for this expedition.

The British Army proceeded up Lake Champlain, in *batteaux*, in the greatest order and regularity, and landed at the River Boquet, near Crown Point. Here a body of Indians joined it. A Congress was held; General Burgoyne opened the meeting with a speech to the Indians, part of which was as follows:

> This war, to you, my friends, is new; upon all former occasions in taking the field, you held yourselves authorised to destroy wherever you came, because everywhere you found an enemy. The case is now very different.
>
> The king has many faithful subjects dispersed in the provinces, consequently you have many brothers there: and these people are the more to be pitied, that they are persecuted, or imprisoned, wherever they are discovered or suspected; and to dissemble, is, to a generous mind, a yet more grievous punishment. Persuaded that your magnanimity of character, joined to your principles of affection to the king, will give me fuller control over your minds than the military rank with which I am invested, I enjoin your most serious attention to the rules which I hereby proclaim for your invariable observation during the campaign.

I positively forbid bloodshed when you are not opposed in arms.

Aged men, women, children, and prisoners, must be held sacred from the knife or hatchet, even in the time of actual conflict.

You shall receive compensation for the prisoners you take; but you shall be called to account for scalps.

Base lurking assassins, incendiaries, ravagers and plunderers of the country, to whatever army they may belong, shall be treated with less reserve, but the latitude must be given you by order, and I must be the judge of the occasion.

After General Burgoyne had ended, an old chief of the Iroquois stood up and made the following answer:

I stand up, in the name of the nations present, to assure our father that we have attentively listened to his discourse. We receive you as your father, because when you speak, we hear the voice of your great father beyond the great lake.

With one common assent we promise a constant obedience to all you have ordered, and all you shall order; and may the Father of days give you many and success!

We rejoice in the approbation you have expressed of our behaviour.

We have been tried and tempted by the Bostonians, but we have loved our father, and our hatchets have been sharpened upon our affections.

In proof of the sincerity of our affections, our whole villages, able to go to war, are come forth. The old and infirm, our infants and our wives, alone remain at home.

In the meantime, the attention of the Americans were exclusively fixed on plans of defence, in order to arrest the progress of the British troops. In the preceding summer, General Gates was ordered by Congress with twelve thousand troops to Ticonderoga, in order to strengthen and fortify that important pass; great was the confidence of the Americans in the strength of this post and the supposed superiority of the forces for its defence.

On the 30th of June, the British advanced to Crown Point, about twelve miles from Ticonderoga. In the evening the following orders were given:

The army embarks tomorrow, to approach the enemy. The services required on this expedition are critical and conspicuous. During our progress occasions may occur, in which, nor difficulty, nor labour, nor life, are to be regarded. This army must not retreat.

From Crown Point they proceeded to invest Ticonderoga. On their approach to it they advanced on both sides of the lake, while the naval force kept in the centre. Within a few days they had surrounded three fourths of the American works at Ticonderoga, and Mount Independence, and had also advanced a work on Sugar Hill, the top of which overlooked and effectually commanded the whole works.

The Americans vainly imagining that the difficulty of the ascent would be sufficient to prevent the British troops from taking possession of it. On the approach of the first Division of the army, the Americans abandoned and set fire to their out works, and so expeditious were the advances, that by the 5th of July, every post was secured which was judged necessary for investing it completely. A road was soon after made to the summit of that eminence, which the Americans had with such confidence supposed could not be ascended; and so much were they disheartened, that they instantly abandoned the fort entirely, taking the road to Skeensborough, a place to the south of Lake George, while their baggage, with what artillery and military stores they could carry off, were sent to the same place by water.

But the British generals were determined not to let them pass so easy; both were pursued and overtaken; their armed vessels consisted only of five galleys, two of which were taken and three blown up, on which they set fire to their boats and fortifications at Skeensborough. On this occasion the Americans lost two hundred boats, one hundred and thirty pieces of cannon, with all their provisions and baggage.

At the break of day, July the 6th, the American land forces, under Colonel Francis, were eagerly pursued by Brigadier-General Fraser, at the head of his brigade, consisting of the grenadiers and light infantry; they were soon overtaken, and made (considering the opposition of raw and undisciplined troops to veteran soldiers) a brave defence.

As they were greatly superior to the British in numbers, they had almost overpowered General Fraser, when General Reidesel, with a large body of Germans, came to his assistance; the Americans were then overpowered in their turn, their commander and above two hundred men killed, and as many taken prisoners. The loss of the British was very inconsiderable; Major Grant of the 24th Regiment, a brave officer, fell on that day.

★★★★★★★★★★

Lord Balcarras, who commanded the British light infantry, distinguished himself in this engagement. The coat which he on that day was pierced through in several places with musket-shot, yet he only received a slight wound.

★★★★★★★★★★

The fort abandoned by the Americans at Ticonderoga, was a place of great importance: the old French lines constructed in the late war, between England and France, which looked towards the encampment, had been repaired the year before, and were in good order. About the centre was a battery of six guns. This occupied about two thirds of the high ground directly opposite to the old fort. The remaining third was open, but some great trees, with their branches outward, were spread about eighty yards for its security. The old Fort was in bad repair, but some guns were mounted on one of its ravelins, that looked toward Lake Champlain. There was also a battery of four guns in the old French lines, which had the same aspect.

On the point above the bridge, was a battery of four guns, and on Mount Independence, another of six or eight. The fort on that side, was nearly a mile from the battery, and formed of picquets. The defence of it might have employed four hundred men. From the battery at the point, a line of entrenchment ran round the mount, upwards of a mile and a half in length. There was a strong abbatis in front of this line. Towards the east of the mount was a block house. Another was on Ticonderoga side. New works were also begun on the mount. A bridge had been constructed, and thrown over the inlet, in order to secure their own vessels, and to obstruct the British fleet.

This bridge was supported by twenty-two piers of timber, the spaces between these piers were filled with separate floats, fifty feet long, and thirteen feet wide, strongly fastened together with large iron chains. It was likewise defended, on the Lake Champlain side, by a boom composed of very large pieces of timber, fastened together by rivetted bolts, and double chains. This bridge, on which the Americans had bestowed so much labour for ten months, and which was deemed by them to le impregnable, was cut through in less time by the British seamen, than it would have cost them, to have described its structure.

The Americans were greatly grieved at the loss of Ticonderoga, and apprehensive of general distress, sought to cover the disgrace by throwing the blame on the general. A court martial was held by order of Congress: cowardice, incapacity, and treachery were brought forward in court, against General St. Clair, who commanded at Ticonderoga. In the course of the trial, it was made to appear, that though thirteen thousand six hundred men had been early called for, as necessary to defend the northern posts; yet on the approach of General Burgoyne the whole force collected to oppose him, was not above half that number. St. Clair was honourably acquitted.

Such was the rapid torrent of success, which in this period of the campaign, swept away all opposition before the British Army. The officers and men, were highly elated with their good fortune. They considered their toils to be nearly at an end; Albany to be within their grasp, and the adjacent provinces reduced to a certainty. The terror which the loss of Ticonderoga spread throughout the New England States was great; but nevertheless, no disposition to purchase safety by submission appeared in any quarter. The army after these successes continued some time in Skeensborough, waiting for their tents, baggage, and provisions.

In the meantime, General Burgoyne detached the 9th Regiment, commanded by Lieutenant-Colonel Hill, to Fort Ann, a place of some strength, in order to intercept such of the enemy as should attempt to retreat towards that fort. They had not proceeded many miles through the woods, before they overtook some boats laden with baggage, women, and invalids, belonging to the Americans rowing up Wood Creek, in order to escape up to Fort Ann, these were immediately secured. They then proceeded on their march, till they came within a quarter of a mile of Fort Ann, which was at that time garrisoned by a strong party of the enemy; they halted and lay upon their arms all night.

Early next morning, 9th July, an American soldier came from the fort; he said that he had deserted, though it was afterwards discovered that he was a spy; he stated that there were one thousand men in the fort, and that they were in the greatest consternation, under an apprehension of the British attacking and storming them; upon this intelligence Colonel Hill dispatched a message to General Burgoyne stating his situation, and how far he had advanced, which was eight or ten miles from the main army.

Not many minutes after this message was sent off, the pretended deserter disappeared; he had viewed the situation and seen the strength of the British, which did not amount to above one hundred and ninety men including officers. It was soon found that he made a faithful report to his friends, for in less than half an hour they came out of the fort with great fury. The British outline of sentries received them with the greatest bravery and steadiness, and obliged them to retreat; they then formed again, and came on with redoubled violence. The officers could be heard encouraging them on to the attack, though their numbers could not be seen, the woods being so thick, but it was soon found that they not only out flanked but were endeavouring to surround the British; in order to prevent this, they were obliged to change their ground, and retire up a high hill, which was in their rear; in performing this manoeuvre several of the men were killed and wounded.

When the troops arrived at the summit of the hill they formed in Indian file, and kept up a well-directed fire till all the ammunition was expended; the enemy observing that the firing ceased, was encouraged to press forward with redoubled vigour, and endeavoured to surround them in order to, cut off all retreat. Just at this critical moment a war hoop was heard, which resounded through the wood; this sound, which was so obnoxious at that time to the Americans, threw them into the utmost consternation.

The war hoop was sounded by Captain Money, deputy quarter master general; he had been detached by General Burgoyne early in the morning from Skeensborough, with a party of Indians, in order to join this detachment when they came within four miles of Fort Ann, they heard the firing; Captain Money ordered them to advance as fast as possible to assist, but they refused to obey him, and either stood still or advanced very slow. Being anxious to join the party at all events, he ran forward by himself with all his might, and came to the bottom of the hill where, just as all the ammunition was expended, he gave the war hoop.

In this affair the British had three officers and nineteen men killed and wounded.

This passage following being literally copied from the author's private *Journal*, he hopes pardon for narrating it in the first person:

Captain Montgomery, son to Sir W. Montgomery, bart. of Dublin, was wounded in the leg and taken prisoner, with the surgeon who was dressing his wound, just before we retired up the hill. I very narrowly escaped myself from being taken prisoner at that time, as I was just in the act of assisting the surgeon in dressing the captain's wound, when the enemy came pouring down upon us like a mighty torrent, in consequence whereof

I was the last man that ascended the hill. I had not been there five minutes when Lieutenant Westrop, who was by my side was shot through the heart; a few minutes after a man, a short distance upon my left, received a ball in his forehead, which took off the roof of his skull! he reeled round, turned up his eyes, muttered some words, and fell dead at my feet!

After the Americans had retreated, we formed on the hill. It was a distressing sight to see the wounded men bleeding on the ground, and what made it more so the rain came pouring down like a deluge upon us; and still to add to the distress of the sufferers, there was nothing to dress their wounds, as the small medicine box which was filled with salve, was left behind with Surgeon Shelly and Captain Montgomery at the time of our movement up the hill. The poor fellows earnestly entreated me to tie up their wounds. Immediately I took off my shirt, tore it up, and with the help of a soldier's wife, (the only woman that was with us, and who kept close by her husband's side during the engagement,) made some bandages, stopped the bleeding of their wounds, and conveyed them in blankets to a small hut about two miles in our rear.

In the meantime, General Burgoyne having heard of our critical situation, moved forward at the head of a strong detachment, in order to support us; but the Americans had set fire to Fort Ann, and fled with great precipitation, before his arrival. Our regiment now marched back to Skeensborough, leaving me behind to attend the wounded, with a small guard for our protection. I was directed, that in case I should be either surrounded or overpowered by the Americans, to deliver a letter, which General Burgoyne gave me, to their commanding officer.

Here I remained seven days with the wounded men, expecting every moment to be taken prisoner; but, although we heard the enemy cutting down trees every night during our stay, in order to block up the passages of the road and river, yet we were never molested. Every necessary which we wanted was sent us from the camp at Skeensborough, and all the wounded men (except three who died) were nearly fit for duty when we arrived at headquarters.

The British were now obliged to suspend all operations for some time, and wait at Skeensborough for the arrival of provisions and tents;

but they employed this interval clearing a passage for the troops, to proceed against the enemy. This was attended with incredible toil. The Americans, now under the direction of General Schuyler, were constantly employed in cutting down large trees on both sides of every road, which was in the line of march. The face of the country was likewise so broken with creeks and marshes, that there were no less than forty bridges to construct, one of which was over a morass two miles in extent. The difficulties of the march through this wilderness were encountered and overcome by the army with a spirit and alacrity which could not be exceeded; and on the 20th of July, it encamped at Fort Edward.

General Schuyler now retreated to Saratoga, and immediately issued a proclamation warning the Americans that they would be dealt with as traitors, if they joined the British Army, and requiring them, with their arms, to repair to the American standard. At the same time numerous parties were employed in desolating the country, felling trees, and throwing every obstruction in the way of the army. Indeed, at first a universal panic intimidated the inhabitants, but they soon recovered from its operation.

The terror excited by the Indians, instead of disposing the inhabitants to court British protection, had a contrary effect. This was chiefly occasioned by the murder of Miss M'Crea, a young lady of the neighbourhood of Fort Edward. As this melancholy transaction made a great noise in Great Britain and America at this time, I shall take the liberty of relating it in the words of that great American partisan Dr. Ramsay:

> This, though true, was no premeditated barbarity The circumstances were as follow: Mr. Jones, (an officer in a new raised American corps attached to our army) her lover, from an anxiety for her safety, engaged some Indians to remove her from among the Americans, and promised to reward the person who should bring her safe to him, with a barrel of rum. Two of the Indians who had conveyed her some distance, on the way to her intended husband, disputed which of them should present her to Mr. Jones. Both were anxious for the reward. One of them killed her with his tomahawk, to prevent the other from receiving it.
>
> Burgoyne obliged the Indians to deliver up the murderer, and threatened to put him to death. His life was only spared, upon the Indians agreeing to terms, which the general thought

would be more efficacious than an execution, to prevent similar mischiefs.

Had the execution taken place, there is every probability that the Indians would have retired from the army, massacring everybody and destroying everything before them; thus, it would have caused the destruction of hundreds of the innocent inhabitants of the frontiers of Canada, if the assassin had been then put to death. When the murder of Miss M'Crea had reached the general's ears, he went to the Indian camp, and insisted in the most determined language that the culprit should be given up to justice, and had it not been for the remonstrances of Monsieur St. Luc le Corne, a Frenchman who then presided over them, the murderer's execution would not have been deferred another day.

St. Luc informed the general that great discontent had reigned among the Indians, at the restraint under which they were kept. To which General Burgoyne replied, "That he had rather lose every Indian in his army than connive at their enormities."

The general afterwards said:

That he ever esteemed the Indian alliances, at best a necessary evil, their services to be overvalued; sometimes insignificant, often barbarous, always capricious, and that the employment of them was only justifiable, when by being united to a regular army, they could be kept under control.

Governed by these sentiments the general acted. In his own expressive language, "he determined to be the soldier, not the executioner of the state." Indeed, it was very remarkable, how he restrained their ferocity during the short time they were with our army; and in order to do this the more effectually, he took to his aid a favourite priest of theirs, who had more control over the passions of the Indians than all their chiefs put together.

By such assistance he was able to enforce obedience to his commands in preventing them from barbarity The following instances are given as proofs of his wisdom and humanity: In a skirmish which happened between the Americans and Indians, two of the American officers were wounded; the Indians, under a heavy fire of the enemy, conveyed the wounded officers on their backs to a place of safety. At another time, a captain, with a detachment of Americans, were placed in ambuscade, in order to cut off part of the British troops on their march; these were discovered by the Indians, who took them all prisoners without a man being hurt. It is also worthy of remark, that no party of the Indians was ever allowed to leave the camp without having a British officer at its head.

Every possible exertion of humanity was used in order to restrain their ferocity. The case of Miss M'Crea excepted, (which was premeditated cruelty) no barbarity or murder was committed by the Northern Army. It is true, that charges of this nature, against that army, were fabricated by the Americans, and propagated in their newspapers, throughout the continent; but this was in order to accomplish the end which they had in view, which was to prevent the loyalists from joining the British standard. This might be pardonable in the Americans at that time, if it be allowed that "stratagems are justifiable in war." But what shall we say to a popular author, fostered in our own country, who, in writing on this campaign, says:

> Such was the sanguine and savage spirit which breathed throughout this infamous proclamation, (alluding to General Burgoyne's proclamation, issued at the camp at Putnam Creek, June 29th, 1777), unparalleled except in *one* very recent instance, that the following lines from Shakespeare's *Timon of Athens,* were not unhappily applied to it as a kind of comment or paraphrase:
>
> ──*Let not thy sword skip one;*
> *Pity not honoured age for his white beard.*
> *Strike me the matron──Let not the virgin's cheek*
> *Make soft thy truncant sword──Spare not the babe*
> *Whose dimpled smiles from fools exhaust their mercy,*
> *Mince it without remorse.*

Lord Harrington, the present, (1809), Commander in Chief in Ireland, was at that time *aide-de-camp* to General Burgoyne, and General Freeman, the present, (1809), Barrack Master General in Ireland, was also in that service, and both His Lordship and the general well know the principle of humanity which dictated even this very proclamation. Its object was to terrify into allegiance, not to massacre to extermination, which the latter quotation of Mr. Belsham more than insinuates: it avows. General Burgoyne in his examination before the house of commons, fully and explicitly explained the motives which induced him to the proclamation. "I have," said he: "Spoken daggers──but *used none*!!!"

After all, it is not much to Mr. Belsham's credit that he does not give the quotation as his own, nor even present the reader with the slightest intimation where, on what occasion, or by whom it was made. The application of such savage motives to one of the most humane and enlightened officers in the service, is more than ungenerous. One of these two facts appears pretty evident—either Mr. Belsham was ashamed of the authority from whence he took the quotation, or too much convinced of its inapplicability to take it upon himself.

The militia was now raised everywhere, and drafted to join the American Army at Saratoga; and that they might have a commander whose abilities could be relied on, General Arnold was appointed, who repaired to Saratoga with a suitable train of artillery; but receiving intelligence that Colonel St. Leger was proceeding with great rapidity in his expedition on the Mahawk River, he moved to Still Water, a place about half way between Saratoga and the junction of the Mahawk and Hudson Rivers.

Before General Burgoyne had crossed Lake Champlain, Colonel St. Leger was sent with a detachment, consisting of two hundred and fifty. British troops, drawn from the 8th and 34th Regiments, Colonel Johnson's corps of New Yorkers, a few German *chasseurs*, a company of Canadians, and another of rangers. These troops were joined by a body of Indians. This detachment, which consisted of near eight hundred men, ascended the River St. Lawrence, crossed Lake Ontario, and commenced the siege of Fort Stanwix, now named by the Americans Fort Schuyler.

A detachment of American militia, consisting of eight hundred men, was immediately ordered to relieve this important fortress. Colonel St. Leger having intelligence of the march of this reinforcement, and knowing the danger of being attacked in his trenches, judiciously detached Colonel Johnson, with a party of regulars and Indians, in order to attack them on their march, either openly or covertly, as circumstances should offer. On the 6th of August, at five o'clock in the morning, Sit John Johnson met the American troops. The Indians, on the sight of the enemy, forgetting the judicious disposition formed by Sir John (which was to suffer the attack to begin with the troops in front, while they should be on both flank and rear) rushed in hatchet in hand, and thereby gave two hundred of the enemy's rear an opportunity to retreat.

Almost all the American officers, with one hundred and sixty men, were slain. Numbers were wounded. Among the latter was General Harkimer, who expired soon after the engagement. Thirty of the Indians were killed and wounded, and the misfortune was doubly aggravated, as some of their favourite chiefs and confidential warriors fell in the carnage. The siege now continued with unabated labour of officers and men. Great was their toil, the smallness of their numbers never admitting the relief of three hours' cessation for sleeping or cooking.

While the British troops were carrying on the siege with vigour, intelligence was brought in, by scouts, of a second corps of a thousand men being on their march. This brigade of continental troops was headed by General Arnold, who was detached from the American headquarters at Still Water, for the purpose of relieving the fort. The following stratagem was practised by Arnold: On his march he took up a gentleman, who resided in that country, of the name of Schuyler, accused him of being a spy in the British service, and threatened him with immediate death. Mr. Schuyler was greatly alarmed, solemnly declared his innocence of the crime laid to his charge, and interceded with Arnold in the most impressive manner for his life. The American general then raising his voice, said:

> Your life and estate shall be given you, on condition that you will repair immediately to the Indians in the British camp before Fort Stanwix, and represent to them that General Burgoyne's army is cut to pieces, and that Arnold is advancing upon them by rapid and forced marches; and be sure to swell the number of my troops to three thousand men.

Mr. Schuyler performed this service very faithfully, for he immediately proceeded to the Indian camp, and being able to converse in their own language, he laid before them every syllable that Arnold told him, adding a great deal more on his own account. This intelligence spread from tent to tent among the Indians. The zeal that they formerly possessed no longer animated them; they complained of the small number of British troops and their former losses.

Colonel St. Leger was greatly alarmed at the change he perceived in them; be immediately called a council of the chiefs, encouraged them by every argument he could suggest; promised to lead them on himself, and bring into the field three hundred of the best troops. They listened to this with great attention; promised to follow him, and agreed that he should reconnoitre the ground most proper for field of battle next morning, accompanied by some of their chief warriors.

But Mr. Schuyler's tale had taken too great hold of their fears; they kept not their word, and the colonel was bigly mortified on being informed next morning that two hundred of them were already decamped; and to add to his mortification, those of them who remained on the ground insisted that he should retreat, or they would abandon him. Hard, indeed, was the situation of Colonel St. Leger at this crisis. The king's troops did not then exceed more than two hundred and fifty men; he was therefore under the necessity of yielding to their resolves, and retired from before the fort at night, sending on his sick, wounded, artillery, &c.

In the meantime, the British Army halted at Fort Edward, while some were employed in bringing forward provisions, stores, &c. over the carrying place from Lake George to Hudson's River. This was found a work of much difficulty, owing to the want of horses and carriages. To remedy this great inconvenience, which retarded the movement of our troops, it was determined to send out a detachment, in order to bring in horses to mount the Brunswick dragoons, if a sufficient number could be found.

Lieutenant-Colonel Baum, a German officer, was ordered on this service with the following troops:—

Brunswick dismounted dragoons	150
Captain Fraser's Rangers	50

(The above company was composed of picked men from different regiments)

Peter's Provincial Corps	150
Provincial and Canadian Volunteers	56
Indians	80
Total	486

Governor Skeene was sent with this detachment, from whose supposed knowledge of the country, and influence among the inhabitants much was expected.

Lieutenant-Colonel Baum was instructed by General Burgoyne to march directly to Bennington, a place about twenty miles east of Hudson's River, intelligence having been received that the Americans had a considerable magazine there.

On the 11th of August, Colonel Baum took post at Batton Kill, and on the 12th, he proceeded to Cambridge, where his advance guard fell in with and defeated a party of American troops, took eight prisoners, one thousand bushels of wheat, and one hundred and fifty bullocks, which he sent to the British camp. Here the colonel was informed that near eighteen hundred of the enemy were posted at Bennington, and that they had a very considerable magazine there, besides two thousand bullocks and three hundred horses. Encouraged by the success of his first attack, the colonel determined to press forward and dislodge the enemy from that post.

He sent every day exact reports of his progress and situation to General Burgoyne, with which the general was perfectly satisfied, and approved his design of attacking Bennington so soon as the colonel could be fully informed of the enemy's number and situation, that it might be attempted with a prospect of success, and without running any risk. Early in the morning of the 14th of August, the colonel was attacked by a body of seven hundred Americans, who, after having a few shot fired at them, retired, and dispersed. By some prisoners taken on this occasion, he was informed that the enemy were strongly entrenched at Bennington, that they expected a large reinforcement from the American Army, and intended to attack him as soon as the reinforcement had joined them.

On receiving this information, the lieutenant-colonel very prop-erly deferred his intention of pushing on to Bennington, and halted in his post, sending off an express to inform General Burgoyne of his situation, and desiring that some troops might be ordered to sustain him. His report was written in such high spirits, that the general was induced to believe that he asked for a reinforcement more to enable him to attack the enemy, than from any apprehension of his corps be-ing in danger of an attack themselves.

In consequence of the above information, Lieutenant-Colonel Breyman was ordered to march with his corps, the battalion of Ger-man grenadiers, and that of Barnier's, (about five hundred men), with two pieces of cannon, to sustain Lieutenant-Colonel Baum: an officer was sent off to inform the latter that Lieutenant-Colonel Breyman had begun his march early on the 15th. The distance between the two corps, rendered this reinforcement useless to Lieutenant-Colonel Baum, as they could not get up time enough, to support him, owing to excessive bad roads, and a continued rain.

August the 16th, in the morning, several bodies of men in arms were observed approaching his post. Lieutenant-Colonel Baum was assured they were loyalists; but their numbers increasing, he ordered out parties to reconnoitre, and soon perceived he was surrounded by the Americans, from Bennington. On a signal being made by the Americans, he was attacked on all sides by superior numbers; he main-tained his post above two hours, and often repulsed the enemy; but finding that his men had expended all their ammunition, and Lieutenant-Colonel Breyman's corps not yet appearing, he was obliged to think of a retreat, with the dragoons, (the Provincials, Canadians, and Indians being already cut off from him).

He twice forced his way through the enemy, and was as often attacked by fresh troops. As a last resource, be ordered his men to draw their swords, and rush in upon the enemy, where, notwithstanding every effort of bravery, this valiant corps, overpowered by superior numbers, was entirely broken, and most of them were either killed or taken prisoners: among the latter was their wounded commander.

Lieutenant-Colonel Breyman had not received the smallest information of this engagement; he arrived on the same ground, and on the same day, but not till the action was over. Instead of meeting his friends, as he expected, he found himself briskly attacked on all sides. Notwithstanding the severe fatigue they had undergone, his troops behaved with great vigour and resolution, and drove the Americans from several bills, on which they were posted. They were, however, at length overpowered, and their ammunition being unfortunately expended, they were obliged with great reluctance to abandon two pieces of artillery they had brought with them, and retreated with good order in the dusk of the evening.

Accustomed to success as the royal troops had been in the preceding part of the campaign, they felt unusual mortification from this unexpected check. Though it did not diminish their courage, it abated their confidence; it deranged every plan for pursuing the advantages which had been previously obtained. Among other embarrassments it reduced them to the alternative of halting till the supplies were brought forward from Fort George, or of advancing without them at the risk of being starved. The former being adopted, the army was detained till the 13th September before they crossed Hudson's River. This unavoidable delay gave time and opportunity to the Americans to assemble in great numbers.

About this period Congress appointed General Gates to command their Northern Army, while the militia, flushed with their recent success, collected in great numbers to his standard.

The affair of Bennington, though of great importance to the Americans, was of still more consequence in a national sense to the British Army, as it gave occasion to a correspondence which tended to wipe off the reproaches of inhumanity from them, which had gone forth and astonished all Europe. Colonel Baum, who commanded the detachment, being wounded and a prisoner in the American camp, General Burgoyne was desirous of sending not only to that officer, but all those whom the fortune of war had put on that occasion, into the enemy's hands, all the succour in his power, and with that view wrote to General Gates to permit the baggage and servants of the prisoners to pass to them unmolested. In this letter, dated 30th of August, after the formal requisition, he says:

It is with great concern I find myself obliged to add to this application, a complaint of the bad treatment the Provincial soldiers in the king's service received after the affair of Bennington. I have reports, upon oath, that some were refused quarter after having asked it: I am willing to believe this was against the order and inclination of your officers; but it is my part to require an explanation, and to warn you of the horrors of retaliation, if such a practice is not in the strongest terms discountenanced and reprehended.

To this complaint, General Gates expressed his astonishment that General Burgoyne should mention inhumanity or threaten retaliation:

Nothing, says he, happened in the action at Bennington but what is common, when works are carried by assault. That the savages of America should in their warfare mangle and scalp the unhappy prisoners is neither new nor extraordinary; but that the famous Lieutenant-General Burgoyne, in whom the fine gentleman is united with the soldier and the scholar, should hire the savages of America to scalp Europeans, and the descendants of Europeans; nay more, that he should pay a price for each scalp so barbarously taken, is more than will be believed in Europe until authenticated facts shall in every *gazette*, confirm the truth of the horrid tale.
Miss M'Crea, a young lady, lovely to the sight, of virtuous character and amiable disposition, engaged to an officer of your army, was, with other women and children, taken out of a house near Fort Edward, carried into the woods, and there scalped and mangled in a most shocking manner. Two parents with their six children were all treated with the same inhumanity, while quietly residing in their once happy dwelling.
The miserable fate of Miss M'Crea, was particularly aggravated by her being dressed to receive her promised husband; but she met her murderers employed by you. Upwards of one hundred

men, women, and children have perished by the hands of the ruffians, to whom it is asserted you have paid the price of blood.

To these specific charges General Burgoyne answered:

I have hesitated, sir, upon answering the charges in your letter. I have disdained to justify myself against rhapsodies of fiction and calumny, which from the first of this contest it has been an unvaried American policy to propagate, but which shall no longer impose upon the world: I am induced to deviate from this general rule, in the present instance, lest my silence should be construed an acknowledgment of the truth of your allegations, and a pretence be thence taken for exercising future barbarities by the American troops.

By this motive, and upon this only, I condescend to inform you, that I would not be conscious of the acts you presume to impute to me, for the whole continent of America, though the wealth of worlds were in its bowels, and a paradise upon its surface.

It has happened that all my transactions, with the Indian nations last year and this, have been clearly heard, distinctly understood, accurately minuted by very numerous, and, in many parts, very unprejudiced persons. So immediately opposite to truth is your assertion that I have paid a price for scalps, that one of the first regulations established by me at the great council in May, and repeated, enforced, and invariably adhered to since, was, that the Indians should receive compensation for prisoners, because it would prevent cruelty, and that not only such compensation should be withheld, but a strict account would be demanded for scalps.

These pledges of conquest, for such you well know they will ever esteem them, were solemnly and peremptorily prohibited to be taken from the wounded, and even the dying, and the persons of aged men, women, children, and prisoners, were pronounced sacred even in assaults.

In regard to Miss M'Crea, her fall wanted not the tragic display you have laboured to give it, to make it as sincerely abhorred and lamented by me as it can be by the tenderest of her friends. The fact was no premeditated barbarity; on the contrary, two chiefs who had brought her off for the purpose of security, not of violence to her person, disputed which should be her guard:

in a fit of savage passion in one, from whose hands she was snatched, the unhappy woman became the victim.

Upon the first intelligence of this event, I obliged the Indians to deliver the murderer into my hands; and though to have punished him by our laws, or principles of justice, would have been perhaps unprecedented, he certainly should have suffered an ignominious death, had I not been convinced, from many circumstances and observations, beyond the possibility of a doubt, that a pardon, under the terms which I prescribed and they accepted, would be more efficacious than an execution, to prevent similar mischiefs.

The above instance excepted, your intelligence respecting the cruelties of the Indians is false.

You seem to threaten me with European publications, which affect me as little as any other threats you could make; but in regard to American publications, whether your charge against me, which I acquit you of believing, was penned from a *gazette* or for a *gazette*, I desire and demand of you as a man of honour, that, should it appear in print at all, this answer may follow it.

It cannot be matter of much surprise, that such reports were fabricated by the Americans to serve their own purposes; but that they should obtain circulation and credence at home is truly astonishing. *Saunders's News-Letter* of August 14, 1777, gravely asserts:

That seven hundred men, women, and children, were scalped on the sides of Lake Champlain; that the light infantry and Indians scoured each bank, women, &c. flying in turns before them.

Now the fact is, that from St. John's to Crown Point there were not more than ten human dwellings, the whole being upwards of eighty miles of woods and wilderness. Could inhabitants, *which never existed in a country*, be scalped, or fly before their enemies?—How necessary is it for those who fabricate such deeds, to acquaint themselves with the topography of a place in which they fix their scene of action!!!!

General Burgoyne being disappointed in his attempt on Bennington, a month's provision for the army was ordered to be brought forward from Lake George. In the meantime, he threw a bridge of boats over the River Hudson, which was crossed on the 13th and 14th of September, the army taking post on the heights and plains of Saratoga.

As the Royal troops advanced towards the enemy along the side of Hudson's River, they found the country covered with thick woods, and the bridges broken down every quarter of a mile; these they were obliged to repair. Every obstacle to impede their march was thrown in their way, and they soon discovered that the Americans were determined to dispute every inch of the ground with them.

September 19th. The Royal Army halted within two miles of the enemy's encampment, and formed for battle, in the order on the page following.

The signal guns, which had been previously settled to give notice that all was ready, now fired, and the troops advanced in the greatest order and regularity.

In the meantime, the Americans came out of their entrenchments in great force, and moved forward to meet the British Army. Their line extended upwards of two miles, while they were supported by several strong columns. The scouts and flankers of both armies were soon in contact, and the firing began a little after mid-day.

The Americans being incapable from the nature of the country, of perceiving the different combinations of the march, (as the country is thickly covered with woods, movements may be effected without a possibility of being discovered), advanced a strong column, with a view of turning the British line upon the right; here they met the grenadiers and light infantry, who gave them a tremendous fire. Finding that it was impossible to penetrate the line at this point, they immediately countermarched and directed their principal effort to the centre. Here the conflict was dreadful; for four hours a constant blaze of fire was kept up, and both armies seemed to be determined on death or victory.

> *Here mingling hands, but not with friendly gripe,*
> *Join in the fight; and breasts in close embrace,*
> *But mortal as the iron arms of death.*
> *Here words austere, of perilous command,*
> *And valour swift t'obey; bold feats of arms*
> *Dreadful to see, and glorious to relate.*

Men, and particularly officers, dropped every moment on each side. Several of the Americans placed themselves in high trees, and as often as they could distinguish a British officer's uniform, took him off by deliberately aiming at his person. Reinforcements successively arrived and strengthened the American line. The 20th, 21st, and 62nd Regiments greatly distinguished themselves. The stress of the action

Canadians, Provincials, and Indians, on their flanks and front;

ORDER

Of the BRITISH and GERMAN Troops at the Battle of Freeman's Farm, between Saratoga and Still-Water, on the 19th of September, 1777.

Lord Petersham,† and Sir James Clarke, Aid-de-camps to Gen. Burgoyne.

RIGHT WING.	CENTRE.	LEFT WING.
LED ON BY	LED ON BY	LED ON BY
BRIG. GEN. FRAZER,	LIEUT. GEN. BURGOYNE,	MAJOR GENERALS PHILLIPS
MAJORS ACKLAND,	AND	AND
AND	BRIG. GEN. HAMILTON.	REIDESEL.
LORD BALCARRES,		
British Light Infantry and Grenadiers,* and 24th Regiment, sustained by Colonel BREYMAN'S German Riflemen.	20th Regiment......Lieut.Col. Lynd. 21st do....Lieut. Col. Brig.Gen. Hamilton. 62d do..............Lieut. Col. Anstruther.	British Artillery, commanded by MAJOR WILLIAMS, Sustained by the German Corps.

9th Regiment....Lieut. Col. Hill, Reserve.

47th Regiment guarding the batteaux.‡
General Hospital in the rear.

* These flank companies belonged to the 9th, 20th, 21st, 24th, 29th, 31st, 34th, 47th, 53d, and 62d regiments.

† Now Earl Harrington, the present Commander in Chief in Ireland.

‡ Two companies of this Regiment were left on Diamond Island in Lake George.

lay chiefly on these regiments, which stood the repeated attacks of three tines their number for four hours.

"Not noise, nor number, nor the brawny limb,
Nor high built size prevails: 'Tis courage fights,
'Tis courage conquers.

Most of the other corps of the army bore a good share in this desperate conflict. The 24th Regiment, with the grenadiers, and part of the light infantry, were for some time brought into action, and charged with their usual spirit and bravery. Breyman's riflemen likewise did good service.

Major-General Phillips, upon hearing the firing, made his way through a difficult part of the wood to the scene of action, and brought up with him Major Williams and four pieces of artillery; this reinforcement animated our troops in the centre, which at that moment were critically pressed by a great superiority of fire, and to which the major-general led up the 20th Regiment at the utmost personal hazard. Major-General Reidesel then brought forward part of the left wing, and arrived in time to charge the enemy with regularity and bravery.

Few actions have been characterized by more obstinacy in attack or defence; the British troops repeatedly tried their bayonet with their usual success.

As the day closed, the Americans retreated on all sides, and left them masters of the field of battle.

It was supposed that during this engagement near fifteen hundred men were killed and wounded in both armies. The British had to lament more than three hundred brave officers and men, who were killed and wounded on that day!

General Burgoyne, in his dispatches to government, says:

The behaviour of the officers and men in general was exemplary, brigadier General Fraser took his position in the beginning of the day, with great judgment, and sustained the action with constant presence of mind and vigour. Brigadier-General Hamilton was the whole time engaged, and acquitted himself with great honour, activity and good conduct. The artillery in general was distinguished, and the brigade under Captain Jones, who was killed in the action, was conspicuously so.

★★★★★★★★★★

The estimation in which these services of the artillery (especially the

Irish drafts) were held at home can be best appreciated by the testimony of distinguished characters. Among many others, the following testimonial is deserving particular notice:

Extract of a letter from lord viscount Townshend, Master-General of the British Ordnance, to Lieutenant-Colonel Straten, Commandant of the Royal Irish Regiment of Artillery.

"Sir,

"By Lieutenant Slack, who this evening arrived from Quebec, and who has related to me many transactions of the late unfortunate campaign in that part of America, I am informed that none among our gallant troops behaved more noble than the drafts from the Royal Irish artillery, who being now exchanged are to return. I am sorry they suffered so much; but it is the lot of brave men, who, so situated, prefer a glorious discharge of their duty to an unavailing desertion of it. Be assured, sir, I have a sincere, a grateful pleasure, in doing this justice to part of that corps, whose zeal for His Majesty's service, and ambition to distinguish themselves, I have never doubted would be equal to any whatever. I am, sir, &c.

Townshend."

****

General Burgoyne during this conflict behaved with great personal bravery, he shunned no danger; his presence and conduct animated the troops, (for they greatly loved the general;) he delivered his orders with precision and coolness; and in the heat, fury, and danger of the fight maintained those true characteristics of the soldier—serenity, fortitude and undaunted intrepidity.

20th. The army moved forward, and took post nearly within cannon shot of the American's fortified camp. Here the English strengthened their camp by cutting down large trees, which served for breast works.

21st. This day a messenger arrived from Sir Henry Clinton, informing General Burgoyne of his intention to attack Fort Montgomery, in about ten days from the date of his letter, which was the 20th of September; this was the only messenger from him or Sir William Howe which had reached our camp since the beginning of August. This messenger was sent back the same night to Sir Henry Clinton, and charged to deliver him a silver bullet, and to give it into the general's own hands. If he should happen to be suspected as an enemy and taken prisoner by the American troops, he was ordered to swallow the bullet which would prevent the message from being detected. Having reached as far as Fort Montgomery, on the North River, he made enquiry for General Clinton; and finding, on being brought before him, that he was not the person to whom he was sent, but that he was Governor Clinton of the state of New York, and a general in the American service, he turned aside and swallowed the silver ball.

Being observed by some of the attendants, he was immediately taken into custody; when being interrogated as to what business he had with General Clinton, and discovering some embarrassment in his answers, it was proposed to administer an emetic, to ascertain what he had swallowed with such precipitation. The idea was adopted, and the consequence was, that he threw up the silver ball, which being unscrewed, was found to contain a letter from General Burgoyne to Sir Henry Clinton, the purport of which was, to explain his situation and the necessity of a diversion up the North River, in order to oblige General Gates to detach troops from his army; and further, that General Burgoyne would wait favourable events in his position to the 12th October. The messenger was immediately hung as a spy.

October 3rd. This day the rations were diminished. The army saw the necessity of this measure, complaint or murmur was heard throughout the British camp.

7th. A detachment of fifteen hundred men, led on by General Burgoyne in person, made a movement to the right in order to discover if there were any possible means of forcing a passage to Albany.

As they advanced, they were checked by a very sudden and rapid attack of the enemy on the left; there Major Ackland was posted with the British grenadiers, who sustained the attack with great resolution and firmness. The Americans extended their attack along the whole front of the German troops, who were posted on the right of the grenadiers, and they also marched a large body round their flanks, in order to cut off their retreat. To oppose this bold enterprise the British light infantry, with a part of the 34th Regiment, were directed to form a second line, and to secure the return of the troops into camp. In the meantime, the Americans pushed forward a fresh and a strong reinforcement to renew the action upon the left; where the troops, overpowered by so great a superiority, gave way, but the light infantry and 24th Regiment, by a rapid movement, came to give succour, and saved the line from being carried; in doing which, Brigadier-General Fraser received his mortal wound.

The action now became very serious, as the British lines lay exposed to the enemy's sudden attack. In this crisis of danger General Burgoyne appeared cool and intrepid. He directed Generals Philips and Reidesel to cover the retreat, while such troops as were most ready were ordered for the defence of the camp. The British troops were hard pressed, but retreated in good order; they were obliged to leave six pieces of cannon behind, all the horses having been killed, and all the artillery men, who had, as usual, behaved with the utmost bravery, being either killed or wounded.

————*Veteran bands*
Here made their last campaign.

General Arnold, with a brigade of continental troops, pushed rapidly forward, for that part of the camp possessed by Lord Balcarres, at the head of the British light infantry, and some of the line; here they were received by a heavy and well directed fire which mowed down their ranks, and compelled them to retreat in disorder. Arnold now left this brigade and put himself at the head of a fresh corps, which he ordered instantly to advance and attack the lines in their front, which were defended by Lieutenant-Colonel Breyman, at the head of the German reserve.

The Americans pressed on with rapidity, and carried the works. Arnold was one of the first who entered them, and was wounded. Lieutenant-Colonel Breyman was killed. The Germans retreated firing, until they had gained their tents in the rear of the entrenchments; but supposing that the assault was general, gave one discharge, after which some retreated to the British camp, but others surrendered prisoners. Night at length put an end to the engagement.

This day's battle added many brave officers and men to the melancholy list of killed and wounded.

Brigadier-General Fraser, on account of his distinguished merit, was greatly lamented by the whole army; Sir James Clarke, General Burgoyne's *aide-de-camp*, was mortally wounded; Majors Ackland and Williams were taken prisoners. The former was wounded. The general himself had some very narrow escapes, a shot passed through his hat and another through his waistcoat. It was with great truth said, that, in the service of this campaign, the officers bled profusely and most honourably.

On the side of the Americans, the loss in killed and wounded was very great, and far exceeded ours.

The enemy, now having made a lodgement on the right of the

British, their rear of course was exposed. In order to avoid this, General Burgoyne, by a judicious manoeuvre, took a position upon the heights above the general hospital; this was executed in the night with the greatest order, regularity, and silence. By this entire change of front, the American Army was under the necessity of forming a new disposition.

October 8th. The British remained under arms all this day, offering the enemy battle, but nothing more than skirmishes took place, in one of which the American General Lincoln was dangerously wounded.

In the meantime, General Burgoyne discovered that the Americans were marching a strong column forward, in order to turn the British right, which, if effected would have enclosed them on every side; nothing could prevent this but an immediate retreat to Saratoga.

The army began to march to this place at nine o'clock at night; Major-General Reidesel led the van, and Major-General Philips brought up the rear. They were under the necessity of leaving the sick and wounded behind.

9th. This evening the van arrived at the heights of Saratoga, having endured much hardships on the march, from a heavy rain and bad road; here it was discovered that a division of the Americans had already arrived, and were employed in throwing up entrenchments on the heights before the British, on whose approach they retired over the ford, and joined a large body there; who likewise were employed for the same purpose of preventing all retreat.

10th. The *batteaux* with what little provisions remained were constantly fired upon, from the opposite side of the river; many of them fell into the hands of the enemy, and several of the men who conducted them, were killed and wounded.

11th. Several men were employed this day in landing the provisions from the boats, and conveying them up to the bill, under a very galling fire from the enemy:

Very great indeed were the distresses which the army had to encounter at this period, yet they were borne with fortitude. The greatest subordination was manifested throughout the British lines. The men were willing and ready to face any danger, when led on by officers whom they loved and respected, and who shared with them in every toil and hardship.

Numerous parties of the militia now joined the Americans and swarmed around the little adverse army like birds of prey. Roaring of cannon and whistling of bullets from their rifle pieces, were heard constantly by day and night.

12th. A council of war, composed of general officers was held, in which General Burgoyne stated the present situation of affairs to the following effect:

Upwards of fourteen thousand of the enemy, with a considerable quantity of artillery almost surround us, threatening an attack every moment. Two large bodies with cannon at Fort Edward guard that passage. A brigade below Saratoga church, by which their two armies can have a free communication. Our *batteaux* destroyed, and the enemy in possession of the immediate passes over Hudson's River. The following routes are those which offer themselves for the retreat of the army:

1st. To cross the river by the ford at Fort Edward.

2nd. To take a passage over the mountains until we arrived at some place higher up the river, where it can be passed by rafts.

3rd. To continue the march on the mountains until we arrive at a ford, reported to be passable, but the passage of which is acknowledged to be attended with much danger.

4th. To persevere in the march over the mountains, until we clear the head of Hudson's River, keeping on the westward of Lake George until the army shall arrive at Ticonderoga. The Indians, and some small bodies of stragglers only, have effected the latter passage.

At the same time, General Burgoyne submitted to the council his readiness to attack the enemy, and attempt forcing a passage through their ranks. The council, however, determined in favour of a retreat by night. It was also stated, that the provisions could not possibly hold out beyond the 20th, and that there were neither rum nor spruce beer. It would be rendering an act of injustice to the memory of General Burgoyne not to copy distinctly the communications which he made to the council, and their answers on each head. This will clearly evince, that he then did nothing *of himself;* but, on the contrary, that he acted from the *collective wisdom* of the army. From the four different statements already given, the general deduced the following propositions, and to them the council gave the annexed replies:

1st. To wait in the present position an attack from the enemy, or the chance of favourable events.

2nd. To attack the enemy.

3rd. To retreat, repairing the bridges as the army moves for the artillery, in order to force the passage of the ford.

4th. To retreat by night, leaving the artillery and the baggage; and should it be found impracticable to force the passage with musketry, to attempt the upper ford, or the passage round Lake George.

5th. In case the enemy by extending to their left, leave their rear open, to march rapidly for Albany.

Upon the first proposition resolved, that the situation would grow worse by delay; that the provision now in store is not more than sufficient for the retreat, should impediments intervene, or a circuit of country become necessary; and as the enemy did not attack when the ground was unfortified, it is not probable they will do it now, as they have a better game to play. The second unadvisable and desperate, there being no, possibility of reconnoitring the enemy's position, and their great superiority of numbers known.

The third impracticable.

The fifth thought worthy of consideration by the Lieutenant-General, Major-General Phillips, and Brigadier-General Hamilton; but the position of the enemy yet gives no open for it.

Resolved, that the fourth proposition is the only resource, *and* that to effect it, the utmost secrecy and silence is to be observed; and the troops are to be put in motion from the right in the still part of the night, without any change in the disposition.

★★★★★★★★★★

It depended upon the delivery of six days provision in due time, and upon the return of scouts who had been sent forward, to examine by what route the army could probably move the first four miles undiscovered, whether the plan should take place on that day, or on the morrow.

★★★★★★★★★★

The arrival of scouts prevented the execution of this determination. They brought intelligence, that the enemy's position on the right was such, and they had so many small parties out, that it would be impossible to move without being immediately discovered. Thus circumstanced,

General Burgoyne again assembled the council. This measure became indispensable, from the situation of the British Army and the character of their general. Rashly to have sacrificed the lives of those over whom he had command, would have been temerity; meanly to save their lives by compromise (unless no other means existed) would have for ever tarnished his own reputation. He summoned the officers for their opinion (the field officers and captains commanding corps were added to this council); and, in this sad dilemma, acted on their resolves. But the minutes of this last proceeding, will best speak for themselves.

Minutes and proceedings of a council of war, consisting of all the general officers, field officers, and captains commanding corps, on the heights of Saratoga, October the 13th, 1777:
The lieutenant-general having explained the situation of affairs as in the preceding council, with the additional intelligence, that the enemy was entrenched at the fords of Fort Edward, and likewise occupied the strong position on the pine plains between Fort George and Fort Edward, expressed his readiness to undertake at their head, any enterprise of difficulty or hazard that should appear to them within the compass of their strength and spirit.

He added, that he had reason to believe a capitulation had been in the contemplation of some, perhaps of all, who knew the real situation of things; that, upon a circumstance of such consequence to national and personal honour, he thought it a duty to his country, and to himself, to extend his council beyond the usual limits; that the assembly present might justly be esteemed a full representation of the army; and that he should think himself unjustifiable in taking any step in so serious a matter, without such a concurrence of sentiments as should make a treaty the act of the army as well as that of the general. The first question, therefore, he desired them to decide was:

Whether an army of three thousand five hundred fighting men, and well provided with artillery, were justifiable, upon the principles of national dignity and military honour, in capitulating in any possible situation? Resolved, *nem. con.* in the affirmative.

Question 2. Is the present situation of that nature? Resolved, *nem. con.* that the present situation justifies a capitulation upon honourable terms.

General Burgoyne then drew up the following letter, directed to General Gates, relative to the negotiation, and laid it before the council. It was unanimously approved, and upon that foundation the treaty opened.

> After having fought you twice, Lieutenant-General Burgoyne, has waited some days in his present position, determined to try a third conflict, against any force you could bring to attack him.
>
> He is apprised of the superiority of your numbers, and the disposition of your troops, to impede his supplies, and render his retreat a scene of carnage on both sides. In this situation he is compelled by humanity, and thinks himself justified by established principles, and precedents of state, and of war, to spare the lives of brave men upon honourable terms.

Should Major-General Gates, be inclined to treat upon that idea, General Burgoyne would propose a cessation of arms, during the time necessary to communicate the preliminary terms by which in any extremity, he, and his army, mean to abide.

General Gates then transmitted the following proposals to General Burgoyne:

General Burgoyne's army being exceedingly reduced by repeated defeats, by desertion, sickness, &c. their provisions exhausted, their military horses, tents and baggage taken or destroyed, their retreat cut off, and their camp invested, they can only be allowed to surrender prisoners of war.

Answer. Lieutenant-General Burgoyne's army however reduced, will never admit that their retreat is cut off while they have arms in their hands.

The troops under his excellency General Burgoyne's command, may be drawn up in their encampments, where they will be ordered to ground their arms, and may thereupon be marched to the river side to be passed over in their way towards Bennington.

Answer. This article inadmissible in any extremity; sooner than this army will consent to ground their arms in their encampment, they will rush on the enemy determined to take no quarter. If General Gates does not mean to recede from this article the treaty ends at once. The army will to a man proceed to any act of desperation rather than submit to that article.

General Gates did recede from this article, and the following was substituted in its stead,

The troops to march out of their camp with the honours of war, and the artillery of the entrenchments, to the verge of the river, where their arms and artillery must be left. The arms to be piled by word of command from their own officers.

★★★★★★★★★★

While the British troops were marching from the heights of Saratoga to the verge of the river, the American drummers and fifers were ordered by General Gates to play the tune of "Yankey Doodle," while at the same time his troops were drawn up in a thick part of the wood out of sight of the British Army. The arms were piled by order of the British officers.

★★★★★★★★★★

A free passage to be granted to the army under Lieutenant-General Burgoyne to Great Britain, upon condition of not serving again in North America during the present contest; and the port of Boston to be assigned for the entry of transports to receive the troops whenever General Howe shall so order. (*This article was never fulfilled.*)

Such was the melancholy catastrophe of these brave men, after undergoing:

> A series of hard toil, incessant effort, stubborn action, till disabled in the collateral branches of the army, by the total defection of the Indians, the desertion or timidity of the Canadians and Provincials, some individuals excepted; disappointed in the last hope of any timely co-operation from other armies; the regular troops reduced by losses from the best parts to three thousand five hundred fighting men, not two thousand of which were British; only three days provisions in store, upon short allowance; invested by an army of sixteen thousand men, and no apparent means of retreat remaining. (General Burgoyne's own words.)

The British Army, under these circumstances, were induced to open the above treaty.

In the meantime, Sir Henry Clinton had sailed up the North River, attacked and carried Fort Montgomery, and passed it in his attempt

137

to favour the descent of General Burgoyne, and in all probability a junction of these two armies would have been effected, had the expedition been earlier adopted, as meditated by Sir Henry Clinton.

Fort Montgomery was erected by the Americans the year before; there was laid a strong boom across the river, guarded by two frigates, the Hudson being navigable for ships of war of sixty guns much higher than this fort, and at spring tides for frigates near to Albany.

After this fort was taken, the town of Esopus (now called Kingston,) situated near the west bank of Hudson's River, was destroyed by General Vaughan; it was here that Captain Rose and Lieutenant Meddagh, two leaders of the loyalists, were executed without a regular form of trial, for their adherence to the British cause; this circumstance, with others of a similar nature, had rendered the place extremely odious to the loyal followers of the British arms, and possibly might have occasioned its conflagration. A large body of loyalists were forming at this time on the eastern shore of the river, to join the Royal Army; but the advanced state of the season prevented the continuance of Sir Henry Clinton's force in the rear, and they were obliged to return to New York.

It should have been mentioned, that, on the very day the Royal forces crossed Hudson's River, the Americans in order to cut off the retreat of the British Army, under General Burgoyne, in the most effectual manner, undertook an expedition against Ticonderoga. They conducted their operations with such secrecy and address, that on the 18th of September a sudden and general attack was made upon the carrying place of Lake George, Sugar Hill, Ticonderoga, and Mount Independence.

The sea officer commanding the armed sloop stationed to defend the carrying place, as also some of the officers commanding at the ports at the Sugar Hill, and at the portage were surprised, and a considerable part of four, companies of the 53rd Regiment were made prisoners. A blockhouse, commanded by Lieutenant Lord of that regiment, was the only post on that side where they had time to make use of their arms, and they made a gallant defence, till cannon taken from the *Surprize* vessel was brought against them.

The enemy having twice summoned Brigadier-General Powell, and received such answers as became a gallant officer, entrusted with so important a post, and having tried during the course of four days several attacks, and being repulsed in all, retreated without doing any considerable damage.

Brigadier-General Powell gave great commendation to the British and German troops stationed at Mount Independence. The brigadier mentioned with great applause the behaviour of Captain Taylor of the 21st Regiment, who was accidentally there on the road to the army, and Lieutenant Beercroft of the 24th Regiment, who, with the artificers in arms, defended an important battery,

On the 24th of September, the enemy enabled by the capture of the gunboats and *batteaux*, (which they had made after the surprise of the sloops,) to embark upon Lake George, attacked Diamond Island in two divisions. Captain Aubrey, and two companies of the 47th Regiment, had been posted at that island from the time the army passed the Hudson's River; the enemy were repulsed by Captain Aubrey, with great loss, and pursued by the gun boats under his command to the east shore, where two of our principal vessels were re-taken, together with all the cannon; they had just time to set fire to the other *batteaux*, and retreated over the mountains,

The sacrifice which, without obtaining its end, was made in the course of this campaign, will the more fully appear on perusal of the following lists of those who suffered and those who fell:

July 2d. Lieutenant Haughton, 53d regiment, wounded near Ticonderoga.
—— 6th. Second Lieutenant Clelland, Royal Artillery, killed at Hubberton.
Volunteer Sutton, wounded at do.
—— 7th. Major Grant,* 24th regiment, killed at do.
Lieutenant Douglas, 29th do.   do.   do.
————— Haggart, marines,   do.   do.

LIGHT INFANTRY.

Major Lord Balcarres, 53d regiment, wounded at do.				
Captain Harris,	34th	do.	do.	do.
———— Craig,	47th	do.	do.	do.
Lieutenant Cullen,	53d	do.	do.	do.
———— Jones,	62d	do.	do.	do.

GRENADIERS.

Captain Staypleton, 9th regiment, died of his wounds, at do.				
Major Ackland,	20th	do. wounded, at	do.	
Captain Ross,	34th	do.	do.	do.
———— Shrimpton,	62d	do.	do.	do.
Lieutenant Rowe,	9th	do.	do.	do.
———— Steele,	29th	do.	do.	do.

* Major Grant was twice wounded at Ticonderoga, under general Amherst, in the former wars.

Lieutenant Richardson, 34th regt.		wounded	{ Hub-berton
Volunteer Lindsay,		do.	do.
July 9th, Lieutenant Westrop,	9th regt.	killed	{ Fort Ann.
Captain Montgomery,	— do.	{ wounded & taken prisoner, }	do.
Lieutenant Stavely,	— do.	wounded	do.
———— Murray,	— do.	do.	do.
Adjutant Fielding,	— do.	do.	do.
Aug. 16, Lieutenant Wright,	— do.	killed	{ Ben-ning-ton.
Ensign Baron De Salons,	— do.	wounded,	do.
Sept. 19, Captain Jones, Royal Artillery,		killed	{ Free-man's Farm.
Lieutenant Cooke,	20th	do.	do.	do.
———— Lucas,	—	do.	do.	do.
———— Currie,	21st	do.	do.	do.
———— M'Kenzie,	—	do.	do.	do.
———— Robinson,	—	do.	do.	do.
———— Reynal,	24th	do.	do.	do.
———— Hervey,	62d	do.	do.	do.
Ensign Phillips,	—	do.	do.	do.
———— Taylor,	—	do.	do.	do.
———— Young,	—	do.	do.	do.
Lt. Col. Lynd,	20th	do.	wounded	do.
*———— Anstruther,	62d	do.	do.	do.
Major Forbes,	9th	do.	do.	do.
—— Agnew,	24th	do.	do.	do.
*—— Harnage,	62d	do.	do.	do.
Captain Sweetenham,	9th	do.	do.	do.
———— Dowling,	21st	do.	do.	do.
———— Stanley,	—	do.	do.	do.
———— Farquire	—	do.	do.	do.
———— Weyms,	—	do.	do.	do.
———— Ramsay,	—	do.	do.	do.
———— Blake,	24th	do.	do.	do.
Lieutenant Prince,	9th	do.	do.	do.
————Rutherford,	21st	do.	do.	do.
Ensign Hervey,	62d	do.	do.	do.

Thus marked * were wounded in two different actions.

Oct. 7th, Brig. general Frazer,   killed, { near Still Water.

SirJames Clarke, Aid de Camp to General Burgoyne, } { mortally wounded & taken prisoner, } do.

Captain Wight,   53d regiment,   killed   do.
Lieutenant Obin,   20th   do.   do.   do.
————— Turnbull,   21st   do.   do.   do.
————— Stewart,   62d   do.   do.   do.
Lt. Col. Anstruther,   —   do.   wounded   do.
*Major Ackland,   20th   do.   do.   do.
——— Harnage,   62d   do.   do.   do.
Captain Strangways,   24th   do.   do.   do.
——— Bunbury,   62d   do.   do.   do.
———Green Aid de de Camp to General Philips } 31st   do.   do.   do.
Captain Bloomfield, Major of Brigade } Royal Artillery, do.   do.
Lieutenant Battersby, 29th light infantry, do.   do.
————— Fisherton,   21st   do.   do.   do.
————— *Richardson, 34th grenadiers, do.   do.
————— Dowling,   29th regiment   do.   do.
————— Doyle,   24th   do.   do.   do.
————— Williams,   29th   do.   do.   do.
————— Richardson,   34th battalion,   do.   do.
————— Houghton,   53d regiment,   do.   do.
————— Smith, Royal Artillery,   do.   do.
————— Howarth,   do.   do.   do.
Ensign Connel,   20th regiment,   do.   do.
——— Blake,   62d   do.   do.   do.

Oct. 11th. Adjutant Fitzgerald,   —   do.   killed { at Saratoga.

——— 7th,   Major Ackland, 20th   do. } taken prisoner, { near Still Water

——— Williams, Royal Artillery,   do.   do.

July 9th. Captain Montgomery,   9th regiment,   do. { Fort Ann.

Oct. 7th. ——— Money, Deputy Quarter Master General, } — do.   do. { near Still Water
Lieutenant Johnson,   29th   do.   do.   do.
——— York,   —   do.   do.   do.

Lieut. Howarth, Royal Artillery, } taken prisoner, { near Still Water

Ensign D'Antroch,   62d regiment,   do.   do.
——— Naylor,   —   do.   do.   do.

July 9th, Surgeon Shelly,   9th   do.   do. { at Fort Ann.

KILLED.	WOUNDED.
1 Brigadier General,	2 Lieutenant Colonels,
1 Major,	5 Majors,
1 Aid de Camp,	16 Captains,
3 Captains,	18 Lieutenants,
15 Lieutenants,	4 Ensigns,
4 Ensigns,	1 Adjutant,
12 Serjeants,	2 Volunteers,
5 Drummers,	38 Serjeants,
313 Rank & File.	4 Drummers,
	715 Rank & File.
355 Total killed.	
	805 Total wounded.

Killed.........................355
Wounded.....................805

Total killed and wounded of the British army......1160

The following numbers surrendered prisoners at Saratoga, on the 17th October, 1777 :—

British troops, including the sick and wounded, in camp..2240
German ditto,   do.   do.......1700
Canadians, Provincials, Batteaux-men, &c................... 480
Sick and -wounded left behind in the British camp, } 460
    when general Burgoyne retreated to Saratoga..... }

Total.............4880

An account of brass ordnance taken :

2———24 pounders.
4———12 ditto.
18——— 6 ditto.
4——— 3 ditto.
5——— 5½ inch royal howitzers.
2——— 8 inch brass mortars.

Total.......35

The loss of General Fraser was a severe shock to the army, and the sensation which it produced was felt by all ranks, from the commander in chief to the private. After he was wounded, he was supported by two officers, one on each side of his horse. When he arrived in camp, the officers all anxiously enquired as to his wound: the downcast look and melancholy that were visible to everyone, too plainly spoke his situation, and all the answer he could make to the many inquiries, was a shake of his head, expressive that all was over with him. So much was he beloved that even the women flocked round, solicitous for his fate.

When he had reached his tent, and was recovered a little from the faintness occasioned by the loss of blood, he told those around him, that he saw the man who shot him; he was a rifle man, and aimed from a tree. The ball entered a little below his breast, and penetrated just under the back bone. After the surgeon had dressed his wound, he said to him, very composedly, "Tell me, to the best of your skill and judgment, if you think my wound is mortal."

When he replied, "I am sorry, sir, to inform you, that it is; and that you cannot possibly live twenty-four hours."

The general called for pen, ink, and paper, and after making his will, and distributing a few little tokens of regard to the officers of his suite, desired that he might be removed to the general hospital. Early the next morning, he breathed his last, and at his particular request was buried without any parade in the great redoubt, by the soldiers of his own corps.

About sunset, the corpse was carried up the hill. The procession was in view of both armies. As it passed, by, Generals Burgoyne, Phillips, and Reidesel, with most of the officers of the army, joined the procession, The troops who fought immediately under General Fraser, not being acquainted with the privacy of burial that was enjoined by his will, construed it into neglect, and urged by a natural wish to pay the last honours to him in the eyes of the whole army, marched after the body in solemn procession to the grave.

The enemy, with an inhumanity deserving the condemnation of every liberal mind, cannonaded the procession as it passed, and during the service over the grave the aggression was repeated. Charity would incline us to hope, although probability is against the fact, that they were unacquainted with the nature of the awful ceremony. Sacred from interruption and hostility, even among the most barbarous of mankind, are the last sad offices which the living pay to the dead.

Nor should the heroism of Lieutenant Hervey, of the 62nd Regiment, a youth of sixteen, and nephew to the adjutant general of the same name, be forgotten. It was characterized by all that is gallant in the military character.

In the battle of the 19th of September, he received several wounds, and was repeatedly ordered off the field by Lieutenant-Colonel Anstruther, but his heroic ardour would not allow him to quit the battle while he could stand, and see his brave comrades fighting beside him. A ball striking one of his legs, his removal became absolutely necessary, and while they were conveying him away, another wounded him mortally.

In this situation, the surgeon recommended him to take a powerful dose of opium, to avoid a seven or eight hours life of most exquisite torture. This he immediately consented to, and when the colonel entered the tent, with Major Harnage, who were both wounded, they asked whether he had any affairs they could settle for him? His reply was, that being a minor, everything was already adjusted; but he had one request, which he retained just life enough to utter: "Tell my uncle, I died like a soldier"——

Major Ackland when wounded, observed the British troops were retreating; he requested Captain Simpson of the 31st Regiment, who was an intimate friend, to help him into camp, upon which, being a stout man, he conveyed the major on his back a considerable way, when the enemy pursuing so rapidly, he was obliged to leave him behind to save himself. As the major lay on the ground, he cried out to the men who were running by him, that he would give fifty guineas to any soldier who would convey him into camp. A stout grenadier instantly took him on his back, and was hastening into camp, when they were overtaken and both made prisoners.

Captain Bloomfield, of the artillery, received a wound which was very remarkable, a shot passing through both cheeks without hurting the inside of his mouth.

Lieutenant Howarth, of the same corps, was wounded in his knee. It was very singular, that he was so strongly prepossessed with an idea of being wounded, that when the orders came for the detachment's going out, being in company with Lieutenant Anburey, after reading the orders, and that his brigade of guns were to go, he said to that officer, "God bless you, Anburey, farewell; for I know not how it is, but I have a strange *presentiment* that I shall either be killed or wounded."

Some letters passed between the opposed generals. The first was from General Burgoyne, by Lady Ackland, whose husband was dangerously wounded, and a prisoner, recommending Her Ladyship to the care and protection of General Gates. Gates's answer was pointed with the sharpest irony, in which he expresses his surprise that his excellency after considering his preceding conduct, should think that he could consider the greatest attention to Lady Ackland, in the light of an obligation. These epistles, although mere communications between individuals, and frequently on private affairs, yet serve to portray the *disposition of the times*, and unveil the cause that gave rise to the unhappy contest. He added:

> The cruelties, which mark the retreat of your army, in burning the gentlemen and farmers houses as they went along, are almost, among civilized nations, without a precedent; they should not endeavour to ruin those they could not conquer; this conduct betrays more the vindictive malice of a monk, than the generosity of a soldier.

What gave rise to this charge, was the following circumstance: on the west bank of Hudson's River, near the height of Saratoga, where the British Army halted after the retreat, stood General Schuyler's dwelling house, with a range of barracks and store houses, &c. The evening the army arrived at these buildings, the weather being very wet and cold, the sick and wounded were directed to take possession of these barracks; while the troops took post on the height above it. In the course of the night, the barracks took fire by accident, and being built of wood, were soon consumed. It was with the greatest difficulty that the wounded soldiers were rescued from the flames. (The author was the in the house when it took fire, and it was with the greatest difficulty he escaped.)

Two days after this, the enemy had formed a plan of attack; a large column of troops was approaching to pass the river, preparatory to a general action: this column was entirely covered from the fire of the British artillery, by some of these buildings. General Burgoyne ordered them to be set on fire; but so far was the sufferer from putting an invidious construction upon that action, that one of the first persons General Burgoyne saw after the convention was signed was the owner, General Schuyler; who, instead of blaming the English general, owned he would have done the same upon the like occasion, or words to that effect. He did more.

He conducted him to his house; presented him to Mrs. Schuyler; continued him in his family during the whole time of his stay in Albany, with a table of more than twenty covers for himself and friends, and with every other possible demonstration of hospitality: a situation painful at that time, but now pleasing, and carrying undeniable testimony how little he deserved the charges thrown out against him.

On this occasion, and at this distance of time, the energetic language of General Burgoyne, when he demanded a trial, cannot be passed by. It speaks the proud, dignified spirit of the soldier, alike conscious of his humanity as his courage, and is a clearer refutation of the calumnies advanced against him, than the most laboured and artful defence, which wealth could purchase, or ingenuity fabricate:

> As for myself, if I am guilty, I fear I am doubly guilty: An army lost! The sanguine expectation of the kingdom disappointed! A foreign war caused, or the commencement of it accelerated! An effusion of as brave blood as ever ran in British veins, and the severest family distresses combined with public calamity! If this mass of miseries be indeed the consequence of my misconduct, vain will be the extenuation I can plead, of my personal sufferings, fatigue, and hardships, laborious days and sleepless nights, ill health, and trying situations; poor and insufficient would be such atonement in the judgment of my country, or perhaps in the eyes of God; yet with this dreadful alternative in view, I provoke a trial. Give me inquiry. I put the interests that hang most emphatically by the heart strings of the man—my fortune—my honour—my head—I had almost said my salvation upon the issue."

There were as many witnesses of the truth of this statement of facts as there were men in the British Army. Indeed, the more these charges were sifted (and the general was very strictly examined in the House of Commons) the more it tended to place the suffering officer in a very high point of view, whether considered as a man, a soldier, or the leader of an army, in the most trying and perilous service.

It proved that he possessed the confidence and affection of his army in so extraordinary a degree, that no loss or misfortune could shake the one, or distress or affliction weaken the other. It established an instance, as far as it could be conclusive, (and a close examination was not able to weaken it), perhaps unequalled in the military history, that notwithstanding so long and continued a scene of unceasing fatigue, hardship and danger, finally ending in general ruin and captivity, not a single voice was heard through the army, to upbraid, to censure, or blame their general, and that at length, when all their courage and efforts were found ineffectual, and every hope totally cut off, they were still willing to perish along with him.

But perhaps the best testimonial of the rectitude of General Burgoyne's character, was what fell from the pen of his illustrious rival. A higher eulogium, and one more just, was never paid by the generous heart of one soldier to another. Near five months after the convention of Saratoga, General Burgoyne, finding his health declining, and hearing that his character had been much traduced in England, solicited Congress to permit him to return, on his parole of honour, to England. He also applied to General Washington for his interference in the matter. The following is Washington's answer:

Headquarters, Pennsylvania, March 11th, 1778.

Sir,—I was, only two days since, honoured with your very obliging letter of the 11th of February.

Your indulgent opinion of my character, and the polite terms in which you are pleased to express it, are peculiarly flattering; and I take pleasure in the opportunity you have afforded me of assuring you, that, far from suffering the views of national opposition to be imbittered and debased by personal animosity, I am ever ready to do justice to the merit of the gentleman and the soldier; and to esteem, where esteem is due, however the ideas of a public enemy may interpose. You will not think it the language of unmeaning ceremony, if I add, that sentiments of personal respect, in the present instance, are reciprocal.

Viewing you in the light of an officer contending against what I conceive to be the rights of my country, the reverse of fortune you experienced in the field cannot be unacceptable to me; but, abstracted from considerations of national advantage, I can sincerely sympathize with your feelings, as a soldier, the unavoidable difficulties of whose situation forbid his success: and as a man, whose lot combines the calamity of ill health, the anxieties of captivity, and the painful sensibility for a reputation, exposed, where he most values it, to the assaults of malice and detraction.

As your *aide-de-camp* went directly on to Congress, the business of your letter to me had been decided before it came to hand. I am happy that the cheerful acquiescence with your request prevented the necessity of my intervention. And, wishing you

147

a safe and agreeable passage, with a perfect restoration of your health, I have the honour to be, &c.

George Washington.

The circumstances relative to Major Ackland and his lady are so very remarkable, and they have been so variously related, that it becomes necessary, on both accounts, to notice them. The accuracy of the following detail may be depended on. The communication comes directly from General Burgoyne. There is scarcely an instance, either in ancient or modern history, that more finely depicts the resolution, affection, and fortitude of woman toward the husband of her heart and vows than this. If war sometimes in bad men, calls forth all the viler passions of our nature, in woman it is otherwise; it reuses into action a heroism otherwise unknown, an intrepidity almost incompatible with the sex, and awakens all the dormant susceptibilities of their mind.

Besides the continuation of general fatigue, this day was remarkable for a circumstance of private distress too affecting to be omitted. The circumstance to which I allude, is Lady Harriet Ackland's passage through the enemy's army, to attend her wounded husband, then their prisoner.

The progress of this lady with the army could hardly be thought abruptly or superfluously introduced, were it only for the purpose of authenticating a wonderful story. It would exhibit, if well delineated, an interesting picture of the spirit, the enterprise, and the distress of romance; realised and regulated upon the chaste and sober principles of rational love and connubial duty.

Lady Harriet Ackland, sister to the Earl of Ilchester, had accompanied her husband, Major John Dyke Ackland, son of Sir Thomas Ackland, to Canada in the beginning of the year 1776. In the course of that campaign, she had traversed a vast space of country, in different extremities of season, and with difficulties that a European traveller will not easily conceive, to attend him, in a poor hut at Chamblee, upon his sick bed.

In the opening of the campaign of 1777, she was restrained from offering herself to, a share of the fatigue and hazard expected before Ticonderoga, by the positive injunctions of her husband. The day after the conquest of that place, he was badly wounded, and she crossed the Lake Champlain to join him.

As soon as he recovered, Lady Harriet proceeded to follow his fortunes through the campaign, and at Fort Edward, or at the next camp, she acquired a two-wheel tumbril, which had been constructed by the artificers of the artillery, something similar to the carriage used for the mail upon the great roads of England. Major Ackland commanded the British grenadiers, which were attached to General Fraser's corps; and consequently, were always the most advanced post of the army. Their situations often called them to be so alert, that no person slept out of his clothes. In one of these posts of danger a tent, in which the Major and Lady Harriet were asleep, suddenly took fire. An orderly sergeant of grenadiers, with great hazard of suffocation, dragged out the first person he caught hold of. It proved to be the major. It happened that in the same instant she had, unknowing what she did, and perhaps not perfectly awake, providentially made her escape, by creeping under the walls of the back part of the tent. The first object she saw, upon the recovery of her senses, was the major on the other side, and in the same instant perceived him again in the fire, in the search of her. The sergeant again saved him, but not without the major being very severely burned in his face and different parts of the body. Everything they had with them in the tent was consumed.

★★★★★★★★★★

This accident was occasioned by a favourite Newfoundland dog, who, being restless, overset the table, on which a candle was burning, and which, rolling to the walls of the tent, instantly set them on fire.

★★★★★★★★★★

This accident happened a little time before the army passed Hudson's River. It neither altered the resolution, nor the cheerfulness of Lady Harriet; and she continued her progress, a partaker of the fatigues of the advanced corps. The next call upon her fortitude was of a different nature, and more distressful, as of longer suspense. On the march of the 19th, the grenadiers being liable to action at every step, she had been directed by the major to, follow the route of the artillery and baggage, which was not exposed. At the time the action began, she found herself near a small uninhabited hut, where she alighted. When it was found the action was becoming general and bloody, the surgeons of the hospital took possession of the same place, as the most convenient for the care of the wounded.

Thus was the lady in hearing of one continued fire of cannon and musketry, for four hours together, with the presumption, from the post of her husband at the head of the grenadiers, that he was in the most exposed part of the action. She had three female companions, the Baroness of Reidesel, and the wives of two British officers, Major Harnage, and Lieutenant Reynal; but, in the event, their presence served little for comfort. Major Harnage was soon brought to the surgeons, very badly wounded; and a little time after came intelligence that Lieutenant Reynal was shot dead. Imagination will want no helps to figure the state of the whole group.

From the date of the action, the 7th of October, Lady Harriet, with her usual serenity, stood prepared for new trials! and it was her lot that their severity increased with numbers. She was again exposed to the hearing of the whole action, and at last received the shock of her individual misfortune, mixed with the intelligence of the general calamity: the troops were defeated and Major Ackland, desperately wounded, was a prisoner.

The day of the 8th was passed by Lady Harriet and her companions in common anxiety; not a tent nor a shed being standing, except what belonged to the hospital; their refuge was among the wounded and the dying.

When the army was upon the point of moving, after the halt described, I received a message from Lady Harriet, submitting to my decision, a proposal (and expressing an earnest solicitude to execute it, if not interfering with my designs) of passing to the camp of the enemy, and requesting General Gates's permission to attend her husband.

Though I was ready to believe (for I had experience) that patience and fortitude, in a supreme degree, were to be found, as well as every other virtue, under the most tender forms, I was astonished at this proposal, After so long an agitation of the spirits, exhausted not only for want of rest, but absolutely for want of food, drenched in rains for twelve hours together, that a woman should be capable of such an undertaking, as delivering herself to the enemy, probably in the night and uncertain of what hands she might first fall into, appeared an effort above human nature.

The assistance I was enabled to give was small indeed. I had not even a cup of wine to offer her; but was told she had found, from some kind and fortunate hand, a little rum and dirty water. All I could furnish to her was an open beat and a few lines, written upon dirty and wet paper, to General Gates, recommending her to his protection.

Mr. Brudenell, the chaplain to the artillery, (the same gentleman who had officiated so signally at General Fraser's funeral) readily undertook to accompany her, and with one female servant, and the major's *valet-de-chambre*, (who had a ball which he had received in the late action then in his shoulder,) she rowed down the river to meet the enemy. But her distresses were not yet to end. The night was advanced before the boat reached the enemy's out-posts, and the sentinel would not let it pass, nor even come on shore. In vain Mr. Brudenell offered the flag of truce, and represented the state of the extraordinary passenger. The guard was apprehensive of treachery, and therefore threatened to fire into the boat if it stirred before daylight. Her anxiety and suffering were thus protracted through seven or eight dark and cold hours; and her, reflections upon that first reception could not give her very encouraging ideas of the treatment she was afterwards to expect. But it is due to justice, at the close of this adventure, to say, that she was received and accommodated by General Gates, with all the humanity and respect that her rank, her merits, and her fortunes deserved.

Let such as are affected by these circumstances of alarm, hardship, and danger, recollect, that the subject of them was a woman of the most tender and delicate frame; of the gentlest manners; habituated to all the soft elegancies, and refined enjoyments that attend high birth and fortune; and far advanced in a state in which the tender cares, always due to the sex, become indispensably necessary. Her mind alone was formed for such trials.

A circumstance of as singular, but altogether of an opposite nature, happened in the desperate adventures of one Whitcomb, who undertook to steal a British officer for the Americans, and who, in executing his scheme, actually murdered Brigadier-General Gordon. Lieutenant Anburey, who was on the spot, thus relates the particulars:

Whitcomb, a native of Connecticut, and a great partisan of the Americans, who, after the defeat upon the lakes, (in 1776, as already related in a former part of this work), offered his service to venture through the woods, and bring in prisoner an English officer, for which purpose he stationed himself among the thickest copses that are between La Praire and St. John's. The first officer who happened to pass him was Brigadier-General Gordon; he was mounted on a spirited horse, and Whitcomb thinking there was little probability of seizing him, fired at, and wounded him in the shoulder,

The general immediately rode as fast as he could to the camp at St. John's, which he had but just reached, when with loss of blood and fatigue, he fell from his horse; some soldiers took him up, and carried him to the hospital, where, after his wound was dressed, and he was a little at ease, he related the circumstance, which being immediately made known to General Carleton, a party of Indians were sent out to scour the woods, and search for Whitcomb; but in vain, as he hastened back to Ticonderoga. General Carleton, however, imagining be might be lurking about the woods, or secreted in the house of some disaffected Canadian, issued out a proclamation among the inhabitants, offering a reward of fifty guineas to anyone that would bring Whitcomb, alive or dead, to the camp.

A few days after this General Gordon died of his wound, in whose death we sincerely lamented the loss of a brave and experienced officer.

When Whitcomb returned to Ticonderoga, and informed the general who commanded there, that although he could not take an officer prisoner, he believed he had mortally wounded one, the general expressed his disapprobation in the strongest terms, and was so much displeased at the transaction, that Whitcomb, in order to effect a reconciliation, offered his service to go again, professing he would forfeit his life, if he did not return with a prisoner.

He accordingly with two other men, proceeded down Lake Champlain, in a canoe, to a small creek, where they secreted it, and repaired to the woods, to the same spot where Whitcomb had stationed himself before; the two men lay concealed a little way in the wood, whilst he skulked about the borders of it.

"The regiment of which our friend S—— is quartermaster, having occasion for some stores from Montreal, he was going from the camp at St. John's to procure them; he was advised not to go this road, but by the way of Chamblee, on account of the late accident; but you know him to be a man of great bravery and personal courage, joined with uncommon strength; resolving not to go so many miles out of his road for any Whitcomb whatever, he jocosely added, that he should be very glad to meet with him, as he was sure he should get the reward; in this, however, he was greatly mistaken, his reward being no other than that of being taken prisoner himself.

Previous to his setting out he took every precaution, having not only loaded his fusee, but charged a brace of pistols. When he came near to the woods I have already described, he was very cautious; but, in an instant, Whitcomb, and the two men he had with him, sprung from behind a thick bush, and seized him before he could make the least resistance; they then tied his arms behind him with ropes, and blindfolded him.

It was three days before they reached the canoe that had been concealed, during which time they had but very scanty fare; a few hard biscuits served to allay hunger, while the fruits of the wood was a luxury! When Whitcomb had marched him to such a distance as he thought he could not make his escape, were he at liberty, through fear of losing himself; for the greater ease on his own part, and to facilitate their march, they untied his hands, and took the cloth from his eyes. Only picture to yourself what must have been his feelings, at seeing himself in the midst of a thick wood, surrounded by three desperate fellows, and uncertain as to their intentions!

At night, when they had partaken of their scanty pittance, two out of the three used to sleep, whilst the other kept watch. The first night he slept through fatigue; on the second, as you may naturally suppose, and from his great anxiety of mind, he could not close his eyes. In the middle of the night an opportunity occurred, whereby he could have effected his escape, for the man whose watch it was, fell fast asleep. He has since told me how his mind wavered for a length of time, what measures to pursue; he could not bear the idea of putting them to death, though justified by the rules of war: if he escaped from them, they might in all probability retake and ill-treat him.

The great hazard of all, which determined him to abide by his fate was, that by being so many miles in a tract of wood, where he could not tell what direction to take (having been blindfolded when he entered it) he might possibly wander up and down till he perished with hunger. In this restless state he remained till daybreak, when they resumed their march, and in the evening came to the creek where the canoe was concealed; they then secured him again, put him in the canoe, and proceeded up the lake to Ticonderoga, where they arrived early the next morning. When they landed him, he was again blindfolded, that he might not see their works, and thus conducted to the general, whose only motive for endeavouring to get an officer was, either by threats or entreaties, to gain information relative to our army. In this, however, he was greatly disappointed, and as he could not obtain the least intelligence from our friend, he ordered him as prisoner of war upon his parole, to some of the interior towns, from which place, as I informed you in my last, he is just returned as hearty and as well as ever.

The same author also relates a circumstance, which was well known to the whole British Army, and which the author of this *Journal* can fully corroborate. It happened after the Battle of Freeman's Farm, on the 19th of September:

We have within these few evenings, exclusive of other alarms, been under arms most of the night, as there has been a great noise, like the howling of dogs, upon the right of our encampment; it was imagined the enemy set it up to deceive us, while they were meditating some attack. The two first nights this noise was heard, General Fraser thought it to have been the dogs belonging to the officers, and an order was given for the dogs to be confined within the tents; any that were seen running about, the provost had orders to hang them.
The next night the noise was much greater, when a detachment of Canadians and Provincials were sent out to reconnoitre, and it proved to have arisen from large droves of wolves that came after the dead bodies; they were similar to a pack of hounds, for one setting up a cry, they all joined, and when they approached a corpse, their noise was hideous till they had scratched it up.

It is a remark which has been frequently made by foreigners of most countries, that there is a feeling, a sensibility observable in the Irish character, which, if not absolutely peculiar to us, forms a most prominent feature in our disposition. The following circumstance, of which many then in the British as well as American Armies were witnesses, may not be altogether inappropriate, particularly to the native reader.

During the time of the cessation of arms, while the articles of capitulation were preparing, the soldiers of the two armies often saluted, and discoursed with each other from the opposite banks of the river, (which at Saratoga is about thirty yards wide, and not very deep,), a soldier in the 9th Regiment, named Maguire, came down to the bank of the river, with a number of his companions, who engaged in conversation with a party of Americans on the opposite shore. In a short time, something was observed very forcibly to strike the mind of Maguire. He suddenly darted like lightning from his companions, and resolutely plunged into the stream.

At the very same moment, one of the American soldiers, seized with a similar impulse, resolutely dashed into the water, from the opposite shore. The wondering soldiers on both sides, beheld them eagerly swim towards the middle of the river, where they met; they hung on each other's necks and wept; and the loud cries of "My brother! my dear brother!!!" which accompanied the transaction, soon cleared up the mystery, to the astonished spectators. They were both brothers, the first had emigrated from this country, and the other had entered the army; one was in the British and the other in the American service, totally ignorant until that hour that they were engaged in hostile combat against each other's life.

CHAPTER 10

Captured Troops March to the Vicinity of Boston

Immediately after their surrender, the British troops, were marched upwards of two hundred miles to the vicinity of Boston, where they were confined in boarded huts on Winter and Prospect Hills. It is true, the court of Massachusetts passed resolutions for procuring suitable accommodations for them, but from the general unwillingness of the people to administer the least civility, and from the feebleness of the authority which the American rulers had at that time over the property of their fellow citizens, their situation was rendered truly deplorable.

Such were the disagreeable and distressing circumstances, which on every side increased the miseries of confinement, that, at this time, the most faithful recital must despair of credence. It was not infrequent for thirty, or forty persons, men, women and children, to be indiscriminately crowded together in one small, miserable, open hut (the officers without any regard to rank, were frequently crowded, six or eight together in one small hut); their provisions and firewood on short allowance; and a scanty portion of straw their bed, their own blankets their only covering. In the night time, those that could lie down, and the many who sat up from the cold, were obliged frequently to rise and shake from them the snow which the wind drifted in at the openings; or, in case of rain, to endure the "chill peltings of the merciless storm."

General Burgoyne, ever attentive to the welfare of his army, remonstrated in a letter to General Gates, and after making use of some strong expostulations, he added, "the public faith is broken;" this letter being laid before Congress, gave an alarm. It corroborated, they said, an apprehension previously entertained, that the captured troops, on their embarkation, would form a junction with the British garrisons, in America.

Some paltry resolutions which were passed, relative to the British soldiers not having faithfully delivered up all their accoutrements, were of so shameful a nature, as to be highly disgraceful to the Congress, and seemed strongly to indicate that they were ready to grasp at any pretence, however weak or futile, by which they could evade the terms of the convention, without incurring the charge of a direct breach of public faith.

Just at this time, a requisition was made by the commander in chief at New York, for the embarkation of the convention troops, either at the Sound near New York, or at Rhode Island, instead of Boston, which was the place appointed for their departure to Europe; and in consequence of the expectation entertained, that the proposals would have been complied with, the transports for the conveyance of the troops were assembled at Rhode Island. The Congress, however, not only refused to comply with the requisition, but made it a ground of a pretended suspicion that the measure was proposed, merely to afford an opportunity to the convention troops to join their fellows, with an intention of making some pretence to evade, or break the terms of the capitulation, and continue to act in America, to the great detriment and danger of the common cause.

To strengthen this colour of suspicion, they pretended that twenty-six transports, which were provided at Rhode Island, were insufficient for the conveyance of above five thousand six hundred men, (here the Congress magnified the numbers of the British, even adding all the women and children belonging to the captured troops), in a winter voyage to Europe; and that, in the present state of things, with respect of provisions, both in the British fleet and army, it was scarcely possible they said, that they could have been victualled for so long a voyage in so short a time.

General Burgoyne offered to pledge himself, that notwithstanding the injurious suspicions entertained of his own honour, and that of his officers, they would still join with him in signing any writing, or instrument, that might be thought necessary for strengthening, confirming, or renewing the validity of the convention. But the Congress was inexorable. It was easily seen that the measure which they had adopted, was not so lightly taken as to be easily given up, and that explanations and securities, could produce no effect on their determination. They had passed a resolution, from which they never receded, that the embarkation of General Burgoyne's army, should be suspended.

When General Burgoyne found that Congress was resolved that no ratification of the convention which was tendered, would be accepted, he applied for leave to return home, which was immediately granted; General Phillips therefore remained to command the captured troops, and General Burgoyne sailed for England.

The reader will here naturally expect some account of the town of Boston. The author's own observation, when a prisoner on Prospect Hill, and which has been much assisted by a gentleman who a few years afterwards travelled through the country, enables him to offer the following. This part of America, (particularly the island of Nantucket), has not been much benefited by the revolution. The proprietors of this island were in a much greater progress to wealth while under the British dominions, than they have been since.

Boston is the most populous, if not the largest city in North America, and stands upon a peninsula of four miles circumference, within forty-four miles of the bottom of Massachusetts Bay. It was greatly damaged by an earthquake in 1727, and by the bombardment of the Americans themselves in the year 1776. It is most advantageously situated for trade. On the north side are several small islands called Brewsters, one of which is called Noddle's Island. The only safe way for entrance into the harbour, is by a channel; so narrow, that three ships can scarce pass in abreast. But there are proper marks to guide them, and within the harbour there is room enough for five hundred ships to lie at anchor in a good depth of water, while they are covered by the cannon of a regular and very strong fortress.

At the bottom of the bay is a very noble pier, near two thousand feet in length, along which, on the north side, extends a row of warehouses. The head of this pier joins the principal street in the town, which is like most of the others, spacious and well built. The town has a fine and striking appearance at entering, as it lies at the very bottom of the bay like an amphitheatre. It has a town-house, where the courts meet, and the exchange is kept. Round the exchange are a great number of shops.

There are several places of public worship. These buildings are lofty and elegant, with towers and spires. It contains upwards of nine thousand houses, and it is supposed near sixty thousand inhabitants.

The trade of New England was very great, before the unhappy contest with the parent country. They were the coasters of all North America, the West Indies, and many parts of Europe.

The activity and enterprise of the inhabitants of this state are wonderful, particularly in the object of their fisheries. Mr. Burke, in his speech in the House of Commons, in 1775, has thus characterized and immortalised them he says:

Behold, the manner in which the people of New England have carried on the whale fishery. Whilst we follow them among the tumbling mountains of ice, and behold them penetrating into the deepest recesses of Hudson's Bay and Davis's Straits! Whilst we are looking for them beneath the arctic circle, we hear that they have pierced into the opposite region of polar cold! That they are at the antipodes, and engaged under the frozen serpent of the south! Falkland's Island, which seemed so remote and romantic an object for the grasp of national ambition, is but a stage and resting place in the progress of their victorious industry! Nor is the equinoctial heat more discouraging to them than the accumulated winter of both the poles.

We know that whilst some of them draw the line and strike the harpoon on the coast of Africa, others run the longitude, and pursue their gigantic game along the coast of the Brazils! No sea but what is vexed with their fisheries; no climate that is not witness to their toils! Neither the perseverance of Holland, nor the activity of France, nor the dexterous and firm sagacity of English enterprise, ever carried this most perilous mode of hardy industry, to the extent to which it has been pushed by this recent people; a people, who are still, as it were, but in the grizzle, and not yet hardened into the bone of manhood.

Nantucket, in the province of Massachusetts, is a small island, about eighty miles from Boston, and one hundred and twenty from Rhode Island; it is the great nursery for seamen, pilots and fishermen. This island appears to be the summit of some huge sandy sea-mount, affording some acres of dry land, for the habitation of man.

The first proprietors of this island, began their career of industry with a single whale-boat, with which they went to fish for cod; the small distance from their shores, at which they caught it, enabled them soon to increase their business, and those early successes, first led them to conceive that they might likewise catch the whales, which hitherto sported undisturbed on their banks; after many trials, and several miscarriages they succeeded. Thus, they proceeded step by step. The profits of one successful enterprise, helped them to purchase and prepare better materials for a more extensive one; as these were attended with little costs, their profits grew greater.

The south sides of the island from east to west, were divided into four equal parts, and each part, was assigned to a company of six, which though thus separated still carried on their business in common. In the middle of this distance, they erected a mast, provided with a sufficient number of rounds, and near it they built a temporary hut, where five of the associates lived, whilst the sixth from this high station, carefully looked toward the sea, in order to observe the spouting of the whales. Thus, they went on, until the profits they made, enabled them to purchase larger vessels, and to pursue them farther. When the whales quitted their coasts, those who failed in their enterprises, returned to the cod fisheries, which had been their first school, and their first resource; they even began to visit the banks of Cape Breton, the Isle of Sable, and all the other fishing places with which this coast abounds.

By degrees they went a whaling to Newfoundland, to the Gulph of St. Laurence, to the Straits of Belleisle, the coast of Labrador, Davis's Straits, even to Cape Desolation in 70° of latitude; where the Danes carry on some fisheries, in spite of the perpetual severities of that inhospitable climate. In process of time, they visited the Western Islands, the latitude of 34° famous for that fish, the Brazils, the coast of Guinea, Falkland's Islands, and the South Sea. Their confidence is so great, and their knowledge of this branch of business so superior to that of any other people, that they have acquired a monopoly of this commodity. Such were their feeble beginnings, such the infancy and progress of their maritime schemes; such is now the degree of boldness and activity to which they are arrived in their manhood.

After their examples several companies have been formed in many of the capitals, where every necessary article of provisions, implements and timber, are to be found. But the industry exerted by the people of Nantucket, has hitherto enabled them to rival all their competitors; consequently, this is the greatest mart for oil, whale bone, and spermaceti, on the continent. They possess like the generality of Americans, a large share of native penetration, activity and good sense, which leads them to a variety of other secondary schemes, too tedious to mention: they are well acquainted with the cheapest method of procuring lumber from Kennebec River, Penobscot, &c. pitch and tar from North Carolina; flour and biscuit from Philadelphia; and beef and pork from Connecticut.

They know how to exchange their cod-fish and West Indian produce for those articles, which they are continually either bringing to their island, or sending off to other places where they are wanted. By means of all those commercial negotiations, they have greatly cheapened the fitting out of their whaling fleets, and therefore much improved their fisheries.

The vessels most proper for whale fishing, are brigs of about one hundred and fifty tons burthen, particularly when they are intended for distant latitudes. They always man them with thirteen hands, in order that they may row two boats; the crews of which must necessarily consist of six, four at the oars, one standing on the bows with the harpoon, and the other at the helm. It is also necessary that there should be two of these boats, that if one should be destroyed in attacking the whale, the other, which is never engaged at the same time, may be ready to save the hands. Five of the thirteen are always Indians, the last of the complement remains on board to steer the vessel during the action. They have no wages, each draws a certain established share, in partnership with the proprietor of the vessel, by which economy they are all proportionably concerned in the success of the enterprise, and all equally alert and vigilant. These whale-men seldom exceed the age of forty.

As soon as they arrive in those latitudes where they expect to meet with whales, a man is sent up to the mast head; if he sees one, he immediately cries out "*Awaite Pawana,*" "Here is a whale;" they then all remain still and silent until he repeats "*Pawana,*" "A whale," when in less than six minutes, the boats are launched, and filled with every implement necessary for the attack. They row toward the whale with astonishing velocity. There are various ways of approaching the whale, according to their peculiar species; and this previous knowledge is of the utmost consequence. When these boats are arrived at a reasonable distance, one of then rests on its oars, and stands off, as a witness of the approaching engagement; near the bows of the other the harpooner stands up, and on him principally depends the success of the enterprise.

He wears a jacket closely buttoned, and round his head a handkerchief lightly bound: in his hands he holds the dreadful weapon, made of the best steel, marked sometimes with the name of their town, and sometimes with that of their vessel; to the shaft of which the end of a cord of due strength, coiled up with the utmost care in the middle of the boat, is firmly tied; the other end is fastened to the bottom of the boat.

Thus prepared, they row in profound silence, leaving the whole conduct of the enterprise to the harpooner and to the steersman, attentively following their directions. When the former judges himself to be near enough to the whale, that is, at the distance of about fifteen feet, he bids them stop; perhaps she has a calf, whose safety attracts all the attention of a dam, which is a favourable circumstance; perhaps she is of a dangerous species, and it is the safest to retire, though their ardour will seldom permit them; perhaps she is asleep, in that case he balances high the harpoon, trying in this important moment to collect all the energy of which he is capable.

He launches it forth—she is struck: from her first movement they judge of her temper, as well as of their future success. Sometimes, in the immediate impulse of rage, she will attack the boat and demolish it with one stroke of her tail; in an instant the frail vehicle disappears, and the assailants are immersed in the dreadful element. Were the whale armed with the jaws of the shark, and as voracious, they never would return home to amuse their listening wives with the interesting tale of the adventure. At other times she will dive and disappear from human sight, and everything must then give way to her velocity, or else all is lost; sometimes she will swim away as if untouched, and draw the cord with such swiftness that it will set the edge of the boat on fire by the friction. If she rises before she has run out the whole length, she is looked upon as a sure prey.

The blood she has lost in her fight, weakens her so much, that if she sinks again, it is but for a short time; the boats follow her course with an almost equal speed. She soon re-appears; tired at last with convulsing the element, which she tinges with her blood, she dies, and floats on the surface. At other times it may happen, that she is dangerously wounded, though she carries the harpoon fast in her body; when she will alternately dive and rise, and swim on with unabated vigour. She then soon reaches beyond the length of the cord, and carries the boat along with amazing velocity; this sudden impediment sometimes will retard her speed, at other times it only serves to rouse her anger, and to accelerate her progress.

The harpooner, with the axe in his hands, stands ready. When he observes that the bows of the boat are greatly pulled down by the diving whale, and that it begins to sink deep and take much water, he brings the axe almost in contact with the cord; he pauses, still flattering himself that she will relax; but the moment grows critical, unavoidable danger approaches; sometimes men more intent on gain, than on the preservation of their lives, will run great risks; and it is wonderful how far these people have carried their daring courage at this awful moment! But it is in vain to hope; their lives must be saved, the cord is cut, the boat rises again. If after thus getting loose, she reappears, they will attack and wound her a second time. She soon dies, and when dead, she is towed alongside of their vessel, where she is fastened.

The next operation is to cut with axes and spades, every part of her body which yields oil; the kettles are set a boiling, they fill their barrels as fast as it is made; but as this operation is much slower than that of cutting up, they fill the hold of their ship with those fragments, least a storm should arise and oblige them to abandon their prize. They frequently produce from one hundred and fifty, to two hundred barrels of oil. After having once vanquished this leviathan, there are two enemies to be dreaded, beside the wind; the first of which is the shark.

That fierce voracious fish, often comes alongside, and shares with them on their prey. They are very mischievous; but the second enemy is much more terrible and irresistible; it is the killer, sometimes called the thrasher, a species of whale about thirty feet long. They are possessed of such a degree of agility and fierceness, as often to attack the largest spermaceti whales; and not seldom to rob the fishermen of their prey, nor is there any means of defence against so potent an adversary. When all their barrels are full, (for everything is done at sea,) or when their limited time is expired, and their stores almost expended, they return home, freighted with their valuable cargo.

The following are the names, and principal characteristics of the various species of whales, known to these people.

The River St. Laurence whale.

The disko, or Greenland *do.*

The right whale, or seven feet bone, common on the coasts of this country, about sixty feet long.

The spermaceti whale found all over the world, and of all sizes; the longest are sixty feet, and yield about one hundred barrels of oil.

The hump back, on the coast of Newfoundland, from forty to seventy feet in length.

The finn back, an American whale, never killed, as being too swift.

The sulphur bottom, River St. Laurence, ninety feet long; they are but seldom killed, being extremely swift.

The grampies, thirty feet long; never killed, on the same account.

The killer, or thrasher, about thirty feet; they often kill the other whales, with which they are at perpetual war.

The black fish whale, twenty feet, yields from eight to ten barrels.

The porpoise, weighing about one hundred and sixty pounds weight.

In 1769, they fitted out one hundred and twenty-five whalemen; the first fifty that returned brought with them eleven thousand and six barrels of oil. In 1770 they fitted out one hundred and thirty-five vessels for the fisheries, at thirteen hands each; four West India men, twelve hands; twenty-five wood vessels, four hands; eighteen coasters five hands; fifteen London traders, eleven hands. All these amount to two thousand one hundred and fifty-eight hands, employed in one hundred and ninety-seven vessels.

★★★★★★★★★★

The Americans were undoubtedly injured in many valuable branches of trade, by the separation from the mother country: Their ship trade, in consequence of the revolution, received a great check. Their market for oil is not equal to France, to that which they formerly found for it in England. Shortly after the American war, the King of France offered the people of Nantucket a settlement at Dunkirk, with many immunities and privileges, such as building them a town, exempting them from taxes, and allowing them the free exercise of their own religion; in consequence of which many went there. But all, or at least the greater part of these privileges have been lost by the changes in the French Government; and they now suffer a diminution in their trade without any equivalent to indemnify them for the loss.

★★★★★★★★★★

Marriage is so highly respected that all persons marry here, and marry early, and the women are almost universally the happy mothers of a numerous offspring. Their children, born by the sea side, hear the roaring of its waves as soon as they come into the world; it is the first noise with which they become acquainted, and by early plunging into the water, they acquire that boldness, that presence of mind and dexterity, which makes them ever after such expert seamen. They often hear their fathers recount the adventures of their youth, their combats with the whales; and these recitals imprint on their opening minds, an early curiosity and taste for the same life.

They often cross the sea to go to the mainland, and learn even in those short voyages, how to qualify themselves for longer and more dangerous ones; they are therefore deservedly conspicuous for their maritime knowledge and experience, all over the continent. A man born here, is distinguishable by his gait, from a hundred other men, so remarkable are they for a pliability of sinews, and a peculiar agility which attends them even to old age.

In the name of honour, humanity, and justice, let not one part of the Quaker's conduct be forgotten! there is not a slave on the whole island, at least, among the Friends; whilst slavery prevails all around them, this society alone, lamenting that shocking insult offered to humanity, has given the world a singular example of moderation, disinterestedness, and Christian charity, in emancipating their negroes.

Idleness is the most heinous crime that can be committed in Nantucket: an idle man would soon be pointed out as an object of compassion; for idleness is considered as another word for want and hunger. This principle is so thoroughly well understood, and is become so universal, so prevailing a prejudice, that literally speaking, they are never idle. Even if they go to the market place, which is, if I may be allowed the expression, the coffee-house of the town, either to transact business, or to converse with their friends; they always have a piece of cedar in their hands, and while they are talking, they will, as it were intuitively, employ themselves in converting it into something useful, either a bung or spoil for their oil casks, or some other article.

In the summer of the year 1778, the captured army was ordered to remove from Prospect-bill to Rutland County, about fifty miles to the south of Boston. Here we were confined in a sort of pen or fence, which was constructed in the following manner: A great number of trees were ordered to be cut down in the woods, these were sharpened at each end, and drove firmly into the earth very close together, enclosing a space of about two or three acres. American sentinels were planted on the outside of this fence, at convenient distances, in order to prevent our getting out.

At one angle, a gate was erected, and on the outside thereof stood the guard house; two sentinels were constantly posted at this gate; and no one could get out unless he had a pass from the officer of the guard; but this was a privilege in which very few were indulged. Boards and nails were given the British in order to make them temporary huts, to secure them from the rain, and the heat of the sun. The provisions were rice and salt pork, delivered with a scanty hand. The officers were allowed to lodge in the farm houses, which lay contiguous to the pen; they were permitted likewise to come in amongst their men for the purpose of roll-call, and other matters of regularity.

While the captured troops remained here, Sir Henry Clinton, the commander in chief in New York, applied again to Congress, in behalf of General Burgoyne's army. In a letter to Henry Laurence, Esq. president of Congress, dated New York, September 19th, 1778, he acquaints the Congress that His Majesty had given him positive injunctions to repeat the demand, that the convention of Saratoga be fulfilled according to the conditions stipulated by Lieutenant-General Burgoyne, in respect to the troops serving under his command, and to require permission for their embarkation; to this letter, Congress sent the following answer;

> Sir,—Your letter of the 19th was laid before Congress, and I am directed to inform you, that the Congress make no answer to insolent letters.
> Signed,   Charles Thompson, Sec.

Soon after the intelligence of the capture of General Burgoyne's army reached Europe, the Court of France openly avowed a treaty of amnesty, commerce, and alliance with the United States. France, from the beginning of the contest, had secretly encouraged the Americans in their opposition, and supplied them liberally with the means of defence, while at the same time they amused Great Britain with declarations of the most pacific disposition.

> On the 7th of April, the Duke of Richmond, in the House of Lords moved an address to the king on the state of the nation. In his speech in support of this address, his grace declared in strong terms, his conviction of the necessity of an immediate recognition of American independence.
> The mischief, whatever might be the magnitude of it, was already done; America was already lost; her independence was as firmly established as that of other states. We had sufficient cause for regret, but our lamentation on the subject was of no more avail than it would be for the loss of Normandy and France.
> The Earl of Chatham in expectation that this point would come under discussion that day, resolved, however enfeebled and afflicted by his corporeal infirmities, to make his appearance before the house, in order to bear his decided testimony against it. The mind feels interested in the minutest circumstances relating to the last day of the public life of this renowned statesman and patriot. He was dressed in a rich suit of black velvet, with a full wig, and covered up to the knees in flannel.
> On his arrival in the house, he refreshed himself in the Lord Chancellor's room, where he staid till prayers were over, and till he was informed that business was going to begin. He was then led into the house, by his son, and son-in-law, Mr. William

Pitt, and Lord Viscount Mahon, all the lords standing up out of respect, and making a lane for him to pass to his own bench: he bowed respectfully to them as he proceeded. He looked pale and emaciated, but his eye retained all its native fire; which joined to his general deportment, and the attention of the house, formed a spectacle very striking and impressive.

When the Duke of Richmond had sat down, Lord Chatham rose, and began by lamenting 'that his bodily infirmities had so long, and at so important a crisis prevented his attendance on the duties of parliament. He declared, that he had made an effort almost beyond the powers of his constitution, to come down to the house on this day, perhaps the *last* time he should ever enter its walls, to express the indignation he felt at the idea which he understood was gone forth, of yielding up the sovereignty of America; My Lords,' continued he 'I rejoice that the grave has not closed upon me, that I am still alive to lift up my voice against the dismemberment of this ancient and noble monarchy.

'Pressed down as I am by a load of infirmity, I am little able to assist my country in this most perilous conjuncture; but, my lords, while I have sense and memory, I never will consent to tarnish the lustre of this nation by an ignominious surrender of its rights and fairest possessions. Shall a people so lately the terror of the world, now fall prostrate before the House of Bourbon? It is impossible. I am not, I confess, well informed of the resources of this kingdom, but I trust it has still sufficient to maintain its just rights, though I know them not. Let us at least make one effort, and if we must fall, let us fall like men."

The Duke of Richmond, in reply, declared himself to be 'totally ignorant of the means by which we were to resist with success the combination of America with the house of Bourbon. He urged the noble lord to point out any possible mode, if he were able to do it, of making the Americans renounce that independence of which they were in possession. His grace added, that if *he* could not, no man could; and that it was not in his power to change his opinion on the noble lord's authority, unsupported by any reasons, but a recital of the calamities arising from things not in the power of this country to alter.'

Lord Chatham, who had appeared greatly moved during the reply, made an eager effort to rise at the conclusion of it, as if labouring with some great idea, and impatient to give full scope to his feelings; but before he could utter a word, pressing his hand on his bosom, he fell down suddenly in a convulsive fit. The Duke of Cumberland, Lord Temple, and other lords near him, caught him in their arms. The house was immediately cleared, and His Lordship being carried into an adjoining apartment, the debate was adjourned. Medical assistance being obtained, His Lordship in some degree recovered, and was conveyed to his favourite villa, of Hayes, in Kent, where, after lingering some few weeks, he expired, May 11, 1778, in the seventieth year of his age.

CHAPTER 11

The Americans Raise an Army

It is now time that we should return to General Howe's army, which we left at the conclusion of Chapter 8, at New Brunswick. The reader will recollect that the American headquarters were then at Morristown.

While the British troops lay at Brunswick and Amboy, Congress was indefatigable in recruiting their army; at Morristown ninety-six battalions were ordered to be raised for the service of the United States, and in some of the colonies the enlisting of apprentices and of Irish indented servants, was permitted; this army was distinguished by the name of Continentals, and in addition to their pay and bounty, they were promised one hundred acres of land at the conclusion of the war.

Early in the spring of 1777, twenty-one thousand stand of arms, and one thousand barrels of powder were sent from France, and arrived in America, for the use of the Continental Army.

On the other side a considerable body of Provincial troops was formed under the auspices of General Sir William Howe. They included not only Americans, but British and Irish refugees, from the different parts of the continent, and were officered by those gentlemen who for their attachment to the Royal cause, had been obliged to abandon their respective provinces. Governor Tryon, who already, in his civil capacity, commanded the militia, and who had taken the utmost pains in its establishment, was now placed at the head of these new levies under the title and rank of Major-General.

Before the Royal Army took the field, in prosecution of the main business of this campaign, two enterprises, for the destruction of the American stores, were undertaken, the first was conducted by Colonel Bird, who in March landed with five hundred men, at Peek Hill, near fifty miles from New York. The Americans upon the approach of the British troops, set fire to the barracks and principal store houses, and then retreated to a strong pass in the mountains. The loss of provisions and other valuable articles was considerable.

In April, Major-General Tryon, Brigadier-General Agnew, and Sir William Erskine, with a detachment of two thousand men, embarked at New York, and passing through the Sound landed between Fairfield and Norfolk the next day. They now perceived that the country was rising to intercept their return, and as no carriages could be procured to bring off the stores, they set fire to the magazine; in the execution of this service, eighteen houses, which were built near the magazine, were unavoidably burned.

The detachment returned by the way of Ridgefield, and was greatly harassed by the enemy under Generals Wooster and Arnold. While Wooster hung upon the rear of the British, Arnold by crossing the country gained their front, and got possession of Ridgefield; here they found the American general covered by an entrenchment which he had hastily thrown up. The village was forced, and the Americans drove back on all sides. The action, while it lasted, was sharp. Arnold displayed his usual intrepidity. His horse having been shot under him, while he was extricating himself, a British soldier advanced to run him through with his bayonet, but he shot him dead with his pistol, and got off safe. (Congress voted that a horse properly caparisoned should be presented to General Arnold, in their name, as a token of his gallant conduct on that day.)

General Tryon remained that night at Ridgefield, and renewed his march the next morning. The enemy having been reinforced with troops and cannon, the British were exceedingly harassed, during their march. Early in the evening the detachment gained the hill of Campo, within cannon shot of their ships, and formed. The Americans were now assembled in great numbers, and seemed determined on an attack. General Tryon ordered the British troops to advance and charge with their bayonets. This order was executed with such impetuosity, that the enemy was totally broken and dispersed.

The troops were now embarked without molestation. The loss of the British in killed, wounded, and missing, amounting to one hundred and seventy-two, of whom more than two-thirds were wounded. No British officer was killed. It was supposed the Americans lost double that number.

Several of the American officers were killed and wounded; among the former Doctor Atwater, a gentleman of respectable character and considerable influence. General Wooster, though seventy years old, behaved with the vigour of youth; and received a mortal wound.

The Americans were very industrious in calling forth all the military talent of the country. Neither the extreme of youth, or advanced age, formed any impediment to their actual service. Brigadier-General Wooster, (like Putnam) was in the decline of life, when the troubles began.

He was born at Newhaven, in Connecticut, a province of New England, in the year 1711. His father was a man of great wealth and connexions; and this, his only son, received a liberal education. High in blood, and fraught with youthful ardour, the whole bent of his disposition seemed turned towards the pursuits of a soldier. For him the military life appeared to possess every attraction. And his father, it should appear, by no means wished or attempted to turn aside the current of his temper. He entered the army when but twenty years, of age; and gained a high reputation from the many events in which he signalised his courage and intrepidity.

In the war between France and England, when America was the scene of action, he distinguished himself in a manner much to his honour. He commanded a company in General Pepperall's regiment of foot, was present at the taking of Cape Breton, to the reduction of which place, the corps in which he served very much contributed, and during the whole war reaped those laurels in America, which raised his name to no inconsiderable height on both sides the Atlantic. After the peace, in 1749, his regiment was reduced, and he returned home to the bosom of his relatives. His father being dead, he became the inheritor of his estate, and the greater part of his wealth.

It was at this period, or shortly after, that he married Miss Boroughs, a young lady of Rehoboth, near Providence. This marriage, brought him a large accession of property; and thus circumstanced, he resolved on retiring from the army, and enjoying the charms of domestic ease and retirement. He accordingly placed himself on the half-pay list, in which he continued till the year 1776.

When the troubles in America proved too violent for any peaceable adjustment, and by repeated acts of hostility, the parent country was at last roused to arms, Clinton, Burgoyne, the Howes, and other distinguished officers were sent to America. The Congress thus opposed by experience and valour took on their part, the wisest resolutions which human sagacity could dictate; they determined likewise to call forth into action the greatest military talents which America could furnish. (More than one third of the soldiers in the American ranks had formerly been in the British service; and what was still worse, these men were indefatigable in training the raw recruits to the use of arms.)

Agreeable to this resolve, it may be naturally imagined that they could not easily pass by such a character as Captain Wooster. A most respectful invitation was sent desiring him "to assist his native country in the hour of her calamity." Embosomed in the affections of a beloved family, he yet felt, and acknowledged the superior motive. He obeyed the mandate, and was appointed a brigadier-general in the service of Congress. This, as might have been expected, caused his name to be immediately struck off the half pay list. He was then far advanced in years; but he entered a second time on the military life with all the avidity of youth.

It was an unhappy circumstance for England, that some of the bravest and most experienced officers in her pay, then residing in America, turned against her and supported the insurrection. To this, perhaps, much more than to any other cause, was America indebted for her ultimate success. This was precisely, the case with regard to General Wooster. In several affairs of minor importance, but which in the end led to matters of the highest consequence, his knowledge of the art of war, rendered essential services to the party to whom he attached himself, until at last, when Montgomery was defeated before Quebec, General Wooster, was ordered to march to the relief of the besiegers. In this, however, his former success deserted him, as the reader has already been informed.

On account of one circumstance which attaches itself to this country, it may be worthwhile to mention General Wooster's issue, a son and daughter. The former was finishing his education in England. When the American troubles broke out, he came over to Ireland, and the rupture between the two countries preventing the regularity of his remittances from America, his circumstances became, from youthful extravagance much involved, until at last he was arrested, and thrown into the Four Courts Marshalsea. All the letters and remittances from his father being of course, intercepted by the British Government, the young man remained in confinement, until General Wooster, through another channel, sent him money to pay his debts, the remainder of which enabled him, (though contrary to his father's commands) to leave the country.

The general, fearful of the issue of the American struggle, had positively enjoined young Wooster to remain in England until the war was terminated. This injunction however he disobeyed; and as soon as he gained the American shore, actually joined that part of the Continental Army which his father commanded.

The following is the inscription on a monument erected in honour of General Wooster, by order of Congress;

IN HONOUR OF
DAVID WOOSTER,
BRIGADIER-GENERAL OF THE ARMY OF THE
UNITED STATES,
IN DEFENDING THE LIBERTIES OF AMERICA
AND BRAVELY REPELLING THE INROADS OF THE BRITISH
TROOPS TO DANBURY, IN CONNECTICUT;
HE RECEIVED A MORTAL WOUND
ON THE 27TH APRIL, 1777,
AND DIED ON THE 2ND MAY FOLLOWING:
THE CONGRESS OF THE UNITED STATES, AS AN
ACKNOWLEDGEMENT OF HIS MERIT AND SERVICES, HAVE
CAUSED THIS MONUMENT TO BE ERECTED.

Four hundred dollars were allowed for erecting this monument.

On the 24th of May, Colonel Meigs, an enterprising American officer, (who had attended Arnold in the expedition to Quebec, and had been taken prisoner in the attempt to storm that city, as before related) having passed his detachment, consisting of one hundred and seventy men in whale boats over the Sound, which separates Long Island from Connecticut, landed on the north branch of Long Island, within four miles of Sagg harbour, and notwithstanding the resistance they met with from the guard and crews of the vessels, they fully completed their design, having burned twelve sloops and brigs which lay at the wharf, and entirely destroyed everything on the shore, they brought off with them about ninety prisoners, consisting of the officer who commanded, with his men, and most of the masters and crews of the small vessels which they destroyed.

A circumstance which renders this expedition particularly curious, that the colonel and his party returned to Guilford in Connecticut, in twenty-five hours from the time of their departure, having in that short time, not only completed the object of their expedition, but traversed by land and water a space not less than ninety miles. However, this may be, Congress ordered an elegant sword to be presented to Colonel Meigs for his good conduct in this expedition. About six weeks after the above transaction, another daring enterprise was executed. The circumstance was as follows. The British troops on Rhode Island, were divided into two large encampments, one covering the town, the other subdivided into three parts, and stationed towards the northern extremity of the island.

For the convenience of being as near as possible to all those encampments, General Prescot, who commanded the troops, slept every night in the middle between them, about five miles distance from each extremity, and about half a mile from the western coast of the island; this place he thought secure, by its great distance from the mainland, and by means of some ships of war which were stationed along that coast, at no greater distance from it than two miles. However, an American colonel of the name of Burton, accompanied by forty volunteers, passed from Warrick Neck to Rhode Island, a distance of ten miles, by water, eluded the guard ships, and landed about twelve o'clock at night at the opening of a ravine, into which they crept, and proceeded undiscovered to the general's quarters, and carried off the general, his *aide-de-camp*, and the sentinel.

The enterprise was conducted with so much silence and address, that no alarm was given, though a guard was at a very little distance from the house, until Burton and his party had nearly reached the continent with their prize, Congress resolved that an elegant sword should be presented to Colonel Burton, as a testimonial of his gallant behaviour.

Towards the latter end of May, General Washington quitted his winter encampment at Morristown, and took a strong position on the high lands round Middlebrook, in the vicinity of Brunswick. In this strong position he threw up works along the front of his lines, but his principal advantage was the difficulty to approach his camp, the ground being so judiciously occupied as to expose the British to every kind of danger in the attempt. On the one side he covered the Jerseys, and on the other, he observed the motions of the British Army at Brunswick, of which he commanded a full prospect.

Many stratagems were employed by the British general, to draw Washington from this strong situation, On the 24th of June, General Howe, suddenly relinquished his position in front of the Americans, and retired to Amboy; at the same time preparations were made for passing the army to Staten Island, this feint had the desired effect, for as soon as the British Army began to move, intelligence was received that Washington had moved down from the mountain, and taken post at Quibble Town, intending to attack the rear of the British Army;

174

General Howe lost no time in endeavouring to profit by this movement of the Americans: he immediately marched the army back, by
different routes, in order to cut off some of the advanced parties of
the enemy, and likewise, if possible, to bring Washington to a general
engagement in the neighbourhood of Quibble Town; at the same time
Lord Cornwallis with his column, was directed to take a considerable
circuit to the right, and by turning the enemy's left, take possession of
some passes in the mountains, which had hitherto afforded them so
advantageous a security.

Soon after Lord Cornwallis marched with his column, he fell in
with a division of American troops, commanded by Lord Sterling,
whom he found advantageously posted in a country much covered
with wood, and his artillery well disposed; the king's troops attacked
them with the greatest impetuosity, and after a short conflict the
Americans dispersed on all sides, leaving behind them three pieces of
brass ordnance, three captains, sixty men killed, and upwards of two
hundred officers and men, wounded and taken prisoners.

The British troops had five men killed, and thirty wounded, Captain Finch of the light company of the guards was the only officer
who suffered; the wound he received proved mortal, and he died at
Amboy on the 29th of June, greatly regretted by the British Army.

The troops engaged in this action were the 1st Battalion of Guards,
Queen's Rangers, 1st Battalion Light Infantry, 1st Battalion of Grenadiers, and 3rd Battalion of Hessian Grenadiers. The enemy was pursued
to Westfield, with little effect; for Washington seeing his error, immediately retook possession of his strong camp on the hills, and secured
those strong passes on the mountains, the possession of which, by the
British troops, would have exposed his whole army to certain ruin.

General Howe, now found it necessary to make an attempt on
Philadelphia by sea.

About this time the following humane order was sent from the
War Office to General Howe:

If a wound shall be received in action by any commissioned officer, which shall occasion the loss of an eye, or a limb, he shall
receive a gratuity in money of one year's full pay, and be further
allowed such expenses relating to his care (if not performed at
the king's charge;) as shall be certified to be reasonable by the
surgeon general of the army, and inspector general of regimental infirmaries, upon examination of the vouchers which he

shall lay before them.

If the wounds received shall not amount to the loss of a limb, the charge of cure only shall be allowed, certified as above. When any commissioned officer shall lose an eye or a limb as aforesaid, the commanding officer of the corps in which he serves, shall deliver to him a certificate, specifying the time when, and the place where the said accident happened; a duplicate of which certificate, shall likewise be transmitted with the next monthly returns. When any commissioned officer shall be killed in action; his widow and orphan children (if he leave any) shall be allowed as follows:

The widow, a full year's pay according to her husband's regimental commission; each child under age, and unmarried, one third of what is allowed to the widow; posthumous children to be included.

All persons dying of their wounds, within six months after battle, shall be deemed slain in action.

The commanding officers of corps, in which the slain officer served, shall, on demand, give a certificate of his being killed in action, to his surviving wife and orphans respectively, specifying the time when, and the place where, the said accident happened, a duplicate of which, shall likewise be transmitted with the next monthly returns.

It was about this time that Colonel Maclean left New York, to join his new-raised troops in Halifax and Canada. He was a meritorious officer, and indefatigable in his exertions to obtain men for the service.

Lieutenant-Colonel Maclean's corps of emigrants, though partly raised in 1775, had not, from their dispersed situation, which compelled them to serve in different parts of America, an opportunity of being reviewed, or of receiving their colours in due form. The battalions however were reviewed in June last, 1777, by General Massey, at Halifax, when their appearance gave universal satisfaction to the general and the spectators. Previous to the review, their colours were consecrated, and their respective chaplains, preached a sermon suitable to the occasion. An oath was then solemnly administered to each individual; and the commanding officer delivered a charge to the men, which it is presumed may not be unacceptable to many readers, particularly to young officers and soldiers, who have never been present at any ceremony of the kind. The substance was as follows:

Man is born under obligations of conforming to the rules of propriety and rectitude, and with a passion for the applause which is due to virtuous actions.

While inferior professions hold out sordid views as a spur to emulation, the object of the military is of the most sublime nature, *viz.* to perform gallant actions, that shall gain the approbation of their sovereign and superior officers, the esteem even of the enemy, the gratitude of fellow subjects, and the admiration of posterity.

Happy those who shall have arrived at this exalted summit! To gain it, the greatest men that ever existed did not think it too much to sacrifice interests, ease, and even life; nor is it inaccessible to private soldiers, whether as a collective body, or as individuals any more than to officers,

In the histories of the most warlike nations of antient times, we find mention of the actions of private soldiers who are recorded by name, with the honours and reward that followed; and instances of the like merit are no less frequent in our modern armies.

Who then does not feel the influence of that divine spark, which prompts us to rise, above the common level? Who has not ambition to transmit his name with applause to posterity? Who does not wish and pant for the opportunity to signalise himself?

It is in the strongest manner recommended to the soldiers, to cherish in their breasts this natural and laudable passion for true glory: it inspires a sentiment of dignity, which leads to cleanliness, and neatness in dress, to abstain from drunkenness and every other abject vice; it renders them attentive and diligent on duty, cool and brave in action; on all occasions they will be patient, obedient, disinterested, and generous.

The approbation of their officers will follow, and from thence many indulgencies; nor will the esteem and rewards of their country be wanting, to enable such illustrious career, to spend the decline of life in tranquillity, ease and comfort. In these their honourable retreats, to recollect the memory of gallant actions, to relate and dwell on their circumstances, to meet now and then a companion of former dangers, will rekindle youthful ardour, and afford the most pure and exquisite pleasures, when the toil and pain that accompanied them are no more.

Duty and prudence dictate to a soldier the greatest care of his arms and accoutrements; they are the instruments of his defence, and of acquiring the honour he contends for; his pride should consist in having them of the best quality possible, always neat and in good order, always fit for instant and certain execution. It is ever natural for a brave soldier to entertain for them the most ardent regard, and to wish that even in death they should not be separated. Thus, it was a maxim with the Spartans, to return from battle with, or on their shields. Epaminondas, one of the best generals of antiquity, being mortally wounded, But,was only anxious lest his arms should fall into the enemy's hands. The arms of the Roman soldiers weighed sixty pounds, and it was death to throw away any part of them. The colours, are above all things the object of a soldier's particular regard, attention, and attachment; this was the case in warlike nations at all times. The Romans worshipped and swore by them, and to lose them was to incur certain death. We have many instances in antient history, of commanders, in a doubtful engagement, throwing the colours among the troops of the enemy, knowing that, therefrom the courage, ardour, and exertion, of the soldiery would instantly redouble, beat the enemy, and retake them.

Though we do not worship the colours, yet the awful ceremony of this day sufficiently evinces, that they are with us, as in antient times, the object of peculiar veneration; they hold forth to us the idea of the prince whose service we have undertaken, of our country's cause which we are never to forsake, and of our military honour which we are ever to preserve.

The colours, in short, represent everything that is dear to the soldier; at the sight of them all the powers of his soul are to rouse, they are a post to which he must repair through fire and sword, and which he must defend while life remains; to this he is bound, besides every other consideration, by the acceptance of a most solemn oath: to desert them is the blackest perjury and eternal infamy: to lose them by such an accident, even as one might otherwise judge unavoidable, is not to be excused, because to lose them, no matter how, is to lose everything; and when they are in danger, or lost, officers and soldiers have nothing for it but to recover them or die.

Penetrated therefore with innate eagerness for glory, mindful of the fame of their ancestors, emulous of the lustre of their countrymen, now on service in other parts of America, and incited by the example already exhibited, and the honour already acquired by officers and fellow soldiers of the regiment, the Royal Highland Emigrants, will, it is hoped, always act with a dignity becoming the military profession, acquit themselves on every occasion, of the oath emitted this day, and not only transmit their honour and colours unsullied to posterity, but let every individual think himself entitled, nay bound, to aim at something that may deservedly shine in the page of history.

The month of July was far advanced before the preparations for the expedition against Philadelphia were completed, and it was the 23rd before the fleet was able to sail from Sandy Hook. The force employed on this occasion, consisted of thirty-six battalions of British and Hessian infantry, a regiment of Light Dragoons, and a corps of loyalists, amounting in the whole to about sixteen thousand men. At the same time a strong detachment was left behind at New York, under Sir Henry Clinton, and seven battalions were stationed on Rhode Island.

After a tedious navigation, the fleet entered Chesapeake Bay, and was conducted as far up the River Elk as was practicable. Here the army landed without opposition, on the 25th of August. Part of the troops was left to guard the stores, while General Howe proceeded with the main body to the head of the Elk.

General Washington, on the news of the arrival of the British in the Chesapeake, left the Jerseys and hastened to the relief of Philadelphia, with fifteen thousand men. In the beginning of September, he met the Royal Army at Chad's Ford, on the Brandywine, a small stream which empties itself into Christiana Creek.

Here Washington adhered to his former method of skirmishing, and harassing the Royal Army on its march; but as this was insufficient to stop its progress, he retired to that side of the Creek next to Philadelphia, with an intent to defend the passage. This brought on a general action. On the 11th, our army advanced in two columns, that under General Knyphausen, to Chad's Ford, had arrived in front of the enemy about ten o'clock, while the other column under Lord Cornwallis, having marched twelve miles round to the forks of the Brandywine, crossed both branches, taking from thence the road to Dilworth, in order to turn the enemy's right at Chad's Ford.

General Washington, having intelligence of this movement, detached General Sullivan to his right, with near 10,000 men, who took a strong position, with his left, near to the Brandywine, both flanks being covered by very thick woods, and his artillery advantageously disposed. About four o'clock the king's troops advanced, and Lord Cornwallis having formed his line of battle, the light infantry and *chasseurs* began the attack; the guards and grenadiers instantly advanced from the right, the whole under a heavy fire of artillery and musketry: but they pushed on with an impetuosity not to be sustained by the enemy, who falling back into the woods in the rear, the king's troops entered with them and pursued them closely for near two miles.

After this success, a part of the enemy's right took a second position in a wood, from whence the 1st Light Infantry and *chasseurs* soon dislodged them; from this time, they did not rally again in force.

The 2nd Light Infantry, 2nd Grenadiers, and 4th Brigade moved forward a mile beyond Dilworth, where they attacked a corps of the enemy, strongly posted to cover the retreat of their army, which corps not being forced till it was dark, the enemy escaped a total overthrow.

A part of the Americans retired to Chester, and remained there that night, but the greater body did not stop until they reached Philadelphia. They had about three hundred men killed, six hundred wounded, and near four hundred made prisoners. In the list of their wounded, were two of their general officers, the Marquis de la Fayette, and General Woodward. The former was a French nobleman of high rank, who had left his native country and offered his service to Congress.

While in France, and only nineteen years of age, he espoused the cause of the Americans; having determined to join them, he communicated his intentions to the American commissioners at Paris. They conceived that a person of so much importance would be of service to their cause, and encouraged his design. Before he left France, intelligence arrived in Europe that the American insurgents, reduced to 2,000 men, were flying through the Jerseys before a British force of 30,000. Under these circumstances, the American commissioners at Paris, thought it but honest to dissuade him from the present prosecution of his perilous enterprise, but their advice was in vain.

Having embarked in a vessel, which he purchased for the purpose, he arrived in Charlestown early in 1777, and soon after joined the American Army. Congress resolved that "in consideration of his zeal, illustrious family, and connections, he should have the rank of major-general in their army." He was wounded in the leg while rallying the

American troops.

The loss on the side of His Majesty's troops, amounted to about three hundred killed, and four hundred and eighty-eight wounded. Eight pieces of cannon and a great quantity of military stores were taken from the enemy.

The British Army lay during the night on the field of battle, and the next day, Major-General Grant, with the first and second brigade, marched to Concord; Lord Cornwallis with the light infantry and British grenadiers, joined him within five miles of Chester.

At this period intelligence being received that the enemy were advancing on the Lancaster road, it was immediately determined to push forward and attack them; but a most violent fall of rain setting in, the intended attack became impracticable.

The enemy apprised of the approach of our army, marched the whole night and got to Yellow Springs, having all their small ammunition damaged by the rain. It being found that General Wayne was lying in the woods with a corps of fifteen hundred men, and four pieces of cannon, Major-General Grey, was detached on the 20th to surprise them; their outpost and pickets were forced without noise, with the bayonet, about four o'clock in the morning; the Americans had scarcely time to turn out, and when they did, they paraded in the light of their fires.

This directed the British how and where to proceed; they rushed in upon them, killed and wounded not less than three hundred on the spot, taking between seventy and eighty prisoners, including officers, their arms, and eight waggons loaded with stores; on our side only one captain of light infantry, and three men were killed in the attack, and four wounded. The horrors of this conflict (although so few of the British Army were lost) almost realised the terrific idea of one of our great poets:

> *Uproar, revenge, and rage, and hate appear*
> *In all their murd'rous forms; and flame, and blood,*
> *And sweat, and dust, array the broad campaign*
> *In horror: Hasty feet and sparkling eyes,*
> *And all the savage passions of the soul*
> *Engage in the warm business of the day."*

On the 22nd of Sept. the British Army crossed the Schuylkill at Fatland Ford without opposition, and on the 25th marched in two columns to Germantown.

Germantown is now one of the most considerable towns of Pennsylvania, and is principally inhabited by High and Low Dutch, it contains near five hundred houses. Peach trees are planted all along before the doors. It is exceedingly pleasant, and situated at the distance of five miles from Philadelphia; it has only one street, which however, is two miles long. Many of the Philadelphians have their country houses in its vicinity. The trade carried on here is at present great; the place is particularly famous for coach-makers, type founders, &c.

Lord Cornwallis with the British Grenadiers, and two battalions of Hessian grenadiers, took possession of Philadelphia the next morning.

The possession of one of the largest cities in the United States, together with the dispersion of the Congress which had hitherto conducted their public affairs, were reckoned by the British as decisive of their fate. One of their first objects after they had obtained possession, was to erect batteries to command the river, and to protect the city against any insult from water. The British shipping were prevented from ascending the Delaware by thirteen gallies, two floating batteries, two *zebecs*, one brig, one ship; besides a number of armed boats, fire ships and rafts were constructed or employed for the purpose. The Americans had also built a fort on Mud Island, and erected thereon a considerable battery.

This island, or rather a bank of mud and sand, which had been accumulated, is admirably situated, for the erection of works to annoy shipping on their way up the Delaware. It lies near the middle of the river, about seven miles below. Philadelphia. No vessel of burden can come up, but by the main ship channel, which passes close by Mud Island, and is very narrow for more than a mile. On the opposite shore, on the Jersey side, is a height called Red Bank. This overlooks not only the river, but the neighbouring country. On this eminence, a respectable battery was erected. Between these two fortresses, which are half a mile distance from each other, the American Navy for the defence of the River Delaware, made their harbour of retreat.

Two ranges of *chevaux de frise* were also sunk into the channel; these consisted of large pieces of timber, strongly framed together in the manner usual for making the foundation of wharfs, in deep water. Several large points of bearded iron, projecting down the river, were annexed to the upper parts of these *chevaux de frise*, and the whole was sunk with stones, so as to be about four feet under the water at low tide. Their prodigious weight and strength, could not fail to effect the destruction of any vessel which came upon them.

Thirty of these machines were sunk about three hundred yards below Mud Island, so as to stretch in a diagonal line across the channel. The only open passage left, was between two piers lying close to the fort, and that was secured by a strong boom, and could not be approached but in a direct line to the battery. Another fortification was erected on a high bank on the Jersey shore, called Billingsport. And opposite to this, another range of *chevaux de frise* was deposited, leaving only a narrow and shoal channel on the one side. There was also a temporary battery of two heavy cannon at the mouth of Mantua Creek, about half way from Red Bank to Billingsport.

In the evening of the 26th, three batteries were begun by the British, in Philadelphia, to act against the enemy's shipping. These batteries were unfinished when they were attacked by a number of gallies, *gondolas* and other armed vessels, and the largest frigate, the *Delaware*, mounting thirty-two guns, anchored within five hundred yards of the town. About ten in the morning, she began a heavy cannonade, but the tide falling, the *Delaware* grounded. In this condition she was compelled to surrender. The smaller frigates and armed vessels were forced (except a schooner that was driven on shore) to return under the protection of the fort already described.

General Washington having received a reinforcement of two thousand five hundred men, and presuming on the British Army being much weakened by the detachments to Philadelphia and Jersey, thought it a favourable time for him to attack their post at Germantown, and where the bulk of the Royal Army was posted in the following order: their line of encampment crossed the town at right angles near its centre: the left wing extended to the Schuylkill, and was covered in front by the mounted and dismounted *chasseurs*; the Queen's Rangers, and a battalion of light infantry were in front of the right: the 40th Regiment, with another battalion of light infantry, were posted on the Chestnut-Hill, road, three quarters of a mile in advance.

The American commander recommended, that the attack should be made in different places, to produce the greater confusion, and to prevent the several parts of the British force from affording support to each other. From an apprehension, that the Americans from a want of discipline, would not persevere in a long attack, it was resolved that it should be sudden and vigorous, and if unsuccessful, they were to make an expeditious retreat.

The divisions of Sullivan, and Wayne, flanked by Conway's brigade, were to enter the town, by the way of Chestnut Hill, while General Armstrong with the Pennsylvania militia, should fall down the Munatawny road, and gain the left and rear of the British. The division of Green and Stevens, flanked by M'Dougal's brigade, were to enter by the Limekiln road; the militia of Maryland, and Jersey, under General Smallwood, and Furman, were to march by the old York road, and to fall upon the rear of their right; Lord Sterling, with Nashe's and Maxwell's brigade, were to form a corps of reserve.

At three in the morning of the 4th of October, the British patrols discovered the enemy's approach, and the army was immediately ordered under arms. About break of day, the enemy began their attack with great impetuosity, the 40th Regiment, and a battalion of light infantry, sustained this severe attack with great bravery, till they were nearly surrounded: they then retreated in good order to the town, where Lieutenant-Colonel Musgrave, with six companies of the 40th Regiment, took post in a large and strong stone house, which lay in front of the enemy. This party being so advantageously posted, kept one half of the American Army in check, and from the windows of the house, did considerable execution. General Washington, says in his letter to Congress, when speaking of this affair:

> The party in Mr. Chew's house, who were in a situation not to be easily forced, had it in their power from the windows, to give us no, small annoyance, and in a great measure to obstruct our advance.

Major-General Grant, now advanced with the right wing of the British, and attacked the enemy's left, which gave way and was pursued through a woody country, between four and five miles; but such was the expedition with which they fled, that it was not possible to overtake them. The whole American Army now retired, near twenty miles to Penibacker Creek, and encamped. General Washington, in relating this action to Congress, says:

> The morning was extremely foggy, which prevented our improving the advantages we gained, so well as we otherwise should have done; this circumstance by concealing from us the true situation of the enemy, obliged us to act with more caution, and less expedition than we could have wished; and gave the enemy time to recover from the effects of our first impression, and what was still more unfortunate, it served to keep our

different parties in ignorance of each other's movements, and hindered our acting in concert; it also occasioned us to mistake one another for the enemy, which I believe more than anything else contributed to the misfortune which ensued. In the midst of the most promising appearances, when everything gave the most flattering hopes of a victory, the troops began suddenly to retreat, and entirely left the field, in spite of every effort that could be made to rally them.

The loss of the Royal Army in this action, amounted to seventy killed, and four hundred and sixty-five wounded; in the number of the former, were unhappily some very brave and distinguished officers, particularly Brigadier-General Agnew, of the 44th Regiment, and Lieutenant-Colonel Bird, of the 15th. The number of officers wounded was considerable. The American loss was esteemed between two and three hundred slain, six hundred wounded, and four hundred taken prisoners; among their slain was General Nash, and his *aide-de-camp*, Major Witherspoon. On the 19th, the British troops removed from Germantown to Philadelphia, as a more convenient situation, for the reduction of Mud Island, which at that time prevented the passage of the river, as the *chevaux de frize* could not be removed until possession of that post was obtained; the British Army was well apprised that without the command of the *Delaware*, their possession of Philadelphia would be of no advantage; every exertion was therefore made to open the navigation of that river.

Colonel Donop, with a strong detachment of Hessians, crossed the Delaware on the 21st, with directions to proceed to the attack of Red Bank; the colonel led on the troops in the most gallant manner to the assault. They carried an extensive outwork, from which the enemy were drawn into an interior entrenchment, which could not be forced without ladders. The detachment in moving up, and returning from the attack, suffered much by the enemy's gallies and floating batteries; Colonel Donop, being mortally wounded and taken prisoner, the command devolved upon Lieutenant-Colonel Linsing, who, after collecting all the wounded that could be brought off, returned with the detachment to camp.

The ships of war designed for the attack of Mud Island, made their way with difficulty, and took the best possible disposition that the situation of the river would admit; they commenced their assault at the same time that Colonel Donop was engaged at Red Bank, but with as little success. The ships could not bring their fire to bear with any great effect upon the enemy's works. The *Augusta* ship of war, of 64 guns, commanded by Captain Reynolds, (afterwards Lord Ducie), and the *Merlin* sloop of war, grounded. In this situation, though the skill and courage of the officers and crews of the several vessels, prevented the effect of four fire ships, which the enemy had sent to destroy the *Augusta*; she afterwards unfortunately took fire in the engagement, which obliged the other vessels to retire with the greatest expedition, in order to get beyond the effect of her explosion. It was at the same time found expedient to abandon the *Merlin*, and destroy her; the greater part of the officers and crew of the *Augusta* were saved, but the second lieutenant, chaplain, and gunner, with no inconsiderable number of the seamen, unhappily perished.

Though this first attempt for opening the navigation of the Delaware, was unsuccessful, it by no means damped the resolution of the naval commanders; new measures were immediately adopted, and on the 15th November, the attack was renewed with the greatest fury on both sides, till the works being nearly demolished, the garrison retreated in the night, across the river in boats to Red Bank; three days after, Mud Island was evacuated.

The Americans, upon the approach of Lord Cornwallis, with a detachment of British troops, hastily withdrew from Red Bank, leaving their artillery and a considerable quantity of cannon and stores behind them. A few of the enemy's gallies and vessels escaped, by keeping close in with the Jersey shore, to places of security above Philadelphia; but seventeen of them were abandoned by their crews, and burned.

On the 30th and 31st of December, the British troops went into winter quarters in Philadelphia, and were well accommodated; while the American Army, excepting a detachment of twelve hundred at Wilmington, were hutted in the woods, in a strong position at Valley Forge, sixteen miles from that city.

In May 1778, General Howe took his departure for England, and the chief command of the British Army devolved on Sir Henry Clinton.

CHAPTER 12.

The Author Makes his Escape into New York

In the beginning of June, 1778, the Earl of Carlisle, (he was Lord Lieutenant of Ireland from the year 1780 to 1782), Mr. Eden, (later Lord Auckland), and Governor Johnston, arrived at New York; these gentlemen, with Sir Henry Clinton, were appointed by the British government, to attempt a reconciliation with the American colonies; but in vain were all their efforts, an implacable spirit of hostility to the parent country had taken place in the breast of the Americans. They had thrown themselves into the arms of France, and no exertion of reason was able to unfetter the embrace. The following reflection, in the commissioners' declaration, roused Congress to such a degree of anger, that they declared:

Were it not under the idea of stopping the effusion of human blood, they would not have read a paper containing expressions so disrespectful to His Most Christian Majesty, the good and great ally of these states, or to consider propositions so derogatory to the honour of an independent nation.

The commissioners in part of their letter to Congress say:

In our anxiety, for preserving those sacred and essential interests, we cannot help taking notice of the insidious interposition of a power, which has from the first settlement of these colonies been actuated with enmity to us both; for notwithstanding the pretended date, or present form, of the French offers to America, yet it is notorious, that these were made in consequence of the plans of accommodation previously concerted in Great Britain, and with a view to prevent our reconciliation, and to prolong this destructive war.

But, we trust, that the inhabitants of North America, connected with us by the nearest ties of consanguinity, speaking the same language, interested in the preservation of similar institutions, remembering the former happy intercourse of good offices, and forgetting recent animosities, will shrink from the thought of becoming an accession of force to our late mutual enemy, and will prefer a firm, a free, and perpetual coalition with the parent state, to an insincere, and unnatural foreign alliance.

But this was not all, General de la Fayette, a young French nobleman then in the American service, and who has since made so conspicuous and gallant a figure in the Gallic revolution, considering the honour of his sovereign wounded, actually sent a challenge to lord Carlisle, to which His Lordship returned the following temperate and dignified answer:

> Sir—I have received your letter, transmitted to me from Monsieur Gimot, and I confess I find it difficult to return a serious answer to its contents. The only one can be expected from me as the king's commissioner, and which you ought to have known, is, that I do and ever shall consider myself responsible to my country and to my king, and not to any individual for my public conduct and language. As for any opinion or expressions contained in any publication issued under the commission, in which I have the honour to be named, unless they are retracted in public, you may be assured I shall never, in any change, be disposed to give an account of them, much less recall them in private.
>
> The injury alluded to in the correspondence of the king's commissioners to the Congress, I must remind you, is not of a private nature, and conceive all national disputes will be best decided by the meeting of Admiral Byron and Count D'Estaing.

On the 13th of June, General Clinton following instructions received from the parent country, evacuated Philadelphia. It is probable that all idea of negotiation was now considered hopeless, as the commissioners accompanied the army. Their accompanying a retreat from a city, which might be properly called the capital of America, was not very likely to procure for them any terms to which Great Britain could possibly listen; on the contrary, this circumstance only swelled the pride and increased the insolence of the American rulers, The whole British Army marched out of the town at three o'clock in the morning, and crossed the Delaware before noon with all its baggage.

★★★★★★★★★★

Several of the Loyalists of Philadelphia went along with the British Army; some, who remained behind, were treated with great severity by the Americans. Messieurs Roberts and Carlisle, gentlemen of respectable characters of the Quaker persuasion, suffered death for their attachment to the Royal cause.

★★★★★★★★★★

General Washington, by some means, was apprised of this movement; in consequence of which he sent expresses into the Jerseys, to collect troops.

The American Army then likewise passed the river, and were hourly joined by reinforcements of the regular troops, and of their militia. General Gates, with an army from the northward, was fast advancing. In this situation, General Clinton retreated across the country towards Sandy Hook, at which place he could with facility effect the passage to New York.

At this juncture, Washington was far from being inactive; he pursued the retreat of the British, and also sent the Marquis de la Fayette, with a strong body of chosen troops, to harass their rear; General Lee, (who had been some time exchanged,) followed with a division, to support him, and the commander in chief finally so managed his own movements, that with the main body he covered and sustained the whole.

On the 27th of June, the British Army encamped in a strong position in the neighbourhood of Freehold Court House, in the county of Monmouth; the following morning the van division of the Americans, under General Lee, commenced the attack. General Clinton had already, with due precaution, directed General Knyphausen to take the baggage of the whole army under his division, which consisted of the 17th Light Dragoons, the 2nd Battalion of Light Infantry, Hessian *Yagers*, 1st and 2nd Brigades, British, Stern's and Lee's brigade of Hessians, Pennsylvania loyalists, West Jersey volunteers, and Maryland loyalists.

General Clinton was induced to this order, under the firm persuasion that the baggage only was Washington's object, it having been his constant practice to avoid a general engagement with the British; the general, therefore, with much wisdom and foresight, placed it in a state of security, and prepared himself to encounter the American Fabius. Under the head of baggage was comprised not only all the wheel carriages, of every denomination, but also the bat horses; a train, which as the country admitted but of one route for carriages, extended near twelve miles. Sir Henry Clinton had with him the 16th Light Dragoons, 1st and 2nd Battalion of British Grenadiers, 1st Battalion of Light Infantry, Hessian Grenadiers Guards, and the Third, Fourth, and Fifth Brigades.

The total disagreement between the British and American accounts of this action, is not a little perplexing to the impartial narrator; both parties claim the advantage, but the Americans, particularly at that time, had their reasons for their misrepresentations-reasons which did not at all influence the reports of the British commanders.

The Marquis de la Fayette, who commanded the American cavalry, began the attack. They were instantly charged with great spirit by the light dragoons. The Americans did not wait the shock, but fell back in disorder upon their own infantry. The British then proceeded on their march; but, on the rearguard descending from the heights above Freehold into a plain near three miles in length, and above one in breadth, several columns of the enemy appeared, and descended into it also. About ten o'clock they began to cannonade the rear of the British. Sir Henry Clinton, as has already been observed, being apprehensive that the baggage was their sole object, determined on the attack of these divisions, in order to oblige those troops who were at that time on his flanks to return. These divisions were endeavouring to gain his front, that they might attack the baggage, and therefore impede his progress.

The British Grenadiers, Guards, light infantry and Queen's Rangers now engaged the enemy with such vigour, that their first line, commanded by General Lee, was completely broken; their second line withstood the attack with great obstinacy, but was also defeated; they both rallied, however, and posted themselves with a morass in their front. They were again charged by the British troops, and were with difficulty preserved from total defeat by the junction of their main body, which was supposed to consist of twenty thousand men, under General Washington,

When Washington found the division under General Lee retreating in disorder, he rode up to Lee, and proposed several questions to him, which implied censure. Lee answered with warmth and unsuitable language. Washington then ordered two of his battalions to form on advantageous ground, which he judged suitable for giving a check to the advancing enemy. Lee was then asked, if he would command on that ground, to which he consented, and added to Washington, in a haughty tone, "Your orders shall be obeyed, and I will not be the first to leave the field." Lee continued until the last on the field of battle, and brought off the rear of the retreating troops.

In this action the bravery and discipline of the British forces were gloriously conspicuous. Facts speak for themselves. They forced an enemy, superior in numbers, from two strong positions, and endured excessive fatigue, both from unremitting toil, and the intense heat of day. The British general took up the position from whence the enemy had first been driven, after they had quitted the plain; and having reposed the troops till ten o'clock at night, to avoid the excessive heat of the day, he took advantage of a fine moonlight-night to rejoin General Knyphausen, which he effected near Middleton. On the 30th of June the whole Royal Army arrived at Sandy Hook, without the loss of either their covering party or baggage; from whence it passed over to New York without further molestation.

After the evacuation of Philadelphia, much praise was due to Admiral Lord Howe for the excellent dispositions which he made to cover the troops passing the *Delaware*. It is pretty evident that Washington was at first deceived by his own caution and dread of being decoyed into a general engagement, and that he then ascribed the slow movements of the British to a design on the part of Sir Henry Clinton, of gaining the strong grounds above him, and se inclosing his army to the river.

The loss of the Royal Army in killed, wounded, and missing, was three hundred and fifty-eight men, fifty-nine of whom, through excessive heat and fatigue, fell dead without a wound. The honourable Lieutenant-Colonel Monckton, who commanded the 2nd Battalion of Grenadiers, fell in the action. One of the writers on the American war says:

> This gallant officer, who had frequently encountered death in all its forms, had the fortune of being more than once grievously wounded, both in the last war and the present; and after the hair-breadth escape of a recovery, when left among the dead on the field, was only reserved to be killed on this day, at the head of the second Battalion of grenadiers.

A braver soldier never expired on the field of battle.

The conduct of Washington on this occasion, (however he might have been self-deceived, relative to some of the movements of Sir Henry Clinton,) was highly creditable to his military skill.

His timely interposition with the main body of the American

Army, prevented the rest from being entirely cut off; and by his subsequent movements, he succeeded in gaining it such an advantageous position, as entirely secured it from attack.

The loss of the Americans, however, in killed and wounded, was very considerable. (According to their own accounts it amounted to three hundred and sixty-one men, including thirty-two officers.) Colonel Bonner and Major Dickinson, officers highly esteemed by their country, fell in this engagement. The emotions of mind, added to the fatigue of a remarkably hot day, brought on such a suppression of the vital powers, that numbers of the Americans, as well as the English, were found dead on the field of battle, without any marks of violence on their bodies.

After the engagement the American general drew off his troops to White Plains, near King's Bridge. Taking up a commanding position, he remained there until the latter end of autumn, watching the motions of the British, when he retired to Middle Brook, in Jersey,

In the meantime, the haughty spirit of Lee could not brook the language which General Washington had hastily used when he met his troops retreating before the British, on the 28th. It is probable that Washington intended to take no further notice of Lee's conduct on the day of the action; but, upon the general's receiving from him a letter couched in the most disrespectful terms, and replete with the most violent invective, he was immediately put under an arrest, and a court martial, of which Lord Sterling was president, was held upon him. His accusation consisted of three principal charges: *viz.* Disobedience of orders, misbehaviour in action, and disrespect to his commander. He was found guilty upon every charge, and suspended from all his military commands for twelve months.

Immediately on the departure of the British troops from Philadelphia, the Congress returned to that city, and gave public audience to Monsieur Gerrard, minister plenipotentiary from the Court of France.

It may now be necessary to revert to the maritime events of the war. Early in the spring, Count D'Estaing had been dispatched from the port of Brest, with twelve ships of the line and six frigates; there were six thousand soldiers on board, for the assistance of the American cause. The whole armament suffered considerably on the voyage, and did not arrive off the coast of America before the beginning of July.

On finding that Lord Howe had sailed to New York, Count D'Estaing followed him, and in a few days the French fleet appeared off Sandy Hook. The British admiral had only eleven ships, very inferior in magnitude and weight of metal. The French commander seemed fully determined to attack the English fleet, and force his way into the harbour of New York. The British admiral ranged his ships with much nautical skill to receive him. He was powerfully supported by the inhabitants. Upwards of one thousand volunteers, from the trading vessels, then lying at New York, entered on board the British ships of war; the masters and mates of the transport-ships took their situations at the guns, with the common seamen; others put to sea in light vessels, in order to watch the motions of the enemy; and in our army, the officers and privates contended with so much eagerness, to serve on board the ships of war, as marines, that it became necessary, to decide the point of honour by lot.

After the French fleet had remained at Sandy Hook for eleven days, they weighed anchor and put to sea. Lord Howe's fleet was, at that time, every way for resistance inferior. Indeed, nothing but the excellent disposition made by the noble admiral, and the determined activity, not only of the respective crews, but also of the volunteers, could possibly have saved it, had the count felt himself inclined to come to action. The tacit compliment that he paid to the skill, the resolution, and the character of Lord Howe, by not daring to attack him with so decided a superiority of strength, raised that nobleman's name to a degree of exaltation which will make it live for ever.

So freely, however, was the matter spoken of in America, that, in order to save the credit of the French admiral, it was reported that he determined to force the harbour; but the American pilots on board, declared it impossible for the large ships of his squadron to pass the bar.

On this curious apology, it is not surely too much for an old subject of the British Empire, (and who has been on the spot,) to declare his belief, that if admiral Nelson had commanded D'Estaing's fleet, he would have found water enough to have brought the largest ships in that squadron alongside the quay of New York.

The next attempt of D'Estaing was against Rhode Island, in order to co-operate with General Sullivan, in an enterprise against Newport. General Sir Robert Pigot, who commanded on the island, having been reinforced, made every preparation for a vigorous defence. In the meantime, Lord Howe being reinforced by some ships from England, (part of a squadron commanded by Admiral Byron), immediately stood out to sea, though still inferior in force, in order to give battle. D'Estaing, finding that he was pursued to Rhode Island so quickly, (as he only had entered the harbour of New Port the day before,) determined to hazard an engagement; accordingly, he put out to sea with his whole fleet.

But, while the two commanders were busily employed, in manoeuvring for the weather gage, a tremendous tempest arose, which separated the fleets. Amidst this conflict of the elements, the *Languedoc*, of ninety guns, D'Estaing's own ship, after losing her masts, fell in with the *Renown*, of fifty guns, commanded by Captain Dawson, who attacked her with great fury, when the appearance of six French ships of the line, compelled him to desist. Captain Raynor, in the *Isis*, and Commodore Hotham, in the *Preston*, each of fifty guns, fought with much gallantry the *Tonnant* of eighty guns, and the *Cæsar* of seventy-four guns; but no ship on either side struck her colours.

Lord Howe, with all possible dispatch, followed D'Estaing to Boston, and entered the bay, under the hope of a favourable opportunity of attack: but, to his great mortification, he found the French fleet lying in Nantucket road, so well defended by the forts and batteries on that island, that it was found to be absolutely impracticable.

In the meantime, General Sullivan and his army in Rhode Island, with the people of the northern colonies, complained loudly of the conduct of D'Estaing. For this they boldly assigned their reasons, which were, that they had, engaged in an expedition of great expense and danger, under prospect of the most effective co-operation of the French fleet; that depending thereon, they had risked their lives on an island, where, without naval protection, they were likely to be enclosed, like wild beasts, in a toil; and that in this situation they were first deserted, and then totally abandoned, at the very time when they stood most in need of help.

It was a fact, at that time pretty generally admitted in America, that it was under these apprehensions their general was deserted by most of the militia, (who composed nearly half of his army) which obliged him to retreat from his lines; and though he was most vigorously pursued, and repeatedly attacked in every quarter by the British forces, yet, his measures were so well conducted, that he gained the north end of the island, from whence he passed his troops over to the continent without any considerable loss.

Indeed, before he quitted the island, the Marquis de la Fayette, who commanded under him, set off for Boston by land, to request the speedy return of the French fleet. To this requisition D'Estaing would not consent. He had been very roughly handled a few days before by a British captain, and he knew very well the great danger his master's fleet would be exposed to, if he again fell in with the British Navy. But he offered to lead the French troops which he had on board against Rhode Island, in co-operation with the American forces.

The most remarkable transactions, during the remainder of this campaign, might, from their nature, almost be termed naval expeditions, at least they were intimately connected with maritime warfare.

In October 1778, Lord Howe sailed for England, on account of his health, and the command of the fleet devolved on Admiral Gambier.

There is no doubt but it was part of the insidious policy of the French Cabinet to strike a blow at the British possessions in the West Indies. How this plan had been methodised, it is impossible at this period to ascertain; but its operations became so intimately connected with American affairs, that it is necessary to take some notice of them.

The projects of D'Estaing being effectually disconcerted at Rhode Island, he sailed in the beginning of November for the West Indies, in order to second the operations of the Marquis de Bouille, Governor of Martinico, who had already captured the island of Dominique. Three days before the French fleet left Boston, the 4th, 5th, 15th, 27th, 28th, 35th, 40th, 46th, 49th, 55th Regiments, and a corps of Hessians, under the command of General Grant, sailed from New York, in order to strengthen the garrisons of the West India Islands.

It may be necessary that the reader may the more clearly understand the sequel of American transactions, to mention the progress of the British arms in the West Indies. Upon the arrival of the troops there, a descent was made on the island of St. Lucia, and by the active exertions of Brigadier-General Meadows, the advanced posts were carried. While these opera rations were going on, D'Estaing appeared in view. That commander upon his arrival at Martinico had been joined by a fleet of transports, with nine thousand land forces on board, with which he had hoped to effect the entire reduction of the British islands.

Admiral Barrington's squadron, which was greatly inferior to the French fleet, was stationed across the entrance of the Carenage, and was supported by several batteries, erected on the shore. The French admiral bore down with twelve sail of the line; but met with so gallant a reception, that he thought proper in a short time to draw off. In the afternoon he renewed the attack, with his whole squadron, and a furious cannonade, directed chiefly against Admiral Barrington's division, was kept up for several hours. This, however, made no impression on the English fleet, and the French admiral was again obliged to desist from the attack. He then landed a body of nine thousand troops, which he formed in two divisions; putting himself at the head of the right, he gave the Marquis de Bouille orders to lead on the left.

They advanced rapidly towards the English lines, keeping up a heavy fire as they proceeded The British troops reserved their fire until they saw them mount their trenches; then a tremendous fire was poured upon the assailants, which immediately stopped their progress, and threw them into disorder; before they could recover, they were charged by the British. The slaughter was dreadful, and it was with difficulty the French reached their ships. The count re-embarked his troops, and left the island to its fate. It soon after surrendered to the British arms.

The American government had, in the beginning of the year projected the reduction of West Florida; and several detachments of their troops had made some successful incursions into that country. This awakened the attention of the British commanders to the southern colonies; and an expedition against them was resolved on. Georgia was the place of its destination; and the more effectually to ensure success, Colonel Campbell, a brave and prudent officer, with the 71st, and two battalions of Hessians, four battalions of Provincials, and a detachment of artillery, embarked at New York; while General Prevost, who commanded in East Florida, was directed to set out with all the force he could spare.

The armament from New York, under commodore Sir Hyde Parker, arrived at the mouth of the Savannah, in the month of December; and though the enemy were very strongly posted in an advantageous situation on the shore, the British troops made good their landing, and the light infantry, under Captain Cameron, of the 71st Regiment, formed and advanced. A body of Americans, however, attacked them with great bravery; but the Highlanders rushed on, and drove the Americans into the woods. Captain Cameron, a spirited and valuable officer, with two Highlanders, were killed, and five were wounded. The British troops then advanced towards Savannah, the capital of the province. The day, however, was destined for still further triumph to the Royal cause.

They had not marched far when they attacked and defeated the American troops, who opposed them with great resolution and bravery. This victory was complete: upwards of one hundred of the Americans were killed, thirty-eight officers, four hundred and fifteen privates, forty-eight pieces of cannon, twenty-three mortars, the fort with its ammunition and stores, the shipping in the river, a large quantity of provisions, with the capital of Georgia, were all, in the space of a few hours, in the possession of the conquerors. The broken remains of the American Army retreated across Savannah River into South Carolina. The different posts upon that river were secured by the British troops, and the province of Georgia was entirely at peace in seven days after the defeat of the American Army. General Prevost now arrived at Savannah, and took the command of the British troops. The conquest of South Carolina was next projected.

While these operations were carrying on in the southern province, the captured troops in New England, as already described, were ordered to march to the east parts of Virginia.

This was universally considered by the privates as a very great hardship, and by the officers as a shameful violation of the articles of capitulation. The application of General Burgoyne to General Gates on this subject, has already been mentioned. It should seem that the origin of the whole delay was ascribable to the Congress; for the members hesitated not to declare, when pushed hard on the violation of the seventh article of the convention, "that if the troops were suffered to embark for Great Britain (according to the spirit of that article,) as soon as they left their coasts, they would form a junction with the British garrisons in America."

Still further to colour their breach of faith, with an apparent shew of justice, they alleged, that it had been often asserted by the British nation, "that faith was not to be kept with rebels," and that therefore, Congress would be deficient in attention to the interests of America, if they suffered the captured troops to depart.

When I saw that the American rulers had no intention of allowing the British troops to return to England, I determined on attempting my escape into New York. The idea immediately suggested itself to me, that it would be much more agreeable, and indeed less dangerous, to have companions in my flight; I therefore resolved to induce as many of my comrades as I could to join me.

I soon made myself acquainted with the route which it was necessary that we should take; I found that we were to cross the North River, only sixty or seventy miles above New York. This then appeared to me the most favourable point from which to attempt our escape. Unfortunately, however, for my scheme, our officers (fearful of their regiments being, at their return to Europe, reduced to mere skeletons) had previously issued orders, that if any soldier should absent himself from his regiment only for one day or night, he should be returned as a deserter; and if brought back to his regiment by any of the inhabitants or American soldiers, he should be tried by a court-martial, and punished accordingly. I was fully aware, that the intention of this order was to keep the men together, and likewise to deter them from remaining in the country, it being the constant practice of the Americans to induce the captive soldiers to become settlers. These orders prevented many from attempting their escape. But for them, numbers like myself, and the companions of my journey, would have made good their escape into New York.

While the Americans protected to the uttermost those deserters, who left the British Army to settle among them, they who were caught by them in the attempt to join the king's forces at New York, had everything to fear; nor was the least their being brought back to their respective regiments under the odium of desertion.

I weighed in my mind all the consequences that would most probably result, should I be taken by the natives; and the more I thought of the attempt, the more I began to feel a degree of enthusiasm, to which I was before a stranger. I looked forward, not without hope, to the prospects before me, and I began already to indulge the exultation of effecting my escape. Indeed, I had wrought myself up to such a pitch of firmness, that I am persuaded, the most agonizing cruelties which the Americans could have inflicted on my body, would have been unable to have effected any alteration in my resolution.

I communicated my scheme to two of my comrades, over whom I had most influence, and persuaded them to join me in the attempt; one of these soldiers understanding the French and German languages, was a powerful assistant in effecting our escape, as our guards were chiefly composed of German troops. By his conversing with these men, we obtained permission to go to a house in order to buy some necessaries which we wanted. When we got to the house, we took care not to return to the line of sentries again; but moved further from the guards, by degrees; until we entirely lost sight of them. We then began to fear, lest the next inhabitants we met, might pick us up and bring us back. We therefore thought it best to conceal ourselves. Just at this critical moment, we perceived a small hut on the verge of a wood. On our entering it, we found a poor woman with two children.

We entreated her to hide us for a few hours, as we were apprehensive that the American soldiers would soon miss us, follow, and make search for us. As the chief inducement to obtain her assistance, we immediately shewed her some silver money, which we promised to give her, if she assisted us in making our escape. To this she readily consented, and as a pledge of sincerity left her little child with us. She gave us some provisions, locked us all up in a small apartment, and went out in order to gain information.

There was a characteristic shrewdness about this woman which highly fitted her for our purpose. She very acutely observed, before she went, that this would be the best method, for if our pursuers should come to the house, and observe it fastened up, they would not, she believed, break it open, unless they had some previous information of our being concealed there; and as nobody had observed our coming into the hut, she hoped there would be no danger.

In this place we remained until dark, under the unpleasant apprehension of being seized every moment by our pursuers, as we were in the very midst of them; however, fortunately for us, not one of them either knocked at the door or demanded entrance.

The woman returned in the evening. She said: "You see, that I have been faithful to you. Your comrades have all crossed the North River, with most of their guards, and there are very few of the Americans at this side of the river."

It may be naturally supposed that we all felt ourselves much indebted to her for her faithfulness; and, as far as was in our power, we rewarded her. We then informed her, that we intended to make our escape into New York. She observed, that that would be a very hard task to accomplish, as there were several American encampments in the Highlands, which lay between us and that city. However, she gave us a recommendation to a man living a few miles off, who, she observed, would assist us in getting forward. Taking an affectionate leave of our faithful hostess, we directed our course to the house of her friend; but before we had proceeded three miles, we were stopped by a deep and rapid stream.

My comrades not knowing how to swim, I proposed to swim across, taking one of them at a time with me, if they would faithfully and courageously follow my advice, which was to lay their hands gently on my loins while in the water, striking out with their feet at the same time. This method would have soon carried us all across, as the river was not very broad; however, they both declined it, as too hazardous an attempt, and proposed to trace the river upwards, in order to discover a fording place. We had not proceeded up the river two hundred yards, when we perceived a tree lying across the stream;

this served the inhabitants for a bridge. Such conveniences for passing rivers are very common in America. We crossed the river in safety, and pursuing our journey, arrived at the house to which we had been directed by our late kind hostess. It stood alone at the edge of a wood, and being unconnected with any other human dwelling, seemed admirably adapted to our purpose. The family were much alarmed when we rapped them up.

We, however, soon made the owner acquainted with our intentions, and informed him, that if he would conduct us to New York, we would give him twenty dollars, exclusive of the reward he would receive from the commander in chief. He listened with attention, and seemed willing to comply; but his wife, overhearing our discourse, opposed it immediately, and declared, with tears in her eyes, that, he should not go. The rude reasonings of this woman appeared so powerful an instance of conjugal feeling, that they made a strong impression on my mind at the time. To the married reader little apology is due for their introduction.

She said: "What! do you mean to break my heart, by foolishly running into the jaws of death, depriving me of a husband, and my children of a father? You know that there are several camps and garrisons between this and New York, that you would not be able to go ten miles before you would be taken up, and then you would be hung up like a dog."

This discourse operated with all the power of simple nature, when the whole force of the passions is brought to bear on any given point. The man changed his mind in a moment. He said: "Gentlemen, this is a very dangerous piece of work; I know that all my wife has said is true; I know that the Americans have very strong outposts all along the North River, as far as King's Bridge, and if I were taken in the act of bringing you into the British lines, I could expect no mercy."

All our arguments after this, could not prevail with him, though we promised to give him twelve dollars in advance, and two new English blankets; however, he at last, for a small present, conducted us to another friend, who lived two miles further on our journey; this person, he observed, might probably go with us.

We set off between one and two o'clock in the morning, and arrived at the poor man's hut, which was situated on the top of a high mountain.

When we entered the hut, we found his wife ill of a fever, and the husband, with a woman, attending her. After much persuasion, and a small present, we prevailed with this man to bring us to another friend that lived six miles onwards, and whom there was every probability we might obtain for a guide. We set off immediately, and after making our way for six hours, through a trackless desert, full of swamps, we found ourselves at daybreak very near the out-posts of an American encampment. Here our guide, on finding where we were, being much terrified, fled from us with the greatest precipitation. As his last act of attention, he pointed out a pathway which led into the woods, and told us to pursue that track, and it would bring us to a friend,

We took his advice, and continued on that track for five or six miles, when we came to a small hut. The inhabitants were astonished at our appearance, but evidently pleased at our company. We informed the woman that we were very hungry. She immediately prepared a repast for us, which I need not add, was at that time highly acceptable, as we had not eaten anything for the space of forty-eight hours.

The fatigue we had undergone during our march, from the extent of country which we had traversed, rendered sleep highly necessary, and we prepared to lie down. This measure, the woman warmly opposed. She said, "the American soldiers often straggled from their camp to her hut, and some of them might probably come upon us while we slept." Her husband now came in, and seemed glad to see us.

We made him acquainted with our intention of escaping into New York. He repeated the observations of our other directors, relative to the number of the American posts, particularly on the North River; and added, "that it would be a hundred chances to one, if we were not taken." We told him that we would reward him liberally, if he would conduct us.

He answered: "There is a young man who lives several miles off, who will, I believe, undertake it: if he should, I have no objection to go; but I will not go by myself, as I well know the dangers which we shall be exposed to without a second guide."

We remained at this place two days, encouraging them by every argument which we could suggest to make the attempt. At last, we prevailed, by giving them ten dollars and the two new English blankets, which we had with us. We set off with our two guides about six o'clock in the evening, and after travelling through deep swamps, thick woods, and over difficult mountains for ten hours, our young guide stopped, and declared that he would not proceed any further with us, unless we gave him forty dollars in hand.

He said: "This is a dangerous, troublesome piece of work. Here is an American encampment within a mile of us; I have been there a few days ago, and I know where all the sentries are posted; if I should be taken, I shall lose my life."

As he uttered this, he seemed to be under great terror and fear, which increased when we said: "We are not afraid of one or two American sentinels, only conduct us the best way you can; and if we unavoidably fall in with any of them, you may leave the matter to us and fly for your life."

All we could say had no effect on him, and although we offered him on the spot twelve dollars, he would not advance one step further.

We then encouraged our other guide to proceed with us, to which, after much entreaty and promises of reward, he consented.

We expected every moment, as we advanced, to fall in with the line of sentries belonging to the Americans; but, happily for us, as it rained very hard during the whole night, and was very dark, we did not encounter one of them, though we passed very near to a log house, which was full of troops. Taking, however, every possible precaution, we immediately struck off into the woods, and after climbing up precipices, and wading through swamps, about five o'clock in the morning, we arrived at the wished-for house.

This was situated only two miles from another encampment. Our guide being well acquainted with this family, told them who we were, and also our intention. They received us very kindly, and gave us refreshment, informing us, at the same time, that it would be highly dangerous for us to remain in the house, as the American soldiery were scattered over almost the whole face of the country.

We held a consultation what was to be done under the then existing circumstances; and it was unanimously agreed, that we should hide ourselves in a haystack, which was near the house, until our guide could explore the country, and find out the safest way for our escape. We were conducted to the spot on which it stood, when each of us buried himself up to the chin in the hay, and waited the event. Our conductor was vigilant in procuring all the intelligence he could with regard to the station of the American Army. This delayed him much longer than we at first imagined. Our not hearing aught from him during the space of thirty hours, made us very uneasy; we were fearful lest he also had forsaken us, and left us to shift for ourselves. At last, he came, and bad us prepare to follow him. We were at that time about forty miles from King's Bridge, the outpost of the British Army.

Thus circumstanced, we determined to accomplish the march,

if possible, that night; we therefore set off in high spirits, about six o'clock in the evening.

Previous to the commencement of our journey, we were informed by our guide of our perilous situation, while we remained concealed in the hay-stack. The Americans had determined to remove it to the camp for forage, which probably would have been done the day before, only that it rained remarkably hard during the whole of it. Fortunately for us, the storm continued, with unabated violence, all night; and the darkness was such, that we were completely shrouded from all observation. These circumstances tended very much to favour our escape.

After as hard a march as any poor fellows ever experienced for the time, over swamps, rivers, and mountains, we arrived a little before daylight at a small house about one mile from the British outposts at King's Bridge, fifteen miles from New York. We boldly rapped at the door, and demanded entrance. The inhabitants were much terrified, on our approach, and their fears began sensibly to increase, when we ordered them to light a candle. They assured us, that if a light were seen in their house, at that hour, the habitation would be soon tumbled about their ears, for the British fort would immediately fire into it; we were, therefore, constrained to remain in that situation until daylight had commenced, as it would have been highly dangerous, to have proceeded to the fort in the dark.

Soon as morning dawned, we left the house, and with joyful hearts proceeded to the fort. The out-sentry challenged us; we answered, "We are British soldiers, who have made good our escape." We were conducted with joy and wonder to the fort, and received with great kindness by the officers and men. I believe we were the first party belonging to General Burgoyne's army, that effected an escape.

It would not be very easy to give the reader an adequate idea, either of my own feelings, or those of my associates on this occasion. The toil and hardships we had sustained, the dangers which we had surmounted; captivity, or death, in its most frightful, shapes, every moment presenting horrid images to our minds; in avoiding destruction or recapture from the Americans, encountering the hazard of still greater calamities; sinking into the morass or quagmire; drowning in the rapid torrent; tumbling headlong from the dreadful precipice; not to mention the terrors of the woods, among which, the least was the encountering the venomous bite of the American serpents: when delivered from all these, we joined our countrymen and fellow soldiers in arms.—Such a moment must be imagined; it cannot be described.

We were, of course, immediately conducted forward to New York, when Major André, the adjutant general, received us with great affability and kindness, at the headquarters. As I was the person who first planned the means of escape, and conducted the whole plan, under the guides, I was the object to which every inquiry was directed. Sir Henry Clinton the commander in chief, was an experienced officer, and a sensible man. He, doubtless, gave private orders, relative to my examination, willing to gain information of every circumstance, however minute, that might by (communicating intelligence of the state of the country,) add to the security of the British Army. I am also inclined to think, that much of the bounty that I and my comrades received, was the result of Sir Henry's secret benevolence.

Major André immediately brought me into the parlour, inquired very minutely into every circumstance of the route I had taken with my party, and the dangers I was exposed to: the number of the enemy, the usage which the British soldiers received when prisoners, &c. &c. &c. When I had given him all the information which I could, he expressed much satisfaction, and told me, that if I chose, I might take my passage to England in the next packet that sailed, (as I was at that time a non-commissioned officer, I had the privilege of being sent home.); but, at the same time, he intimated a wish that I would continue to serve in America. I answered, "That I would rather remain, and serve His Majesty in America, than go home to England."

The major then, with much feeling and politeness, informed me, that he was authorised by Sir Henry Clinton, to offer me my choice of entering in any regiment, then serving in America. I came to the resolution of serving in the 23rd, or Royal Welch Fusiliers, then quartered in New York. I was soon after appointed sergeant by Colonel, now General Balfour, to whose kind attention I must ever feel myself much indebted. I was immediately sent to an officer, (Colonel Handfield, the present—1809—Commissary General of Ireland), who was appointed to pay the men who made their escape from confinement, the usual bounty.

The distinction made in cases like mine, by General Burgoyne himself, was highly flattering to the military feelings of the soldier. The general used to term them, "honourable desertions." This distinction he made, even in the house of commons, between these soldiers, who, through every difficulty, made their way to, and joined His Majesty's forces, and those who left their regiments, for the purpose of settling among the Americans.

CHAPTER 13

Southern Affairs

It may now be necessary to pursue the thread of this narrative in a different direction, and to turn the reader's attention to the southern affairs.

The reduction of Georgia by General Prevost and Colonel Campbell excited great alarm in the Congress; nor were the apprehensions of ruin and discomfiture to American independence less without doors, particularly among the inhabitants of South Carolina. In this critical posture of affairs General Lincoln, who served under Gates in the northward, as already related, was appointed to the command of the southern American Army. Being reinforced by a considerable body of troops, he encamped within twenty miles of Savannah. Another strong body of troops was posted at Briar's Creek, farther up the river.

Thus, the extent of ground for the exercise of the British Government was likely to be circumscribed within very narrow bounds. General Prevost therefore determined to dislodge the party at Briar's Creek. Lieutenant-Colonel Prevost (the general's brother) with three companies of the 60th Regiment, Sir James Baird's light infantry, the Second Battalion of the 71st Regiment, Captain Tawe's Provincial troop of light dragoons, and some militia, amounting in the whole to nine hundred men, were directed to make a circuit, in order to come upon the rear of the American encampment; whilst Major Macpherson, with the First Battalion of the 71st Regiment, and two field pieces, appeared in their front. These two dispositions proceeded in strict obedience to orders.

It was on the 30th of March, that the Americans were attacked in front and rear, and totally routed, with the loss of seven pieces of cannon, several stand of colours, almost all their arms, and the whole of their ammunition and baggage. Upwards of four hundred men were killed, wounded, or taken prisoners; among the latter was General Elbert, the second in command. This victory entirely broke the American measures in the province; of consequence the communication was again opened between the British posts and South Carolina.

This victory proved of considerable service. General Lincoln was thereby reduced to a state of cautious inactivity, and at last moved off towards Augusta.

Lincoln had no sooner quitted his post than the British general determined on the invasion of Carolina. The time was chosen with the most profound judgment, but many difficulties lay in his way. The River Savannah was so swelled by the excessive rains of the season, that it seemed impassable; the shores were so full of swamps and marshes, that no army could march over it without the greatest difficulty; to obstruct the passage still more, General Moultrie was left with a considerable body of troops, to oppose any attempt that might be made by the British. In defiance of every opposition, the constancy and perseverance of the British forces at last prevailed. General Moultrie was defeated, and obliged to retire towards Charlestown, while the victorious army, after having waded through the marshes, at last arrived in an open country, over which they pursued their march with rapidity, towards the capital.

A general alarm, throughout all Carolina, now took place. Their capital was in danger. Lincoln, with a numerous army, took possession of all the avenues leading to. Charlestown, and prepared for a vigorous defence. But all opposition proved ineffectual; the Americans were defeated in every encounter, and retreating continually, at last allowed the British Army to come within cannon shot of Charlestown, on the 12th of May, 1779.

The town was summoned to surrender. The inhabitants would gladly have agreed to have observed a neutrality during the war, and would have engaged for the rest of the province; but these terms not being accepted, every preparation was made for a vigorous defence of the place. It was not in the power of the British commander (without being guilty of that rashness, the danger of which, could not escape his enlarged and consummate judgment, as an officer) at that time to make an attack with any prospect of success. His artillery was not of sufficient weight, there were no ships to support his attack, and General Lincoln, advancing rapidly with a superior army, threatened to enclose him between his own force and the town.

The British commander was too wise not to be aware of the danger; if he had failed in the first attempt, certain destruction would have been the consequence, General Prevost's force was about two thousand four hundred strong, and the garrison three thousand three hundred, including the militia. For these reasons the British general withdrew his forces from before the town, and took possession of two islands, called St. James's, and St. John's, lying to the southward; where, having waited some time, his force was augmented by the arrival of two frigates. With these he determined to make himself master of Port Royal.

This island, from its excellent harbour, and many other natural advantages, became an object of no small importance, its situation commanding all the sea coast from Charlestown to Savannah River. These measures, however, were not accomplished without opposition from the American general. Perceiving that the British had occupied an advantageous post on St. John's Island, preparatory to their enterprise against Port Royal, he attempted, on the 20th of June, to dislodge them from it; but after an obstinate conflict, the Americans were as usual obliged to retire with considerable loss.

This disappointment was instantly followed by the loss of Port Royal, of which General Prevost took immediate possession. He then proceeded to Savannah, and left the command to Lieutenant-Colonel Maitland. The troops were put in proper stations, and the whole waited the arrival of such reinforcements as were necessary for the intended attack on Charlestown.

It would swell this volume far beyond its prescribed limits, to point out the merits of the British officers and soldiers, who were engaged in these actions; but the singular gallantry of one exploit; performed by Captain Moncrief, of the engineers, in the sight of both armies, ought not to be omitted: that officer, with only twenty soldiers, sallied out in the face of the American Army, took an ammunition waggon, and brought it safe within the lines. This was a most seasonable supply of what was greatly wanted: for such was the scarcity of ammunition in the garrison, that the last charge was in, the guns when the enemy gave way.

The affairs of the American campaigns were sometimes of a very complicated nature: clearly to comprehend several leading events of the history of the war, it is necessary in many instances, that the reader should be in possession of the joint movements of the British Armies, acting far distant from each other; but on the co-operation of which the issue of the contest finally depended. It is hoped that this remark will be received as a sufficient apology for breaking off rather abruptly from the affairs, transacting in the Carolinas, and proceeding to detail those of the north.

Sir Henry Clinton proceeded up the North River. By great exertions of valour, he carried the two important posts of Stoney Point and Verplanks. These forts securing the communication between the eastern and western colonies, had been fortified with much skill and diligence by the Americans. After leaving garrisons in them, the fleet, with the rest of the troops, fell down the river and returned to New York,

The province of Connecticut was the great source from whence the Americans recruited their armies and supplied them with provisions. It had, from its situation, hitherto sustained little of that rage of war, which most of the other provinces had endured. The British commander, to convince the inhabitants that their province was not inaccessible, and that it was to our lenity, and forbearance they were indebted, planned an expedition against it. It formed also part of the general's plan, to compel Washington to quit his strong situation on the North River, and descend into the country, for the defence of the sea coast.

As this expedition has been greatly misrepresented, both by Ramsay and Belsham, the author takes the liberty to transcribe from his *Journal* the following account of this affair, as he was himself personally employed on the service. He is happy to state, that many respectable British officers are still living, (particularly General Garth, second in command on the expedition,) who can bear full accord to the truth of the following account. Indeed, such refutation becomes the more necessary, as the British Army still lies under the odium thrown on it by those virulent party writers, which has never yet, to the author's knowledge, been answered by anyone.

The transports, on board which were troops amounting to two thousand six hundred men, weighed anchor at the entrance into the sound, and sailed towards New Haven, the capital of Connecticut, the 4th of July. Major-General Tryon commanded the land forces. Commodore Sir George Collier, in the *Camille* frigate, with the *Scorpion* sloop, *Halifax* brig, and *Hussar* galley, was appointed to the naval command, and escorted the transports. The first Division of the troops, under Brigadier-General Garth, of the Guards, disembarked at some distance below the town of New Haven. He had to pass the head of a creek, and was in consequence compelled to take a march of seven miles, amidst the continued opposition of the inhabitants; he, nevertheless, forced his way, and succeeded in gaining possession of the town.

Meanwhile Major-General Tryon, with the 2nd Division, landed on the opposite side of the harbour, and took a fort on the heights, the artillery of which commanded it; a direct communication was thus established between the two divisions of the army, one of which was. in possession of the town, The vessels in the harbour, artillery, ammunition, public stores, &c. were taken or destroyed; but, notwithstanding the opposition of the inhabitants, and their even firing from the windows, after the troops were in possession of the town, such was the British humanity, that, instead of indiscriminate death, which by the laws of war they were liable to, the town was saved from damage, and private houses, as much as possible, exempted from plunder, by placing sentinels before them, many of whom, (such was the American gratitude,) were actually wounded on their posts!

The next day a proclamation was issued, promising protection and pardon to all who should return to their allegiance, and threatening to punish as traitors those who did not. The fort was then dismantled; the troops were re-embarked, and New Haven was left in a far better situation than many less offending places have experienced in all countries during war.

The expedition next proceeded to Fairfield. After the landing of the troops, the opposition from the inhabitants was far more desperate than at New Haven. The lenity already shewn to the offenders, serving only to make them more outrageous, an example of severity became indispensable. All the public stores, and the vessels in the harbour, were therefore either taken or destroyed, and the town itself was laid in ashes. This example had not its desired effect. As the troops proceeded, the opposition became more determined, and of a nature which no regular army could patiently endure: no established system of warfare pardon. Norwark and Greenfield, places taken immediately afterward, therefore underwent a similar fate.

New London, the rendezvous for the American privateers, was the last place, the reduction of which General Tryon had in view; but as still more obstinate resistance was apprehended there, it was judged that a supply of ammunition, and an augmentation of troops should be obtained before it was attacked, though the loss of the British in the expedition amounted only to twenty killed, ninety-six wounded, and thirty-two missing. The fleet, therefore, returned to Huntington Bay, in Long Island, and the commodore went to Frog's Neck, where a conference was held with the commander in chief of the army, fully to arrange the future plan of attack.

The immediate occasion of this conference was the intelligence received by Sir Henry Clinton, that the inhabitants of Connecticut, who certainly had suffered much loss, both public and private, during the nine days of the expedition, were highly dissatisfied both with Congress and General Washington; in particular they loudly complained of the latter, in permitting the destruction of so many towns on the sea-coast, and remaining fixed, if not inattentive, in his strong position near the North River; and further, Sir Henry had been secretly and positively informed, that many were hesitating, from these circumstances, about withdrawing their support from Congress and making terms with the parent country.

Such is the simple, impartial, and unbiassed narrative of an expedition, which Ramsay, and after him Belsham, have endeavoured, with all the artifice of wilful misrepresentation, so to colour as to render the British name odious to humanity. No doubt, in such excursions many scenes occur, at which the feeling heart must revolt; but in war, all that the brave and the humane can do, is to soften and alleviate its horrors; to prevent them entirely, is altogether beyond the power of man.

And that this was done almost in every point, by the commanding officers, the Author can aver from his own personal knowledge. But if persons, whose residence unfortunately becomes the seat of war, will not govern themselves prudently, whom have they to blame, except themselves, for all the disastrous consequences that may ensue?

Mr. Ramsay makes the strange assertion, that at New Haven:

> The inhabitants were stripped of their household furniture and other moveable property; and the harbour and water-side were covered with feathers, which were discharged from opened beds!

Strange, indeed, that soldiers weighed down with arms, ammunition, and provisions, should carry feather beds so far to destroy them! and as for the household furniture what were they to do with it? Such slanderous improbabilities refute themselves: I never saw anything of the kind. But further, he has the hardihood to assert, that, "an aged citizen, who laboured under a natural inability of speech, had his tongue cut out by one of the Royal Army;" and that "a sucking infant was plundered of part of its clothing, while a bayonet was presented to the breast of its mother." It is literally impossible for one who has been in America during great part of the war, and who has actually fought in several of the engagements, to read such gross falsehoods without feeling more indignation than he can readily express, and hearing a sigh for the depravity of human nature. I am certain, that either of these actions, proved on a British soldier, would have been punished by his officers with the greatest severity.

Mr. Belsham, although somewhat more cautious and guarded in his assertions than Ramsay, is equally rancorous; and from the art with which he fabricates his deceptions, is a far more dangerous writer. His allusion to the words of the proclamation, that "the existence of a single house on the coast, was a striking monument of British mercy," is highly uncandid. This was an act of mercy after their cruel behaviour to the troops. And the assertion that all the buildings and farmhouses for two miles in extent round the town, were laid in ashes, I can take upon me to contradict as a gross and malignant falsehood. And yet these are the men who assume the pompous name of historians, and who transmit the most wanton misrepresentations of public events, together with the most wicked slander of illustrious individuals, to generations yet unborn!

In the meantime, the American general made a diversion in another quarter, which broke all the measures which had been taken, with bravery equal to the wisdom with which they were planned. Such is the fate of war, and such sometimes the result of the best laid schemes of man. In the night of the 15th of July, the fort at Stoney Point was taken by surprise. The Americans having had perfect knowledge of all its works, knew well, at what points to attack it, with advantage; it was still an enterprise of much difficulty, and greater danger. General Wayne was much praised for his conduct in the assault. He divided his troops into two columns, which entering the works in opposite quarters met in the centre of them about one in the morning of the 16th.

The surprise was not so sudden, but that a brave resistance was made: so that the killed and wounded were nearly equal. There were about six hundred men in the fort, commanded by Lieutenant-Colonel Johnson. They consisted of the 17th Regiment, the Grenadier company of the 71st, a company of the Regiment of Loyal Americans, and a detachment of artillery. One hundred and fifty-two were either killed or wounded; the remainder with their commander were made prisoners. General Wayne's force was supposed to be about one thousand five hundred. It is but just, here to praise the conduct of the American commander; he stopped the carnage, and when the place was entirely calmed, not a man of the garrison was put to the sword.

The bravery of General Wayne commanded the highest praises of all parties. As he passed the last abbatis he was wounded in the head by a musket ball; in which state, he insisted on being carried forward, declaring, "That if he died, he wished it might be in the fort."

To the loss of this important fortress must be added, one which was at the time sensibly felt through the whole army. Captain Tew, a brave and distinguished officer, fell in defending the first barrier. He, with the most rare and undaunted heroism, even refused the quarter that was offered him by the Americans, being determined to make a stand until the rest of the garrison were alarmed, or perish on the spot. The effort proved unavailing; and unfortunately, he fell a sacrifice!

His name, however, must be always dear to the mind of the brave; nor did there an officer fall, during the whole campaigns, who deserved a more splendid monument.

He was most dangerously (and it was at first thought mortally) wounded when serving under General Amherst, in the French war, at Louisbourg. He was shot five times through the body, once through each arm, and likewise in the thigh. Through one of the apertures made by a bullet, which penetrated the body, a large stripe of linen was passed from the belly out at the back during some months. After the engagement, his wounds were so firmly believed to be mortal, that they were not dressed for three days, the surgeon expecting his death every half hour. At length, however, with great care some hopes were entertained; but his recovery was as tedious as his situation had been dangerous, until, at length he was able to accompany the shattered remains of his regiment to England.

At last, by the assistance of the first surgeons, and a good constitution, his wounds so far healed, as to permit his return to the public duties of his profession, and he served at those hazardous expeditions, both with regard to health and life, the sieges of Martinico and the Havannah, In both places the dangers encountered from the enemy, admitted no comparison whatever with those which arose with the deadly exhalations and descended with the pestiferous dews of the climate, Notwithstanding all these services, he still remained unpromoted, continuing in the rank of a lieutenant, the same in which he left Europe in 1757.

Sometime after the peace, he returned to Great Britain; and an opportunity soon offering, he purchased the captain lieutenancy of the regiment. When they were reviewed by the king, he was pointed out to His Majesty, to whom his singular fate was related. His Majesty walked up to him, and after conversing with him very familiarly for some time, put his name down in his memorandum book, in order that he might not forget him when an occasion for promoting him should occur.

In 1771, he was, by His Majesty's Royal Favour promoted to a company in the regiment, which was then sent to Scotland, where it continued three years; but being again reviewed by the king, on their return to London, His Majesty instantly recognised Mr. Tew's person, and again most graciously condescended to converse with him, giving him hopes of still further preferment.

In the year, 1776, he again embarked for America, where, becoming eldest captain in the regiment, on the appointment of the then lieutenant-colonel and major to other duties, he was promoted to its command. Many and important were the services rendered by this gallant officer to the royal cause, until, at last, we behold him, like the Spartan, Leonidas, nobly falling in defending the pass. I have already mentioned the affairs of Princetown and Germantown, at both which places he bravely distinguished himself. Indeed, in those two actions his regiment rendered such essential service, that they received the public thanks of the commander in chief. It is such men who are the best guards of the throne, and on whom a nation may with safety fix its firmest dependence.

Washington's arrangement for the attack on the North River, included Fort Fayette with Stoney Point. They were to have been assaulted at the same time. The detachment which had the attack of Fort Fayette in charge, did not arrive in time; it, however, advanced under the command of the American General Howe; and, to favour its operations, General Wayne turned the cannon of Stoney Point against Fort Fayette, Lieutenant-Colonel Webster commanded there. The garrison was formed of the 33rd Regiment, part of the Regiment of Loyal Americans, a detachment from the 71st, and another of Royal Artillery.

Sir Henry Clinton was not unapprised of the danger; the expedition against New London was suspended, the transports and troops were recalled from the sound, and the army moved on to Dobb's Ferry, on the North River. Brigadier-General Sterling, with a detachment, sailed up the river; and the commander in chief, with a superior force, followed, hoping that Washington might be tempted, for the safety of Stoney Point, to quit his fortresses, and risk an engagement.

The American general was too prudent, and on the contrary, gave immediate orders for the evacuation of Stoney Point, and the demolition of all the works which the time would permit. Colonel Webster bravely defended his post at Fort Fayette or Verplank's Neck. He sustained the cannonade of Stoney Point without returning it, and bent the whole of his attention to the attack, under General Howe. This conduct succeeded. Before the Americans were able to effect anything against the fort, the arrival of Brigadier Sterling put an end to the contest; Stoney Point was retaken, and on the arrival of Sir Henry Clinton, the works were repaired, and Brigadier-General Sterling, with a more numerous garrison, took the command. As no manoeuvre whatever seemed likely to draw Washington from his hold of security in the Highlands, the transports fell down the river, and the troops returned to their quarters.

The idea of forming a settlement on the bay of Penobscot, had been adopted by the British commander. Six hundred men from the 74th and 82nd Regiments sailed in transports for that purpose, escorted by three sloops of war. The command of this detachment was given to General Maclean. It was suggested that forming a post in this settlement would not only check the incursions of the Americans into Nova Scotia, but also facilitate the supply of timber for the royal yards at Halifax, &c. that part of the country abounding with forests. The bay of Penobscot is about seven leagues broad at the entrance, and seventeen in length. The River Penobscot empties itself into its head. About nine miles below the mouth of the river, on the east side of the bay is a small, but convenient harbour. The point of land on the peninsula forming one side of the harbour, was the spot General Maclean fixed on for the erection of a fort to protect the settlement.

The Americans lost no time in opposing the measure. A fleet, consisting of nineteen armed ships and brigantines, and twenty-seven transports, with three thousand troops, under the command of General Lovell set sail from Boston harbour, under the protection of Commodore Saltonstal, to oppose the undertaking.

His detachment arrived in Penobscot Bay on the 25th of July, but could not effect a landing until the 28th; three sloops of war, under the direction of Captain Mowat commanding the mouth of the harbour. The fleet could not enter to land the troops on one side the peninsula, and the other was so steep and rugged that it was almost inaccessible. At last, it was accomplished on the morning of the 28th, before daybreak: various and ineffectual assaults and skirmishes, took place until the twelfth of August, (a period of fifteen days) when a deserter brought intelligence to General Maclean, that the day following, a general assault was to be made on the fort; but the arrival of Sir George Collier caused them to forego their design, and they hastily reimbarked, with the greater part of their cannon.

The utmost confusion took place on board, and at last, not daring to wait the shock of the British squadron, they sought safety by flight. Two of the armed ships in endeavouring to get to sea by passing round Long Island, were lost to them, the one being taken, and the other was ran ashore, and blown up by the crew. The rest, with the transports, fled in disorder to the head of the bay, and entered the mouth of the river, closely pursued by the British. Here they landed in a wild uncultivated country; destitute of provisions and every necessary, they had to explore their way through a trackless desert, more than a hundred miles before they could reach any place of safety, or obtain succour. A quarrel ensued between the seamen and the landsmen, each throwing the blame on the other. It terminated in a battle, wherein fifty or sixty men were killed, and numbers, before they reached the cultivated part of the province, perished in the woods.

Such, (with all their vast superiority of numbers, was the event of the American opposition at Penobscot. General Maclean was entitled to, and received the highest praise. Stedman says:

In the progress and issue of this expedition, we see how much may be effected by a very inconsiderable force, when British officers act with zeal and unanimity in the service of their king and country.

On the English side, seventy were killed, wounded, and missing; on board the fleet, fifteen killed and wounded.

The loss of the American soldiery was never ascertained; but it must, on the whole, have more than exceeded two-thirds of their force. Of their fleets there were—

TAKEN.

Warren,	32 guns,	Defence,	16 guns,
Monmouth,	24 do.	Hazard,	16 do.
Vengeance,	24 do.	Diligence,	14 do.
Putnam,	22 do.	Tyrannicide,	14 do.
Sally,	22 do.	Providence,	14 do.
Hector,	20 do.	Spring Bird,	12 do.
Black Prince,	18 do.	Together with 24 sail	
Sky Rocket,	16 do.	of transports.	
Active,	16 do.		

BURNT.

Hampden,	20 guns,	Nancy,	16 guns,
Hunter,	18 do.	Rover	10 do.

Once more the reader's attention is solicited to other scenes, and following the operations of the southern armies, let us pursue the narrative of affairs before Savannah.

Count D'Estaing, after taking St. Vincent's and Grenada, sailed for America, and arrived an unexpected visitant on the coast of Georgia. His fleet consisted of twenty sail of the line, two of fifty guns, and eleven frigates, with which he surprised and took the *Experiment* of fifty guns and three frigates.

As soon as his arrival was known to the Americans, General Lincoln marched for Savannah, and in a short time place was invested both by sea and land. The British were diligent in making every preparation for its defence. Before the arrival of Lincoln, the count sent a peremptory summons, demanding the surrender of the place to the arms of France. To this General Prevost replied, by inquiring on what terms? The French commander rejoined, "That it was for the besieged to offer terms," A truce for twenty-four hours was then demanded and granted. During this time Colonel Maitland, after encountering incredible difficulties, arrived from Beaufort, which place he had been ordered to abandon.

The difficulties he had overcome in his march were astonishing. His arrival decided the fate of Savannah: for when some of the officers in council were for capitulating, the colonel resolutely arose, though almost worn out with fatigue, and said, "that the word *capitulation* was what he abhorred;" adding, in a firm tone, "that if he should survive, and go home to Britain, he would report to the king the name of the first officer who should dare to propose a capitulation." Thus encouraged, the, garrison determined on the most vigorous resistance. The works of the garrison were strengthened by the incessant labour of the troops and the negroes, under the direction of that excellent engineer Major Moncrief.

The siege commenced with nine mortars, and thirty pieces of cannon from the land side, and fifteen from the water. It was at this period that General Prevost solicited leave to send the women and children out of the place. This was tauntingly refused on the part of the Americans. Ramsay says (with his usual *candor* and *truth!*) that they were fearful lest the plunder of the Carolinas should be thus conveyed away; but I am almost weary with noticing the misrepresentations of this writer.

The hurricane season, so fatal on that part of the American coast, had now commenced, and the sailors began to murmur at delay. This forced them on the desperate attempt of storming the place, which was commenced at Springhold battery, October 9th, early in the morning, by three thousand five hundred French troops, six hundred continentals, and three hundred and fifty of the inhabitants of Charlestown. These troops, under the command of D'Estaing and Lincoln, resolutely marched up to the lines; but the tremendous and well directed fire of the batteries, joined to that in a cross direction from the gallies, threw their whole columns into confusion; not before, however, they had planted two standards on the British redoubts.

There were two feints made by the American militia to draw the attention of the garrison from the real point of attack, to their centre and left. Meanwhile it was intended that Count Dillon should secretly pass the edge of the swamps, the redoubts, and batteries, and attack the rear of the British lines.

The troops were in motion before daylight, but a heavy fog arising with the morning, they lost their way in the swamp, and were finally exposed to the view of the garrison and the fire of the batteries, which was so hot and tremendous, that they in vain attempted to form, and their whole design was defeated.

Lieutenant Tawes, of the 71st Regiment, nobly fell with his sword in the body of the third of the assailants he had killed. It was in defending the gate of the redoubt that he fell. The enemy rushed forward, and two standards (one American and the other French) were fixed on the parapet. They were soon displaced, and the conflict for possession of the redoubt became hot and bloody.

At last, when everything hung in suspense, Lieutenant-Colonel Maitland seized the critical moment, and ordered the grenadiers of the 60th Regiment, with the marines, to charge the enemy, who began to give way, being annoyed at once by the slaughter in the redoubt, the heavy fire from the batteries, and the guns of the *Germaine* armed brig, which played incessantly upon them. This judicious movement decided the contest. The enemy were driven out of the redoubt with immense slaughter; they fled in all directions; six hundred and thirty-seven French and two hundred and sixty-four of the Americans were left upon the spot, either killed or wounded.

General Prevost did not order any pursuit, as the enemy, notwithstanding their loss, were three times the number of the garrison. However, their ranks were still further thinned, during their flight, by the heavy and well directed fire of the British garrison, under the command of Captain Charleton. The loss of the besiegers, upon the whole, was upwards of one thousand men, among whom were forty-four officers.

Count D'Estaing was wounded in two places, neither of the wounds were mortal, and Count Polaskie received a ball, of which he died shortly after the engagement.

The event, in Polaskie's life, which will long render him an object of public curiosity, and also of public execration, was the attempt to assassinate the king of Poland. He was, at the time he planned the atrocious enterprise, a general in the Army of the Confederates. The conspirators who carried it into execution, were about forty in number, and were headed by three chiefs, named Lukawskie, Strawenskie, and Kosinski. These three chiefs had been engaged for that purpose, by Polaskie, who, in the town of Cyetscho, now (1809), in Great Poland, obliged them to swear in the most solemn manner, by placing their hands between his, either to deliver the king alive into his hands, or, in case that was impracticable, to put him to death.

On the 2nd of November, 1771, about a month after they had quitted Cyetscho, they obtained admission into Warsaw, unsuspected, by the following stratagem: they disguised themselves as peasants, who came to sell hay, and concealed their saddles and clothes under the loads in the waggons. On Sunday night the 3rd of November, 1771, a few of these conspirators remained in the skirts of the town, and the others repaired to the place of rendezvous, the streets of the Capuchins, where His Majesty was expected to pass by, about his usual hour of returning from visiting to the palace. The king had to visit his uncle Prince Zartoriski, Grand Chancellor of Lithuania, and was on his return from thence to the palace between nine and ten o'clock.

He was in a coach, accompanied by at least fifteen or sixteen attendants, besides an *aide-de-camp* in the carriage. Scarcely was he two hundred paces from Prince Zartoriski's palace, when he was attacked by the conspirators, who commanded the coachman to stop on pain of instant death. They fired several shots into the carriage, one of which passed through the body of a *hey-duc*, who endeavoured to defend his master from the violence of the assassins. Almost all the persons who preceded and accompanied His Majesty, were dispersed; the *aide-de-camp* abandoned him, and attempted to conceal himself by flight.

Meanwhile the king had opened the door of his carriage, with the design of effecting his escape, under shelter of the night, which was extremely dark. He had even alighted, when the assassins seized him by the hair, exclaiming in Polish, with horrible execrations, "We have thee now; thy hour is come."

One of them discharged a pistol at him, so very near, that he felt the heat of the flash, while another cut him across the head, with his sabre, which penetrated to the bone. They then laid hold of His Majesty by the collar, and mounting on horseback, dragged him along the ground between their horses at full gallop, for near five hundred paces, through the streets of Warsaw.

It is astonishing that none of the balls which passed through the carriage should hurt or wound the king, several went through his *pelisse*, or *sur great coat*. That celebrated writer, Nathaniel Wraxal, Esq says:

"I have seen this, and the holes made in it by the pistol bullets."

It is no less wonderful that the assassins should carry him through such a number of streets without being stopped. A Russian sentinel did hail them, but as they answered in Russian, he allowed them to pass, imagining them to be a patrol of his nation. The night besides was exceeding dark, and Warsaw has no lamps. All these circumstances contribute to account for the extraordinary event.

All was confusion during this time at the palace, where the attendants spread the alarm. The foot guards ran immediately to the spot from whence the king had been conveyed; but they found only his hat all bloody, and his bag; this increased their apprehensions for his life. The whole city was in an uproar. The assassins profited by the universal confusion, terror, and consternation, to bear away their prize. Finding, however, that he was incapable of following them on foot, and that he had already nearly lost his respiration, they set him on horseback; and then redoubled their speed for fear of being overtaken. When they came to the ditch which surrounds Warsaw, they obliged him to leap his horse over.

In the attempt the horse fell twice, and at the second fall broke his leg. They then mounted His Majesty on another, all covered as he was with dirt.

The conspirators had no sooner crossed the ditch, than they began to rifle the king, tearing off the order of the black eagle of Prussia, which he wore round his neck, and the diamond cross hanging to it. He requested them to leave him his handkerchief, to which they consented; his pocket book escaped their rapacity.

A great number of the assassins retired, after having thus plundered him, probably to notify to their respective leaders the success of their enterprise, and the king's arrival as a prisoner. Only seven remained with him, of whom Kosinski was the chief. The night was exceedingly dark; they were absolutely ignorant of the way; and as the horses could not keep their legs, they obliged His Majesty to follow them on foot, with only one shoe; the other being lost in the dirt.

They continued to wander through the open meadows, without following any certain path, and without getting any great distance from Warsaw. They again mounted the king on horseback, two of them holding him on each side by the hand, and a third leading his horse by the bridle. In this manner they were proceeding, when His Majesty finding they had taken the road, which led to a village called Burakow, warned them not to enter it, because there were some Russians stationed in that place, who might probably attempt to rescue him.

★★★★★★★★★★

This intimation may at first sight appear unaccountable; but was really dictated by the greatest address and judgment. He apprehended, with reason, that on the sight of a Russian guard, they would instantly put him to death and fly; whereas, by informing them of the danger they incurred, he in some measure gained their confidence. In effect, this behaviour of the king seemed to soften them a little, and made them believe he did not mean to escape from them.

★★★★★★★★★★

Finding himself, however, incapable of accompanying the assassins in the painful posture in which they held him, he requested them at least to give him another horse and a boot. This request they complied with; and continuing their progress through almost impassable lands, without any road, and ignorant of their way, they at length found themselves in the wood of Bielany, only a league distant from Warsaw. From the time they had passed the ditch, they repeatedly demanded of Kosinski, their chief, "If it was not yet time to put the king to death?" and these demands were reiterated in proportion to the difficulties they encountered.

Meanwhile the confusion and consternation increased at Warsaw. The guards were afraid to pursue the conspirators, lest terror of being overtaken should prompt them in the darkness to massacre the king: and on the other hand, by not pursuing, they might give them time to escape with their prize, beyond the possibility of assistance. Several of the first nobility at length mounted on horseback, and following the track of the assassins arrived at the place where His Majesty had passed the ditch. There they found his *pelisse*, which he had lost in the precipitation with which he was hurried away: it was bloody, and pierced with holes made by the balls or sabres. This caused them to imagine that he was no more.

The king was still in the hands of the seven remaining assassins, who advanced with him into the wood of Bielany, when they were suddenly alarmed by a Russian patrol or detachment. Instantly holding council, four of them disappeared, leaving him with the other three, who compelled him to walk on.

Scarce a quarter of an hour, after a second Russian guard challenged them anew. Two of the assassins then fled, and the king remained alone with Kosinski, the chief, both on foot. His Majesty, exhausted with the fatigue he had undergone, implored his conductor to stop, and suffer him to take a moment's repose. Kosinski refused it, menacing him with his naked sabre; and at the same time informed him, that beyond the wood they should find a carriage. They continued their walk until they came to the door of the convent of Bielany. Kosinski appeared lost in thought, and so much agitated by his reflections, that the king, perceiving his disorder, and observing that he wandered without knowing the road, said to him, "I see you are at a loss which way to proceed. Let me enter the convent of Bielany, and do you provide for your own safety."

"No," replied Kosinsksi, "I have sworn."

They proceeded till they came to Mariemont, a small palace belonging to the house of Saxony, not above half a league from Warsaw. Here Kosinski betrayed some satisfaction at finding where he was, and the king still demanding an instant's repose, he at length consented. They sat down together on the ground; and the king employed these moments in endeavouring to soften his conductor, and induce him to favour or permit his escape. His Majesty represented the atrocity of the crime he had committed, in attempting to murder his sovereign, and the invalidity of the oath he had taken to perpetrate so heinous an action. Kosinski lent attention to this discourse, and began to betray some marks of remorse. "But," said he, "if I should consent and reconduct you to Warsaw, what will be the consequence? I shall be taken and executed."

This reflection plunged him into new uncertainty and embarrassment. "I give you my word," answered His Majesty, "that you shall suffer no harm; but if you doubt my promise, escape while there is yet time; I can find my way to some place of security, and I will certainly direct your pursuers to take the contrary road to that which you have chosen." Kosinski could not any longer contain himself, but throwing himself at the king's feet, implored forgiveness for the crime he had committed, and swore to protect him from every enemy; relying totally on his generosity for pardon and preservation.

His Majesty reiterated his assurances of safety. Judging, however, that it was prudent to gain some asylum without delay, and recollecting that there was a mill at some considerable distance, he immediately made towards it. Kosinski knocked, but in vain; no answer was given. He then broke a pane of glass in the window, and entreated for shelter, to a nobleman who had been plundered by robbers. The miller refused, supposing them to be a *banditti*, and continued for more than half an hour to persist in his denial. At length the king approached, and speaking through the broken pane, endeavoured to persuade him to admit them under his roof; adding, "If we were robbers, it would, be easy for us to break the whole window, instead of one pane of glass." This argument prevailed: they at length opened the door, and admitted His Majesty. He immediately wrote a note to General Coccei, Colonel of the Foot Guards. It was literally as follows:

By a kind of miracle, I have escaped from the hands of the assassins. I am now at the mill of Mariemont. Come as soon as possible and take me from hence. I am wounded, but not dangerously.

It was with the greatest difficulty that the king could persuade anyone to carry this note to Warsaw, as the people of the mill, imagining that he was a nobleman who had just been plundered by robbers, were afraid of falling in with the troop. Kosinski then offered to restore everything he had taken, but His Majesty left him all, except the blue ribband of the White Eagle. When the messenger arrived with the note at Warsaw, the astonishment and joy was incredible. Çoccei immediately rode to the mill, followed by a detachment of the guards. He met Kosinski at the door with his sabre drawn, who admitted him, as soon as he knew him. The king had sunk into a sleep caused by his fatigue, and was stretched on the ground covered with the miller's cloak.

Coccei immediately threw himself at His Majesty's feet, calling him his sovereign and kissing his hand. It is not easy to describe the astonishment of the miller and his family, who instantly imitated Coccei's example, by throwing themselves on their knees. This mill is still standing, rendered memorable by such singular an event. It is a wretched Polish hovel, at a distance from any house. The king rewarded the miller to the extent of his wishes, in building him a mill upon the Vistula, and allowing him a small pension. His Majesty returned to Warsaw in General Coccei's carriage, and reached the palace by five in the morning. His wound was found not to be dangerous, and he soon recovered the bruises and injuries which he had suffered during this memorable night.

The king in his speech to the *Diet*, on the trial of the conspirators, interceded strongly for Kosinski, or John Kutsma, to whom he gratefully expresses himself indebted for these favours, in the following words:

> As I was in the hands of the assassins, I heard them repeatedly ask John Kutsma, if they should not assassinate me, but he always prevented them. He was the first who persuaded them to behave to me with greater gentleness; and obliged them to confer on me some services, which I then greatly wanted; namely, one to give me a cap, and another a boot; which at that time were no trifling presents; for the cold air greatly affected the wound in my head; and my foot, which was covered with blood, gave an inexpressible torture, which continued every moment increasing.

Lukawski and Strawenski were both executed. They both suffered without manifesting the least contrition for their guilt; the latter behaved with that fortitude which was worthy a better cause.

After the conclusion of these troubles, Polaski escaped from Poland, and repaired to America, where he raised a regiment of horse, and was appointed by Congress a Major-General of their armies.

But although death thus swept away from the American service a most active and dangerous character, the triumph of the British garrison was alloyed by an event, on their part of the most distressing nature. This was the loss of that highly esteemed and much beloved officer, Colonel Maitland. The noxious vapours which rise from the American marshes during the summer season, proved fatal to his constitution. Before he left Beaufort, he was attacked with a bilious disorder, which was increased by his route through the marshes to Savannah.

The anxiety and hardships of the siege served only to aggravate the complaint, which terminated in the dissolution of an officer whose name will be dear to Britons, until patriotism ceases to be a virtue, and loyalty becomes a crime. Soon after his death a character of him appeared in Rivington's *New York Royal Gazette*, the elegance, strength, and beautiful diction of which (I have no other reasons) inclines me strongly to suspect that, it was written by his friend Major André.

The late Colonel Maitland was one of the most active officers at the commencement, and during the progress of the American war: his zeal and gallantry were sufficient incitements to lead where danger dignified and rendered a post honourable. Though he possessed an easy fortune, had a seat in the House of Commons, and was of an advanced age, yet he never availed himself of such powerful pretensions, or expressed a desire of returning from the field of honour.

Unshaken loyalty, genuine patriotism, undaunted bravery, judicious conduct, steady coolness, and unremitting perseverance, constituted his character as an officer. His benevolence was ever exerted when indigence presented; he not only relieved, but sympathized with the distressed: to inform him of any person that required charitable exertion, was an ample recommendation. His disposition was so extremely amiable that to know him was to admire him.

His address was easy and engaging; his language strong, nervous and persuasive: his affability rendered him pleasing to every observer: he was beloved by his friends, respected by his acquaintances, and revered by every officer and soldier under his command. His country will feel the loss of so accomplished a chief; his acquaintance will long lament the loss of so venerable a friend; the indigent search in vain for another so eminently benevolent, and the soldiers, long accustomed to his pleasing command, lament his death, and revere his memory.

About this time the Congress, in order to terrify the Indians into neutrality, gave orders for an expedition which should convince them that the inhabitants of the sea coast were possessed of the means of carrying devastation into the heart of their territory. It was imagined that such a measure would deter them from again invading and ravaging the American settlements. Five thousand men with artillery and field pieces, under the command of Major-General Sullivan, entered the Indian possessions.

The natives fled as they approached, and a general destruction of everything commenced; "more," says Stedman, "than one hundred and fifty thousand bushels of corn were destroyed;" their gardens were laid waste, even the fruit trees were cut down; and one wide and spreading desolation everywhere met the eye." Meantime the Indians invaded the Provincial towns and settlements, and thus mutual destruction commenced. The Indians were enraged, but not overcome; and the little benefit and great expense of the measure, rendered it very unpopular—Congress became dissatisfied—it never had General Washington's approbation and General Sullivan, on his return, resigned all his employments and retired. While the northern Indians were thus suffering under the invasion of General Sullivan, those of the south, were also made to feel the effects of American retribution. Such a system of warfare is shocking to humanity, and, after all, its very policy seems to be at best but problematical.

CHAPTER 14

Charlestown Capitulates to the British Forces

Towards the latter end of the year 1779, Sir Henry Clinton entrusted the command of the Royal Army in New York, to Lieutenant-General Knyphausen, and embarked for the southward, with a formidable force, provisions, ammunition, &c. The whole sailed from Sandy Hook on the 26th of December, under convoy of Admiral Arbuthnot.

The passage proved both tedious and dangerous. Part of the ordnance, some of the artillery, and most of the cavalry horses were lost; nor did the fleet arrive at Tybu, in Georgia, until the 31st of January, 1780.

In a few days the transports sailed with the army for North Edisto. They landed about thirty miles from Charlestown (after a short passage) and took possession of John's Island, Stono Ferry, James's Island, and Wappo-Cut. A bridge being thrown over the canal, part of the forces took post on the banks on Ashley River, opposite Charlestown.

The tedious passage from New York, afforded opportunity to the Americans to fortify Charlestown; and from the losses which the expedition had sustained, Sir Henry Clinton deemed it prudent to send orders to New York for a reinforcement of men and stores. He also drew twelve hundred men from the garrison at Savannah. Brigadier-General Patterson who commanded this detachment, crossed the River Savannah, and traversing the country, arrived on the banks of Ashley River.

The siege was immediately commenced. A depot was formed at Wappo, on James's Island; fortifications were erected there, and on the main land, opposite the southern and western ends of Charlestown. An advanced party crossed the river, and broke ground at eight hundred yards from the American works; and batteries were erected on

Charlestown Neck. Nor were the Americans idle during this period: they put the town into every possible state of defence.

Charlestown is said to contain about one thousand four hundred houses, and about eight thousand inhabitants, including the blacks, who are by far the more numerous, almost every white man, in this boasted land of liberty, keeping a great number of slaves! The inhabitants are very extravagant in their living, splendid equipages, &c. But the merchants suffered so much during the war that it is doubtful if they will ever regain their former wealth. They boast of their town as the most polite place in America; but it is far exceeded by several others, in riches as well as convenience; the waters are frequently putrid; its climate unhealthy, and every necessary of life much dearer than in any other part of America.

But there is one circumstance, which, in the opinion of every wise as well as of every good man, must operate as a drag chain of Almighty vengeance about the neck of any state, practised here to a greater extent than in all the other cities of America, *viz.* that abominable and notorious traffic, the slave trade. How any people pretending, as the Americans do, to the profession of Christianity, can dare to drive on a horrible traffic in the blood of their fellow creatures, their co-heirs in redemption, and thus stab the religion which they profess in one of its most vital parts, is a dreadful solecism, at which a pagan may laugh; a Mahometan triumph; a *deist* exult, and which even a Jew might pity. But the sincere Christian must lament the continuance of the deplorable evil, alike ashamed of the practice, as incompetent to its cure. These reflections struck the mind of the author, when he perused the following paragraph, relative to the inhabitants of Charlestown, in the historical review of North America:

> In the midst of every appearance of festivity and joy, scenes of misery, with the horrors of slavery, momentarily intervene to assault the eye and ear! The feelings of humanity are shocked, with the hardships of incessant toil! The very ground is damp with the sweat and tears of the unhappy Africans. The crack of the whip too frequently intercepts the joys of convivial mirth! Here may be seen every day, and all day long, thousands of our fellow people branded, chained, and treated like cattle in every respect, but that of humanity! They are indeed fed the same, but are harder worked, and more severely abused.

The British troops carried on their parallel from the 3rd to the

10th of April. Immediately on the completion of the first parallel, the town was summoned to surrender; the batteries were opened; and from that time, a constant fire commenced. On the Wando River, at Simpson's Port, and Santic Ferry, posts were established, and works thrown up by the Americans, to guard their reinforcements and secure their retreat.

Meanwhile, Admiral Arbuthnot passed Fort Moultrie, on Sullivan's Island, though strongly opposed from the American batteries, and anchored under James's Island, with the loss of twenty-seven seamen killed and wounded, some damage to the shipping, and the burning of the *Acteus* transport, which grounded within gunshot of the island. The American commander, with his fleet, fell back to Charlestown.

The Americans, to keep up the communication with the country, formed a camp at Monk's Corner, which was the rendezvous of their militia. This post was surprised by Lieutenant-Colonel Tarleton, which gave the British the command of the country, and enabled them to intercept the supplies of provisions,

Our batteries soon obtained a superiority over those of the enemy, a council of war was held by the Americans, in consequence of which, the town offered to surrender, on condition of "security to the persons and property of the inhabitants, and leave being given for the Americans to withdraw."

These terms were instantly rejected by General Clinton, as soon as they were offered; but the garrison would not alter their conditions, under the hope that succours would soon arrive from the neighbouring states, in consequence of which, the town was closely invested, both by land and water, Fort Moultrie surrendered, and the American cavalry, which had escaped from Monk's Corner were all either killed, captured, or dispersed.

On the 9th of May, the town was again summoned, and Lincoln was inclined to surrender his army prisoners of war; but the inhabitants thought to obtain better terms, and the siege recommenced. The third parallel was opened, shells and carcasses thrown into the town, and the cannon and mortars played on the garrison at less than one hundred yards distance; the pickets, crossed the ditch by sap, and advanced within twenty-five yards of the American works.

Matters continued in this state till the 11th, when the inhabitants addressed General Lincoln to capitulate, which was accordingly done, and Major-General Leslie took possession of the town on the 12th. There were in it upwards of four hundred pieces of artillery. The garrison, as prisoners of war, marched out of the town; their drums were not allowed to beat, a British march, nor their colours to be uncased. They laid down their arms in front of the works; the militia returned home, on parole; the inhabitants were considered as prisoners on parole, and like the militia, held their property accordingly; a vessel was allowed to proceed to Philadelphia, with General Lincoln's dispatches, unopened; upwards of five thousand troops, and near one thousand sailors surrendered; all the ships of war, and other vessels were taken.

Among the officers were, two major-generals, five brigadier-generals, three majors of brigade, sixteen colonels, nine lieutenant-colonels, fifteen majors, eighty-four captains, one commodore, eighty-four lieutenants, thirty-two second lieutenants or ensigns. The deputy governor, council, and civil officers were all made prisoners. The total loss of the British from their debarkation to the surrender, was as follows,

Ensign M'Gregor, 71st, Regiment, killed.			
---- Cameron, do. do.		do.	
1 Serjeant.		do.	
73 Rank and File,		do.	
Lieut. White, grenadier company, 22d Regiment, wounded.			
---- Bever,	33d	do.	do.
---- Grant,	42d	do.	do.
---- Freeman, light infantry,	64th	do.	do.
Captain M'Leod,	71st	do.	do.
Lieutenant Wilson,	do.	do.	do.
2 Serjeants,			do.
176 Rank and File.			do.

(A few days after the capitulation, a magazine took fire in Charlestown, and Captain Collins, a valuable officer, with several men of the Royal Artillery, perished by the explosion.)

Captain Grattan received a severe contusion in the head, by the bursting of a shell in one of the trenches. He however recovered, returned to Ireland, and died during the rebellion in Wexford. Of this brave and amiable officer, the author has received the following brief account, from authority, which is indisputable.

Captain William Grattan, studied surgery under the celebrated Mr. Cleghorn of the city of Dublin. When he had attained a perfect knowledge of his profession, he was appointed assistant surgeon to His Majesty's 64th Regiment of Foot, at that time commanded by his friend and patron General Pomeroy. The regiment lay in Cashel, in the county of Tipperary, when they received orders for the theatre of war. They marched to the Cove of Cork, and embarked for the continent of America.

When they arrived at the place of destination, Mr. Grattan, who was at that time very young, glowed for more ardent employment, and possessing the soul of a soldier, he longed to wield the sword in the field of battle, to espouse his country's cause, and amidst the dreadful terrors of war, to meet the hostile foe. He purchased a commission in his own regiment, and shortly after a lieutenancy. Our young soldier avoiding the follies and extravagancies, of which too many are guilty, applied himself closely to the knowledge of the military science, in all its various departments, which he soon acquired. He was often heard to say, "Gambling and extravagance were the bane of a soldier."

What he disapproved in others he never allowed in himself. He lived with economy and frugality, and in the course of a few years, he purchased a company. Captain Grattan possessed a strong understanding, sound judgment, and deep penetration; these, with a perfect knowledge of his profession, made him an invaluable officer. He became the soul of his own regiment, which he never exchanged for another. Merit like his could not be hid. He was honoured with the confidence of his commanding officer, consulted on all matters of importance, appointed assistant engineer to Sir Henry Clinton, and was universally beloved by all, as well the privates of his own regiment, as the generals of the army.

In September 1781, when Count De Grasse, with a powerful French fleet, had the entire possession of the Chesapeake, and General Washington had formed a junction with the French troops, commanded by the Marquis De La Fayette, for the purpose of surrounding Lord Cornwallis, at Yorktown, Sir Henry Clinton dispatched Captain Grattan, with information that eight thousand British troops would immediately march to reinforce him. Captain Grattan encountered most imminent danger on this service; but he arrived safe with his dispatches at Yorktown, the 15th of September, and had the honour of receiving Lord Cornwallis's thanks in public orders.

Captain Grattan was seventeen years absent from Europe; he served in all the American war, and was in the West Indies. During this period, he was not one day absent from his regiment, unless when engaged on business of great importance, or in public employ.

Captain Grattan was in many battles, and displayed the greatest valour and intrepidity. He served at the Battles of Long Island, Germantown, Monmouth, Danbury, Brandywine, in Pennsylvania, the Eutaw Springs, in South Carolina, Brooklyn, on Long Island; Monmouth, at the burning of the enemy's stores on Peek Hill, at the siege of Charlestown, where he was wounded; at the affair of Chamblee River, where the famous Colonel Laurens, son to the President of Congress, was killed, and his party defeated by the 69th and a party of the 17th, besides a most fatiguing duty of two years in South Carolina, where the regiment lost upwards of four hundred men.

On Saturday morning, the 15th of May, 1784, Captain Grattan landed at Portsmouth, with six other commissioned officers, and the remains of his regiment. On his arrival in England, he wrote to his friends in Ireland; the September following he arrived in Edenderry, in the King's County, where he was joyfully received by his aged parents, three brothers, and two sisters, as one restored from the dead.

In the year 1792 he married Miss Giffard, a lady of amiable qualifications, the daughter of Sir Duke Giffard, of Castle Jordan, baronet. He then retired from the army, and settled in Rathangan. He was magistrate for the county, and sovereign of Kildare. When the penetrating mind of Captain Grattan foresaw the approaching rebellion, he did not think it his duty to be an idle spectator; be applied to government for an appointment, and was shortly after made deputy general in the commissariat department.

In the year of 1793, while in Dublin, he received orders to join General Needham, and march to the relief of Wexford. He fought at the Battle of Arklow. He was also at the taking of Enniscorthy, and Vinegar Hill. On the 20th of June, after the fatigue of the day's action was over, Captain Grattan who had been on such arduous duty since he had left Dublin, felt the need of refreshment. Invited by the lovely appearance of the Slaney, flowing under the hill, and attended by a faithful servant, he proceeded to it, to enjoy the refreshment of bathing; as he had not been in the cold bath since be returned to Europe, we may naturally suppose it was the cause of what followed.

Sometime after he arrived in Wexford he was confined to his bed. He experienced the greatest kindness and attention from Mrs. Hattan, a lady of fortune, who resides near the town, and Colonel Finley, of the county of Dublin Militia. They hardly ever left him. Colonel Finley wrote to Mrs. Grattan, who was at that time in Dublin, and informed her of his illness. His amiable wife, with no other companion but her sister, immediately set out to join him, and faced all the dangers of the counties of Wicklow and Wexford at that perilous time. She arrived safe; but though she did, how afflicting must her anguish have been, when her good and amiable husband expired shortly after her arrival!

The finest perfections enriched his character. He was an obedient and dutiful child to his parents, to the latest moments of their lives—a kind and good brother—an affectionate husband—a sincere friend—an elegant gentleman, and an experienced and valiant soldier. The former are known by his friends, and the latter can be proved by his military zeal in the service of his country, and the following letters of thanks from Lord Cornwallis:

Wynnsborough, Nov. 21, 1780.

Sir—I have just heard from Colonel Balfour, that you are returned from your expedition to General Leslie, where you have succeeded to my most sanguine wishes. I beg you will accept of my sincere acknowledgments for your *zeal, prudence,* and *good management* in this important business.

I am, Sir, your most obedient,
And most humble servant,

Cornwallis.

To Captain Grattan, 64th Regiment.

Culford, August 19, 1784.

Sir—It gives me great concern to hear of the particular hardships of your situation, in regard to your commission of Quartermaster of the 64th Regiment. I shall, at all times, be ready to bear testimony of your *merit,* and *good services,* when you were under my command; and I shall ever acknowledge my obligations to you, for your *zeal* and *diligence* for the public service, in executing an important commission at my request in 1780.

I am, Sir, your most obedient,
And most humble servant,

Cornwallis.

To Captain Grattan, 64th Regiment.

As the besiegers made no sallies or desperate assaults, their loss amounted to only eighty-nine killed, and one hundred and forty wounded. This was the first instance in which the Americans had ventured to defend a town. The event demonstrated the policy of Washington's system, who never during the whole war, attempted the defence of any town, against the investment of regular troops. In favour of General Lincoln, it is however but just to remark, that Charlestown was the only considerable place in the southern boundary of the confederacy; for its preservation South Carolina and the neighbouring states seemed willing to make great exertions: the Congress and both states of the Carolinas promised an army of near ten thousand men to its support. These were actually on their march; but the British had taken such a position, that succours could not be thrown into the place, or any retreat successfully made.

Sir Henry Clinton, with a liberal policy, held forth every inducement to the inhabitants that was likely to draw them back to their allegiance, and issued strong and salutary threats, to those who should continue contumacious. In a few days, in conjunction with Admiral Arbuthnot, as commissioners for restoring peace, the inhabitants were offered "pardon for their past treasonable offences, and a reinstatement in the possession of all their rights and immunities, which they heretofore had enjoyed, under a free British Government, exempt from taxation, except by their own legislatures."

The next object with General Clinton, was to bring back to their allegiance the whole southern states. Garrisons were therefore posted in different parts of the country, to awe the inhabitants. The troops marching for the relief of Charlestown were encountered on the borders of North Carolina, by different bodies sent out for that purpose.

One of these consisting of three hundred Americans, commanded by Colonel Buford, was overtaken at Wacsaws, by Lieutenan-Colonel Tarleton, and completely defeated. Colonel Tarleton, in his own *History of the Campaign,* says:

> Upwards of one hundred officers and men were killed on the spot, three colours, two six-pounders, and above two hundred prisoners, with a number of waggons, two royals, quantities of new clothing, other military stores, and camp equipage were taken.

Colonel Tarleton ascribes much of the "complete success" of this difficult enterprise, to the blunders and mistakes of the American commanders. Sir Henry Clinton (leaving between three and four thousand men for the southern service) embarked early in June for New York. On his departure the command devolved on Earl Cornwallis.

Almost the whole of South Carolina was now restored to its legal government; but the calm was only temporary: the submission was only nominal: for when a levy was attempted to be raised among the young men who had no families, to form a body to act against the hostile Americans, the spirit of disaffection broke out in various ways; and it evidently appeared that they possessed a hatred to the British Government.

In the meantime, the Americans marched an army through Jersey and Pennsylvania, which embarking at the head of the Elk, landed soon after at Petersburgh, and thence proceeded through the country toward South Carolina. It consisted of Maryland and Delaware troops, commanded by Major-General Baron de Kalb, who afterwards resigned to General Gates, The Americans expected much from the popularity of the latter.

As the American Army approached to South Carolina, our army, which then consisted of seventeen hundred infantry, and two hundred cavalry was concentrated at Camden. The army with which Gates advanced, was by the arrival of the militia, increased nearly to six thousand men. On the night of the 15th we marched from Camden, intending to attack the Americans in their camp at Rugeley's Mills. In the same night Gates put his army in motion, with an intention of surprising our camp, or posting himself on an eligible position near Camden.

Our army was ordered to march at ten o'clock p. m. The American Army was ordered to march at the same hour. The advance guard of both armies met about two o'clock in the morning. Some of the American cavalry, being wounded in the first fire fell back on others, who recoiled so suddenly, that the first Maryland Regiment was broken, and the whole line of their army was thrown into confusion, The enemy soon rallied and both they and we kept our ground, and a few shots only from the advanced sentries of each army were fired during the night. A Colonel Patterfield, on whose abilities General Gates particularly depended, was wounded in the early part of this skirmish. As soon as daylight appeared, we saw at a few yards distance our enemy drawn up in very good order in three lines.

Our little army was formed in the following plan:

Four companies of light infantry, Royal Welch Fusiliers, or 23rd Regiment, on the right wing, led on by Lieutenant-Colonel Webster.

Volunteers of Ireland, Legion Infantry, two American Loyal corps, on the left wing, led on by Lord Rawdon.

Two six- and two three-pounders were placed in the centre, between the two wings.

71st, the Legion Cavalry Regiment, with two six-pounders, formed the reserve.

It happened that the ground on which both armies stood, was narrowed by swamps on the right and left, so that the American's could not avail themselves of their superior numbers in out flanking us. We immediately began the attack with great vigour, and in a few minutes the action became general along the whole line; there was a dead calm with a little haziness in the air, which prevented the smoke from rising; this occasioned such thick darkness, that it was difficult to see the effect of the fire on either side. Our army either kept up a constant fire, or made use of their bayonets as opportunity offered.

After an obstinate resistance for some time the Americans were thrown into total confusion, and were forced to give way in all quarters. The continental troops behaved well, but some of the militia were soon broken. In justice to the North Carolina militia, it should be remarked, that part of the brigade commanded by General Gregory acquitted themselves well; they were formed immediately on the left of the continentals, and kept the field while they had a cartridge to fire. Gregory himself was twice wounded by a bayonet in bringing off his men: several of his regiment, and many of his brigade who were made prisoners had no wound except from bayonets.

About one thousand prisoners were taken, two hundred and ninety of which being wounded were carried into Camden, and more than twice that number killed. The Americans lost the whole of their artillery, eight brass field pieces, upward of two hundred waggons, and the greatest part of their baggage, tents, &c. with a number of colours. Almost all their officers were separated from their respective commands. The fugitives who fled on the common road, were pursued above twenty miles by Colonel Tarleton's cavalry, and the way was covered with arms, baggage, and waggons.

Baron de Kalb, the second in command, a brave and experienced officer in the American service, was mortally wounded, having exhibited great gallantry in the course of the action, and received eleven wounds; he was taken prisoner, and died on the next day of his wounds; we buried him in Camden with all the honours of war.

The baron, who was a German by birth, had long been in the French service. He had travelled through the British provinces, about the time of the stamp act, and is said to have reported to his superiors on his return, "that the colonists were so firmly and universally attached to Great Britain, that nothing could shake their loyalty." The Congress resolved that a monument should be erected to his memory in Annapolis, with a very honourable inscription.

In compiling an eventful history, like the present, many circumstances must unavoidably be taken on the authority of others. For these the author is no farther responsible than in selecting that report which appears the nearest to truth. Far different, however, are those matters which come beneath my own personal observations. On those a writer can dwell with precision. What he thus produces is the evidence of fact. As in this engagement, I had the honour of carrying one standard of colours belonging to the 23rd Regiment, I was of course, near the centre of the right wing. I had an opportunity of beholding the behaviour both of the officers and privates; it was worthy the character of the British troops. The recollection still dwells deeply in my memory.

Lord Cornwallis's judgment in planning, his promptitude in executing, and his fortitude and coolness during the time of action, justly attracted universal applause and admiration. The Earl of Moira, (then Lord Rawdon, who was only twenty-five years of age): bore a very conspicuous part in the contest. Colonel Webster also ought to be particularly mentioned. His conduct was completely consistent with his general character in the army, cool, determined, vigilant, and active; he added to a reputation established by long, service the universal esteem and respect of the whole army, as an officer, whose experience and observation were equal to his personal bravery, and the rigid discipline which he maintained among the troops. Captain (later General) Champaigne, who commanded the Royal Welch Fusiliers, also evinced the most perfect intrepidity and valour. Thus far I speak, not from the report of others, but from my own immediate observation.

In all the various engagements, which the safety, the honour, the interests of the empire have demanded, the Irish soldier, has seldom, if ever, lagged behind in the career of glory. On the present occasion, Lord Rawdon was so well pleased with the conduct of his regiment (the volunteers of Ireland) that he ordered a silver medal to be struck off, and presented to several of his men who had signalised themselves in the action.

The author cannot conclude the account of this day's victory, without entreating pardon from the reader, while he remarks that three years (excepting two months and a day) had elapsed since he was made prisoner at Saratoga by General Gates! He had at length, the satisfaction of seeing the same general to whom His Majesty's forces, under Burgoyne surrendered, sustain a signal defeat. What were his feelings at that eventful moment! How did he bless that Providence which inspired him with the idea of effecting his escape, and preserved him to be a partaker of that triumph which the soldier feels, when his sovereign's troops are victorious over his enemies! More especially when that victory was obtained in the hard-fought field over a general whose former success at Saratoga, had been trumpeted from one end of America to the other, and who had injured the British name, by charging the officers and privates with depredations that never existed but in his own imagination.

The River Wateree ran near the scene of action, on the other side of which the famous American flying General Sumpter was posted. On the news of the defeat, he immediately shifted his situation, picking up in his retreat a number of the fugitives from Gates's army. Lieutenant-Colonel Tarleton, whose exertions in the late action were deserving the highest praise was detached with some cavalry and light infantry, in the whole about 350, to attack him. With great exertion and military skill, by forced marches, he surprised the party at mid-day on Fishing Creek, near Catawba Fords. The greater part was destroyed, or taken, and the small remainder dispersed; one hundred and fifty were killed, two pieces of brass cannon, three hundred prisoners and forty-four waggons were immediately in possession of the British.

The remainder of Gates's army rendezvoused, at Charlotte, from whence they retreated to Salisbury. This retreat presented perhaps the most lamentable spectacle of misery and wretchedness exhibited during the war.

In addition to the incursions of Sumpter and Morgan, Colonel Clarke made an ineffectual attempt on the post of Augusta in Georgia. This induced Lord Cornwallis to detach Major Ferguson, with some militia, and the small remains of his own corps, without baggage or artillery, to Tyson County, under the idea of intercepting Clarke's party. They pursued the track along the mountains, far distant from the main army. A select body of the American troops, about one thousand of their best men, mounted on fleet horses, attacked the major on the top of King's Mountain, on the confines of the Carolinas.

They formed three parties; Colonel Lacy, of South Carolina, led on, and attacked the west end. The two others were commanded by Colonels Campbell and Cleveland; one of which attacked on the east, and the other in the centre. Major Ferguson, with great boldness, defended himself with fixed bayonets, and compelled them successively to retreat. They formed again, and getting behind trees and rocks renewed their fire in almost every direction.

The American marksmen took deliberate aim at our uncovered men, and numbers were found among the slain, shot through the head. Ramsey, in his account of the battle acknowledges, that "riflemen took off riflemen with such exactness, that they killed each other when taking sight, so instantaneously that their eyes remained, after they were dead, one shut and the other open, in the usual manner of marksmen when levelling at their object."

Major Ferguson shewed all possible bravery; but his valiant spirit disdained either to flee or surrender. After a severe contest, he received a mortal wound, nobly fell, and the submission of the survivors, eight hundred in number, terminated the carnage: one hundred and fifty were killed or wounded; and ten of the refugees who surrendered, were inhumanly hanged by the conquerors.

The fall of Major Ferguson was in itself a great loss to our army. He possessed superior abilities as a soldier, and his spirit of enterprise was uncommon. To a distinguished capacity of planning great designs, he also added the practical abilities necessary to carry them into execution. The advantage which the Americans gained over him and his party in a great degree frustrated a well concerted scheme for strengthening our army, by the co-operation of the well affected inhabitants, whom he had undertaken to discipline and prepare for active service.

The military science possessed by Major Ferguson was profound, and his adoption of it to the use of the smaller arms more correct than any other officer who preceded him. His execution in firing was such that it almost exceeded the bounds of credibility; he very nearly brought his aim at any given object to a mathematical certainty. On the 1st of June 1776, he made some experiments at Woolwich, before Lord Viscount Townshend, Lord Amherst, General Harvey, Deragliers, and several other officers, with the rifle gun, on a new construction, which astonished all beholders. The like had never before been done with any other small arms. Notwithstanding, a heavy rain and a high wind, he fired, during the space of four or five minutes (after the rate of four shots per minute) at a target two hundred yards distance. He next fired six shots in one minute. He also fired (while advancing after the rate of four miles per hour) four times in the minute.

He then poured a bottle of water into the pan and barrel of the piece when loaded, so as to wet every grain of the powder; and in less than half a minute, he fired with her, as well as ever, without extracting the ball. Lastly, he hit the bull's eye, lying on his back on the ground. Incredible as it may seem, to many, considering the variations of the wind, and the wetness of the weather, he only missed the target three times, during the whole course of the experiment. A patent was afterwards granted him for all his improvements. It passed the great seal on the 4th of December following.

Sumpter, soon after the dispersion of his troops, found means to collect a large body of volunteers, with whom he carried on from time to time, a kind of skirmishing warfare. He took his chief positions about Evorce, Broad and Tyger Rivers, and was a sore annoyance to the British. He was at last attacked at Black Stocks, near Tyger River, by Lieutenant-Colonel Tarleton, and defeated; three American colonels were killed, and Sumpter himself dangerously wounded. The enemy lost one hundred and twenty, and the British only fifteen men. Lieutenant Skinner, of the 16th Regiment of Infantry, who did duty with Colonel Tarleton's legion greatly distinguished himself on this occasion. Lieutenants Gibson and Caope, of the 63rd, were killed, and Lieutenant Money, a most promising young officer, *aide-de-camp* to Lord Cornwallis, died of his wounds a few days after.

During the remaining part of the year, General Gates was preparing to take the field. He collected a large force at Hillsborough, and advanced to Charlotte. Congress, however, resolved to suspend him, and ordered a court of inquiry into his conduct. So much for the gratitude of a republican government. The people of Virginia, however, did not so soon forget Saratoga; and when he was at Richmond they complimented him with a very handsome address, replete with expressions of the deepest confidence.

Such was the issue of this campaign. The minds of the Americans were totally alienated from the British Government, and to keep them under subjection when conquered, was an enormous expense to the parent country. The struggle had almost exhausted the resources of America; but the cause of Great Britain had not in the least point been forwarded.

CHAPTER 15

Northern Campaign

The northern campaigns of 1780, commenced with unfavourable auspices on the part of America. Their army was in great want of clothing; and, when with the co-operation of France, they fondly expected to strike an important blow by the capture of New York, Admiral Gucher sailed back to Europe, and left their most favourite schemes in a broken disjointed state. Their principal force lay in the strong holds of the Highlands, on the other side of the North River.

During the summer the British troops made frequent incursions into the Jerseys, and an unsuccessful attempt was made by General Knyphausen, with seven thousand men, to surprise the advanced posts of Washington's army.

On the 11th of July, 1780, a French fleet of seven ships of the line, and four frigates, besides armed vessels and transports, commanded by the Chevalier de Termoy, arrived at Rhode Island, with five regiments of troops, and a battalion of artillery, under the Count de Rochambeau. (The British troops had sometime before evacuated the island.)

The arrival of the French troops produced a remarkable circumstance in Washington's camp. Hitherto the Americans had worn blue cockades; but their general now ordered them to wear blue and white intermixed, to denote the alliance of the French and American Nations.

Admiral Arbuthnot now proceeded with the British fleet from New York to Rhode Island, and so completely blocked up the French fleet and army, as to prevent their co-operation with the Americans.

In the meantime, Sir Henry Clinton returned with his victorious army, from Charlestown.

A circumstance now claims attention, which, if it had been successful on the part of the British, most probably would have decided the American contest forever. This was the defection of the celebrated

American commander, General Arnold.

On the high ground of North River Banks, stood that Gibraltar of America, West Point. It was built by the Americans after the loss of Fort Montgomery, for the defence of the North River, and was deemed the most proper for commanding its navigation. Rocky ridges rising behind one another, rendered it incapable of being invested by less than twenty thousand men. This was the strongest post the Americans had; the thoroughfare of communication between the Eastern and southern states; and was the repository of their most valuable stores; the loss of it would have been severely felt.

Of this important fortress General Arnold had the command. He was a native of Connecticut, a state remarkable for the republican principles of its inhabitants. He was among the first who took up arms against the parent country. Ramsay, his mortal enemy says:

> His distinguished military talents, had procured him many honours from the state; poets and painters had marked him as a suitable subject, for the display of their respective abilities. He possessed an elevated seat in the hearts of his countrymen, and was for some time in the full enjoyment of substantial fame.

Perhaps the real motive in which Arnold's conduct originated, will never be clearly ascertained. If we may credit himself, his conduct was the result of reflection, conviction, principle; if we give credit to Ramsay and the other republican writers, "he betrayed the American cause for a stipulated sum of money." But this assertion has never been fairly proved.

General Arnold's own declarations are tolerably explicit. He says:

> That when he first engaged in the contest between Great Britain and her colonies, he conceived the rights of his country to be in danger, and that duty and honour called him to her defence: a redress of grievances was his only aim and object. He however acquiesced in the declaration of independence, although he thought it precipitate. But the reasons that were then offered to justify that measure, no longer could exist, when Great Britain with the open arms of a parent, offered to embrace the Americans as children and to grant the wished for— redress. From the refusal of these proposals, and the ratification of the French alliance all his ideas of the justice and policy of the war were totally changed, and from that time he had become a professed loyalist. In these principles he had only re-

tained his arms and command, for an opportunity to surrender them to Great Britain.

On the contrary, the Americans declared that his country had loaded him with honours and forgiven him crimes; that though he was brave, yet he was mercenary; fond of parade and extremely desirous of acquiring money to defray the expenses of it; that when he entered Philadelphia after the evacuation of the British, he made Governor Penn's, the best house in it, his headquarters, this he furnished in a very costly manner, and lived in a stile far beyond his income. That he continued this extravagant course of living during his stay in Philadelphia; that the generosity of the states was not able to keep pace with the extravagance of their favourite officer. That about July, 1779, he exhibited heavy accounts and demands against the public; that the commissioners upon examination, rejected about one half of the amount. That he then appealed to Congress, and a committee was appointed, who were of opinion, that the commissioners had allowed more than the general had a right to expect or demand: that this provoked him to outrageous proceedings.

Disgusted at the treatment he had met with, embarrassed in his circumstances, and having a growing and expensive family, he turned his thoughts toward bettering his fortune by a change of sides, which afforded the only hope of evading a scrutiny, and at the same time held out a prospect of replenishing his exhausted coffers.

In what precise manner the negotiation was first opened between Arnold and Sir Henry Clinton has never been revealed. One thing, however, the author can report from the most authentic source of information, that the unfortunate Major André, who fell the devoted victim to it, was a *volunteer* in the business. He was neither commanded nor solicited by Sir Henry Clinton to undertake it.

In the year 1779, Major André commenced a correspondence with Mrs. Arnold, "under the pretence of supplying her," says Ramsay "with millinery," (a strange kind of service for a British officer!). It was asserted and believed by many, that this correspondence was continued and improved by General Arnold without the lady's being at all aware of the designs in which he was engaged. But this was never satisfactorily proved. And after all, for various reasons that might be assigned, it is highly probable that the manner in which this negotiation commenced will for ever remain unknown.

To facilitate the intercourse between General Arnold and the British commander, the *Vulture* sloop of war had been previously stationed in the North River. It should likewise be mentioned that letters had passed, by several conveyances, between General Arnold and Major André, under the fictitious signatures of Gustavus and Anderson. The negotiation was in some state of forwardness when a personal interview was thought necessary. For this purpose, a boat was sent by Arnold to the *Vulture* to fetch Colonel Beverley Robinson, who was the person appointed to negotiate with him. Colonel Robinson was ill in his berth when Mr. Smith (brother to the Chief Justice of New York), arrived with the boat, and Major André *volunteered* to go in his stead. Mr. Smith having recently published a narrative of the whole transaction (and his authority being that on which reliance can be placed) this important event may perhaps be best narrated in his own words:

> Colonel Robinson pleaded indisposition, and said Mr. Anderson (Major André) could as effectually answer all the purposes by going on shore as himself; there seemed no reluctance on the part of Anderson to supply Colonel Robinson's place, and he appeared in a dress equipped for the purpose, wearing boots and a large blue great-coat. For my own part it made no difference to me who bore me company, so that the object of my mission was fully answered, and the great national ends obtained, which Arnold assured me would be the result of the affair.
>
> Mr. Anderson being ready, we left the ship, and were rowed in a short time to the western shore, to the place which General Arnold had appointed for the interview; this was at the foot of a mountain called the Long Clove, near the low water mark, whither my servant had conducted General Arnold on horseback, he being still lame from his wounds.
>
> On my approach to the place of appointment, I found General Arnold ready to receive me; *he was hid among firs.* I mentioned to him Colonel Beverley Robinson's reason for not accompanying me, and the delegation of a young gentleman, a Mr. Anderson, whom I had brought with me, and who was then with the watermen on the strand. He appeared much agitated, and expressed chagrin at the disappointment of not seeing Colonel Robinson. He desired me, however, to conduct Mr. Anderson to him, which being done, he requested me to remain with the hands at the boat. I went as directed, but felt greatly mortified at not being present at the interview, to which I conceived myself

entitled from my rank in life, and the trouble I had taken to effect the meeting.

At length they continued such a time in conference, that I deemed it expedient to inform them of the approaching dawn of day. Shortly afterwards both came down to the boat, and General Arnold, with much earnestness, solicited me to return with Mr. Anderson to the *Vulture*; but I pointed out the impracticability of effecting his wish, from the great distance, and the fatigue of the hands. He then applied to the men, who declared themselves unable to gratify his wish, through want of strength to accomplish it, and the ebb tide being against them.

Convinced of the apparent impracticability of the attempt to reach the ship, and return before day without being discovered from either shores by the inhabitants, whose eyes were constantly watching the movements on the water, not only from the forts, but the surrounding shores, he relinquished his solicitations, and desired I would endeavour to return the boat to the place from whence we first embarked; this, with much labour, and taking the circuit of the eddies, was nearly effected, (as we left the boat at Crane's Island) when our attention was called to the cannonade from Gallows Point against the *Vulture*, which was compelled to fall down the river, and appeared to be set on fire; Colonel Livingston, however, must have been totally unacquainted with General Arnold's designs, or he never would have fired at that time upon the ship.

On my return home, I found that General Arnold and Mr. Anderson had arrived long before, Mr. Anderson having mounted the horse my servant had rode, when he followed General Arnold to the Long Clove, the place of Anderson's landing. He appeared vexed that the ship had been compelled to leave her position. General Arnold and Mr. Anderson were left alone the far greater part of the day. Toward the evening Arnold came to my house, and proposed that I should convey Mr. Anderson back to the *Vulture*, which had nearly regained her former situation. With a fit of the ague upon me, I was unable to gratify him; on which he proposed my accompanying him part of the way on his return to New York by land, as soon as my health would permit, to which I made no objection.

He soon after returned, and told me a difficulty had occurred, of which he was not before apprised; for that Anderson had come on shore in a military dress, which he had borrowed, from pride or vanity, from an officer of his own acquaintance at New York; that it would be impossible for him to travel in that uniform, he requested the loan of one of my coats. Being nearly of my size, I lent him a coat: the other part of his dress, he said, did not require change. General Arnold then proposed returning to his command at West Point, leaving Mr. Anderson very disconsolate with me; he cast an anxious look towards the *Vulture*, and with a heavy sigh wished he was on board.

I endeavoured to console him by the hope of his being at the White Plains, or New York, before her. Finding myself better I promised to accompany him on his way. I could not help remarking to him, that I thought the general might have ordered a flag of truce from Stony Point, to have returned him to the *Vulture*, without the fatigue of his going to the White Plains, that appearing to me a circuitous route, unless he had business to transact at that place of a public nature. From this time, he seemed shy, and desirous to avoid much conversation; he continued to urge preparations for his departure, and carefully avoided being seen by persons that came to the house,

General Arnold had prepared a passport for him to go to the White Plains, and a flag of truce for me to go thither and return. We reached the ferry at Stoney Point before it was dark, intending to proceed as far as Major De La Van's that night, we rode on with an increased speed, and had reached it about five or six when we were challenged by a patrol party. On advancing, the commanding officer, a Captain Bull, demanded a countersign before we should pass, and drew his corps about us, he inquired who we were, the reason of our travelling in the night, and from whence we came?

I told him who I was, and that we had passports from General Arnold, the commanding officer at West Point, which we had received from the general that day; that we were on public service, on business of the highest import, and that he would be answerable for our detention one moment; he insisted on seeing the passports, and conducted us to a house in the vicinity where there was a light, on approaching the house Mr. Anderson seemed very uneasy; but I cheered him by saying our papers would carry us to any part of the country to which they were directed, and that no person dare presume to detain us.

When we came to the light, I presented the passports, which satisfied the captain.

With no small difficulty we gained admittance into a house for the night, while such was the caution and danger of admitting nocturnal inmates, that we were obliged to take to bed or keep the family up, who would not retire until they saw us safely lodged. We slept in the same bed; and I was often disturbed with the restless motions, and uneasiness of mind exhibited by my bedfellow, who, on observing the first approach of day, summoned my servant to prepare the horses for our departure. He appeared in the morning as if he had not slept an hour during the night; he at first was much dejected, but a pleasing change took place in his countenance when summoned to mount his horse.

We rode very cheerfully towards Pine's Bridge without interruption, or any event that excited apprehension; here I proposed to leave my companion; but I observed that the nearer we approached the bridge, the more his countenance brightened into a cheerful serenity, and he became very affable; in short, I now found him highly entertaining; he was not only well informed in general history, but well acquainted with that of America, particularly of New York, which he termed the *residuary legatee* of the British Government (for it took all the remaining lands not granted to the proprietary and chartered provinces.) He had consulted the muses as well as Mars, for he conversed freely on the *belles lettres*; music, painting, and poetry, seemed to be his delight. He displayed a judicious taste in the choice of the authors he had read, possessed great elegance of sentiments, and a most pleasing manner of conveying his ideas, by adopting the flowery colouring of poetical imagery.

He lamented the causes which gave birth to and continued the war, and said if there was a correspondent temper on the part of the Americans, with the prevailing spirit of the British ministry, peace was an event not far distant; he intimated that measures were then in agitation for the accomplishment of that desirable object, before France could establish her perfidious designs. He sincerely wished the fate of the war could alone be determined in the fair, open, field-contest, between as many British in number as those under the command of count Rochambeau at Rhode Island, whose effective force he seemed clearly to understand; he descanted on the richness of the scenery around us, and particularly admired from every eminence, the grandeur of the Highland mountains, bathing their lofty summits in the clouds from their seeming watery base at the north extremity of Haverstraw Bay.

The pleasantry of converse, and mildness of the weather, so insensibly beguiled the time, that we at length found ourselves at the bridge before I thought we had got half the way; and I now had reason to think my fellow traveller a different person from the character I had at first formed of him.

This bridge crosses Croton River, a branch of the Hudson; here we halted, and I mentioned my determination to proceed no farther. Having discharged the bill to the woman, in the local money of the country, my companion requested me to lend him some, and I cheerfully supplied him with the half of my pocket amount, although I was afraid it was not current below that place; the bridge being accounted the south boundary of the American lines. He was affected at parting, and offered me a valuable gold watch in remembrance of him, as, a keepsake, which I refused.

The passport given the major by General Arnold particularly mentioned "to go to lines of White Plains, or lower, if he thought proper, he being on public business." When he had passed the American lines and thought himself out of danger, he was stopped by three of the New York militia, who with others were on a scouting party between the outposts of the two armies. What strange infatuation seized the major, not to produce his pass, defies all conjecture: had he done so, this would have let him pass; or, if they had proved British scouts, they would only have conducted him where he wanted to go, to the Royal lines. On the contrary, he imprudently asked the man who stopped him, "Where he belonged to?"

The man answered, "To below," meaning to New York. Thinking himself then perfectly safe, and mistaking them, by this equivocal reply for a party of English, he hastily replied, "So do I," declared himself a British officer, and pressed that he might not be detained, as he was on urgent business. He was soon convinced of his mistake, by the party proceeding to search him. Papers, in General Arnold's hand writing, were discovered in his boots, which contained exact returns of the state of the forces, ordnance, and defences at West Point, with the artillery orders, critical remarks on the works, &c. The major offered them his purse and gold watch, if they would let him pass; which they refused, and delivered him a prisoner to Lieutenant-Colonel Jameson, who commanded the scouting parties.

When Major André appeared before him it was under the name of Anderson, which he supported, choosing to hazard the greatest danger, rather than let any discovery be made which could involve Arnold, before he had time to provide for his safety. With a view to the general's escaping, he requested that a line might be sent to acquaint him of Anderson's detention, which Jameson granted. General Arnold on the receipt of this letter abandoned everything. He immediately seized the messenger's horse and instantly proceeded down a precipice, almost perpendicular, to the river where boats were always ready to pass to and from West Point. He sprang into one, and directed the hands to row him down the river and make for the *Vulture*; but he had scarcely passed Stoney and Verplanks Point, when Colonel Hamilton arrived at the latter, with orders to stop him; for by the time General Washington had searched the house, the packet from Jameson arrived.

Colonel Jameson forwarded to General Washington all the papers found on Major André, together with a letter, of which the following is a correct copy. Here he manfully assumed his character, bursting with a noble dignity from that false appearance, which the safety of General Arnold alone had caused him to assume. This was the only point on which the board of American officers could at all criminate him as a spy: thus, he generously sacrificed his own life to the preservation of General Arnold's.

Sir—What I have as yet said concerning myself, was in the justifiable attempt to be extricated; I am too little accustomed to duplicity to have succeeded.

I beg Your Excellency to be persuaded, that no alteration in the temper of my mind, or apprehension for my safety, induces me to the step of addressing you, but that it is to secure myself from an imputation of having assumed a mean character for treacherous purposes or self-interest; a conduct incompatible with the principles that actuated me, as well as with my condition in life. It is to vindicate my fame I speak, and not to solicit security.

The person in your possession is Major André, Adjutant-General of the British Army.

The influence of one commander, in the army of his adversary, is an advantage taken in war. A correspondence for this purpose I held as confidential (in the present instance,) with His Excellency Sir Henry Clinton.

To favour it, I agreed to meet, upon ground not within the posts of either army, a person who was to give me intelligence; I came up in the *Vulture* sloop of war for this effect, and was fetched by the boat from the ship to the beach; being there I was told the approach of day would prevent my return, and that I must be concealed until the next night. I was in my regimentals, and had fairly risked my person.

Against my stipulation, my intentions, and without my knowledge beforehand, I was conducted within one of your posts. Your Excellency may conceive my sentiments on this occasion, and will imagine how much more I must have been affected by a refusal to reconduct me back the next night as I had been brought; thus become a prisoner, I had to concert my escape. I quitted my, uniform, and was passed another way in the night, without the American posts, to neutral ground; and being informed I was out of the reach of all armed parties, and left to proceed for New York, I was taken at Fairy Town by some volunteers.

Thus, as I have had to relate, I was betrayed (being Adjutant General of the British Army) into the vile condition of an enemy within your posts.

Having avowed myself a British officer, I know nothing to reveal but what relates to myself, which is true on the honour of an officer and a gentleman.

The request I have to make to Your Excellency, and I am conscious I address myself well, is, that in any rigor, policy may dictate, a decency of conduct towards me may mark that, though unfortunate, I am branded with nothing dishonourable, as no motive could be mine, but the service of my king, and as I was involuntarily an impostor.

Another request is, that I may be permitted to write an open letter to Sir Henry Clinton, and another to a friend for clothes and linen.

I take the liberty to mention the condition of some gentlemen in Charlestown, who being either on parole, or under protection, were engaged in a conspiracy against us; though their situation is not similar, they are objects who may be sent in exchange for me, or are persons, whom the treatment I receive, may in some degree affect.

It is no less, Sir, a confidence in the generosity of your mind, than on account of your superior station, that I have chosen to importune you with this letter. I have the honour to be, with the greatest respect, Sir, Your Excellency's most obedient,

And most humble servant,

John André, Adj. Gen.

His Excellency, George Washington, &c. &c.

Major André had been removed under a strong escort to Tappan for Orangetown, when General Washington referred his whole case to the examination and decision of fourteen general officers, (of whom were the Marquis De La Fayette and Baron De Steubin) with the assistance of the judge advocate, General Lawrence. Major André disdaining all subterfuge and evasion, and studying to place his character in so fair a light, as might prevent its being shaded by the present circumstances, voluntarily confessed everything that related to himself, while he concealed with the most scrupulous nicety whatever might involve others. Being interrogated by the board with respect to his conception of coming on shore, under the sanction of a flag, he said with a noble frankness of mind, that if he had, he might certainly have returned under it. The board was exceedingly struck with his candour and magnanimity. They did not examine a single witness, but founded their report merely upon his own confession. In this they stated the following facts:

That Major André came on shore on the night of the 21st of September in a private and secret manner; that he changed his dress within the American lines; that under a feigned name, and a disguised habit, he was taken on his way to New York, and when taken, several papers were found in his possession, which contained intelligence for the enemy."

That Major André, ought to be considered as a spy, and that agreeable to the laws and usages of nations he ought to suffer death.

It may be naturally imagined that the British officers were indefatigable in their exertions to save Major André from his impending fate. Sir Henry Clinton and Lieutenant-General Robertson wrote letters, which every suggestion and entreaty were used to General Washington on the subject; but in vain. General Arnold went so far as to take the whole guilt of the transaction on himself. He urged, that everything done by Major André was transacted at his particular request, and at a time when he was acknowledged commanding officer in the department.

He contended, "that he had a right to transact all those matters, for which, though wrong, Major André ought not to suffer death."

An interview also took place between General Robertson on the part of the British, and General Greene on the part of the Americans. Everything was urged by the former that ingenuity or humanity could suggest for averting the proposed execution; Greene made a proposal for delivering up Arnold instead of André; but found this could not be acceded to by the British, without offending against every principle of honour and policy, General Robertson urged "that André went on shore under the sanction of a flag, and that being in Arnold's power, he was not accountable for the subsequent actions, which were said to be compulsory."

To this it was replied that "he was employed in the execution of measures very foreign to the object of flags of truce, and such as they were never meant to authorise or to countenance, and that Major André in the course of his examination had candidly confessed, "that it was impossible for him to suppose that he came on shore under the sanction of a flag." As Greene and Robertson differed so widely in both their statements of facts, and the interference they drew from them, the latter proposed to the former that the opinion of disinterested military gentlemen might be taken on the subject, and Generals Knyphausen and Rochambeau were mentioned; General Robertson also urged that André possessed a great share of Sir Henry Clinton's esteem, and hinted, as his last resource that he would be infinitely obliged if he should be spared.

He offered that in case André should be permitted to return with him to New York, any person whatever, that might be named, should be set at liberty. All these arguments and entreaties having failed, Robertson presented a long letter from Arnold, in which he endeavoured to exculpate André, by acknowledging himself the author of every part of his conduct, "that he had particularly insisted on his coming from the *vulture* under a flag which he had sent for that purpose," He declared that if André suffered, he should think himself bound to retaliate. He also observed:

That forty of the principal inhabitants of South Carolina had:

justly forfeited their lives, which had hitherto been spared only through the clemency of Sir Henry Clinton, who would no longer extend mercy if Major André suffered; an event which would probably open a scene of bloodshed, at which humanity must revolt.

He entreated Washington by his own honour, and for the sake of humanity, not to suffer an unjust sentence to touch the life of André, but if that warning should be disregarded, and André suffer, he called "heaven and earth to witness that he alone would be justly answerable for the torrents of blood which might be spilt in consequence."

Indeed, every exertion was made by our commanders to save André, but without effect; it was urged, on the contrary, that the general opinion of the American Army, was, that his life was forfeited, and that national dignity and sound policy required that the forfeiture should be exacted.

General Greene was originally a Quaker, a stern republican, and such was the rancour displayed throughout the whole transaction, both by him and the Marquis De La Fayette that they may almost literally be said to have thirsted for the blood of the unfortunate victim whom fate had put in their power.

Here again I am compelled to notice the misrepresentation and detect the falsehood of the account given by Belsham. He says the unfortunate André was apprehended. in disguise, *and with a false passport.*"; True the major was apprehended, in disguise, but his passport was *not a false one.* It was signed by the commanding officer of the American, district from whence he came. Was the signature "*Arnold,*" a forgery?

It was a true passport on the part of Major André, and General Arnold who signed it alone was accountable to the American Government for it. But this is Belsham's constant practice, by coupling a truth with a falsehood, (as the Jews vend a damaged article with a sound one) they both pass muster with the great mass of mankind, until a critical examination detects the fraud.

The same writer tells us, with an air of triumph, that:

The major suffered death in that degrading mode which gives the brave, the keenest wound, notwithstanding the urgent solicitations and *the impotent, injudicious menaces* of Sir Henry Clinton.

What injudicious menace escaped from Sir Henry Clinton during the whole unfortunate negotiation? His letter to General Washington is a master piece of prudence, of humanity, of temperate, energetic remonstrance, conjoined with manly dignity. I have not the vanity to suppose myself capable of determining the merits of the great body of historians; but certainly, if I may be permitted to give an opinion on those who have published the American transactions, Mr. Belsham is of all the most artful and dangerous. His misrepresentations are of deep design, and his false colourings are laid on with so much adroitness, that it is no easy matter completely to detect him. But on some points, I think he has been sufficiently unmasked.

I introduce here a quotation from Smith, which places Sir Henry Clinton's character in the most amiable point of view.

> The noble humanity in his breast, which at the moment when every agonised feeling must have been wounded to its greatest height, alone prevented him from making that sacrifice which the laws of arms and the manes of the murdered André seemed, almost imperiously to require at his hands.
>
> The *Greyhound* schooner, flag of truce which brought General Robertson's last letter to General Washington, dated, on board the schooner, on the 2nd of October, the day Major André suffered, carried to New York the melancholy account of that event.
>
> No language can describe the mingled sensations of: horror, grief, sympathy, and revenge, that agitated the whole garrison; a silent gloom overspread the general countenance; the whole Royal Army, and citizens of the first distinction, went into mourning. Sir Henry Clinton, (although stung with the deepest sorrow for the loss of so valuable an officer,) who best knew how to appreciate his merits, could not indulge a spirit of resentment, in exercising the dictates of passion or policy, by, a retaliation on a number of Carolina prisoners, of, the first distinction, who had forfeited their lives agreeable to the usage of war. In almost every instance, where humanity could be exercised, the lenity of Sir Henry Clinton was eminently conspicuous, both in civil and military matters.

It is to be regretted, that, we have benefitted so little by so great a literary genius as Major André was. The following letters (which are extracted from Smith's *Narrative*) prove him to have been a young man of very considerable intellect,

Major André to Sir Henry Clinton,

dated Tappan, September 29th:

Sir—Your Excellency is doubtless already apprised of the manner in which I was taken, and possibly of the serious light in which my conduct is considered, and the vigorous determination that is impending.

Under these circumstances, I have obtained General Washington's permission to send you this letter; the object of which is, to remove from your breast any suspicion, that I could imagine I was bound by Your Excellency's orders to expose myself to what has happened. The events of coming within an enemy's posts, and of changing my dress, which led me to my present situation, were contrary to my own intentions, as they were to your orders; and the circuitous route which I took to return, was imposed (perhaps unavoidably) without alternative upon me.

In addressing myself to Your Excellency on this occasion, the force of all my obligations to you, and of the attachment and gratitude I bear you, recurs to me.

With all the warmth of my heart, I give you thanks for Your Excellency's profuse kindness to me: and I send you the most earnest wishes for your welfare, which a faithful, affectionate, and respectful attention can frame.

I have a mother and three sisters, to whom the value of my commission would be an object, as the loss of Grenada has much affected their income. It is needless to be more explicit on this subject, I am persuaded of Your Excellency's goodness, &c. &c.

I have the honour to be, &c.

John André, Adj. Gen.

On October the 2nd, the tragedy was closed. The major was superior to the terrors of death: but the disgraceful. mode of dying which the usage of war had annexed to his unhappy situation, was infinitely dreadful to him: he was desirous to be indulged with a death worthy of his profession; and accordingly, he wrote the day before, the following letter to General Washington:

Sir—Buoy'd above the terror of death, by the consciousness of a life devoted to honourable pursuits, and stained with no action that can give me remorse, I trust that the request I make to Your Excellency at this serious period, and which is to soften my last moments, will not be rejected.

Sympathy towards a soldier will surely induce Your Excellency, and a military tribunal, to adopt the mode of my death to the feelings of a man of honour.

Let me hope, Sir, that if aught in my character impresses you with esteem towards me, if aught in my misfortunes marks me as the victim of policy, and not of resentment, I shall experience the operation of these feelings in your breast, by being informed that I am not to die on a gibbet.

I have the honour to be, &c.

John André, Adj. Gen.

General Washington consulted his officers upon the subject. Pity and esteem wrought so powerfully, that they were all for shooting him, till Greene insisted on it that his crime was that of a common spy, that the public good required his being hanged, and that if he was shot the public would think there were favourable circumstances entitling him to notice and lenity. His observations had their desired effect, and they resolved that there would be an impropriety in granting the major's request; but his delicacy was saved from the pain of receiving a negative answer. The guard which attended him in his confinement marched with him to the place of execution. The way, over which he passed, was crowded on all sides with anxious spectators, as he went along between two officers of his guard, his arms being locked in theirs, he bowed himself familiarly to all those with whom he had been acquainted in his confinement.

A smile of complacency expressed the serene fortitude of his mind. Upon seeing the preparations on the fatal spot, he asked with some degree of concern, "Must I die in this manner?" He was told it was unavoidable. He replied, "I am reconciled to my fate, but not to the mode." Soon after recollecting himself, he added, "It will be but a momentary pang." He ascended the cart with a pleasing countenance, performed the last offices to himself, with a composure which excited the admiration of all the spectators."

Being told the final moment was at hand, and asked if he had anything more to say, "nothing but to request that you will witness to the world *that I die like a brave man*." He died universally esteemed and regretted. The sympathy he had excited in the American Army was perhaps unexampled, under any similar circumstances, Numbers condemned, very few justified, but all regretted the fatal sentence which put an end to his valuable life.

He was a young officer of great abilities, and of uncommon merit. Nature had bestowed on him an elegant taste for literature and the fine arts, which by industrious cultivation he had greatly improved. He possessed many amiable qualities, and very great accomplishments. His fidelity together with his place and character, eminently fitted him for the negotiation with Arnold, but his high ideas of candour, and his abhorrence of dishonourable conduct, made him inexpert in practicing those arts of deception which it required. It may not be improper to add, that our gracious sovereign, who never suffers any public service to pass unrewarded, has caused an elegant monument to be erected in Westminster Abbey, which, with the historic page both of England and America will perpetuate the virtue and gallantry of Major André, through ages yet unknown.

Description of the Monument in Westminster Abbey, for Major John André, designed by Robert Adam, Esq. Architect, and executed in statuary marble, by Mr. P. M. Van Gelder.

This monument is composed of a *sarcophagus*, elevated on a pedestal, upon the panel of which is engraved the following inscription:

SACRED TO THE MEMORY
OF
MAJOR JOHN ANDRÉ,
WHO, RAISED BY HIS MERIT, AT AN EARLY PERIOD
OF HIS LIFE, TO THE RANK OF
ADJUTANT-GENERAL OF THE BRITISH FORCES
IN AMERICA,
AND, EMPLOYED IN AN IMPORTANT BUT HAZARDOUS ENTERPRISE,
FELL A SACRIFICE
TO HIS
ZEAL FOR HIS KING AND COUNTRY,
ON THE 2ND OF OCTOBER, 1780, AGED 29,
UNIVERSALLY BELOVED AND ESTEEMED BY THE ARMY
IN WHICH HE SERVED, AND LAMENTED EVEN
BY HIS FOES.
HIS GRACIOUS SOVEREIGN
KING GEORGE III.
HAS CAUSED THIS MONUMENT TO BE ERECTED.

The following description of the characters on the *sarcophagus*, and remarks on the lamented catastrophe are copied from Smith's *Narrative*.

On the front of the *sarcophagus*, General Washington is represented in his tent, at the moment when he had received the
report of the court martial held on Major André; at the same
time a flag of truce arrived from the British Army, with a letter
for General Washington to treat for the major's life. But the fatal
sentence being already passed, the flag was sent back without
the hoped-for clemency in his favour.

Major André received his condemnation with that fortitude
and resolution which had always marked his character, and is
represented going with unshaken spirit to meet his doom.

On the top of the *sarcophagus*, a figure of Britannia reclined,
laments the premature fate of so gallant an officer. The British
Lion too, seems instinctively to mourn his untimely death.

Ancient or modern history does not exhibit an instance, where
an officer fell so universally lamented by adversaries and friends;
an irrefragable proof of unsullied honour, and superior merit.

Eulogy cannot do sufficient justice to the deserts of this rarely
accomplished hero; and it must be some consolation to his surviving friends, that his and their foes drop the tear of sympathy,
and mingle their sorrows at the same shrine, made sacred to
virtue and truth.

It has already been noticed, as matter of regret, that distinguished
as Major André was by literary talent, so little of his compositions survived him. The following poem however the author is enabled to lay
before the reader; from the authority of a respectable person, a native
of America; where it is generally acknowledged to have been the major's composition. It was written a few days previous to his execution.

Other testimony of its authenticity it is now impossible to produce,
as no British officer was permitted to attend his last moments, console
the heroic sufferer, or receive the dying injunctions of the man, who
fell a martyr to the interests of his country.

But if such report carries with it full conviction to the author, it
will to the mind of the loyal and unprejudiced reader, and as for those
who were instrumental, in robbing the major of life, or who *can* approve the deed, it would be a waste of words to attempt the removal
of their doubts. Under these circumstances, to have suppressed it altogether would have been criminal, and on this authority, it is inserted,
leaving the reader to his own unbiassed judgment as to its authenticity.

Hail sovereign love, which first began,

The scheme, to rescue fallen man!
Hail matchless, free, eternal grace,
Which gave my soul a Hiding Place!

Against the God who built the sky
I fought with hands uplifted high,
Despis'd the mention of his grace,
Too proud to seek a Hiding Place.

Enwrapt in thick Egyptian night,
And fond of darkness more than light
Madly I ran the sinful race,
Secure, without a Hiding Place.

But thus, the eternal council ran,
Almighty love, arrest that man!"
I felt the arrows of distress,
And found I had no Hiding Place.

Indignant justice stood in view,
To Sinai's fiery mount I flew,
But Justice cry'd with frowning face,
This mountain is no Hiding Place.

Ere long a heav'nly voice I heard,
And mercy's angel soon appear'd,
He led me in a placid pace,
To Jesus as my Hiding Place.

On him Almighty vengeance fell,
Which must have sunk a world to hell,
He bore it for a sinful race,
And thus became their Hiding Place.

Should sevenfold storms of thunder roll,
And shake this globe from pole to pole:
No thunder bolt shall daunt my face,
For Jesus is my Hiding Place.

A few more rolling suns at most,
Shall land me on fair Canaan's coast,
Where I shall sing the song of grace,
And see my glorious Hiding Place.

Major André's remains were interred in an open field, belonging to a Mr. Mabie, in the vicinity where he suffered.

The end of the year 1780 was now arriving; winter set in with great severity. The Americans, in addition to the inclemencies of the season, had many hardships to encounter. The three years, for which period the American troops were originally enlisted, being expired; and enraged at the hardships which they had suffered, a spirit of insurrection manifested itself: at first in the troops of the Pennsylvania line, which soon spread to the New Jersey line. The American governors, well acquainted with the grievances endured by the army, wisely redressed them, and passed a general amnesty

The soldiers which were under the immediate command of General Washington also began to betray the most alarming discontent; but actuated by that wisdom for which he was so conspicuous, he remained in his quarters, and by his presence prevented their murmurs from breaking out into absolute resistance.

Meantime the paper currency of the Americans became every hour more and more depreciated. The financial arrangements of the Congress, of course fell into the utmost confusion: a general discredit began to prevail, and it was clearly perceived by the most intelligent members of their government, that nothing could possibly preserve their affairs from utter ruin but a foreign loan, and that to a considerable amount. This they attempted with the Dutch, and by means of French influence, in opposition to the *stadtholder* and the British interest, it was brought into a state of forwardness under the negotiation of a Mr. Lee, (formerly an alderman of London, and brother to the American General Lee,) agent for the Congress, and John de Neufville, an Amsterdam merchant.

This measure, although resorted to at a moment of the most distressing exigence, had been in contemplation ever since the year 1778, at which time the parties first met at Aix-la-Chapelle. It was sanctioned by Van Berkel, Grand Pensionary of Amsterdam. Provisionary articles were signed by the parties, and copies transmitted to America and Holland. This was all transacted with that secrecy, so consonant to the insidious policy of the Dutch, who negotiated in that crafty manner which left them at liberty, according as the affairs of America prospered or failed, to avow or disavow, the treaty to Great Britain.—A remark here must press on the minds of most readers. How strikingly has Providence placed before the world, an awful lesson on national duplicity, by the present humiliation of that money-loving, cunning people, under the French domination!

To ratify this nefarious bargain, Mr. Henry Laurens, the late President of Congress, was dispatched from America. He embarked at Philadelphia for Holland, but in the progress of the voyage the vessel was captured by the British, and Laurens, with all his official documents, sent to England; the box which contained the papers was thrown overboard; but a loyal and determined sailor secured it from sinking. The name of the ship which captured Mr. Laurens was the *Vestal*, commanded by Captain Keppel. He was landed in Devonshire, and arrived at the admiralty on the 7th of October, 1780. On his examination he disclaimed all allegiance to Great Britain, and boldly avowed himself an agent and a subject of the American Government.

The administration on this occasion, acted with a becoming spirit. The papers of Mr. Laurens had put them in full possession of the perfidy of the Dutch. A memorial was accordingly presented by the British Ambassador at the Hague, requiring the States General to disavow the proceedings of the Pensionary Van Berkel and his adherents, and demanding their immediate trial and punishment. The Dutch, conscious of their guilt, attempted to delay the business; but the English ambassador was finally recalled, and hostilities commenced between the two nations.

Mr. Laurens was committed to the Tower on a charge of high treason, but from circumstances which afterwards arose, never brought to trial.

This extraordinary character was of French descent, His ancestors fled to America upon the revocation of the edict of Nantz, under Lewis XIV. They settled in South Carolina, in the capital of which his father carried on the business of a saddler, for which employment he intended his son. Mr. Laurens was born in the year 1724; his education was very limited, and for some time he followed the business of his father. But, being of an aspiring turn of mind, and eager for the attainment of wealth, he quitted the business of saddler, and commenced merchant. Remarkable for a rigid punctuality in all his dealings, he established a high character for integrity and attention to business.

It is this which does everything in America for the man of business: he became rich, and by degrees respectable. He was appointed a Provincial Colonel in the war with France, and commanded an expedition against the Indians. At the time of passing the stamp act, he was among the friends of government and supported the authority of the parent country.

Charlestown at that time became the seat of much civil dissention; to avoid taking a part in which he left America and went over to England. Strange to record! it was there that all his principles of loyalty were shaken, and he returned to America a staunch and sturdy republican.

He immediately took part with the American oppositionists, and professed himself a patriot, ready to make any sacrifice in what he termed the common cause, and to defend that cause in every extremity: this was in the year 1775. The Americans at that time were indefatigable in uniting to their side, men of talent, enterprise and integrity. Mr. Laurens possessed the very requisites which they desired to constitute a leading character, and he was accordingly advanced to be president of the Provincial Congress of Carolina. From that province he was nominated a delegate to the Continental Congress.

There he became a distinguished member, and was eventually appointed president of that assembly. The moderation, good sense, and ability which he displayed in that office commanded the respect, even of the first men among those, who neither approved his principles, nor wished success to his cause, The importance to America of the Dutch loan, can best be estimated, by the Congress sending such a man to transact the business: his capture by Captain Keppel was a sore blow to their interests.

It may be necessary here to rest a moment, and notice the difference in point of humanity between the British Government, and the American partisans. With the bleeding wounds of the untimely, and remorseless fate of Major André, still fresh on recollection, the cabinet of St. James paused before they retaliated on America, in the person of the late president of her senate (the highest officer in time of peace, and in war second to none but the commander in chief, Washington.) The shade of the murdered André seemed from the grave to cry for vengeance. Yet British magnanimity, in the worth of the individual, ameliorated the punishment of the traitor and Mr. Laurens, with his friend Turnbull, Deputy-Adjutant-General of the American Forces, suffered only a partial confinement, for deeds which would have doomed them to the gibbet, if not to the torture, under any other state. Surely the sons of many of the Americans must blush, for the cruel violence of their forefathers in this unhappy contest.

★★★★★★★★★★

Mr. Turnbull, son to the Governor of Connecticut, and Deputy-Adjutant-General to the American Forces, who left America for France with a Major Tyler, and who from thence came to England, was also apprehended and his papers seized. Several letters to and from his father and other persons in America being produced, and his conferences at Paris with Dr. Franklin fully established, he was committed to the New Prison, Clerkenwell, about a month after the commitment of Mr. Laurens to the Tower.

★★★★★★★★★★

CHAPTER 16

Southern Campaign under Lord Cornwallis

Quitting the affairs of the north, which were conducted by General Clinton, we shall now revert to events in the south under Lord Cornwallis.

The capture of Charlestown, and the reduction of almost all the whole of South Carolina, naturally inclined the British commanders to extend their views to the conquest of North Carolina. The Americans on their part saw the necessity of reinforcing the Southern Army; and General Greene, at the recommendation of Washington, was appointed to its command, which was transferred to him at Charlotte by General Gates. A country thinly inhabited, and abounding with swamps, afforded every advantage to a partisan warfare over a large and regular army. This system was acted on by Greene, and accordingly General Morgan, with a numerous detachment was directed to threaten the British post at Ninety-Six, on the western extremity of South Carolina; the main body under General Greene at the same time, moving on to north side of Pedee, opposite Cheraw-Hill.

The British Army, at that time, had marched two hundred miles from the sea-coast, and was preparing for an invasion of North Carolina. In order therefore to drive Morgan from its rear, and deter the inhabitants from joining his standard, Lieutenant-Colonel Tarleton with six hundred men (three hundred of which were cavalry) proceeded against him. The engagement took place at Cowpens. The British, led on by the colonel himself, advanced, confident of victory, with a shout, and poured a tremendous fire on the enemy.

The American line gave way, and filed; the British advanced, and engaged the second. At that critical moment, Colonels Washington and Howard rallied the flying troops, and, joined by the militia, led them on to the support of the second line. The British were thrown into confusion: three hundred were killed and wounded; the whole of the artillery-men (who worked the guns) that did not share their fate, were taken, with two three pounders. Colonel Tarleton, with about fifty of the cavalry, made a last, desperate, but glorious effort: he charged and repulsed Washington's horse, retook the baggage of the corps, cut the detachment who had it in possession to pieces, destroyed the greater part, and retired with the rest to Hamilton's Ford.

★★★★★★★★★★

In Lord Cornwallis's dispatches to government concerning this engagement, he says, "In justice to the detachment of the Royal Artillery, I must here observe, that no terror could induce them to abandon their guns, and they were all killed and wounded in the defence of them."

★★★★★★★★★★

This defeat (particularly the loss of the light infantry) was a severe loss to the royal camp. The prisoners were conveyed by forced marches to Richmond; so that all attempts of the main army to recapture them were unavailing. The army halted during two days collecting provisions, and destroying superfluous baggage. We then marched through North Carolina, to the banks of the Dan, on the utmost extremities of the province.

On the 1st day of February, at daylight in the morning, we were directed to cross M'Cowan's Ford, in order to dislodge a party of the Americans under the command of General Davison, which were strongly posted on the opposite hills. Lord Cornwallis, according to his usual manner, dashed first into the river, mounted on a very fine spirited horse, the brigade of guards followed, two three pounders next, the Royal Welch Fusiliers after them. Colonel Webster had been previously directed to move with a strong Guard Division to Beattie's Ford, six miles above M'Cowan's in order to divide the attention of the Americans,

The place where we forded was about half a mile over. The enemy stood on the hills of the opposite shore, which were high and steep, hanging over the river, so that they had every advantage over us, to facilitate their firing on those who attempted to cross there. Lord Cornwallis's fine horse was wounded under him, but His Lordship escaped unhurt. Amidst these dreadful oppositions, we still urged through this rapid stream, striving with every effort to gain the opposite shore; just in the centre of the river, the bombardier who was employed in steering one of the three pounders, unfortunately let go his hold of the helm of the gun, and being a low man, he was forced off his feet, and immediately carried headlong down the river.

At that very instant, I was bringing up the division that covered this gun, and encouraging the men to hold fast by one another, and not to be dismayed at the enemy's fire, or from the rapidity or depth of the water, which was at this place more than four feet deep, and very rocky at the bottom. I knew that if this artillery man was either killed or drowned, his loss would be great indeed, as we had no man at hand that could supply his place in working the gun; this consideration darted through my mind in an instant, and I was determined to save his life or perish in the attempt. I therefore quitted my hold of the right hand man of my division, and threw myself on my belly on the surface of the water, and in nine or ten strong strokes, I overtook him.

By this time, he was almost exhausted, having been carried down the stream heels overhead, upwards of forty yards. I got him on his feet, and led him back in safety to his gun. It was very remarkable, and taken particular notice of by the British troops, that during this transaction not one shot was, fired at us by the Americans; indeed, they might have easily shot us both in the head, as the current of the river carried us very near to them. After this affair the enemy began again a very heavy fire upon us, nevertheless our divisions waded on, in a cool intrepid manner, to return their fire, being impossible, as our car touch boxes were all tied at the back of our necks. This urged us on with greater rapidity, till we gained the opposite shore, where we were obliged to scramble up a very high hill under, a heavy fire; several of our men were killed and wounded, before we reached the summit.

The American soldiers did all that brave men could do, to oppose our passage across the river, and I believe not one of them moved from his post, till we mounted the hill, and used our bayonets; their general was the first man that received us sword in hand, and suffered himself to be cut to pieces sooner than retreat; after his death, his troops were soon defeated and dispersed.

Let the reader only for a moment consider what a situation the British troops were placed in, while they were wading over this ford, upwards of five hundred yards wide, up to their breast in a rapid stream, their knapsacks on their back, sixty or seventy rounds of powder and ball in each pouch, tied at the pole of their necks, their firelocks with bayonets, fixed on their shoulders, three hundred of their enemies (accounted the best marksmen in the world) placed on a hill as it were

265

over their heads, keeping a continual and very heavy fire upon them.

Yet such was the resolution with which they encountered the danger, and such the determined regularity which was observed, that only one officer, (Lieutenant-Colonel Hall) and three privates were killed, and thirty-six wounded. A striking instance of what may be effected in situations, deemed by many as invincible impediments to the progress of an army, by coolness, courage, and resolution. It may be necessary to mention, that Lord Cornwallis's horse, though he was shot in the water, did not fall until he reached the shore. General Leslie's horses were carried down the river; and such was the rapidity of the stream, that Brigadier-General O'Hara's horse rolled with him down the current, for near forty yards.

Lord Cornwallis's division having made good the dangerous passage of the Catawba, landed, and the 23rd Regiment, with the cavalry under Colonel Tarleton, set out in pursuit of the militia. Intelligence being gained that the American militia had rendezvoused at Tarrant's Tavern, ten miles from Beattie's Ford, the 23rd Regiment halted half way, and the colonel proceeded with the cavalry alone. About five hundred were then prepared to receive him, who were immediately charged, their centre broken through, fifty killed and the rest dispersed.

The gallantry of these actions made such an impression on the inhabitants, that the troops made their way without molestation to the Yadkin, notwithstanding the inveterate prejudice which this part of North Carolina bore to the British name. General Greene's plan of waiting till Huger and Williams joined him, was thus completely frustrated, the troops at the different fords were withdrawn, and Morgan began a precipitate retreat to the Yadkin.

Meantime Colonel Webster's division passed Beattie's Ford, on the Catawba, and joined that of Lord Cornwallis on the road to Salisbury. They immediately began to pursue Morgan; but he reached the Trading Ford, and passed the Yadkin, with the loss of his baggage, which the flight of the rifle men left in possession of the king's troops. A heavy rain which fell during the night, rendered the fords impassable, and so swelled the river, that General Morgan having secured all the boats and flats on the opposite shore, the pursuit was rendered impossible, except by marching up the western banks of the Yadkin, and passing by the shallow fords near its source.

This gave time for the junction of the American Armies. In this situation, it was the aim of Lord Cornwallis to get between the American Army and Virginia, and thereby cut off General Greene's retreat to that place. His Lordship was, by some means, misled by false information relative to the lower fords being impassable, and began his march to the upper fords of the Dan. Of this, General Greene took advantage, and by a rapid flight, reached Boyd's and Irwine's Ferries, and passed the river; but so closely was he pursued by His Lordship, that the last Division had scarcely crossed, when the British reached the opposite banks.

The difficulties, and hardships which the troops endured in this ineffectual pursuit, were sustained with a heroism that was inspired by the idea of terminating the contest in this part by one decisive blow, which certainly would have been done, but for the mistake relative to the fords. General Greene having thus made his escape from North Carolina Lord Cornwallis returned to Hillsborough, where he erected the Royal Standard, and issued a proclamation inviting all the loyal inhabitants to join him.

General Greene receiving intelligence of this, and dreading the consequences, took the daring measure of again crossing the Dan, with the legion of Colonel Lee, and returning to North Carolina.

A transaction here forces itself on record, more foul, inhuman and abominable than anything which took place during the war. The loyalists on the branches of Haw River, having risen in numbers, Lieutenant-Colonel Tarleton was dispatched to forward their organisation, and give them succour. Colonel Lee was sent with his legion to counteract the measure.

On the 25th of February, the assembled loyalists were proceeding in a body to the standard of Tarleton, when they were met in a narrow lane by his legion. They mistook the American cavalry for Tarleton's dragoons, and were surrounded before they perceived their error. In this situation they immediately begged for quarter; but the relentless American refused it, and in the very act of supplicating mercy, two or three hundred were inhumanly butchered.—When did such a deed as this stain the British arms. Had twenty Americans thus fallen, how would the pages of Ramsay, Belsham, and the other republican historians have foamed with the charges of murder, massacre, blood, and malice!!!! However, the historian may weep over the record, this is a specimen of republican mercy, as horrible as it is true.

Such was the scarcity of provisions at Hillsborough, that it was found impossible to support the army in that place. They were even obliged to kill some of their best draft horses. They therefore passed the Haw, and encamped in Allamance Creek. This movement much dispirited the loyalists, and raised the drooping hopes of the Americans. As the British retired, Greene advanced, crossed the Haw, and posted himself between Troublesome Creek and Reedy Fork, carefully changing his position every night, to avoid an engagement.

In this situation, Lord Cornwallis gave orders to beat up the American posts at Reedy Fork, in order to compel them to a greater distance, or perhaps allure Greene, who lay in the direction of Guildford Court-House, to a general engagement. Early in the morning of the 6th of March, the army passed Allamance Creek, and marched towards Reedy Fork. The Americans were not unapprised of the movement, and hastily retreated across the fork. General Greene instead of marching to their assistance, abandoned them to their fate. At Wedzell's Mill, they were overtaken by Lieutenant-Colonel Webster, and numbers fell. The supplies and reinforcements which Greene anxiously expected, arrived at last, under Lawson, Butler, and Eaton, with the North Carolina militia, from the frontiers, commanded by Campbell and Preston, making his numbers in the whole upwards of five thousand men.

Thus reinforced, he determined to offer Lord Cornwallis battle. He repassed the Haw, and marched to Guildford Court-House, but twelve miles from the British Army, at the Quakers' meeting house in the forks of Deep River.

On the 15th of March, about four miles from Guildford, the engagement began; Colonel Tarleton led on the British advance. The Americans were commanded by General Lee, who behaved with the most undaunted bravery, and maintained himself against the most formidable opposition, until the 23rd Regiment advancing to the support of Tarleton, compelled him to give way.

Greene formed his order of battle on a commanding site. It consisted of three lines. Two brigades of the North Carolina militia flanked by a wood, composed the first. That of Virginia, commanded by Stephens and Lawson, formed the second. These were completely encompassed in the wood, three hundred yards in the rear of the first. Four hundred yards behind them, in open ground, near the Court House, the third was formed, consisting of two brigades of continental troops. Two corps of observation were placed on the right and left flanks; the one commanded by Colonel Washington, the other by Colonel Lee.

The British advance was formed by a column of Royal Artillery, under the command of Lieutenant Macleod; and the disposition of the main attack was as follows: the 71st, the Regiment of Bose, commanded by General Leslie, and the 1st Battalion of Guards, Colonel Norton, formed the right line; the 23rd and 3rd led on by Colonel Webster, and supported by Brigadier-General O'Hara, and the Grenadiers and 2nd Battalion of Guards, constituted the left; corps of observation, light infantry of the Guards, and *Yagers*, on the left of the artillery, and the cavalry in column behind on the road.

These masterly dispositions preluded one of the most signal battles ever gained by British valour. The details are so accurately laid down by Stedman, who had every opportunity of ascertaining even the minutest circumstance, that it may be better to quote his account of it, than by aiming at originality, fall short of the particulars.

This disposition being made, the line received orders to advance, and moved forward with that steady and guarded, but firm and determined resolution which discipline alone can confer.

It has been remarked by an eye-witness, (Lieutenant-Colonel Tarleton), that:

The order and coolness of that part of Webster's brigade which advanced across the open ground, exposed to the enemy's fire, could not be sufficiently extolled.

At the distance of one hundred and forty yards they received the enemy's first fire, but continued to advance unmoved. When arrived at nearer and more convenient distance, they delivered their own fire, and rapidly charged with their bayonets: the enemy did not wait the shock, but retreated behind their second line. In other parts of the line the British troops behaved with equal gallantry, and were not less successful. The second line of the enemy made a braver and stouter resistance than the first. Posted in the woods, and covering themselves with trees, they kept up for a considerable time a galling fire, which did great execution.

At length, however, they were compelled to retreat, and fall back upon the continentals. In this severe conflict the whole of the British infantry were engaged. General Leslie, from the great extent of the enemy's front, reaching far beyond his right, had been very early obliged to bring forward the 1st Battalion of the Guards, appointed for his reserve, and form it into line and Lieutenant-Colonel Webster, finding the left of the 33rd Regiment exposed to a heavy fire from the right wing of the enemy, which greatly out-flanked him, changed its front to the left, and the ground become vacant by this movement, was immediately occupied by General O'Hara, with the grenadiers, and 2nd Battalion of the Guards.

Webster moving to the left with the 33rd Regiment, supported by the light infantry of the Guards, and the *Yagers*, routed and put to flight the right wing of the enemy, and in his progress, after two severe struggles, gained the right of the continentals; but the superiority of their numbers, and the weight of their fire obliged him, separated as he was from the British line, to re-cross a ravine, and occupy an advantageous position on the opposite bank, until he could hear of the progress of the king's troops on the right. The British line being so much extended to the right and left, in order to shew a front equal to the enemy, was unavoidably broken into intervals in the pursuit of the first and second American lines; some parts of it being more advanced than others, in consequence of the different degrees of resistance that had been met with, or of other impediments arising from the thickness of the woods, and the inequality of the ground.

The whole, however, moved forward; and the second Battalion of the guards, commanded by the honourable Colonel Stuart, was the first that reached the open ground at Guildford Court House. Impatient to signalise themselves, they immediately attacked body of continentals, greatly superior in numbers, that was seen formed on the left of the road, routed them and took their cannon, being two six-pounders; but pursuing them with too much ardour and impetuosity towards the wood on their rear, were thrown into confusion by a heavy fire received from a body of continentals, who were yet unbroken, and being instantly charged by Washington's dragoons, were driven back with great slaughter, and the loss of the cannon that had been taken. Lieutenant Macleod, advancing along the road with the Royal Artillery, had by this time reached the open ground.

By a spirited and well-directed cannonade be checked the pursuit of the Americans. Fortunately, also, the 71st Regiment, belonging to General Leslie's division, was seen emerging from the woods on the right, and the 23rd not long afterwards, made its appearance on the left. To the right and left of these regiments, General O'Hara, although severely wounded, rallied with much gallantry and great expedition, the remains of the 2nd Battalion of the Guards; and the Americans were quickly repulsed and put to flight, with once more the loss of the two six-pounders: two other six-pounders were also taken, being all the artillery which they had in the field, and two ammunition waggons.

The 71st pushed forward to an eminence at the Court House, on the left flank of the continentals. Lieutenant-Colonel Webster again advanced across the ravine, defeated the corps that was opposed to him, and connected himself with the centre of the British line. The continentals of the American Army being now driven from their ground, as well as the militia, a general retreat took place; but it was conducted with order and regularity. The 23rd and 71st, with part of the cavalry, were at first sent in pursuit of the enemy, but afterwards received orders to return. It is probable that, as the British commander became more acquainted with all circumstances of the action, and the number of the killed and wounded, he found it necessary to countermand his orders, and desist from the pursuit.

The action being now ended in the centre and left of the British line, a firing was still heard on the right, where General Leslie with the 1st Battalion of the Guards and the Regiment of Bose, had been greatly impeded in advancing, by the excessive thickness of the woods, which rendered their bayonets of little use. The broken corps of the enemy were thereby encouraged to make frequent stands, and to throw in an irregular fire; so that this part of the British line was at times warmly engaged in front, flank, and rear, with some of the enemy that had been routed in the first attack, and with part of the extremity of their left wing, which, by the closeness of the woods, had been passed unseen.

At one period of the action the first Battalion of the guards was completely broken. It had suffered greatly in ascending a woody height to attack the second line of the Americans, strongly posted upon the top of it, who, availing themselves of the advantages of their situation, retired, as soon as they had discharged their pieces, behind the brow of the hill, which protected them from the shot of the guards, and returned as soon as they had loaded, and were again in readiness to fire. Notwithstanding the disadvantage under which the attack was made, the guards reached the summit of the eminence, and put this part of the American line to flight: but no sooner was it done, than another line of the Americans presented itself to view, extending far beyond the right of the guards, and inclining towards their flank, so as almost to encompass them.

The ranks of the guards had been thinned in ascending the height, and a number of the officers had fallen: Captain Maitland, who at this time received a wound, retired to the rear, and having had his wound dressed, returned immediately to join the battalion of guards to which he belonged. Some of the men, too, from superior exertions, had reached the summit of the eminence sooner than others; so that the battalion was not in regular order when it received the fire of the third American line. The enemy's fire being repeated and continued, and, from the great extent of their line, being poured in not only on the front but flank of the battalion, completed its confusion and disorder, and notwithstanding every exertion made by the remaining officers, it was at last entirely broken.

Fortunately, at this time, the Hessian Regiment of Bose, commanded by Lieutenant-Colonel de Bury, which had hitherto suffered but little, was advancing in firm and compact order on the left of the guards, to attack the enemy: Lieutenant-Colonel Norton thought the fortunate arrival of the regiment of Bose presented a favourable opportunity for forming again his battalion, and requested the Hessian lieutenant-colonel to wheel his regiment to the right, and cover the guards, whilst their officers endeavoured to rally them. The request was immediately and most gallantly complied with; and, under the cover of the fire of the Hessians, the exertions of Lieutenant-Colonel Norton, and his few remaining officers, were at last successful in restoring order.

The battalion, being again formed, instantly moved forward to join the Hessians: the attack was renewed, and the enemy were defeated. But here the labours of this part of the line did not yet cease. No sooner had the guards and Hessians defeated the enemy in front, than they found it necessary to return and attack another body of them that appeared in the rear; and in this manner they were obliged to traverse the same ground in various directions, before the enemy were completely put to the rout. The firing heard on the right, after the termination of the action in the centre, and on the left, induced Lord Cornwallis to detach Tarleton, with part of the cavalry, to gain intelligence of what was doing in that quarter, and to know whether General Leslie wanted assistance.

But before Tarleton's arrival on the right, the affair was over, and the British troops were standing with ordered arms; all resistance having ceased on the part of the Americans, except from a few hardy riflemen, who lurking behind trees, occasionally fired their pieces, but at such a distance as to do no mischief. These Colonel Tarleton, when requested, readily undertook to disperse with his cavalry, and rushing forward under cover of a general volley of musketry from the Guards and the Regiment of Bose, quickly performed what was expected of him. In this affair Colonel Tarleton himself received a slight wound, but the rest of his corps returned unhurt.

In this battle the British troops obtained a victory most honourable and glorious to themselves, but in its consequences, of no real advantage to the cause in which they were engaged. They attacked, and defeated an army of more than three times their number, not taken by surprise, but formed in regular order of battle, and ready to engage; an army too, that is allowed on all hands to have been strongly and judiciously posted, on ground chosen with care, and most excellently adapted to the nature of the troops that occupied it.

★★★★★★★★★★

By the return of the adjutant of the day, it appears that the British troops engaged in the action, amounted to fourteen hundred forty-five. The cavalry are not included in this return, and indeed they were not engaged, except for an instant on the right, after the action in the centre, and on the left, was over. The Americans were generally supposed to amount to seven thousand men, and a letter, found in the pocket of one of their sergeants that was slain, specifies seven thousand to be the number of their army: but Gordon in his history, who appears to have taken their numbers, from official documents, states them to be fourteen hundred and ninety continentals, and two thousand seven hundred and fifty three militia; in all, four thousand two hundred and forty three foot soldiers, and two hundred cavalry. But he seems not to have included the backwoods men, under Campbell and Preston; so that their whole number probably exceeded seven thousand men.

★★★★★★★★★★

The resistance of the enemy was in proportion to the advantages they possessed; nor did they yield, but with extreme reluctance. Even the militia, encouraged by their position, fought with bravery, and greatly weakened the British line before it reached the continentals. The Virginia militia, who composed the second American line, did not quit their ground, it is said until their commander, seeing them no longer able to withstand the attack of regular troops, and ready to be overpowered, gave orders for a retreat. A victory achieved under such disadvantages of numbers and ground, was of the most honourable kind, and placed the bravery and discipline of the troops, beyond all praise; but the expense at which it was obtained rendered it of no utility.

Before the Provincials finally retreated, more than one third of all the British troops engaged had fallen. The whole loss, according to the official returns, amounted to five hundred and thirty-two: of these ninety-three were killed in the action, four hundred and thirteen were wounded, and twenty-six missing. Amongst the killed were the Honourable Lieutenant-Colonel Stuart of the Guards, Lieutenant O'Hara of the Royal Artillery, brother of the Brigadier-Lieutenant Robinson of the 23rd Regiment, Ensign Talbot of the 33rd, and Ensign Grant of the 71st; amongst the wounded, were Brigadier-Generals O'Hara, and Howard; Lieutenant-Colonels Webster, and Tarleton; Captains Swanton, Schutz, Maynard, Goodricke, Lord Dunglass, Maitland, Peter, Wilmonsky, and Eichenbrodth; Lieutenants Salvin, Winyard, Schewener, and Graise; Ensigns Stuart, Kelly, Gore, Hughes, and De Troot; and Adjutant Colgahoun, and Fox.

The loss of the Americans in this action has been variously estimated, and does not appear to have been fully ascertained. If we are to credit their official returns, their whole loss in killed and wounded, as well of militia as continentals, did not exceed two hundred and fifty men. But, by Lord Cornwallis's dispatches, it appears that between two and three hundred of their dead, were found upon the field, after the action; and if we proportion their wounded according to the number of the slain, their whole loss in killed and wounded, must have greatly exceeded that of the British troops. The number of those who were missing, according to their own returns, was confessedly great; but as the British troops took but few prisoners, is probable that the greatest part of the missing, consisted of militia, who, escaping from the action, fled to their own houses, and did not afterwards return.

The wounded of both armies were collected by the British, as expeditiously as possible after the action: it was, however, a service that required both time and care, as from the nature of the action, they lay dispersed over a great extent of ground. Every assistance was furnished to them, that in the then circumstances of the army could be afforded; but unfortunately, the army was destitute of tents, nor was there a sufficient number of houses near the field of battle to receive the wounded.

The British Army had marched several miles on the morning of the day on which they came to action. They had no provisions of any kind whatever on that day, nor until between three and four in the afternoon of the succeeding day, and then but a scanty allowance, not exceeding one quarter of a pound of flour, and the same quantity of very lean beef.

The night of the day on which the action happened was remarkable for its darkness, accompanied with rain, which fell in torrents. Near fifty of the wounded, it is said, sinking under their aggravated miseries, expired before morning. The cries of the wounded, and dying who remained on the field of action during the night, exceeded all description. Such a complicated scene of horror and distress, it is hoped, for the sake of humanity, rarely occurs, even in a military life.

What loads of mangled flesh and limbs
(A dismal carnage!) bath'd in reeking gore,
Lay welt'ring on the ground; while fitting life,
Convuls'd, the nerves still shivering, nor had lost
All taste of pain! Here an old vet'ran lies
Deform'd with years, and scars, and groans aloud
Torn with fresh wounds; but inward vitals firm
Forbid the soul's remove, and chain it down
By the hard laws of nature, to sustain
Long torment; his wild eye balls roll; his teeth,
Gnashing with anguish, chide his ling'ring fate.

History, perhaps, does not furnish a similar instance of a battle gained under all the disadvantages with which the British troops, (assisted by a regiment of Hessians, and some *Yagers*,) had to contend against, at Guildford Court House. Nor is there, perhaps, on the records of history, an instance of a battle fought with more determined perseverance than was shewn by the British troops on that memorable day. The Battles of Cressy, of Poictiers, and of Agincourt, the glory of our own country, and the admiration of ages, had in each of them, either from particular local situation, or other fortunate and favourable circumstances something in a degree to counter-balance the disparity of numbers; here, time, place, and numbers, all united against the British.

The American general had chosen his ground, which was strong, commanding, and advantageous; he had time not only to make his disposition, but to send away his baggage, and every incumbrance. His cannon and his troops, in numbers far exceeding the British, were drawn out in readiness to commence the action, when Lord Cornwallis approached to attack him."

★★★★★★★★★★★★★★★★★★★★★★★

General Greenie fled to Reedy Fork Creek, where, when he had passed the river, he halted on the opposite banks to collect his stragglers. When he had partly accomplished this, he pushed on to Troublesome Creek, about twelve miles further. Lord Cornwallis, (from the army being in want of provisions, and its several other distresses,) found it would be inadvisable to pursue the fugitives. It on the other hand became indispensably necessary to move towards some place where supplies might be obtained. Accordingly, about seventy wounded were left at the Quaker's meeting house, under protection of a flag of truce, and the army slowly retired to Cross Creek.

It was part of Lord Cornwallis's plan for the operation in the north, that Colonel Balfour, the *commandant* at Charlestown, should dispatch a force by water, sufficient to take Wilmington, as a post of communication, and a medium of obtaining supplies. This service was executed by Major Craig in the end of January, and put in a proper state of defence, Wilmington lies near the mouth of Cape Fear River; and Cross Creek (a settlement of loyal Highlanders) is on a branch of it, about one hundred miles up the country.

From thence it was expected the army would obtain supplies, and it was moreover admirably adapted, from its central situation, as a rallying point for those who were well affected to the Royal Cause.

Lord Cornwallis began his march from Guildford Court House by issuing a proclamation, inviting the loyal to his standard, and offering pardon to those who should return to their allegiance. His Lordship then proceeded by slow marches to Cross Creek; General Greene following him as far as Ramsey's Mill, on Deep River. Nothing but slight occasional skirmishes ensued during the march. On his arrival at the Creek, every hope was disappointed. Four days forage could not be had in twenty miles, all communication, with Wilmington from the narrowness of the river, was impracticable, and the scattered inhabitants on its lofty banks were irreconcilably hostile.

The troops therefore began their march to Wilmington, at which place they arrived on the 7th of April. During these toilsome movements, the British Army sustained an almost irreparable loss, by the deaths of Colonel Webster of the 33rd, Captains Schutz and Maynard of the Guards, and Captain Wilmouski and Ensign De Trott of the Regiment of Bose.

★★★★★★★★★★

It was reported in the army, that when Lord Cornwallis received the news of Colonel Webster's death, His Lordship was struck with such pungent sorrow, that turning himself, he looked on his sword, and emphatically exclaimed, "I have lost my scabbard."

★★★★★★★★★★

They all received their mortal wounds at Guildford Court House. Of Colonel Webster's great military talents and virtues, mention at large has already been made in this *Journal*; but:

The sympathetic manner in which Lord Cornwallis communicated to the Rev. Dr. Webster, of Edinburgh, the intelligence of his son's death, is at once a proof of His Lordship's goodness of heart, his tender sensibility, and of the high estimation in which he held the deceased. The following is a copy of his letter on that occasion:

Wilmington, April 23, 1781.

Dear Sir—It gives me great concern to undertake a task which is not only a bitter renewal of my own grief, but must be a violent shock to an affectionate parent.

You have for your support, the assistance of religion, good sense, and the experience of the uncertainty of human happiness. You have for your satisfaction, that your son fell nobly in the cause of his country, honoured and lamented by all his fellow soldiers; that he led a life of honour and virtue, which must secure him everlasting happiness. When the keen sensibility of the passions begins to subside, these considerations will give you real comfort.

That the Almighty may give you fortitude to bear this severest of trials, is the earnest wish of your companion in affliction, and most faithful servant,

Cornwallis.

As the author belonged to Colonel Webster's brigade, he is enabled, (and the reader will naturally expect it from him,) to state some circumstances unnoticed by any historian, from his own personal observation. After the brigade formed across the open ground, the colonel rode on to the front, and gave the word, "*Charge.*" Instantly the movement was made, in excellent order, in a smart run, with arms charged: when arrived within forty yards of the enemy's line, it was perceived that their whole force had their arms presented, and resting on a rail fence, the common partitions in America. They were taking aim with the nicest precision.

Twixt host and host but narrow space was left,
A dreadful interval, and, front to front,
Presented, stood in terrible array.

At this awful period a general pause took place; both parties surveyed each other for the moment with the most anxious suspense. Nothing speaks, *the general* more than seizing on decisive moments: Colonel Webster rode forward in the front of the 23rd Regiment, and said, with more than even his usual commanding voice (which was well known to his brigade,) *"Come on, my brave Fusiliers."* This operated like an inspiring voice, they rushed forward amidst the enemy's fire; dreadful was the havoc on both sides,

Amazing scene!
What showers of mortal hail! What flaky fires!

At last, the Americans gave way, and the brigade advanced, to the attack of their second line. Here the conflict became still more fierce. Before it was completely routed, where I stood, (it is not from egotism, but to be the better understood, that I here, without breaking the thread of precision, assume the first person) I observed an American officer attempting to fly. I immediately darted after him, but he perceiving my intention to capture him, fled with the utmost speed. I pursued, and was gaining on him, when, hearing a confused noise on my left, I observed several bodies of Americans drawn up within the distance of a few yards. Whoever has been in an engagement well knows that, in such moments all fears of death are over. Seeing one of the guards among the slain, where I stood, I stopped and replenished my own pouch with the cartridges that remained in his; during the time I was thus employed, several shots were fired at me; but not one took effect.

Glancing my eye, the other way, I saw a company of the guards advancing to attack these parties. The reader may perhaps be surprised at the bravery of troops, thus with calm intrepidity attacking superior numbers, when formed into separate bodies, and all acting together; but I can assure him this instance was not peculiar; it frequently occurred in the British Army, during the American war. It was impossible to join this company, as several of the American parties lay between me and it. I had no time for deliberation. How to act I knew not.

On the instant, however, I saw Lord Cornwallis riding across the clear ground. His Lordship was mounted on a dragoon's horse (his own having been shot;) the saddle-bags were under the creature's belly, which much retarded his progress, owing to the vast quantity of underwood that was spread over the ground; His Lordship was evidently unconscious of his danger. I immediately laid hold of the bridle of his horse, and turned his head. I then mentioned to him, that if His Lordship had pursued the same direction, he would in a few moments have been surrounded by the enemy, and, perhaps, cut to pieces or captured.

I continued to run alongside of the horse, keeping the bridle in my hand, until His Lordship, gained the 23rd Regiment, which was at that time drawn up in the skirt of the woods.

CHAPTER 17

Lord Rawdon Forces Greene to Retreat

It was the intention of Lord Cornwallis to have moved on to Camden, to obtain supplies, and messengers were accordingly dispatched to Lord Rawdon, but unhappily they never reached His Lordship. The intelligence that Greene had marched to attack Lord Rawdon, and that probably the fate of Camden was already decided, inclined His Lordship to pursue a different direction, and the army set out for Virginia, to join General Arnold.

An able and heroic defence of Camden was made by Lord Rawdon, and Greene was compelled, after suffering severely from a sortie made by the garrison, to retreat to Rugeley's mills, about twelve miles distant.

Amidst all this display of British valour, the presence of an American Army, although retreating before the king's troops, occasionally harassed them severely, by acting in small parties, and this produced the open avowal of disaffection among the inhabitants. Fort Watson, a British post on the Santee River, was surrendered to Lee and Marion. Colonel Watson, however, with a detachment of five hundred men, notwithstanding every obstacle, made his way through the country, and reinforced Lord Rawdon at Camden.

With this accession of strength, His Lordship attempted once more to bring General Greene to an engagement but he filed before him. The universal disaffection of the Americans in this part, determined Lord Rawdon to contract the limits of the British posts, by abandoning Camden: the stores not removable, were destroyed, and the army retired to Monk's Corner, for the greater safety of Charlestown. In consequence of this movement, Fort Motte was surrendered to Lee and Marion, Orangeburgh to Sumpter, and Forte Granby to Lee alone.

Flushed with these partial successes, the American commander, began his operations on the western frontiers. Lee and Pickens formed a junction, and the two commanders sat down before Augusta, which was defended by Lieutenant-Colonel Brown, with all his former gallantry when Clarke besieged it. But at length, after a brave defence, it was surrendered to the Americans on the fifth of June.

These disasters to the Royal Cause were in a great measure ascribable to the British officers, commanding at the different posts, being ignorant of each other's operations, by the vigilance of the disaffected inhabitants, who intercepted almost all their letters, dispatches, &c. Thus, the orders sent from Charlestown, and also by Lord Rawdon, for the evacuation of Ninety-Six, never reached Lieutenant-Colonel Cruger, and he acted, on local circumstances only, and accordingly fortified the place instead of evacuating it. In this situation it was invested by General Greene.

During the course of the siege, which was carried on with a fury almost amounting to desperation by the Americans, that in open day they attempted to set fire to the abbatis with lighted combustibles. And Colonel Lee had the meanness and inhumanity to march the British prisoners he brought with him from Fort Augusta in full sight of the garrison, accompanied by music, playing Yankee tunes, and preceded by a British standard reversed.

At length the garrison became much distressed for want of water. Their only supply depended on the negroes, who were sent out at night naked, and whose colour, in darkness, rendered them objects not distinguishable by the Americans.

Thus, dreadfully circumstanced, the British commander did not despair. He still depended on relief from Lord Rawdon. Nor were his hopes in vain. A brave and determined American loyalist, in midday rode through the American picquets, notwithstanding their fire, and delivered a verbal message from His Lordship, "that he had passed through Orangeburgh, and was in full march to raise the siege." How this operated on a British garrison, need not be recorded. Three Irish regiments had arrived at Charlestown, which placed that capital in a state of security, and left His Lordship at liberty to attempt the relief of Ninety-Six. With the fank companies of these regiments and the army from Monk's Corner, he began his march in a direction to get between General Greene and his force on the Congaree.

General Greene was not unapprised of this intended relief, and as a last and desperate effort, attempted to take the place by storm. In the morning of the 13th of June, a heavy cannonade was begun from all the American batteries: at noon two parties advanced under cover of the trenches which approached nearest to the works, and made lodgements in the ditch: these were immediately followed by other parties with hooks to draw down the sand bags, and tools to reduce the parapet.

The riflemen, in the meantime, posted on their battery, were ready to take aim at every British soldier that appeared; and the Virginia and Maryland brigades, having manned the lines of the third parallel, fired from them by platoons. The right flank of the enemy was exposed to the fire of a three pounder, as well as to that of the block houses in the village; and Major Greene, who commanded in the *Star*, with much honour to himself, and benefit to the service, from the beginning of the siege, had his detachment ready to receive them on the parapet with bayonets and spears. As the main body of the American Army did not advance beyond the third parallel, and was contented with supporting the parties in the ditch, by an incessant fire from the trenches, the garrison determined to put a speedy period to the assault by an effort of gallantry which confounded the enemy.

Two parties of thirty men each, one under Captain Campbell of the New Jersey volunteers, and the other under Captain French of Delancy's, issued from the sally port in the rear of the *Star*, entered the ditch, and taking opposite directions, charged the Americans who had made the lodgement with such impetuosity, that they drove everything before them, until they met in the opposite quarter. The bayonet being the only weapon used, the carnage was great: even the American accounts admit, that two thirds of their people who entered the ditch, were either killed or wounded. General Greene, seeing it useless any longer to continue so hopeless an attempt, called off his troops, and in the evening of the following day, finally raised the siege.

His baggage having been previously sent off, his army marched with great expedition, and on the 20th crossed the Saluda. The loss of the enemy, during the siege, according to their own accounts amounted to one hundred and sixty-six men, including one colonel, three captains, and five lieutenants: but as the loss of the militia, who, it is said, on this occasion bore the proportion of three to one of the troops, in the pay of Congress, was not included in their returns, their total loss must have been much greater. That of the garrison amounted to twenty-seven killed, and fifty-eight wounded. (Stedman.)

The following day Lord Rawdon arrived before the place, and without delay, in the evening, in defiance of heat and fatigue, set out in pursuit of Greene, who fled before him with the utmost precipitancy:

The fugitives were pursued to the banks of the Enorce; but at last, the American general found safety in the celerity of his movements.

On His Lordship's return, preparations were made for the evacuation of Ninety-Six, and the loyal inhabitants, with their effects, were, under the escort of Lieutenant-Colonel Cruger, removed within the new frontier. After the abandonment of Ninety-Six, His Lordship proceeded to the Congaree, and from thence to Orangeburgh, where he was joined by Lieutenant-Colonel Stuart with the 3rd Regiment, from Charlestown.

The sultry heat of the American climate, now partially suspended the operations of both armies. General Greene retired to the lofty hills of Santee, where he was joined by Lee, Sumpter, and Marion, Lord Rawdon's health was much impaired, and, on leave of absence, His Lordship returned to Europe; the command, of course, devolved on Lieutenant-Colonel Stuart,

It now became the aim of General Greene to attempt the recovery of South Carolina. Accordingly, he marched from the Santee Hills, and came up with the British, who had passed by the Congaree, at its junction with Wateree, at Eutaw Springs, about forty miles from the former river. The regulars were drawn up on the height, across the road, the right wing of the army consisted of the flank battalion, under the command of Major Marjoribanks, the remainder of the army on the left, in an oblique direction. A party of infantry; with two pieces of artillery, defended the pass of the road. Four battalions of American militia composed their first line; three brigades of continental troops their second; Lee's legion covered their right flank, the South Carolina state troops, under Henderson, their left.

Colonel Washington's cavalry, and the Delaware troops were the body of reserve; two three pounders were in front of the line, and two six pounders with the second line. The legion and state troops constituted the advance guard. The attack began with great impetuosity, some of the new raised troops were giving way, when the 63rd and 64th Regiments rushed on the enemy with bayonets in hand. The contest was severe on both sides, the artillery was several times taken, and retaken. At the first fire, Colonel Washington was wounded, and taken prisoner. Often, when the parties seemed overpowered, the contest was renewed with increased vigour on both sides.

The Americans, however, were at last compelled to retire, leaving behind them two brass six pounders, and upwards of two hundred killed on the field, and sixty taken prisoners, besides the wounded which were carried off during the action. The total loss, according to the return which was published by Congress, was more than seven hundred, including sixty commissioned officers, of whom seventeen were killed, and forty-three wounded, among the latter was Lieutenant-Colonel Washington. The British lost six hundred and ninety-three men, eighty-five killed, three hundred and fifty-one wounded, two hundred and fifty-seven missing. Of twenty-nine commissioned officers, three were killed, sixteen wounded, ten missing. It might well be said, in this bloody and hard-fought battle, that

Frowning war
All gloomy, like a gather'd tempest, stood
Wav'ring, and doubtful where to bend its fall.

Congress voted a British standard and a gold medal to General Greene *for the victory;* but the British commander *remained on the ground* the night after the action, and during the following day! This was the last battle of any note which took place in South Carolina.

As we hear no more of General Greene during the American war, some readers may perhaps be curious to know what became of him. There is a brief account of the latter part of his life in Smith's *Narrative,* which may not be altogether improper to quote here:

Congress effectually remunerated Greene, by giving him a valuable plantation, in the state of Georgia, the meed of his indefatigable services, but which was, ultimately, his bane, and the cause of his premature death; for depending too much upon his hardy constitution, contrary to the advice of his friends, he would, to accomplish the duties, and acquire the simple character of a planter, venture out, and subject himself to the meridian blaze of the sun, in order to superintend his negro labourers: in one of these perambulations he received the *coup de soliel,* or, stroke of the sun, as the French West Indians term the effects which Europeans feel from too great an exertion, while subjected to the solar heat; and fell a victim to his own obstinacy, unrelented by some, and deplored by others: for political attachments bore their preponderance in that unhappy, divided, and distracted country, till the last hour of the unfortunate war; and even now they are far, very far, from extinction. In the minds of some this general still lives, and is considered as the *deputy*-saviour of his country. Hosanna one hour, and crucify the next, was the prevailing principle among the Americans) *Sic transit gloria mundi!*

CHAPTER 18

Lord Cornwallis Joins General Arnold

A deep laid, but ineffectual plan was about this time formed by Washington, for entrapping General Arnold. A reinforcement of two thousand British, under General Phillips, were arrived in the Chesapeake: that officer being superior in rank, took the command from Arnold, and became general of the whole British force there. He finished the works at Portsmouth, left a sufficient force for its defence, and proceeded up James's River in the smaller vessels of the fleet. The army after twice landing, and re-embarking, joined Lord Cornwallis at Petersburgh, at which place General Phillips, (equally beloved and respected for his virtues, and his military talents,) died of a fever, a short period before the junction of the royal forces. The command again devolved on General Arnold; but shortly after, as matter of course, the superior direction of both armies became vested in Lord Cornwallis.

The Marquis de la Fayette, had followed the route of the British Army, under General Phillips; but when he learned the junction of the whole under Lord Cornwallis, he took a position on the North of James's River, between Richmond and Wiltown. From this place he however, fled on the approach of Lord Cornwallis. Meantime Colonel Tarleton with a patrol pushed on to Warwick Court-House, fell in with a party of four hundred militia in that neighbourhood, who were routed with great loss to the Americans. Sometime after the colonel, and Captain Champagne of the 23rd Regiment, surprised Charlotteville, (at which place the general assembly was sitting) and took seven of their members prisoners. Brigadier-General Scott, and several officers and men, were killed, wounded, or taken.

The attempt to secure Mr. Jefferson was ineffectual, he discovered the British dragoons from his house, which stands on the point of a mountain, before they could approach him, and he provided for his personal safety, by a precipitate retreat. The gentlemen taken on this expedition, were treated with kindness and liberality. (Colonel Tarleton.)

A great quantity of stores were found in Charlotteville, which were all destroyed. A successful stratagem of Colonel Simcoe, also put the British in possession of all the stores under the care of Baron Steuben, at the point of Fork. At this period the American affairs became much deranged from the want of supplies. Their bills of credit suffered a dreadful depreciation: few would take them for anything wanted by the army, and they were obliged to have recourse to bills of impress, to compel individuals to part with provisions. For want of pay and clothing, the troops were on the verge of mutinying. Even General Washington confessed this in one of his letters.

From the posts of Saratoga to that of Dobb's Ferry, inclusive, I believe there is not, at this moment on hand, one day's supply of meat for the army.

Their marine was, if possible, in a worse condition than their army. In short, a general bankruptcy seemed to be fast approaching. Washington saw that the only chance of continuing the war, was by some bold and decisive operation, and New York became his object. But to carry this or any other decisive operation into effect, the co-operation of the French fleet and army, were necessary. This had been promised, and Congress during the three preceding years had anxiously expected it.

At the end of the last year, they laid before the Court of Versailles, the desperate situation to which the American cause was reduced, and the inevitable ruin which awaited them, without powerful succour from France. When all was suspense and terror, intelligence arrived at Washington's camp, that M. de Barras was at Rhode Island, and that he brought dispatches for Count de Rochambeau. The general accordingly set out for Connecticut, to meet him. At this, conference which was held on the 21st of May, it was agreed to attack New York, and on the arrival of Count de Grasse, to strike some important blow.

General Washington wrote to Congress, requesting the full completion of his own battalions, and the further aid of six hundred and twenty militia, from the New England States. His dispatches were intercepted in the Jerseys, and immediately sent to Sir Henry Clinton. He accordingly wrote to Lord Cornwallis, for part of the troops under His Lordship's command, to be sent to the succour of New

York. Agreeably to General Clinton's request, Lord. Cornwallis left Williamsburg, and passed James's River in his way to Portsmouth. Previous to passing the river he encamped on a spot that covered the ford into the island of James's Town; and in the evening the Queen's Rangers made their way over: the wheel carriages, the bat horses, and baggage followed on the 5th and 6th.

The Marquis de la Fayette pursued by forced marches, hoping to surprise the rear guard, when the main body had passed over. Of this Lord Cornwallis gained intelligence, he permitted the picquets to be driven in to deceive the *marquis*. The attack began about sunset. The enemy were routed, and the approach of night alone saved the whole from ruin.

The 43rd, 76th, and 80th Regiments, were in the fiercest part of the action, opposed by the Pennsylvania line, and Lieutenant-Colonel Dundas, their commander displayed a bravery, and firmness, which obtained the applause of the whole British Army.

The British main body quietly passed the river; the troops destined for embarkation moved on to Portsmouth, and His Lordship followed with the rest. After these troops were embarked, and just as they were putting out to sea, an express arrived from Sir Henry Clinton to prevent their sailing, and directing Lord Cornwallis to regain Williamsburg, as the means of saving a defensive post for the larger ships, either at Point Comfort, or, at Hampton Road. Lord Cornwallis, on due examination found the two places untenable, and accordingly ordered part of the army to sail up the York River in transports, and take possession of York Town and Gloucester. On the 20th of August, His Lordship evacuated Portsmouth, and fixed his headquarters at York and Gloucester.

On the 30th of August, in a fatal moment which may be said to have turned the wavering scale in favour of the Americans, Count de Grasse arrived in the Chesapeake, with twenty-eight ships of the line. An officer from La Fayette's army was waiting his arrival at Cape Henry. He communicated to the count the perilous state of American affairs; and a disposition was instantly formed for blocking up York River, on the banks of which Lord Cornwallis was posted, and for conveying the French land force, which the count had brought up James's River to reinforce La Fayette. All this was performed by four line of battle ships, the others remaining in Lynhaven Bay, within the Capes,

The British admiral (Graves) quitted the entrance of the Delaware, and came within sight of the French squadron, when a partial engagement took place; but from the wind, and other circumstances, it was impossible for him to force the French to a general battle, and it was their object to decline it; for during this partial contest, while both fleets were at sea, M. de Barras sailed into the Chesapeake, conveying fourteen: transports, laden with heavy artillery and stores.

In the meantime, the commander in chief at New York, with a view of making a diversion in Connecticut, and drawing General Washington's attention that way, detached Brigadier-General Arnold with a considerable force to make an attempt upon New London. The troops embarked on this expedition, consisted of the 38th, 40th, and. 54th Regiments, the third Battalion of New Jersey volunteers, the Loyal Americans, the American Legion, some refugees, a detachment of *yagers*, and another of the Royal Artillery. They passed through the Sound in transports, and, landed in the morning of the sixth of September, about three miles from New London, in two divisions, one on each side of the harbour.

That on the Groton side, consisting of the 40th and 54th Regiments, the third Battalion of New Jersey volunteers, with a detachment of *yagers* and artillery, was commanded by Lieutenant-Colonel Eyre, and that on the New London side, consisting of the rest of the troops, by Brigadier-General Arnold. On the New London side no great opposition was made: a redoubt, from which the enemy had begun a cannonade, was abandoned by them upon the approach of General Arnold with part of his division; and soon afterwards Fort Trumbull, that commanded the harbour, was entered by Captain Millet at the head of four companies of the 38th Regiment, through a shower of grape-shot, which the enemy discharged from their cannon, but without doing much mischief, only four or five being killed or wounded in the assault.

General Arnold lost no time in taking possession of New London: He was opposed by a small body of the enemy with a fieldpiece; but they were soon so hard pressed as to be obliged to fly, and leave their piece of artillery behind. On the Groton side of the harbour was Fort Griswold, a regular work of considerable strength. It was assaulted on three sides by the 40th and 54th Regiments, under Lieutenant-Colonel Eyre, and defended by the enemy with the most obstinate bravery.

At length the gallant efforts of the assailants were successful; and with fixed bayonets they entered the works through the embrasures, in the face of the enemy, who were armed with long spears to oppose them. A considerable carnage now ensued, until the enemy were driven from the ramparts, and had ceased from all farther resistance. The honour obtained by the British troops in this assault was great, but too dearly purchased. Two officers, and forty-six soldiers, were killed, and eight officers, with one hundred and thirty-five soldiers, wounded. General Arnold, upon his landing, had been informed that that the works at Fort Griswold were incomplete, and its garrison inconsiderable: but when he arrived at New London, and from an eminence, had viewed its great strength, he dispatched an officer to countermand his orders for an assault, who unfortunately reached Colonel Eyre a few minutes too late.

The fort had refused to surrender, and the action was begun. Of the garrison eighty-five were killed, including Colonel Ladyard, their commander; sixty were wounded, most of them mortally, and seventy made prisoners. Ten or twelve of the enemy's ships were burnt, that contained an immense quantity of European and West India goods. Unluckily they also contained some gunpowder, unknown to General Arnold, by the explosion of which the flames were communicated to the dwelling-houses in the town, and a great part of it was consumed, notwithstanding every endeavour to stop the progress of the conflagration. Upwards of fifty pieces of cannon, and a great quantity of military stores found in the different works, were also destroyed. (Stedman.)

Notwithstanding the heavy loss which the Americans sustained by the destruction of New London, Washington continued his progress to Virginia, passed through Philadelphia, and at the head of the Elk River embarked his troops in transports sent thither by the French. The whole reached Williamsburg on the 25th of September, General Washington and Count de Rochambeau went on board the *Ville de Paris*, and with Count de Grasse settled the future operations of the Allied Armies.

On the 28th the investiture of York Town commenced. In the evening dispatches arrived from Sir Henry Clinton, promising the relief of five thousand troops, and that twenty-three ships of the line, would sail, as a further support by the fifth of October: the next day the investment of the town was pursued; in the night the enemy began to break ground; the French made their approach on the right, the Americans on the left, forming a junction at a morass, which was opposite the centre of the British works, at the same time Gloucester Town was blockaded by the Duke De Lauzan. The garrison made a brave resistance, annoying the besiegers at every possible point of attack, particularly from two redoubts, which were carried out near three hundred yards in front of the works. These it became necessary for the besiegers to silence in the night of the 14th, the one was carried by the Americans, and the other by the French.

A sortie was made by three hundred and fifty men, under the command of Lieutenant-Colonel Abercrombie, against two of the enemy's batteries; a detachment of the guards, with the 80th Grenadiers, under Lieutenant-Colonel Lake, executed the one, and another of light infantry, under Major Armstrong, carried the other; eleven heavy cannon were spiked, one hundred of the French troops were killed and wounded, and the whole party returned, with very little loss, within the British lines. However gallant this enterprise, the garrison was reduced to the last extremity, not a gun remained on that part of the works attacked by the enemy, scarcely a shell was left, and nothing remained to Lord Cornwallis but to attempt an escape, with the army, or immediately to surrender the place. "He determined (says Stedman) to attempt the latter."

On the Gloucester side of the river, Brigadier De Choise now commanded, and lay with a small corps at some distance, in front of the works. It was determined that he should be, attacked before break of day by the whole British force; and the success of the attack was not in the least doubted. The horses taken from him, (for he had a considerable corps of cavalry) would in part mount the infantry, and the rest might be supplied by others collected on the road. As no baggage was to be carried, His Lordship intended to have proceeded to the upper country by rapid marches, leaving his future route uncertain, until he came opposite to the fords of the great rivers; when he meant to have turned off suddenly to the northward, upon a supposition, that the enemy's measures would be principally directed to prevent his escape to the southward.

After turning to the northward, it was His Lordship's design to force his way through Maryland, Pennsylvania, and the Jerseys, and join the commander in chief at New York, Undoubtedly the attempt was beyond calculation hazardous, and the issue totally precarious, but if it afforded even a glimpse of hope, it was preferable to an immediate surrender.

In pursuance of this design the light infantry, the greatest part of the guards, and part of the 23rd Regiment, were embarked in boats, and transported to the Gloucester side of the river before midnight, when a violent storm arose, which not only prevented the boats from returning, but drove them a considerable distance down the river.

The passage of the rest of the troops was now become impracticable, and, in the absence of the boats, those that had already crossed, could not possibly return. In this divided state of the British force, the enemy's batteries opened at break of day: fortunately, the boats returned soon afterwards, and brought back, in the course of the forenoon, the troops that had been carried over in the night, without much loss, although the passage between York and Gloucester, was greatly exposed to the enemy's fire. In the meantime, by the force of the enemy's cannonade, the British works were tumbling into ruin: not a gun could be fired from them, and only one eight-inch, and little more than one hundred coehorn shells remained. They were in many places assailable already; and if the fire continued a few hours longer, it was the opinion of the engineer, and principal officers of the army, that it would be madness to attempt to maintain them with the present garrison, exhausted by the fatigue of constant watching and unremitting duty, and reduced in its numbers by sickness even more than by the enemy's fire.

Under such circumstances His Lordship, on the 17th of October, unwilling to expose the remains of his gallant army to the danger of an assault, which, from the enemy's numbers, and the ruined state of the works, could not fail to be successful, made proposals for a capitulation. The terms were adjusted in the course of the next day, which, though not altogether agreeable to Earl Cornwallis's wishes or proposals, were, nevertheless, such as his desperate situation, obliged him to accept; and on the 19th, the posts of York and Gloucester were surrendered to General Washington as commander in chief of the combined army; and the ships of war, transports, and other vessels, to the Count de Grasse, as commander of the French fleet.

By the articles of capitulation, the garrisons of York and Gloucester, including the officers of the navy, and seamen of every denomination, were to surrender as prisoners of war to the combined army: the land force to remain prisoners to the United States, and the seamen to the most Christian king. The garrison was to be allowed the same honours which the garrison of Charlestown had obtained, when it surrendered to Sir Henry Clinton. The officers and soldiers were permitted to retain their private property; and the officers had liberty to proceed upon parole either to Europe, or any maritime post on the continent of America, in the possession of the British troops.

Although the article for exempting from punishment such of the natives, or other inhabitants of America, as had joined the British

Army, and were then at York, was rejected by General Washington, the same thing was in effect obtained in a different form, by the permission granted to Earl Cornwallis, to send the *Bonetta* sloop of war to New York, with his dispatches without being searched, and with as many soldiers on board as he should think fit, so that they were accounted for in any future exchange. By this permission, he was tacitly empowered to send off such of the inhabitants as were obnoxious to punishment, which accordingly was done.

By the surrender of the posts of York and Gloucester, the Americans became possessed of a large train of artillery, many of which were of brass, together with a considerable quantity of arms, ammunition, warlike stores, and provisions; and to the French were delivered up, one frigate, two sloops of war of twenty guns, and a number of transports, and other vessels. The *Charon*, of forty-four guns, and another ship of war, were set on fire by the enemy's shells, and destroyed during the siege. The combined army consisted of seven thousand French, and nearly the same number of continental soldiers, and about five thousand militia, on the day previous to the surrender, the rank and file of the garrisons of York and Gloucester, amounted to five thousand nine hundred and fifty, but so great was the number of the sick and wounded, that only four thousand and seventeen were reported fit for duty.

Sir Henry Clinton in this moment of distressful exigence, embarked seven thousand troops from New York to relieve Lord Cornwallis. I have already mentioned that he apprised His Lordship that he would send him assistance by the 5th of October; but from intervening circumstances, they did not sail from Sandy Hook, until the 19th, the very day on which the surrender took place. Sir Henry embarked with the expedition himself, nor was it until they arrived off the Capes of Virginia, that Sir Henry received the disastrous intelligence of the capitulation. A writer on the American War, whom I have frequent occasions to quote, and who like myself was an eye-witness to many of the events which he narrates observes:

> Such was the fate of an army, which, if success were the uniform result of merit, would have undoubtedly shared a different fate: if bravery in the field, and patient, and even cheerful, submission to fatigue, inclement skies, and the want, not only of the comforts, but sometimes even of the necessaries of life, have any claim to esteem and admiration.

It is truly grievous to perceive the style of exultation, in which the party writers indulge on this capture of Lord Cornwallis. One of them, in direct terms, speaks of "the pride of Lord Cornwallis."— What pride? The very reverse was His Lordship's true character. In this campaign (I declare these facts from my own knowledge) he fared like a common soldier. He assumed; he would admit of no distinction. Every private under His Lordship must acknowledge,

> "*He bare no hardships but his leader bore.*"

Sometimes we had turnips served out for our food, when we came to a turnip field; or arriving at a field of corn, we converted our canteens into rasps and ground our Indian corn for bread; when we could get no Indian corn, we were compelled to eat liver as a substitute for bread, with our lean beef. In all this His Lordship participated, nor did he indulge himself even in the distinction of a tent; but in all things partook our sufferings, and seemed much more to feel for us than for himself. General indignation ought to follow such a tissue of falsehood and calumny. But when a beloved officer is the object of this viperous attack, it must rouse a resentment in the mind of every old soldier still living, *who knew the contrary to be fact,* which it is not very easy for military feeling to bear, or even Christian forgiveness to pardon.

Ramsay, too, has a very prettily manufactured tale on this occasion:

> The doorkeeper of Congress, an aged man, died suddenly, immediately after hearing the capture of Lord Cornwallis's army. His death was universally ascribed to a violent emotion of political joy!!!

Mr. Ramsay, strongly reminds me of a celebrated republican preacher, in England, who had the impiety to take for his text, the words of good old Simeon, "Lord now lettest thou thy servant depart in peace, for mine eyes have seen thy Salvation," when he preached a sermon to celebrate the French Revolution!!!

As a testimony of what the enemies of Lord Cornwallis, *in America,* thought and said of him, I subjoin the following curious extract from a speech delivered in Congress by the famous Dr. Witherspoon; without, however, joining him in the severe censure he passes on one of our admirals:

> It is incumbent on us to thank heaven for the victory which we have just obtained, and though over a handful of troops, yet they were flushed with success, and led on by a general, whose,

valour is no less illustrious than his discretion; by a general not equalled in courage by the Macedonian madman, or in wise and solemn deliberation, by the Roman Fabius; nor has his defeat tarnished his fame; for he was encompassed about with a mighty host of the picked troops of France and America, aided by a formidable navy; and to sum up his difficulties, he was attacked by famine in his camp.

It would be criminal in me to be silent on this occasion, which has diffused such joy in every breast. To procure America freedom and happiness has ever been my study, ever since I arrived among you; for this I have encountered a variety of hardships, and suffered not a little in my private fortune and reputation.

Now, gentlemen, since victory irradiates our arms, let us snatch this opportunity of securing to ourselves advantageous terms of peace, so shall we reap a profitable benefit from the example of all the wise, states so eminent in history.

Some may think it very censurable, and highly, derogatory to the dignity of this mighty commonwealth to crouch and offer terms of peace, when we have been gathering such blooming laurels; but when we duly weigh all the circumstances of our overrated victory, the reasonableness of my advice may more fully appear to every dispassionate man.

Lord Cornwallis's troops had boldly marched through the heart of our country, opposed not only by woods, rivers, and swamps, but also by all the force we could send against him, which was greatly superior to him in numbers; his whole army, I would say this foraging party (for it does not deserve the name of army) did not exceed four thousand; and small as it was, it had spread universal dismay; it had struck terror even into General Washington's camp, and wondrous to relate! brought that man of valour out of his lurking place, (which it would seem he had taken a lease of) at the head of no less than thirteen thousand troops, whom he had been training to arms, and teaching to storm mock castles these three years, in a strong impregnable camp, where no enemy would ever think it worthwhile to disturb his slumbers; and so panic struck was the American hero, that even with the great and formidable army under his command, would he not dare to attack an English foraging party; no, he must first be sure the French were before him with eight thousand of the *gens d'armes*, as a breastwork, to save his gallant troops, whose blood has ever been so precious to him. And to complete his safety, that thirty sail of the line of battle ships, manned with twenty-five thousand seamen (half of whom might act ashore) were within call of him.

Heavens! Gentlemen, if every victory is to cost us so dear, if we must send into the field fifty thousand men before we can capture four thousand fatigued, half-starved English, we must view at a very remote distance, our so much wished for independency: to bring this about if we go on as we have, for these long seven years, we ought to have more than all the wealth of all Mexico and Peru, and our women must bring forth four males at one birth. O dauntless spirit of immortal Cromwell, behold how enervated are thy descendants? Gentlemen, trivial and contemptible as our success is, we got it by mere accident; we got it not by the vigilance of our allies, or the prowess of our arms; we got it by the neglect or cowardice of the British admiral, who would not, when he had the golden opportunity, take possession of the Chesapeake; and to this gross blunder alone are we to ascribe our good fortune.

But, gentlemen, although one commander has abandoned his post, and betrayed the best interests of his country, can we suppose that his guilt will not meet that severe and exemplary punishment it deserves? Can we hope that British vengeance will never wake, that it will always sleep? When that culpable admiral is put to death, do you foolishly imagine his successor will not be alarmed for himself, and, profit by his fate? Yes; he will exert himself, he will be master of the Chesapeake, upon which you know our destiny hangs; for if that is once shut up, Virginia and Maryland, the springs of all our resources, the objects which enticed your good and great ally to aid you, are no more! Then a few British soldiers may harass our planters, lay waste their lands, set their tobacco in flames, destroy their docks, and block up such ships as they cannot burn or capture. It is a painful task, gentlemen, for me to set before your eyes a true picture of your affairs, but it is the duty of a friend. He who flatters you at this awful period smiles in your face while he stabs you in the vitals; it is by exhibiting to you such a picture, that you will be convinced you ought to send commissioners to treat with Britain for peace, without a moment's delay. Our enemies, I own, are surrounded with danger; a strong confederacy is in arms against them: yet although they possess but a speck of land, the fortitude of Britons, their exertions and supplies have astonished the wondering world; they are by no means exhausted: they have hitherto asked for no alliance, they have singly and alone kept all their combined foes at bay.

Britain has yet in store very tempting offers to hold out to any potentate whom she may court; she is mistress of our seaports; the large and fruitful colony of Canada is hers; her fleets have all arrived from Quebec, the Baltic, the West Indies, and East Indies, without the loss of a ship; her arms in Asia have carried conquest before them; so long as they hold their dominions there, they will have a perennial source of riches. Such is the situation of our foe; but how much more terrible may she become, if she joins to her already resistless marine the fleet of another power!

Suffer me to use the words of the prophet Jeremiah, and ask you, 'If thou hast run with footmen, and they have wearied thee, how then canst thou contend with horses?' When your enemy has once made such an addition to her strength, she will rise in her terms upon you, and in the paroxysm of her fury insist upon your submission, your unconditional submission! In order that I may not displease some of you, who hold a man a traitor for telling you wholesome truths, I will suppose all I have said to be exaggerated; I will suppose Britain to be in a galloping consumption: then, let me interrogate you. Do you increase in power and wealth? The very reverse is your case.

Your maladies, I am sorry to tell you, are incurable. Where are your numerous fleets of merchant ships, which were wont to cover old ocean? Have you so much as one to convoy your cargoes, or save them from capture? Have you any goods to export? Where are your luxuriant glebes and smiling meads? Alas! they are now an uncultivated waste. Your commerce is extinct; the premium of insurance on the very few ships which dare to peep out, never more to see their natal shore, so enormous, seamen's wages so high, (for nothing but death or an English dungeon is before them!) that ruin and bankruptcy have overwhelmed all descriptions of men; hardly any possess the conveniences, none the luxuries of life but faithless secretaries, avaricious commissaries, and griping contractors.

These, indeed, loll in their coaches, live in princely palaces, have

a numerous train of vermin to attend them, and fare sumptu-
ously every day. 'Curse on the wretch who owes his greatness to
his country's ruin!' Would to *God I* could here draw a veil over
our calamities! but the zeal I have to serve you will not allow
it. I must thunder in your ears, that your trade is annihilated;
your fisheries, that fertile nursery of seamen, that fountain of all
we could ever boast, is no more! Our ploughshares beat into
bayonets, our soldiers mutinying for want of pay; our planters
beggared, and our farmers ruined!

You are oppressed with taxes; not to emancipate you from
bondage—No: with taxes to support the lazy; to pamper the
proud; to exalt mean, cunning knaves, and dissipated gamblers,
to the first offices of the state; to pay armies who have the
figures of men, but the hearts of hares; they are, God knows,
numerous enough; but of what use? Why do we call in soup-
meagre soldiers? Are our own cowards? Are they not disciplined
after so many years dancing a jig to the fife and drum? Will they
not look an enemy in the face when their religion, their liberty,
is at stake; when their wives and children are butchered before
their eyes.

O America! America! thou art now ruined, and past redemption, consigned to destruction! Curse on this French connexion! I see thee prostrate on the ground, imploring mercy at the
feet of the Gallic monarch. If France conquers Britain, which,
for your sakes, I pray God to prevent! I tremble when I think of
the accumulated miseries with which you will be loaded.

★★★★★★★★★★

It was said that it was the late Queen of France's party which forced
on the king the treaty with America, in the view of depressing Great
Britain, Louis considered it as an unfair measure, and threw away the
pen, when urged to sanction it with his signature. But in an evil hour
for himself and his family, he relented, on repeated importunity, he
signed the fatal instrument, which involved both hemispheres in the
horrors of war, and, in so doing, he remotely signed the warrant for
his own execution. What a lesson is this to men of all ranks, to be just
and honourable in all their dealings!
Simpson's *Plea for Religion.*

★★★★★★★★★★

The French have already cheated you out of Rhode Island,
from whence, as from a flaming volcano, will stream fire to burn
your ships, and lay your seaports in smoking ruins. Methinks,

I see already the Canadians rush upon your possessions in the North, and the French and Spaniards overrun your southern colonies! like an impetuous torrent they sweep all before them! And even those of your own flesh and blood, whose lands you have confiscated, whose fathers and brother's you have murdered, join to lay you desolate! I see you turned into a desert, exposed to the ruthless elements, calling upon some hospitable roof to hide you from the storm! May heaven save you from calamities, and dispose you to sue for peace! Now is the appointed time; now is the day of salvation!

CHAPTER 19

The Author's Own Narrative

In consequence of this disastrous capitulation, the author became a second time a prisoner of the Americans. Fortunately for him, he was not recognised as one who had formerly made his escape, but ordered to march with the rest of the British troops to Winchester, situate in the back parts of Virginia, upwards of two hundred miles distant from York Town, In this part of his *Journal* (which, in absence of a better phrase, he almost ventures to call an historical episode) as in the narrative of his escape, after being made prisoner at Saratoga, and for the same reasons, he takes the liberty of conveying what befell him to the reader's attention in the first person.

Escape From York Town.

After the army under Lord Cornwallis became prisoners, I was attached to the general hospital. I had frequently officiated as an assistant surgeon, both in the 9th and 23rd Regiments; and sometimes, when we had not a professional surgeon, I had endeavoured to do that duty, to the best of my knowledge. The great fatigue which I underwent during the siege, brought on a severe illness, from which having somewhat recovered, I determined to attempt my escape to New York, (the distance from York Town to New York is upwards of five hundred miles.) I accordingly waited on the surgeon general, and resigned my situation in the general hospital, acquainting him that I intended to follow the troops to Winchester. Having received the balance due to me, I changed my dress, and appeared as a private soldier. The next consideration was, how to elude the French and American sentinels who guarded the prisoners.

This I fortunately accomplished while the guards were relieving, and got outside of the two barriers, on the great road which led to Fredericktown in Maryland. I immediately struck into the woods, to avoid the picquet guard, which I knew was posted on it. Night approaching, and finding myself very weak, I made every exertion to extricate myself from the wood. Before it was completely dark, I perceived a few houses, and went into one of them. I entreated the inhabitants to let me remain there all night; this they refused in the most peremptory terms, and immediately turned me out of doors, threatening, that if I did not instantly depart, they would take me back a prisoner to Gloucester Point. I went away with a very sorrowful heart, and after remaining sometime in the woods, scarcely able to determine what course to take, the weather being very severe and cold, and finding myself becoming very weak, I made a desperate effort, and went into a house, where there was a woman surrounded by a number of children.

I asked her the favour of remaining in her house for the night. She looked at me very sternly, and said, "How can you expect such a favour from me, or any of the Americans, seeing you came from England with an intent to destroy our country?" As I stood talking with her, her husband came in.

He seemed to be a humane man, and said, "It would be very hard indeed to turn you out of my door such a severe evening as this. I will permit you to remain here this night."

He then desired his wife to get a little straw, and make me a bed near the fireplace. After supper I lay down; and not being disturbed by the roaring of cannon, and the alarm of war, which had been my portion for many months before, I slept soundly, and awaked in the morning greatly refreshed. I gave the children some trifling presents, with which they and their parents seemed much gratified, and left them with the warmest emotions of thankfulness.

During this day (the 29th of November) I marched very hard on the main road, without encountering any interruption, this arose from its being the route which our troops had taken, the inhabitants thinking that I had not been able to keep up with the party, had lagged behind, and was endeavouring to overtake them. In the evening I came to a large building, when a gentlemen accosted me, observing; "there are a great many of your men in this house, who are determined to remain in the country, they have hired themselves to different gentlemen. You had better join with them: you shall be well used, and in a short time you may become a citizen of America."

Upon my entering the house, I found that there were above forty British soldiers, who had hired themselves to different gentlemen about the country. Early on the next morning, their masters came with horses, &c. and took them away. I was strongly importuned to go with them; but my mind revolted at the thought.

When I was preparing to leave the house, the gentleman said to me, "You had better remain with me. I am told you can write a good hand, and understand accounts; I will build a schoolhouse for you, and make you as comfortable as I can."

I felt my whole frame agitated at the proposal, and notwithstanding the weather was stormy and severe, and that I was very unwell, I immediately left his house with indignation.

This dishonourable practice of enticing the British soldiers to become settlers, was but too common, during the greater part of the American war. When a prisoner with them, I was often strongly solicited, and promised many rewards, if I would desert, and remain in the country.

But I was determined to die rather than serve any state hostile to Great Britain: indeed, I could not even patiently support the idea of remaining a prisoner among them. I had not travelled many miles when I overtook a sergeant of the 71st, and a drummer of the 23rd. I immediately began persuading them to venture with me in attempting to escape. They both consented. How entwined about the very heart of man, is the love of liberty! From that source more than the soundness of my arguments, or the probability of realizing them, I prevailed. It is very easy to talk about going through a tract of land, five or six hundred miles covered with enemies; but when entangled in the wood, sinking in the swamp, or fording the rapid torrent, we find it an enterprise of much difficulty and danger.

However, we addressed ourselves to our journey with confidence; but the next day our drummer complained that we marched too hard for him, and that it was impossible for us ever "to make good our escape. And (said he) for my part, I will stay where I am, and solace myself after all my hardships." No arguments which we could urge, appearing sufficient to cure his despondency, or alter his determination, we left him, and proceeded on our journey. The next day we overtook a waggon which was going to Philadelphia.

By a short conversation, we soon discovered that the waggoner was a loyalist, and in consequence informed him, that we were making our escape to New York. He proposed to conceal us in his waggon as far as Philadelphia at which place his master lived. This was gladly received on our part, and we promised him an adequate reward; we proceeded with him in high spirits: but, unfortunately for us, we overtook an American soldier, who insisted on his being taken into the waggon. This disconcerted our plan for the present. We were fast approaching Frederick-town, through which we could not pass concealed in the waggon, on account of the presence of the American soldier: we therefore thought it far more prudent to quit the waggon entirely, and boldly march through the town on foot. The faithful waggoner, before he left us, promised to wait a few miles on the other side of the town, until we should rejoin him. But how vain are all human schemes! Soon as the waggon entered the town, the American gave the alarm, and a party of soldiers was ordered out to apprehend us. We were seized and brought through the town, in triumph.

Many British soldiers were prisoners in this town, and among them the regiment to which my companion belonged. We were huddled among them. Indeed, our place of confinement was a most deplorable. situation. Forty or fifty British soldiers crowded together in a small room. It is true we had a large parade to walk about in the day; but as the winter was remarkably cold, very few availed themselves of that privilege.

I examined this place of confinement minutely, and soon discovered, that it was surrounded by a chain of American sentinels. I likewise gained information, that small parties of the prisoners (under a strong guard) were often ordered out to get wood for firing. It immediately occurred to me that the only chance for my escape, lay in getting myself enrolled in one of these wood cutting parties, I soon obtained this favour, and immediately began to take my measures: I strove to persuade as many of the party as I could to venture an escape with me. All my arguments proved ineffectual, except with one man, and my old companion the sergeant.

I waited with anxious suspense for the moment we were to be called out to wood cutting. I emptied my knapsack, and distributed my superfluous necessaries, putting on three shirts, and taking an additional pair of shoes in my pocket. With my blanket wrapped about my shoulders, I sallied out when the call came, bearing my hatchet: the intended companions of my flight were privately directed to keep as near to me as possible. When we had arrived at the wood, about half a mile from the place of confinement, we set to the work of cutting. I observed to one of our guards, that I saw a fine large maple tree a few yards beyond him; and begged permission for me and my two companions to cut it down.

With that rudeness which ever characterizes the low mind when in office, he, in a surly manner, acquiesced in the proposal, little dreaming that we all intended to give him the slip. The better to colour our pretence, and to cover our: escape, we immediately set about cutting down the tree, keeping our eyes constantly fixed on the guard. At last, he turned himself about, to watch the other prisoners.

We seized the opportunity, and darted into the thickest part of the wood. Fear and hope (being pretty nearly balanced in our minds,) were the wings which urged our flight. Our guards must have possessed the feet of deer before they could possibly have overtaken us. We ran on through the woods, as near as I could conjecture, during two hours, scarcely stopping to take breath. At last, we arrived at a deep and rapid river. Fortunately for us, we soon discovered a ferry-boat, and on paying the fare, we crossed, without being examined, and pursued our way through the woods.

It should have been mentioned, that though we had on our regimentals, we disguised ourselves by wrapping our blankets about us, which rather gave us the appearance of Indians than of British soldiers. We had not, however, proceeded far, when we were met by an armed party of Americans, who instantly surrounded us, and brought us back prisoners to the town. The sergeant, my companion, was then separated from me, as his regiment were prisoners near the town; he was turned in along with them, while I was sent a prisoner to their guard-house, where I was used in the most cruel manner. The weather was extremely cold, (the latter end of November,) the guard-house was an open block-house, through which the snow and frost made their way in every direction.

I procured, with much trouble, a little straw to lie upon, in one corner. But I soon found that my lodging would be a very hard one; for when the guard used to discover that I had fallen asleep, they applied a firebrand to the straw, and as it blazed, they set up a yell like the Indians, rejoicing in my distress, and deriding my endeavours to extinguish the flames, When the relief used to be turned out, I sometimes took the liberty of drawing near the fire, to warm my half frozen limbs, but this indulgence was of short duration, for when the sentinels were relieved they came pouring into the guard-house, and, if found near the fire, I was usually buffeted about from one to the other, and perhaps a dozen fixed bayonets at once placed at my breast.

When I found that I could obtain no mercy from these savages, and that every day I was worse used than on the preceding; I wrote a letter to the American commanding officer, informing him of the cruel usage which I daily received, and entreating him to permit me to be confined in the town goal. This request was at last granted; but my condition was not bettered by it. There I was confined in the upper part of the prison, which I had to ascend by a long board, which was almost perpendicular. In this dreary situation, without any fireplace, were twelve criminals. These men received a very small allowance of provisions; but, as for my part, not a morsel was allotted me. All my poor fellow prisoners took compassion, and shared their pittance with me. Had it not been for their compassion, I should have been starved to death.

I remained in this place during twelve days, suffering the bitings of hunger by day, and shivering all night with the cold. It can scarcely be imagined that aught could possibly have added to my sufferings: yet was the case worse, for we were continually annoyed with the yellings of a woman, who was confined for the murder of her child at the bottom of the jail. She used to yell the whole night long.

The reason of the bad usage which I in particular received, originated, it is most probable, in two distinct causes. This town had suffered much by the deaths of several young men, who had been killed during the war: the regiment of horse which was cut to pieces at Long Island was composed almost entirely of the inhabitants of this part of the country. This was a source of general inveteracy to all British prisoners. I had every mischief arising from this cause to support in common with my fellow prisoners. But what rendered me still further an object of their particular severity was, their firm conviction that I still meditated my escape. This principally, if not entirely arose, I believe, from one of Burgoyne's army, who had deserted from his regiment, and was then in town.

This man certainly informed the Americans that I had made my escape from that army into New York, and that I would do so again if I was not well taken care of. However, I was determined, if possible, to extricate myself from my present dreadful situation. With that intent I wrote a letter to Major Gordon of the 80th Regiment, who was then prisoner in the town, letting him know my distressed situation, and entreating his intercession with the American commander, to obtain my liberation from jail, and my being placed with the rest of my comrades, in their confinement near the town.

The major was not unmindful of me; for although he was at that time labouring under a complication of disorders, arising from the excessive fatigue, he had undergone during the siege, and the sufferings of his confinement, he referred my case to Captain Coote of the 33rd Regiment, (now Lieutenant-General Sir Eyre Coote) with his desire that application might be made to the American commanders for the privilege which I desired: Captain Coote most humanely interceded for me, and obtained my request.

While the faculties of my nature remain entire, I never can forget the affecting interview which took place between the captain and me. A guard was ordered to conduct me from the jail to his quarters. While I was relating to him the sufferings which I had undergone since my being captured at York Town, and my determination and hope still to effect my escape into New York, the tear of sympathy filled his eyes, he condoled with me in our common lot, and encouraged me to persevere. He then directed the sergeants of the 33rd Regiment to build me a hut upon the ground where they were confined, and to take me into their mess. He gave me a guinea, and I went off to my companions in triumph.

But my joy was only of short duration. Scarcely was I settled in my hut (in some degree of ease and comfort, in comparison to my former sufferings,) when I was ordered to be moved under a guard to Winchester, where the regiment to which I belonged was confined. The officers and men were all glad to see me: they had heard of the hardships I had endured in attempting my escape, and they condoled with me: part of the British troops remained here until January 1782, when Congress ordered us to be marched to Little York, in Pennsylvania. I received information, that as soon as I fell into the ranks to march off, I should be taken and confined in Winchester jail, as the Americans were apprehensive, that when I got near to New York I should again attempt my escape to that place, I was advised by my officers to conceal myself until the troops had marched.

I took the hint and hid myself in the hospital among the sick, here I remained until the American guards had been two days on their march with the British prisoners. I then prepared to follow them, but at a cautious distance. The troops arrived at Little York, and were confined in a prison similar to that which I have already described earlier, only a little more limited. About two hundred yards from this pen, a small village had been built by the remains of General Burgoyne's army, who were allowed very great privileges with respect to their liberty in the country. When some of my former comrades of the 9th Regiment, were informed that I was a prisoner in Lord Cornwallis's army, and that I was shortly expected at Little York, they immediately applied to the commanding officer of the Americans for a pass in my name, claiming me as one of their regiment.

This was immediately granted, and some of them, kindly and attentively placed themselves on the watch for my arrival, lest I should be confined with the rest of Lord Cornwallis's army. When I entered Little York, I was most agreeably surprised at meeting my former companions; and more so when a pass was put into my hands, giving me the privilege of ten miles of the country round while I behaved well and orderly. I was then conducted to a hut, which my poor loving comrades had built for me in their village before my arrival. Here I remained some time, visiting my former companions from hut to hut; but I was astonished at the spirit of industry which prevailed among them. Men, women, and even the children were employed making lace, buckles, spoons, and exercising other mechanical trades which they had learned during their captivity.

They had very great liberty from the Americans, and were allowed to go round the country and sell their goods; while the soldiers of Lord Cornwallis's army were closely confined in their pen. I perceived that they had lost that animation which ought to possess the breast of the soldier. I strove, by every argument, to rouse them from their lethargy. I offered to head any number of them, and make a noble effort to escape into New York, and join our comrades in arms; but all my efforts proved ineffectual. As for my own part, I was determined to make the attempt. I well knew, from experience, that a few companions would be highly necessary.

Accordingly, I sent word of my intention to seven men of the 23rd Regiment who were confined in the pen, and that I was willing to bring them with me. I believe in all the British Army that these men (three sergeants and four privates) could not have been excelled for courage, and intrepidity. They rejoiced at the idea; and by the aid of some of Burgoyne's army, they were enabled, under cover of a dark night, to scale their fence and assemble in my hut. I sent word of my intention to my commanding officer, Captain Saumarez of the 23rd, (later assistant quartermaster general, and Inspector of Militia in the Island of Guernsey), and likewise the names of the men whom I purposed to bring with me. As my money was almost expended, I begged of him to advance me as much as convenient. He immediately sent me a supply.

It was on the 1st of March, 1782, that I set off with my party. My pass which had been procured from the American commander would only protect us to Susquehanna River which was not further than ten miles: we therefore marched those ten miles free from any dread of being apprehended. But when we arrived at the river, which was about a mile in breadth, we found that it could not be crossed on the ice, as it had thawed all that day. However, when the evening drew on it began to freeze again, which encouraged us to remain until morning, under the hope that it would then be hard enough to bear us. At this place I found a man who had deserted from the Royal Welch Fusiliers about two years before. He seemed at first very shy of us; but after a little conversation he began to be more free.

He acquainted us that since his desertion he had been roving about the country working very hard for his livelihood, and further, that, finding himself universally despised by the Americans, he had become very uneasy in his mind. Perceiving him well acquainted with the country, and possessing a thorough knowledge of all the loyal inhabitants, I thought in our present situation, he would be a valuable acquisition to us as a guide. In consequence, I held out to him every inducement, which I imagined might persuade him to accompany us.—I urged, that we would as soon as we arrived at New York, intercede with Sir Henry Clinton for his pardon, which we had no doubt whatever would be immediately granted.

He was also made thoroughly acquainted with the considerable rewards which he would receive both from the commander in chief, and from ourselves. After much entreaty, and supplying him with repeated drams of peach whiskey, he at last consented to guide us through Pennsylvania and the Jerseys, with which part of the country, and the temper of its inhabitants he seemed perfectly acquainted.

As it had froze all night, we ventured to cross the river at daylight the next morning. Though the ice was exceeding weak, and broken up in many places, the love of liberty had such a powerful effect, that we ventured with the firmest resolution, although the ice cracked under our feet every step we took, while we marched in Indian file. Having crossed this mighty river, we held a consultation what was best to be done. We had exceeded the bounds of my pass, and consequently were liable to be arrested in our progress by the first party of American soldiers we met, or by any of the inhabitants who were disaffected; and even the loyalists, who might have succoured an individual or two, would most probably be fearful of giving assistance to such a party.

Our guide, the deserter, informed us, that it would be impossible for us to march a mile further, unless we divided—that nine in number were too many together, as such a body of British soldiers would soon spread an alarm through the country and cause immediate pursuit. He also strongly advised us to change our regimental clothes for coloured ones. We all saw the propriety of this advice; with aching hearts we took leave of each other. I divided the party; Sergeant Collins of the 23rd, (a brave soldier, and a sensible man,) took three men under his care, and I took the remaining four and our guide. We parted with great reluctance; but in full expectation of meeting each other at New York.

The party which I commanded lay all day in the woods: but in the evening our guide brought us to the house of one of the king's friends, (the Loyalists were so termed in America) where we changed our regimental clothes for very bad coloured ones. There we remained until eleven o'clock, when, favoured by the night, we began our march towards Lancaster. We kept in the woods as much as possible, and about the dawn of morning arrived at a small village. We entered into a house under the hope of procuring some refreshment. Almost immediately we perceived a man rising hastily out of bed. He dressed himself, and ran out of the house in great haste.

Apprehensive, that he had ran out to alarm the neighbours, (indeed our appearance was very suspicious,) we left the house immediately, and took shelter in the woods; where we remained, almost perishing with hunger and cold until night. We then began our march. About the dawn of the succeeding day, we espied a large barn and a dwelling house contiguous. With one consent, we resolved to repose our weary limbs in this barn. We soon got in, and concealed ourselves under some sheaves of wheat which were in the loft. We had not remained in this place more than half an hour, when a boy came up to remove the corn for thrashing.

He was greatly alarmed when he discovered us, and immediately ran down as fast he could. We thought it most prudent to follow him into the house, lest he should alarm the country. We entered the dwelling house almost as soon as him, saluted the farmer, and were desired to sit down. Our host ordered breakfast to be got ready, which consisted of ground Indian corn, boiled like stirabout. No doubt, from the situation in which we had been discovered, and perhaps more from our looks, he perceived that we were hungry, and he was very right in his observation, for none of us had eaten anything during more than fifty hours!

After we had taken a hearty, I might add voracious breakfast, he said, "Gentlemen, I perceive who you are, and what is your intention, but I'll have nothing to do with you. Depart in peace." We offered him money; but he would not accept of it. We then thanked him warmly, and withdrew to our usual hiding place, the woods; where we remained for several hours. Our guide informed us, that ten miles further, on the great road leading to Philadelphia, lived one of the king's friends, from whom we should certainly receive entertainment, and who would probably furnish us with a list of persons disposed, from principle, to assist us for forty miles on the way. Encouraged with this information, we set off towards the house in high spirits, which we reached at dusk in the evening.

We sent our guide into the house, while we remained concealed in the orchard. He soon returned, and desired us to come in. We were received most cordially by the old man, who bad us to sit down at a fine large fire, until refreshment could be got ready for us. He then, in the most feeling manner observed, "you know the great hazard I run in receiving you as friends. It is now (continued be) eight o'clock. I will let you remain under my roof till twelve. You must then depart."

Having said this, a good supper was set before us, with plenty of cider. The night proved very stormy, and the rain poured down like a deluge, which continued increasing every hour. However, the hour of twelve arrived, and gratitude to our kind host, as well as fear for ourselves forbade our stay; and we resolutely faced the terrors of the midnight storm. What will not a captive endure to gain his freedom? The night was very dark: we therefore ventured to march on the main road to Philadelphia. It should have been mentioned, that before we departed from the house, our host kindly gave us a list of the king's friends who lived in our line of march, the nearest of whom was seventeen miles from his house: we therefore proceeded, notwithstanding the inclemency of the weather, with a degree of spirit animated by hope.

The rain still continued to increase, which in a very short time drenched us to the skin; and, what rendered our journey more distressing, in consequence of the great fall of water, was, that the road was exceeding deep. Our guide also began to murmur at the hardships which he endured: his shoes were almost worn out. Indeed, all our shoes were in a wretched condition. They were so bad that we could scarcely keep them on our feet. We used every suggestion that could possibly encourage him to proceed; but his spirit at last failed, and he declared, that he was unable to go any further with us: adding, with a deep sigh, "Perhaps, after all my hardships, if I should succeed, and get into New York, I shall not get my pardon."

Just as he had pronounced these words, we espied a small hovel on the road side, and a house at a very little distance from it. We therefore, in order to keep him in temper, agreed to shelter ourselves from the storm under this hovel; assuring him at the same time that we would provide him a pair of shoes, and give him the best clothes we had in exchange for his bad ones. We drew near to the house, in order to rest our weary limbs; but, to our great mortification, we were saluted with the roaring and loud grunting of pigs which were in it. We soon found it necessary to march off as fast as we could from our noisy neighbours, lest by their outcries the inhabitants of the house should be alarmed. Thus, circumstanced we were compelled to march on. At last, we came within sight of a large barn. Here we again thought to take shelter, and were again disappointed; for, as we approached nearer, we perceived a light in it.

Our guide began now to lose all his fortitude, declaring once more that he was utterly unable to proceed any further. A large dunghill happened to be behind this barn, and as the last resource to humour our guide, we agreed to rest our limbs on it, and cover ourselves with the loose litter. Here we remained about half an hour, being unable to continue longer, from the effects of the extreme cold. We all felt severe pains in our bones, which were occasioned by the damp of the dung. It therefore became the general resolve to march on and gain our wished-for house, which, from the distance we had already travelled, we judged could not be far off. We were further confirmed in this resolution by the morning breaking fast on us. At this place we arrived about the dawn.

It was a tavern; but, to our unspeakable disappointment, we found that several American officers lodged in the house. Thus circumstanced, we were obliged immediately to proceed to another friend a few miles forward. We now thought it best to quit the great road, and turn off towards Valley-Forge. In the course of our march, we fortunately happened to come to a shoemaker's dwelling, where we got all our shoes repaired, and having supplied our guide with a new pair, and given him our best clothes in exchange for his bad ones, and (above all) having supplied him with plenty of peach-whiskey, wherever we could procure it, he seemed determined for the present, to proceed with us to New York.

In the evening we gained the house to which we had been directed. The lady who inhabited it, was a near relation of General Lee. Both herself and husband were firmly attached to the Royal Cause. The house was situate on the banks of the Schuylkill. Here we halted for two days, during which time we were nobly entertained. At twelve o'clock on the night of the second day the master of the mansion provided a canoe, and sent his servant to put us across the river, giving us the name and place of abode of another friend. We now continued for some days going from one friend to another, still keeping our course towards New York. Early one morning we came to a river, which was very broad but only about four feet deep. In the middle of this river was a small island.

We prepared ourselves to wade over. The morning was exceeding frosty which made the water very cold. Our guide now lost all his resolution. He declared with tears in his eyes "That his heart was almost broken with hardships, that he was sure he would never survive if he waded that river;" and all his fears about his pardon returned in full force upon him. We proposed to carry him over on our backs, to give him half the money we had, and renewed our former promises of interceding for him, and procuring his pardon; but all in vain. He turned about, under great terror, and fled from us. We afterwards were informed, that this unfortunate man was, in the course of a few days, taken up, and the fact being proved, that he was seen conducting four men, supposed to be British soldiers, into New York, he was condemned, and hanged.

When we found it impossible to reclaim our guide, we waded across the river ourselves, and were almost deprived of the power of our limbs when we got on the other side. Our last protector had directed us to another friend, whose house was situate about two miles from this river. We therefore made what haste we could before the day advanced. We gained the hospitable mansion, and were concealed in the barn, and plentifully supplied with provisions. Thus far we had been successful in our enterprise. We were near the Delaware River, about twenty miles above Philadelphia. That river we were to cross in our progress. But in crossing it our protector could give us neither assistance or recommendation. He had no connexion on its shores which he durst trust.

Soon however, as day closed, we set off, and arrived on the banks of the Delaware about nine o'clock the same evening. We boldly ventured into a house to inquire for the ferry-house. Contrary to expectation we were kindly entertained, and informed that we were two miles from it. We remained at this place all night, and proceeded to the ferry-house early in the morning. A number of boatmen had just entered the house before us; they were employed in carrying wood to Philadelphia, and landed there (the house being a tavern) to refresh themselves. They were eight in number, and seemed, by their looks and conversation, to suspect who we were. As soon as we perceived this we called for some refreshment, and appeared cheerful and undismayed.

After some time, they withdrew into an inner room, to consult (as we supposed) how they were to attack and take us. We held a consultation, and were determined to part with our liberty at as dear a rate as we could. Just at this crisis, when we were preparing to act on the defensive, one of our party, said, "Let us seize the ferry-boat; and make across the river." This proposal was immediately agreed to; and, after discharging our reckoning, we sallied out of the house, jumped into the ferry-boat and insisted on the negro, who had the charge of her rowing us across with all expedition. This the terrified man performed with such celerity, that we were, halfway over the Delaware before the alarm was given.

The negro being in the boat with us, prevented their firing on us. We soon pulled to the opposite shore, and ran into the woods, where we were soon secure from all our pursuers, as, we had above a mile and a half the start of them. We lay concealed in the thickest part of the wood that day; and at night proceeded, in quest of a house to which we had been directed. After much search we found it, and were, entertained a few hours, when we proceeded to the abode of another friend.

Such was the benevolent assistance which we received in this part of the country, that an imperative duty forces itself on me, here to notice the malignant assertions of Belsham, (*Memoirs of the Reign of George II. Vol. I*) who says, that when the British troops were retiring to Brunswick, through the Jerseys "the licentious ravages of the soldiery, particularly of the German mercenaries, during the time they were in possession of the Jerseys, had excited the utmost resentment and detestation of the inhabitants;" and that "such havoc, spoil, and ruin, were made by the forces under General Howe's personal inspection and command, as were well calculated to obviate the suspicion that any secret partiality to America yet remained in the breast of the English general.".

To this charge (with the most awful appeal for the verity of my assertion) I can aver, that in all the different places in America, through which I have marched as a soldier, been carried as a captive, or travelled in regaining my freedom, I never found people more strongly attached to the British government, than in the very place where Belsham says, "such havoc, spoil, and ruin, were made by the British forces." This we now experienced in a very great degree. These very inhabitants ventured their own lives to secure ours, and at the risk of their whole property, and the jeopardy of all their relatives and friends gave us the means of safe conduct into New York.

Why Belsham cherished, and on almost every occasion manifested such inveterate malice against our commanders and soldiers in America, is matter of astonishment to me, and I might add, remains matter of mystery to the discerning and loyal part of the public. If the British troops in America had been capable of coolly and deliberately murdering his father, mother, and all his relatives, nay if they had actually perpetrated the horrid deed, he could scarcely have been more rancorous. An historian ought to record the *truth,* and the truth only, whether of friend or foe. The officers who served in the American campaigns were gentlemen (some of them noblemen, or noblemen's sons who have since succeeded to their hereditary titles) of the first families in the empire, for wealth as well as honour. Men who had no earthly temptation to such acts, and whose high spirits independent of that circumstance would have revolted at the bare mention of the atrocities charged on them.

★★★★★★★★★★

I am bold to assert that one British regiment was possessed of more property in gold, silver watches, &c. than was in General Washington's whole army: even the inhabitants were destitute of gold and silver.

★★★★★★★★★★

However, they ultimately failed in accomplishing the reunion of England and America, still it was the grand object of all their toils, both bodily and mental; and they were as far removed from "amassing fortunes by plunder and rapine," (as is asserted) by Ramsay, as Mr. Belsham and Ramsay are from acquiring fame by condor and truth. But to return to my narrative. We now entered into a country, which was full of American troops, and the nearer we proceeded to New York, the more numerous they were. This constrained us to act with great caution and circumspection: we made but short stages among our friends. On the 16th of March, we found ourselves within thirty miles of Staten Island, at which place was the British outposts. Our American friend, in whose barn we lay concealed, advised us strongly to take a guide, which he said he could procure for us.

To this we readily consented, and waited three days for our conductor. The wished-for moment arrived; our guide came, the agreement was made, our friend procured us a bottle of strong spirits, and we set off with our conductor about nine o'clock at night, under the expectation of arriving before morning in the vicinity of Amboy; which town lay opposite Staten Island, being divided only by a river. In two hours march we came to a village which our guide told us we might safely march through, as the inhabitants were all in bed, and no American troops were stationed in it.

"But lest," said he, "I should happen to be seen with you, I will take a circuit and meet you on the great road on the top of the hill, on the other side of the village."

We consented to this plan and marched through the village unperceived, and arrived at the place appointed for meeting; there we remained, expecting our guide every moment; but after remaining two hours we gave up all hopes, and saw clearly that he had given us the slip. It snowed all the time very hard accompanied with a piercing north wind. Our clothes and shoes being all torn, made our situation, while we waited, almost insupportable: we at last came to the resolution of proceeding by ourselves, though we were entirely unacquainted upon what point of the compass Amboy lay. But the stars being rather bright we knew we could not be materially wrong if we proceeded due north.

We marched very hard over a broken uneven ground, sometimes on the road and sometimes through the woods. At four o'clock in the morning one of our companions dropped down and declared with tears in his eyes, he was not able to proceed any farther: the soles of his shoes had been worn off and his feet were all bruised and cut. Indeed, we were all much in the same way. We proposed to carry him by turns till daylight, when we would repose ourselves.

"No," said he, "leave me here to die; for I am quite exhausted: if I live till morning, I will strive to creep to the next house; and if I survive, I will endeavour to follow you."

We were greatly affected at parting with him. To me indeed it was peculiarly distressing, as he was one of the men, I had brought in with me to New York from General Burgoyne's army, and was the man whom I have already mentioned, who understood several languages, and who was of so much service in effecting our escape.

We marched on until the morning when we concealed ourselves

in the woods, until the night came on. During this time, we were without provisions. Soon as the evening set in we prepared as well as we could, for our march. About two o'clock in the morning we perceived a house, on the side of a narrow road, it was unconnected with any other building. Not knowing, where we were, we agreed to stop, and obtain all the information which we could. We rapped at the door, which was quickly opened by an old man, who with his wife were the only persons in the house. Without discovering who we were, we entered into conversation with them both. It came out, during our discourse, that he was a native of Dublin and had left it about thirty years before. Here my being a native of Ireland was of inestimable service to the whole party.

As I could mention several places in Dublin, and many of the transactions which had happened in his time, he became highly pleased with my conversation, and with true native hospitality brought out provisions to entertain his countryman. From several of his answers which he gave to some of the questions which I occasionally, and I may say accidentally, put to him, I perceived he was a loyalist; but being unwilling to commit the whole party, I did not discover to him whom we were. Having gained all the information which we wanted, we left his house.

He had informed us where the American guards were stationed along the banks of the river, who could at all interfere with us, which was only the distance of two miles off. We immediately proceeded towards it, carefully avoiding the American posts. About an hour before daylight, we arrived on its banks, and as soon as morning dawned, we saw with pleasure Staten Island. But a deep and broad river rolled between us and our place of refuge. We wandered up and down the shore in hope of finding a canoe or boat; but in vain.

After a fruitless search for near an hour, the broad appearance of day much alarmed us, as we dreaded lest some of the American sentinels, who were posted along the coast, should discover us. In this dangerous situation, we held a consultation what was best to be done; when it was unanimously agreed to return to my countryman's house, discover who, we were, and throw ourselves upon his protection. We returned, and were not disappointed: we found him to be a staunch loyalist. He observed, "The coast is full of troops I will bring you to a place of concealment."

He then conducted us to a thick, part of a wood, while he went to two friends, who owned a boat, in which we could at night safely cross the river. There we remained until a late hour in the evening, when his two friends, with the boatmen, came to us; and having agreed for our passage, we proceeded to the boat. The river, where we had to cross, was more than three miles, broad.

Our friends informed us, that an English sloop of war was stationed there, in order to intercept the American privateers and other craft, and likewise to keep the coast in alarm. We entered the boat with joy, and put off from the shore. They had not rowed a quarter of a mile, when the wind, which had hitherto been fair for us, changed against us, and blew very fresh. The boat, being very small, made a great deal of water. This greatly alarmed the boatmen; and they immediately made for the shore from whence we came. When we perceived what they were about, we insisted that they should turn the boat, and endeavour to gain the sloop; or, failing in that, row us across to Staten Island. They were greatly alarmed at our resolution; and declared, that it was impossible for a boat to live in that gale of wind; and that we should be all certainly lost, if we persisted in the attempt.

But we were resolved to venture, and peremptorily commanded them to proceed. After beating against the wind and waves for near two hours, and being almost perished with wet and cold, we espied a square-rigged vessel, the boatmen were apprehensive at first that she was an American privateer. However, as our boat was every moment in danger of sinking, we determined to make towards her. As we approached, we were hailed, and ordered to come along side. To our unspeakable joy, we saw British soldiers standing on the deck.

Such was the effect of our sufferings, that we had almost lost the power of our limbs and speech: for when I was ordered down to the cabin to Captain Skinner, to give him an account who we were, I could not articulate a word.

Perceiving my situation, he humanely ordered a large glass of rum to be given me. This soon brought me to my speech, and I then briefly recapitulated to him our whole story. The ship's company being informed that we were British soldiers who had escaped from the Americans, were eager to express their joy. We were ordered the best refreshments the vessel could afford. In the morning we were put on shore on Staten Island, with a letter to the captain's father, Colonel Skinner, who commanded a regiment of Loyal Americans, and who was the commanding officer on Staten Island.

I need not tell the reader what we felt when we were marching across the island, where we considered ourselves perfectly safe within the British lines. We waited on Colonel Skinner, who immediately ordered a boat to convey us to New York. We landed at the wharf, and with cheerful steps marched to headquarters. When the inhabitants, and the soldiers in garrison, understood that we were three sergeants of the Royal Welch Fusiliers, they were struck with astonishment. We had had no opportunity of shaving ourselves for more than three weeks; our shoes were worn out; out clothes all in tatters; our looks wan and meagre. In short so wretched was our appearance, that they commiserated our condition, and with kind attention conducted us to the commander in chief. This was on the 23rd of March, 1782.

Sir Henry Clinton received us with great kindness. We communicated to His Excellency all the information of which we were possessed, which in any manner tended to the good of the service. After this, we were sent to receive the usual bounty, which was given as an encouragement to those soldiers who made good their escape. After the officer who was appointed to pay us had entered my name in the book, he turned his eye to the top of the first page, and said, "Here is the same name of a non-commissioned officer of the 9th Regiment, one of the first who had made his escape from General Burgoyne's army, more than four years ago."

I answered, "I am the man."

On which he replied, "if you are the man, your colonel (Colonel Hill) who was exchanged, and went to England, has left here all your arrears of pay. But," added he, "you must prove that you are the identical person."

This I soon did, as there were officers both of the 9th and 23rd Regiments, who knew me well at that time in New York. In consequence, I received a very considerable sum, which was due to me. I then wrote out this narrative, and presented it to Major Mackenzie, (later Colonel Mackenzie, and Secretary to the Military College, London), deputy quartermaster general. The major recommended me to Brigadier-General Birch, the *commandant* of New York, and I was appointed his first clerk, for which I had a good salary. The major's kindness did not stop there; but through his interest I was made adjutant to the Merchants Corps of volunteers, who were then on permanent duty in the town.

At this place, during two months, I enjoyed a comfortable respite from the hard duty to which I had been accustomed: the only repose, I may truly say, which I had during the eight years I was in America.

Colonel Balfour, having arrived in New York from Charlestown, it being evacuated, ordered to proceed to King's Bridge, the outpost of the British Army, and take charge of the recruits of the 23rd Regiment, who were doing duty there; to which place I repaired accordingly.

The reader will doubtless feel some anxiety for the fate of the party which I left on the banks of the Susquehanna River. These poor fellows, after enduring innumerable hardships, and travelling through the woods for some hundreds of miles, were unfortunately taken prisoners in Pennsylvania, and confined in Philadelphia jail, the foundation of which they undermined, and the whole four came safe into New York, the latter end of April.

Much about the same time, my former companion, whom I had left on the road, likewise arrived at New York, conducted by the last guide, who had divided from us in passing through the village. Thus, though by different routes, the whole party which I took with me from Little York, arrived safe at the British headquarters.

When I reflect on the hardships which I endured, the dangers which I escaped from my first setting out from Gloucester, after our army was taken prisoners, in a march of perhaps not less than one thousand miles, through a wilderness interspersed with swamps, I feel (and senseless must I be if I did not feel it) a degree of thankfulness to that Providence, who, not only preserved my life in several hard fought battles, skirmishes, &c. but also guided my footsteps through those desert tracks, and brought me in safety once more among my friends. It is true, I can state the fact in the language of the great heathen poet:

From the din of war,

Safe I returned without one hostile scar;
Though balls in leaden tempests rained around,
Yet innocent they flew, and guiltless of a wound.

But I must acknowledge, as a Christian, (however I may by some persons be charged with enthusiasm for it) that in all these wonderful events of my past life, I see and adore a higher direction—an arm Omnipotent which has been my safe guard; and penetrated with the recollection of which I may truly say—"O God the Lord, the strength of my salvation; Thou hast covered my head in the day of battle."

CHAPTER 20

The Author's Return, &c.

From the capture of Lord Cornwallis, to the period when the independence of America was acknowledged by the British government, and peace between the two countries concluded, little occurred to interest the reader, except the circumstance of Captain Asgill. (Now, 1809, Lieutenant-General Sir Charles Asgill, Bart. commanding the Eastern District, in Ireland.) As I am in possession, of more accurate information on this subject than most who have written on American affairs, I shall take the liberty of detailing on the facts.

The spirit of political rancour in America had at this period risen to an uncommon height. It raged beyond all bounds. Nor was it possible for the British commanders wholly to restrain the exercise of that retaliation by the Loyalists who fought under them, which was inspired, by the violence of the opposite party, Smith, who wrote from observation and not mere report, thus characterizes this party violence.

The malignity, virulence, and savage barbarity, that, at the above mentioned time, pervaded all ranks, classes, and denominations, whether in the civil or military line, cannot be delineated in any terms, but such as must agonise the heart of sensibility, and cause a blush on the cheek of civilized humanity; and the baneful effects of which were not eradicated so late as the year 1801; when at a place called Ninety-Six, and at Augusta, in Georgia, in a large company, among the gentry of the country, where, it would be supposed, humanity would prevail, were it only through decency, and with a view to example, I heard them boast of having committed barbarities shocking to human nature. One instance was that of an old, grey-headed justice of the peace, who solemnly declared, he had during the war, shot, at different actions, and in cold blood, ninety-nine Tories, (American Loyalists), and felt unhappy he had not accomplished the complete hundred.

At New York an association was formed among the American Loyalists, for the purpose of warfare on the opposite party: but which was abused into a retaliation on the continentals, for the death and sufferings of the king's friends. A block-house in Monmouth County was taken by a party of these, and Captain John Huddy made prisoner. He was conveyed to a prison-ship, lying in the river, near New York, and there kept in close custody fifteen days, and then told "That he was ordered to be hanged." Four days after he was sent out with a party of refugees, and hanged on the heights of Middleton. The following label was affixed to his breast:

"We the refugees having long with grief beheld the cruel murders of our brethren, and finding nothing but such measures daily carrying into execution; we therefore determine not to suffer without taking vengeance, for the numerous cruelties, and thus begin, and have made use of Captain Huddy as the first object to present to your view, and further determine to hang man for man, while there is a refugee existing. Up goes Huddy for Philip White."

Philip White in retaliation for whom Huddy was hanged, had been taken by a party of the Jersey militia, and was killed in attempting to make his escape. (Ramsay.)

Sir Henry Clinton as soon as he was informed of the circumstance of Huddy's execution, ordered a court-martial on the captain who commanded at the transaction; but being superseded in command by Sir Guy Carleton, the court broke up without coming to any determination. The American commander flushed with conquest, was not disposed to await or abide by the judgment of an English court martial, but dispatched the following haughty and indignant letter to Sir Henry Clinton.

Headquarters, April 21st. 1782.

Sir—The enclosed representation, from the inhabitants of the county of Monmouth, with testimonials to the fact, (which can be corroborated by other unquestionable evidence,) will bring before Your Excellency the most wanton, cruel, and unprecedented murder that ever disgraced the arms of a civilized people. I shall not, because I conceive it altogether unnecessary, trouble Your Excellency with any animadversions on this transaction. Candour obliges me to be explicit—to save the innocent I demand the guilty.

Captain Lippencot, therefore, or the officer who commanded at the execution of Captain Huddy, must be given up; or if that officer was of inferior rank to him, so many of the perpetrators as will, according to the tariff of exchange, be an equivalent. To do this, will mark the justice of Your Excellency's character. In failure of it, I shall hold myself justified in the eyes of God and man, for the measures to which I shall resort.

I beg Your Excellency to be persuaded, that it cannot be more disagreeable to you to be addressed in this language, than it is to me to offer it; but the subject requires frankness and decision. I have to request your speedy determination, as my resolution is suspended but for your answer.

 I have the honour to be, &c.

George Washington.

To which His Excellency, General Clinton, returned the following answer:

Sir—Your letter of the 21st instant, with the enclosed testimonials, respecting Captain Huddy's execution, was delivered to me yesterday; and though I am extremely concerned for the cause, I cannot conceal my surprise and displeasure at the very improper language you have made use of, which you could not but be sensible was totally unnecessary.

The mildness of the British Government does not admit of acts of cruelty, or persecuting violence; and as they are notoriously contrary to the tenor of my own conduct and disposition, (having never yet stained my hands with innocent blood) I must claim the justice of having it believed, that if such have been committed by any person under my command, they could not have been warranted by my authority, nor can they have ever the sanction of my approbation.

My personal feelings, therefore, required no such incitements to urge me to take the proper notice of the barbarous outrage against humanity, which you have represented to me, the moment it came to my knowledge; and accordingly, when I heard of Captain Huddy's death, (which was only four days before I received your letter) I ordered a strict inquiry to be made into all its circumstances, and shall bring the perpetrators of it to an immediate trial.

To sacrifice innocence under the notion of preventing guilt, in place of suppressing would be adopting barbarity, and raise it to the greatest height! Whereas, if the violators of the laws of war are punished by the generals under whose powers they act, the horrors which those laws were formed to prevent, will be avoided, and every degree of humanity war is capable of maintained.

Could violations of humanity be justified by example, many from the parts where your power prevails, that exceed, and probably gave rise to this in question, could be produced. In hopes the mode I mean to pursue, will be adopted by you, and prevent all future enormities,

I remain, &c.   H. Clinton.

His Excellency General Washington.

This mild and dignified reply of the British commander, produced no other effect than the immediate selection of one the British officers to be the sacrifice, which was to atone for the death of Captain Huddy. Soon, however, as Sir Guy Carleton arrived, and took on him the command, he dispatched the following letter to General Washington:

Headquarters, New York, 7th May, 1782.

Sir—Having been appointed by His Majesty to the command of the forces of the Atlantic Ocean, and joined with Admiral Digby in the commission of peace, I find it proper in this manner to apprise Your Excellency of my arrival at New York,

The occasion, Sir, seems to render the communication proper, but the circumstances of the present time, render it also indispensable, as I find it just to transmit here with to Your Excellency certain papers, from the perusal of which Your Excellency will perceive what dispositions prevail in the government and people of England towards those of America, and what further effects are likely to follow; if the like pacific dispositions should prevail in this country, both my inclination and duty will lead me to meet them with the most zealous concurrence. In all events, Sir, it is with me to declare, that, if war must prevail, I shall endeavour to render its miseries as light to the people of this continent as the circumstances of such a condition will possibly permit.

I am much concerned to find that private and unauthorised persons have on both sides given way to those passions which ought to have received the strongest and most effectual control, and which have begot acts of retaliation, which without proper preventions, may have an extent equally calamitous and dishonourable to both parties, though, as it should seem, more extensively pernicious to the natives and settlers of this country. How much soever, Sir, we may differ in other respects, upon this one point we must perfectly concur, being alike interested to preserve the name of Englishmen from reproach, and individuals from experiencing such unnecessary evils as can have no effect upon a general decision. Every proper measure that may tend to prevent these criminal excesses in individuals, I shall ever be ready to embrace!

And as an advance on my part, I have, as the first act of my command, enlarged Mr. Levingston, and have written to his father on the subject of such excesses as have passed in New Jersey, desiring his concurrence in such measures, as, even under the condition of war, the common interests of humanity require.

I am further to acquaint you, Sir, that it was my intention to have sent this day a similar letter of compliment to Congress, but am informed it is previously necessary to obtain a passport from Your Excellency, which I therefore hope to receive, if you have no objection, for the passage of Mr. Morgan to Philadelphia, for the above purpose.

I have the honour to be, with great respect, Your Excellency's most obedient humble servant,

Guy Carleton.

To this letter Washington returned a cool and evasive answer, and finally the Congress refused the passport requested.

Perhaps a scene more awful can scarcely be imagined, than a number of military men convened to determine by lot which shall become the victim of political rancour.

Thirteen captains of Lord Cornwallis's army were, by the command of General Washington assembled at Lancaster, in Pennsylvania, to draw lots, one of which contained the mandate of death. Captain Asgill drew the 12th lot, which was the fatal one. The word "*Unfortunate*" was written inside it. The captain that did not draw, who was the owner of the 13th lot, is now the honourable Sir G. J. Ludlow,

K. B. Lieutenant-General and Lieutenant Governor of Berwick. Five minutes were allowed between the drawing of each lot. A dreadful pause of suspense!

Soon after Captain Asgill had drawn the "unfortunate" lot, his friend, Major Gordon of the 80th Regiment, who commanded the British prisoners belonging to Lord Cornwallis's army, wrote to General Washington, soliciting permission to accompany the captain in his confinement. This arose from the most generous of motives, to soothe and comfort him under his misfortune. The major humanely supposed that he must want a friend, more especially when he considered his youth, (as the captain was not at that time seventeen years of age) General Washington answered this letter, by declaring, "that he would not grant the major's request, unless he would submit to all the rigors of confinement and usage, which the captain should receive."

To these terms the major acceded, with the most heroic magnanimity, and voluntarily went into confinement with the captain. No writer on American affairs has recorded this circumstance, which is as exalted an instance of the power of friendship, between two British officers, as can be produced from the most boasted stories of antiquity

It should also have been mentioned, (to the honour of Major Gordon's memory) that when Lord Cornwallis's army surrendered at York Town, a field officer was appointed to remain with the captured troops; and Lieutenant-Colonel Lake (afterwards Lord Lake) was the officer to whom that service was assigned. Here the major gave another instance of friendship, as rare as it was disinterested. Knowing the situation of the colonel's health, and that he had a family in England, he voluntarily submitted to remain prisoner in his room, and take command of the captives.

Captain Asgill was conveyed under a strong guard to the Jerseys. Indeed, it was with General Washington's usual policy (a policy which his advocates ascribed to the purest humanity) that he was sent there. Huddy's friends lived on the spot, and being spectators of the usage Captain Asgill received, they might thereby have ceased their clamours, and even felt something for the innocent victim of retribution.

The officer who guarded him, boasted to him on the road, "that he was a very fortunate officer! for he had had the honour of guarding Major André after he was taken." This must have been very distressing to young Asgill. Indeed, the captain received very bad usage throughout his confinement; he was constantly fed upon bread and water. This hard treatment constrained him to send his faithful servant to New

York, to receive and carry letters for him. This man ran great hazard in passing over the North River into New York:

During Captain Asgill's confinement some letters passed between him and General Washington. The captain pleaded the 14th article of the capitulation of York Town; that it would therefore be the highest breach of faith according to the laws of nations that he should suffer death: this article, which the captain alluded to, contains the following sentence:—

> No article of the capitulation shall be violated under presence of *reprisals;* and if it should contain any doubtful expression, it shall be interpreted according to the ordinary sense and tenor of words.—Granted.

To this strong plea General Washington replied, that on several occasions during the war the British commanders had broken many articles of capitulation, he therefore would not be bound, by one solitary article.

This was most erroneous reasoning in so great a man. Is recrimination a proof of innocence or integrity? It amounts merely to this:

> Others have committed many wrongs, I have therefore a right to commit one.

This was justifying evil by the perpetration of evil.

Captain Asgill had frequent opportunities of making his escape into New York; his whole guard (so greatly was he beloved by them) offered to come in along with him, if he would provide for them in England. Although these offers must have been very tempting to a prisoner, under sentence of death! yet he scorned to comply, as it would have involved more British officers in trouble. He nobly said, "As the lot has fallen upon me, I will abide by the consequence."

Meantime General Washington wished to hurry on the execution of Captain Asgill; but that wise general, Sir Guy Carleton (afterwards Lord Dorchester) delayed sending the determination of the court martial, which sat on Captain Lippencot, to the American general. This he did in order to give time to Captain Asgill to send home word to his father and mother, to make speedy application to the King and Queen of France and Count Vergennes, to use their powerful intercession with Washington for his life. At last General Carleton, after delaying the report of the court martial on Captain Lippencot as long as he could, transmitted intelligence to General Washington, that he was acquitted.

★★★★★★★★★★

It appeared in the course of this trial that Governor Franklin, the President of the Board of Associated Loyalists, gave Lippencot verbal orders for what he did, and that Huddy had been designated as a proper subject for retaliation; having been, as the refugees stated, a persecutor of the loyalists, and particularly as having been instrumental in hanging Stephen Edwards, who had been one of that description. The court having considered the whole matter, gave their opinion, "That, as what Lippencot did was not the effect of malice or ill-will, but proceeded from a conviction that it was his duty to obey the orders of the Board of Directors of Associated Loyalists, and as he did not doubt their having full authority to give such orders, he was not guilty of the murder laid to his charge, and therefore they acquitted him"—*Ramsay's American Revolution*.

★★★★★★★★★★

The reception of this intelligence decided the doom of young Asgill, and he prepared to die. He wrote to his family "that before they would receive that letter he should be no more." His parents, although they knew that letters from the Court of France were sent to America to save their son's life, imagined that they had arrived too late. Concluding that he had suffered, the whole family went into mourning for him. The reader must already know, that during this period, Lady Asgill had applied to Count Vergennes. Her letter contains so much of all that is endearing in maternal feeling that I am induced to transcribe it.

Sir—If the politeness of the French court will permit the application of a stranger, there can be no doubt but one in which all the tender feelings of an individual can be interested, will meet with a favourable reception from a nobleman, whose character does honour, not only to his own country, but to human nature. The subject, Sir, on which I presume to implore your assistance, is too heart piercing for me to dwell on; and common fame has, most probably, informed you of it; it therefore renders the painful task unnecessary.

My son (an only son) as dear, as he is brave, amiable as he is deserving to be so, only seventeen, a prisoner under articles of capitulation at York Town, is now confined in America, an object of retaliation. Shall an innocent suffer for the guilty? Represent to yourself, Sir, the situation of a family under these circumstances: surrounded as I am, by objects of distress; distracted with fear and grief; no words can express my feeling, or paint the scene.

My husband given over by his physicians a few hours before the news arrived, and not in a state to be informed of the misfortune: my daughter seized with a fever and delirium, raving about her brother, and without one interval of reason, save to hear heart aggravating circumstances. Let your feelings, Sir, suggest and plead for my inexpressible misery. A word from you, like a voice from heaven, will save us from distraction and wretchedness.

I am well informed General Washington reveres your character; say but to him you wish my son to be released, and he will restore him to his distracted family, and give him back to happiness. My son's virtue and bravery will justify the deed. His honour, Sir, carried him to America. He was born to affluence, independence, and the happiest prospects.

Let me again supplicate your goodness; let me respectfully implore your high influence on behalf of innocence, in the cause of justice, of humanity, that you would, Sir, dispatch a letter to General Washington, from France, and favour me with a copy of it, to be sent from hence. I am sensible of the liberty I take in making this request; but I am sensible, whether you comply with it or not, you will pity the distress that suggests it: your humanity will drop a tear on the fault, and efface it. I pray that Heaven may grant you may never want the comfort it is in your power to bestow upon,

Asgill.

The French minister, moved by so pathetic an appeal, interceded with General Washington; however, before his letter arrived, the determination of the British court-martial, on Captain Lippencot was received, and young Asgill was ordered for execution. In "The very lucky minute of his fate," the letter from the minister of France arrived, (of which the following is a copy) and he was pardoned. Its elegance, as a literary composition, stands almost unrivalled, and its delicate adaption to all the characteristic feelings of the American commander is such, as to speak no common interest in the life of Captain Asgill.

Sir—It is not in quality of a king, the friend and ally of the United States, (though with the knowledge and consent of His

Majesty) that I now have the honour to write to Your Excellency. It is as a man of sensibility, and a tender father, who feels all the force of paternal love, that I take the liberty to address to Your Excellency my earnest solicitations, in favour of a mother and family in tears. Her situation seems the more worthy of notice on our part, as it is to the humanity of a nation, at war with her own, that she has recourse for what she ought to receive from the impartial justice of her own generals.

I have the honour to enclose to Your Excellency a copy of a letter which Lady Asgill has just wrote to me. I am not known to her, nor was I acquainted that her son was the unhappy victim, destined by lot, to expiate the odious crime that a formal denial of justice obliges you to revenge. Your Excellency cannot read this letter without being affected; it had that effect upon the king and queen to whom I communicated it. The goodness of Their Majesties' hearts induces them to desire, that the inquietudes of an unfortunate mother may be calmed, and her tenderness re-assumed. I feel, Sir, that there are cases where humanity itself exacts the most extreme rigor; perhaps the one now in question may be of the number: but allowing reprisals to be just, it is not less horrid to those who are the victims; and the character of Your Excellency is too well known, for me not to be persuaded that you desire nothing more than to be able to avoid he disagreeable necessity.

There is one consideration, Sir, which, though it is not decisive, may have an influence on your resolution. Captain Asgill is, doubtless your prisoner, but he is among those whom the arms of the king contributed to put into your hands at York Town. Although this circumstance does not operate as a safe guard, it however justifies the interest I permit myself to take in this affair. If it is in your power, Sir, to consider and have regard to it; you will do what is very agreeable to their majesties. The danger of young Asgill, the tears, the despair of his mother, affect them sensibly; and they will see with pleasure the hope of consolation shine out for those unfortunate people.

In seeking to deliver Captain Asgill from the fate which threatens him, I am far from engaging you to seek another victim; the pardon to be perfectly satisfactory, must be entire. I do not imagine it can be productive of any bad consequences. If the English general has not been able to punish the horrible crime you complain of, in so exemplary a manner as he should, there is reason to think he will take the most efficacious measures to prevent the like in future.

I sincerely wish, Sir, that my intercession may meet success, the sentiment which dictates it, and which you have not ceased to manifest on every occasion, assures me that you will not be indifferent to the prayers, and to the tears of a family which has recourse to your clemency through me. It is rendering homage to your virtue to implore it. I have the honour to be, with the most perfect consideration,

De Vergennes."

The pardon of Captain Asgill was sent to him in the following letter from General Washington, enclosing the act of Congress by which it was granted.

Copy of an order of Congress releasing Captain Asgill, by the United States in Congress assembled, Nov. 7, 1782.

On the report of a committee, to whom was referred a letter of the 19th of August, from the commander in chief, a report of a committee thereon, and motion of Mr. Williamson and Mr. Rutledge relative thereto, and also another letter of the 25th of October from the commander in chief, with a copy of a letter from the Count de Vergennes, dated the 29th of July last, interceding for Captain Asgill.

Resolved, that the commander in chief be directed, and he is hereby directed, to set Captain Asgill at liberty.

Copy of a letter from General Washington to Captain Asgill, covering the above resolve.

Headquarters, November 13, 1782.

Sir—It affords me singular pleasure to have it in my power to transmit you the enclosed copy of an act of Congress of the 7th instant, by which you are released from the disagreeable circumstances in which you have so long been. Supposing you would wish to go into New York as soon as possible, I also enclose a passport for that purpose.

Your letter of the 18th of October, came regular to my hands; I beg you to believe, that my not answering it sooner, did not proceed from inattention to you, or a want of feeling for your situation. I daily expected a determination of your case; and I thought it better to await that, than to feed you with hopes that might in the end prove fruitless. You will attribute my detention of the enclosed letters, which have been in my hands about a fortnight, to the same cause.

I cannot take leave of you, Sir, without assuring you, that in whatever light my agency in this unpleasing affair may be received, I never was influenced through the whole of it, by sanguinary motives, but by what I conceived a sense of my duty, which loudly called upon me to take measures, however disagreeable, to prevent a repetition of those enormities, which have been the subject of discussion; and that this important end is likely to be answered, without the effusion of the blood of an innocent person, is not a greater relief to you, than it is to, Sir, your most obedient, and humble servant,

George Washington.

In consequence of the passport transmitted to Captain Asgill by General Washington, he gained New York, from whence he sailed for England; and arrived but a very few days after his mother received his last letter. He thought it prudent not to go immediately to her ladyship; but sent the captain of the ship, gradually to prepare her for an interview. Lady Asgill was so overwhelmed with grief, at the supposed death of her son, that she would see no stranger. She shut herself up from almost every visitant. The captain of the ship knocked at the door, and requested to see Lady Asgill. He was answered, that she saw no person, (the captain's father was in the country.)

"Tell her," said the captain, "I am just arrived from New York, and that I have lately seen her son; and perhaps things are not so bad as she imagines."

The captain was admitted to see her; his mission was soon disclosed; and the mother and son meet once more a meeting which I will not attempt to describe, and which none but those who, to their utmost extent, have experienced the parental and filial ties can imagine.

Lady Asgill with her son and family went over to France personally, to thank the king and queen, and Count Vergennes; previous to which Her Ladyship wrote the following letter to the count, a translation of which I subjoin.

Epuisée par de longues souffrances, suffoquée par un excès de bonheur inattendu, retenue dan mon lit par la foiblesse & par la langueur, anéantie enfin, Monsieur, au dernier degré, il n'y a que mon extrême sensibilité qui puisse me donner la force de vous écrire. Daignez accepter,

Monsieur, ce foible effort de ma reconnoissance. Elle a été mise aux pieds du tout-puissant, & croyez moi, elle a été présentée avec la même sincérité, à vous, Monsieur, & à vos illustres souverains; c'est par leur auguste & salutaire entremise, ainsi que par la vôtre, que moyennant la grace de Dieu, j'ai recouvré un fils à la vie, auquel la mienne étoit attachée. J'ai la douce assurance que mes veux pour mes protecteurs & pour vous, sont entendus du ciel, à quí je les offre. Oui, Monsieur, ils produiront leur effet vis-à-vis du redoutable & dernier tribunal où je me flatte que vous et moi nous paroîtrons ensemble, vous pour recevoir la récompense de vos vertus, moi celle de mes souffrances. J'éleverai ma voix devant ce tribunal imposant.

Je réclamerai ces gistres saints où l'on aura tenu note de votre humanité. Je demanderai que les bénédictions descendent sur votre tête, sur celui qui, par le plus noble usage du privilége qu'il a reçu de Dieu, (privilége vraiment céleste) a changé la misère en félicité, a retiré le glaive de dessus la tête d'un innocent, & rendu le plus digne fils à la plus tendre & à la plus malheureuse des mères.

Daignez agréer, Monsieur, ce juste tribut de reconnoisance que je dois à vos sentimens vertuex. Conservez-le, ce tribut, & qu'il passe jusqu'à vos descendans, comme un témoignage de votre bienfaisance sublime & exemplaire envers un étranger dont la nation étoit en guerre avec la vôtre, mais dont la guerre n'avoit point détruit les tendres affections.

Que ce tribut atteste encore la reconnoisance longtems aprés que la main qui l'exprime aura été réduite en poussiére, ainsi que le coeur qui dans ce moment-ci, ne respire que pour donner l'explosion à la vivacité de ses sentimens; tant qu'il palpitera, ce sera pour vous offrir tout le respect & toute la reconnoisance dont il est pénetré.

Therese Asgill

TRANSLATION.

Exhausted by long sufferings, overcome by an excess of unexpected happiness, detained in my bed by weakness and languor; in short, humbled before God to the last degree, it is only, Sir, my extreme sensibility that can give me strength to write to you. Deign to accept, Sir, this feeble effort of my gratitude. It has been placed at the feet of the Almighty, and believe me, it has been presented with the same sincerity to you, Sir, and to your illustrious sovereigns; it is by their august and salutary interposition, joined to yours, that under the influence of divine grace, I have recovered a son to life, to whom mine was attached. I have the sweet assurance, that my vows for my protectors, and for you, are heard in heaven, by him, to whom I offer them.

Yes, Sir, they will produce their effect, before that last and formidable tribunal, where I flatter myself, that you and I shall appear together, you in order to receive the reward of your virtues; I, that of my sufferings. I will raise my voice before that commanding tribunal, I will *sue* for those holy registers, where your humanity shall have been noted down. I will ask, that blessings may descend upon your head, upon him, who by the most noble use of the privilege that he has received from God, (a privilege truly celestial) has changed misery into felicity, has withdrawn the sword from the heart of an innocent person, and restored the most worthy son, to the most tender and agonised of mothers.

Deign to receive kindly, Sir, this just tribute of gratitude, that I owe to your virtuous sentiments; preserve this tribute, let it pass to your descendants, as a testimonial of your exemplary and sublime beneficence towards a stranger, whose nation was at war with yours, but which war had not destroyed the tender affections. May this tribute still attest that gratitude a long time after the hand which expresses it shall have been reduced to dust, as well as the heart which at this moment breathes only to give vent to the energy of its sentiments. So long as it shall palpitate, it will be in order to offer you all the gratitude and respect with which it is penetrated.

Terese Asgill.

★★★★★★★★★★

The following are the reflections of a French writer who had occasion to publish the letters. They are placed in the work from whence they are copied, introductory to the letter itself, and may serve to shew the sentiment which at that time prevailed in France on Captain Asgill's situation.

"Do you not think that the unfortunate Lady Asgill, in the agonies arising from so cruel an expectation, had raised her maternal hands to Heaven a hundred times a day. She remained dumb at the first rumour of her son's deliverance. O my Readers, you would know the affecting facts! She was expiring her heart was dried up, her voice was dying away, the tomb was half open before her. Her son lives, she knows it, a consolatory report has resounded in her ears. I ought to be silent, she is going to speak, she is going to write to that humane minister, who has restored her son to her: she is going to soften him again by her gratitude."

****

I shall conclude this account of Captain Asgill's providential escape, with an extract taken from the *Hibernian Magazine* for 1782, (this article was written when the news arrived here that Captain Asgill was to die); which may serve to shew what was the prevailing opinion of the day relative to that officer.

Captain Asgill is only seventeen years of age, a captain in the first Regiment of foot guards, and only son of Sir Charles Asgill, Bart. possessed of every virtue that can endear him to his family or acquaintance, and in the last campaigns in America, has given sufficient earnest of a spirit and conduct under the different commands, (which have devolved on him by the illness or absence of his senior officers,) that would render him an honour to his profession and country.

General Washington expressed deep concern, when he was informed the unhappy lot had fallen on this worthy young gentleman, so well-known to him by his bravery and humanity in different instances, particularly when the command devolving on him by the illness of his colonel, he took a post from the Americans, commanded by Colonel Gregory, who being old and wounded, be supported him himself, with an awful and tender respect most filial, evincing the true greatness of his amiable mind.

At length in 1792, preliminaries of peace were signed betwixt Spain, France, America, and Great Britain.—Thus ended a contest, which dismembered England of far more than half her territory; but how far her commerce, or her local interests as a nation, were affected by it is a point which I presume not to determine. Various and contradictory have been the opinions of the most profound politicians, concerning it. This work being merely a *Journal* of events (most of which passed under my own immediate observation) during the war, it may with far more propriety, than the investigation of such a subject, terminate with my own return to my native land.

I sailed from Sandy Hook on the 5th of December 1783, and on the 17th of January, 1784, landed at Portsmouth with the 23rd Regiment: from that place we marched to Winchester, where I requested my discharge. At that time, I had very great privileges allowed me in the army, and was making money fast; but peace being proclaimed through all Europe, I thought it my duty to come home to my friends in Dublin, after an absence of near twelve years, during which time I had served my country to the best of my power. Colonel Balfour, who commanded the regiment (well knowing that I was making money in my situation,) kindly and humanely reasoned with me, in order to prevail on me to remain in the army: but seeing my determination was fixed, he signed my discharge, and I marched up to London with a number of my companions, in order to pass the board.

When the board sat, I was considered as too young to receive the pension; and likewise, that I had not been long enough in the service. It is true, the general officers who composed the board at that time were unacquainted with me; and besides, as nothing was mentioned in my discharge but the time of my servitude, and "that I was discharged," they could not possibly be aware of the nature and extent of my services, or the claims which I possessed on the bounty of my sovereign.

Lieutenant Calvert, (later Major-General and Adjutant General of the British Forces), of the 23rd being then in London, I communicated my disappointment to him. He was sorry for me; and said, "Anything that lies in my power I will do for you." He advised me to remain in London until another board would sit; but I was determined not to wait. Lieutenant Calvert was well acquainted with me; we had served together in America for some years; I have frequently had the honour of obeying his command, and of fighting by his side in many battles and skirmishes. Even twenty-five years after these services, he was not unmindful of me; for when I took the liberty of writing to him in September 1808, he kindly answered the letter, and renewed his former acts of friendship by recommending me to the duke of York.

Attachments of persons in the army to each other terminate but with life, the friendship of the officer continues with the man who has fought under his command, to the remotest period of declining years, and the old soldier venerates his aged officer far more than perhaps he did in his youthful days: it is like friendship between schoolboys, which increases in manhood, and ripens in old age.

I left London on the 15th of March, and landed in Dublin on the 19th, to the inexpressible joy of an aged mother, two sisters, and other relations, who had long given up every hope that I was alive.

Since that period, I have been frequently asked by various friends to whom I related the circumstances of the Battle of Guildford Court House, why I did not apply to Marquis Cornwallis for some situation, when Lord Lieutenant of Ireland, in the year 1798? My answer was, and is, that at that time I had a young family, and was moreover tolerably well settled. I knew His Excellency would have recognised me immediately, as I had been employed by him during the campaign to write the duplicates of his dispatches. A commission in a marching regiment would most probably have been my reward, which I could not have accepted, from the state of my health as well as the reasons assigned.

However, to the honour of Lord Cornwallis, it should be mentioned, that when in America His Lordship did not forget the service which I rendered him. A few days after the Battle of Guildford Court House, I was ordered to mount guard over the prisoners which we had taken at that battle. Among them was an American captain who had committed various depredations on the loyal inhabitants of the country.

This man was particularly mentioned to me, by the provost marshal. I was ordered to be very careful that he should not make his escape, for Lord Cornwallis was apprehensive he might murder and destroy the inhabitants, whom he knew had assisted us in our march. Unfortunately, he bribed one of my sentries, who permitted him to effect it. When the circumstance was made known to His Lordship, he was highly displeased, and command the sergeant of the guard to be brought before him, in order to be confined. But when I was approaching towards him, his countenance changed into a smile, and he directed his *aide-de-camp* to tell me to go to my regiment, and to confine the sentinel who had permitted the captain to get out of confinement.

Having thus brought this volume to a conclusion, I have only to solicit the indulgence of the candid, and the protection of the loyal reader. My wish has been to state *facts* as I knew they happened, in opposition to that tissue of falsehood, which but too many writers have produced on the subject. To elegance of composition, I prefer no claim; but I think, on such matters as the revolution of governments, it is the duty of every man to let the present and the future ages know those *truths* with which he is acquainted, and not to lock them up in his own breast, until the grave closes on all communication, and buries them in oblivion forever.

If any circumstances have been misrepresented, accident and not intention was the cause. Since the fourth number of this work was printed, the author has been informed, that General Matthews, whose murder by Tippoo Saib he relates, was not the General Matthews, who so gallantly assisted in the reduction of Fort Washington. That brave officer was never in the East Indies; but immediately after the termination of the American War, he went to the West Indies, was appointed Governor of St.Vincent, and remained in that island many years.

He died a full general in the service. In the account of the Battle of Camden, particular mention ought to have been made of the 33rd Regiment. The services which they rendered on that day, were long the theme of the soldiers and officers present.

Thus, under the assistance of the Almighty, has this account been brought to a period. It has not been unattended by many impedimental circumstances. The heavy duties of a crowded school frequently compelled the author to break in on the hours of rest, in order to finish the narrative. This produced sickness, an alarming sickness, that at one time seemed to threaten life itself. Providence in mercy spared the author; but it was to consign a son (a beloved child!) to the grave. Amidst personal and family afflictions, therefore has this *Journal* been finished. Had the author been more at his ease, it might in some points, perhaps, have been better executed. But it would be superfluous in him again to press on the reader's attention, that the flowers of literature are not to be expected from an old soldier, whose only object in the publication was the unfolding of truth in defence of his country's honour, and the humanity of her officers.

Free School, Whitefriar-Lane, June 26, 1810

A Brief History of Lamb's Regiments During the American War of Independence

Richard Cannon

In the spring of 1777, the Ninth Foot were selected to form part of the force under the orders of Lieut.-General Burgoyne, for the purpose of forcing a passage from Canada to Albany. Fifty men of the regiment were left in Canada for the defence of that province; and five hundred and fifty embarked, under Lieut.-Colonel John Hill, on board the flotilla on Lake Champlain. After a pleasant voyage of several days, they landed at Crown Point, where they halted a short period, and were formed in brigade with the Twenty-First and Forty-Seventh Regiments, under Brigadier-General Powell.

From Crown Point the troops moved forward to invest the fort of Ticonderago, situate on the western shore of Lake Champlain, a few miles from the narrow inlet which unites Lakes George and Champlain. On the 3rd of July the regiment was in position at Mount Hope, where it was exposed to a cannonade from the American batteries. As the British environed the fort, the garrison evacuated it and made a precipitate retreat.

This conquest achieved, the regiment repaired on board the flotilla and pursued the Americans towards Skenesborough. About three o'clock on the afternoon of the 6th of July, the ships *Royal George* and *Inflexible*, with the best sailing gunboats, arrived within three miles of the enemy's stockaded fort at Skenesborough, when the Ninth, Twentieth, and Twenty-First Regiments leapt on shore, and ascended the mountain with great alacrity, to gain the rear of the fort and cut off the enemy's retreat; but as the soldiers were climbing the hill, the Americans were alarmed, and, setting fire to the fort and magazines, fled with such precipitation that they escaped the British regiments: about thirty men were intercepted and made prisoners. Another body

GRENADIER OF THE 9TH FOOT

of the enemy was pursued towards Castletown, and, being overtaken, a sharp fight occurred, in which the Americans sustained a severe loss.

On the 7th of July, the Ninth were detached in pursuit of a party of the enemy retreating by Wood Creek, and marching along difficult roads, and pausing rivulets, where the bridges had been broken, the regiment took post near the enemy's station at Fort Anne. At this place the regiment passed the night, and on the 8th of July, it was attacked by very superior numbers of the enemy. The two other regiments of the brigade were sent to its aid, and the twentieth were ordered forward with two field pieces.

A violent storm of rain which lasted the whole of the day, prevented the troops from getting to Fort Anne so soon as was intended; but the delay gave the Ninth Regiment an opportunity of distinguishing itself, by standing and repulsing an attack of six times its number. The enemy, finding the position not to be forced in front, endeavoured to turn it, and from the superiority of their numbers, that inconvenience was to be apprehended. Lieut.-Colonel Hill, found it necessary to change his position in the height of action. So critical an order was executed by the regiment with the utmost steadiness and bravery.

The enemy after an attack of three hours, were totally repulsed, and fled towards Fort Edward, setting fire to Fort Anne; but leaving a sawmill and a blockhouse in good repair, which were afterwards possessed by the King's troops. The Ninth Regiment acquired during the expedition, about thirty prisoners, some stores and baggage, and the colours of the Second Hampshire Regiment. Captain William Stone Montgomery, an officer of great merit, was wounded early in the action, and was in the act of being dressed by the surgeon when the regiment changed ground; being unable to help himself, he and the surgeon were taken prisoners. (*Journal* of Lieut.-General Burgoyne.)

The gallant conduct of the Ninth, on this occasion, was commended in orders; the repulsing of an enemy six times as numerous as themselves, and capturing the colours of one of the opposing regiments, were held up to the admiration, and for the example, of the army. Their loss was Lieutenant Richard Westropp, one sergeant, and 11 rank and file killed; Captain Montgomery wounded and taken prisoner; Lieutenants James Murray, Joseph Stevelly, Adjutant Isaac Fielding, and 19 rank and file wounded.

In the skirmish on the 7th of July, Captain Francis Samuel Stapleton, of the grenadier company, was mortally wounded, and several private soldiers were killed and wounded.

After this success, preparations were made for a forward movement towards the Hudson's River; but this was a work which required time and labour: fallen trees, stones, and other obstacles, having to be removed from Wood Creek. The Americans retreated without hazarding an engagement; but the country to be passed was covered with obstructions. Large forest trees had been cut so as to fall across the roads, and their removal took up much time; creeks and marshes had to be crossed; forty new bridges had to be constructed, others had to be repaired, and one made of log-work crossed a morass two miles in extent.

The soldiers, emulous of enterprise, and in high spirits, overcame these difficulties with cheerful alacrity, and on the 30th of July, the army arrived at the banks of the Hudson's River. Having taken post at Fort Edward, the troops were obliged to halt; great difficulty was experienced in bringing up provision, and the soldiers began to experience many hardships, at the same time the enemy's numbers were increasing, and the British diminishing.

On the 13th and 14th of September, the army crossed the Hudson's River, and encamped on the heights and plains of Saratoga. On the 19th it advanced towards the enemy's position on the island of Still-Water, some sharp fighting occurred, which lasted until dark, when the Americans, who had evinced firmness and intrepidity, retreated from the field. The Ninth were in reserve on this occasion, and did not sustain any loss.

The British lay on their arms all the night on the field of battle; and the Canadian Indians, who formed part of the force, deserted in a body and went back to their own country. Although thus weakened, the army continued to confront the enemy, who was becoming more superior in numbers every day. In vain the few British who had thus daringly pushed forward into the heart of a hostile country, looked for the expected co-operation of other armies; environed by crowds of opponents; cut off from supplies of provision, their situation became perilous, and they were placed on half allowance of food. A retreat was become the only means of preservation, and this was almost impracticable.

Fifteen hundred men moved against the enemy's posts on the left, to facilitate a retrograde movement, but they were forced to retreat with loss, and the Americans carried the entrenchments occupied by the German troops which formed part of the Allied Army. To avoid being surrounded, the army fell back to Saratoga, and the Americans pressing forward, nearly enveloped the British. A resolution to abandon the artillery and endeavour by a night march to gain Fort Edward, could not be carried into execution, the Americans having gained possession of the roads.

Numerous skirmishes occurred in which the Ninth took part, and they evinced firmness and intrepidity, but the strength of the soldiers was diminished by incessant toil and a scarcity of provision. The regiment had Lieutenant James Wright and about 10 men killed; Major Gordon Forbes, behaved with great gallantry, and was twice wounded; Captain George Swettenham and about 20 men were also wounded; and Captain J. Money was taken prisoner.

The climax of difficulty and danger had arrived; only three thousand five hundred men remained able to bear arms; they were nearly exhausted, their provisions were expended, and they were environed by sixteen thousand Americans. Under these dismal circumstances, the British concluded a convention with the American General, (Gates); and laid down their arms, on condition of being sent to England, and they engaged not to serve again in North America during the war. Lieut.-Colonel Hill of the Ninth, being anxious to preserve the colours of the regiment, took them off the staves, and concealed them in his baggage, which he was permitted to retain.

The American Government violated the conditions of the convention, and detained the troops until 1781, when the Ninth proceeded to England, and Lieut.-Colonel Hill producing the colours, presented them to King George III., who rewarded his faithful services with the appointment of *aide-de-camp* to His Majesty, and the rank of colonel in the army.

On the death of Lieut.-General Earl Ligonier, King George III. appointed Colonel Thomas Lord Say and Sele, from Major in the First Foot Guards, to the Colonelcy of the Ninth, his commission bearing date the 19th of June, 1782.

In August, of the same year, county titles were conferred on the several regiments of foot, to facilitate the procuring of recruits, and this corps was designated the Ninth, or East Norfolk Regiment of Foot.

In the summer of 1773, the Royal Welsh Fusiliers (Fuzileers) embarked at Plymouth for North America, and disembarked at New York on the 14th of June.

SOLDIER OF THE 9TH FOOT

In the following year, 1774, the regiment was removed to Boston, where, in consequence of an anticipated outbreak by the Americans, a strong military force had been assembled under the command of General Gage.

During the winter a firm determination of resistance to the acts of the mother-country became general in the American States; and on the 19th of April, 1775, the Royal Welsh Fusiliers were engaged in the first hostile collision that took place between His Majesty's troops and the colonists, in the unhappy contest which was soon to assume a most formidable character. Information having been received that the Americans were forming a considerable depot of military stores at a place called Concord, about twenty miles from Boston, a detachment, consisting of the flank companies of the army, was despatched under the command of Lieutenant-Colonel Francis Smith, of the Tenth Regiment, for the purpose of destroying it.

Though the greatest secrecy had been observed in the preparations for the expedition, and the detachment marched with the utmost caution, they soon perceived, by the ringing of bells, the firing of guns, &c., that the country was alarmed; and, on arriving at Lexington, about fifteen miles from Boston, they found a considerable body of people assembled under arms. These dispersed in confusion on the approach of the detachment; some shots were exchanged, though it does not seem certain which party was the first to fire. One soldier and several of the Americans were killed. The detachment continued its march to Concord, where a strong party of the militia of the country was found posted on an eminence at the entrance of the town; these were attacked and dispersed by the light infantry, not without further loss on both sides, while the grenadiers carried into execution the purpose of the expedition, by destroying the stores.

In the affair at Lexington, the regiment had four rank and file killed; Lieutenant-Colonel Benjamin Bernard, and twenty-six rank and file, wounded.

By this time the alarm was spread far and near; and an immense multitude appeared, who opposed the return of the detachment to Boston, by keeping a galling fire on its front, flanks, and rear, under cover of the houses, hedges, and walls, which lined the road; the colonists displaying, at this early stage of the contest, that skill in this species of warfare, by which they were subsequently so much distinguished. Thus harassed, the detachment reached Lexington, where it met another detachment, consisting of the remaining eight companies of the Royal Welsh Fusiliers, and the same number of the Eighth Regiment, which had been sent to its support under the command of Colonel Earl Percy.

These formed a square, under protection of which the wearied soldiers of Colonel Smith's detachment took some rest and refreshment, the first since leaving Boston: so much were they exhausted, that they are described in Stedman's *History of the American War*, as "having their tongues hanging out of their mouths like those of dogs after a chase." Both detachments soon resumed their march, still harassed by the Americans, till they arrived at Boston about sunset.

The British force amounted in all to about eighteen hundred men, of whom seventy-one were killed, one hundred and thirty-six wounded, and forty-nine missing; the loss of the Americans is stated by themselves at about sixty, of whom two-thirds were killed.

On the 11th of May, 1775, His Majesty was pleased to appoint Major-General the Honourable Sir William Howe, K. B. (from the Forty-Sixth Regiment), to be Colonel of the Twenty-Third Royal Welsh Fusiliers, in succession to Lieutenant-General the Honourable George Boscawen, deceased.

Boundless was the exultation of the Americans at the result of this unhappy affair—they talked of nothing but driving the king's forces out of Boston; the militia poured in from all quarters, till twenty thousand men were assembled under commanders who had acquired some military experience as militia officers. This formidable force was even still further increased, and a line of encampment was formed thirty miles in extent, enclosing Boston in its centre. At the same time the provincial congress was busily employed, in framing regulations and providing equipments, which should give to their forces some semblance of a regular army. Meanwhile the British troops were kept blockaded in Boston, their numbers being considered inadequate to any hostile operations, though about the beginning of June reinforcements arrived from England with Major-General the Honourable Sir William Howe, which placed the army on a more respectable footing as to numbers than it had hitherto been.

Separated from the peninsula of Boston by the River Charles is the peninsula of Charlestown, in the centre of which rises an eminence called Bunker's Hill, which commands the whole of Boston. This eminence, General Gage, owing probably to the insufficiency of his force, had not occupied; but the Americans perceiving the advantages of the position, formed the hardy design of taking possession of it, which they soon executed with singular skill. As soon as it was dark, on the evening of the 16th of June, a strong body moved with great precaution across Charlestown Neck, and gained unobserved the summit of the hill. Being provided with the necessary tools, they commenced throwing entrenchments, with such order and silence, that before morning they had completed a considerable line well flanked, and in many places cannon-proof.

The first alarm was given by the fire of some of the men-of-war, by which the peninsula was nearly surrounded; this was soon followed by that of the batteries of Boston. About noon of the 17th of June, a detachment from Boston was landed at Charlestown, and soon after a reinforcement, which increased the whole to two thousand. These, under cover of the artillery, advanced to attack the works: the Americans, with the steadiness of veterans, kept close behind their entrenchments, and reserved their fire till the near approach of their enemy, when they poured it in with such effect, that the British ranks were literally mowed down, and the soldiers forced to recoil in several places.

Rallied by their officers, and stung by the reflection of having been repulsed by an enemy whom they held in contempt, they again mounted to the assault, with such impetuosity that they forced their way over the entrenchments, driving the colonists from them at the point of the bayonet. The success was complete; the Americans fled with precipitation; but the reduced and exhausted state of the victors did not admit of a pursuit.

The casualties of the day amounted to about one-half of the numbers engaged, being two hundred and twenty-six killed, and eight hundred and twenty-eight wounded; among the former nineteen, and among the latter seventy officers. Of this severe loss, the Royal Welsh Fusiliers, eager to distinguish themselves the first time they were engaged under the immediate eye of their colonel, Major-General the Honourable Sir William Howe, appear to have borne their full proportion. No return has been preserved of the casualties of the regiment generally; but the grenadier company went into action with three officers and forty-six rank and file, and returned with five effective; the rest were all killed or wounded.

★★★★★★★★★★

Journal of Captain Julian, one of the surviving veterans of the day. If it may be permitted to quote a work of fiction as an authority, it may be observed, as a confirmation of the severe loss of the regiment, that the celebrated American novelist, J. Fennimore Cooper, in his

ROYAL WELSH FUZILEER, EARLY 1750's

work entitled *Lionel Lincoln* after describing the Battle of Bunker's Hill, states, "*The Welsh Fusiliers had hardly men enough left to saddle their goat;*" and after alluding to the keeping of a goat, with gilded horns, by the regiment, adds, "*that the corps was distinguished alike for its courage and its losses.*"

Mrs. Adams, in a letter to her husband John Adams Esq. (afterwards the second President of the United States), dated 25th June, 1775, has thus alluded to the Battle of Bunker's Hill:—

"But in the midst of sorrow we have abundant cause of thankfulness, that so few of our brethren are numbered with the slain, while our enemies were cut down like grass before the scythe. *But one officer of all the Welsh Fusiliers remains to tell his story.*"—*Letters of Mrs. Adams.*

★★★★★★★★★★

The loss of the Americans is estimated by themselves at one hundred and forty-six killed, and three hundred and four wounded.

After the Battle of Bunker's Hill nothing of importance was attempted on either side; the besieged and besiegers remained in a state of equal inactivity, till the commencement of 1776, when General Washington began to carry on his operations with more vigour, in the hope of reducing Boston before the arrival of some expected reinforcements from England. Among the besieged, the slow but sure effects of the long blockade began to show themselves; provisions were scarce, and a supply could not be procured, and the men were worn out with incessant toil.

On the 2nd of March, two batteries opened their fire on the town with such effect, that Major-General Sir William Howe, who had succeeded to the command, soon became sensible that nothing now remained but to evacuate the place. Accordingly, the garrison, and such of the inhabitants as adhered to the cause of the mother-country, were embarked, and conveyed to Halifax, in Nova Scotia.

The troops having recovered from the sickness and fatigue produced by the blockade of Boston, Sir William Howe sailed for Staten Island, near New York, where he landed on the 2nd of July, and was joined by considerable reinforcements from England. On the 4th of July, the American Congress issued their Declaration of Independence, abjuring their allegiance to the Crown of Great Britain, and all hope of accommodation failed. Shortly afterwards another body of troops arrived from the southern provinces, commanded by Major-General Sir Henry Clinton, and the operations of the campaign commenced on the 22nd of August, by the army crossing over to Long Island, where the Americans had raised a strong line of defence across a narrow neck of land, near Brooklyn, for the protection of New York, which it commanded.

The Americans were soon compelled to retire to their works, which the British Commander prepared to attack in form; this was no sooner perceived by the enemy than he resolved to abandon his lines, which he was sensible were incapable of resisting a regular attack. This resolution was carried into effect on the 29th of August, with extraordinary secrecy and good order—an army of nine thousand men being transported from New York, with all its cattle, artillery, and stores, without the loss of a single individual. Early in September the British crossed over to New York Island, and soon after took possession of New York without opposition.

After a series of movements and skirmishes, which terminated with the Battle of White Plains, on the 28th of October, the Americans were driven from all their positions in York Island, with the exception of the important fort of Fort Washington, which kept open the communication with the Jerseys: this place was reduced on the 16th of November, the garrison of 2,500 men surrendering prisoners of war. The Royal Welsh Fusiliers, having assisted in all these operations, went into winter quarters on New York Island.

On the 12th of April, 1777, the regiment embarked, under command of Major-General Tryon, and proceeded to Norwalk Bay, in Connecticut, where it landed. From thence it marched about twenty miles, to Danbury, and destroyed the magazines of warlike stores belonging to the enemy. The following day the troops marched to Ridgefield, where the Royal Welsh Fusiliers had an opportunity of distinguishing themselves, being attacked by very superior numbers, stationed to protect very large magazines of military stores of every description, which were burnt, after the Americans had been defeated and dispersed. (*Journal* of Lieutenant-General Sir Thomas Saumarez, then a lieutenant in the Twenty-Third Royal Welsh Fusiliers.)

The intention, for which the expedition had been undertaken, having been fully accomplished, the British troops returned to embark, when they were constantly harassed and attacked, night and day, by a very superior force of the enemy; particularly when they came in sight of their ships, they saw more than three times their own numbers, drawn up in a very advantageous position, with the intention of disputing their passage. After much manoeuvring on the part of the British, they at length attacked the Americans with the bayonet, and totally defeated them, with great loss in killed and wounded. While the embarkation was proceeding, a strong party of the enemy, under General Arnold, attacked a British regiment with so much vigour as to make it give way.

Upon this the Royal Welsh Fusiliers were ordered by Brigadier-General Erskine, Quartermaster-General of the army, to charge; this they did, after firing a volley so effectually, aided by the other regiment, which had rallied, that, after killing and wounding a great number of the Americans, the latter dispersed, and did not fire another shot, but allowed the rear-guard to embark without further molestation.

In this expedition the regiment had five rank and file killed; second Lieutenant Edward Price, one serjeant, and eighteen rank and file wounded.

The Royal Welsh Fusiliers received the particular thanks of Brigadier-General Erskine, and of the other general officers, for their gallant conduct on this and every other occasion since they disembarked: after this the troops returned to New York.

Early in June the commander-in-chief crossed over with the army, to Staten Island, and subsequently to New Jersey. He, however, found General Washington's position at Middlebrook too strong to be attacked with any prospect of advantage, and every scheme to draw that cautious officer from his fastnesses having proved unavailing, Major General the Honourable Sir William Howe returned to Staten Island on the 20th of June, and on the 24th the Royal Welsh Fusiliers were again in New York.

Having failed in his attempt to penetrate to Philadelphia through the Jerseys, Sir William Howe now resolved to embark the army, and to arrive at that place by sailing up the Delaware. The troops destined for this service, among which were the Royal Welsh Fusiliers, embarked on the 21st of July, and sailing two days afterwards, arrived on the 30th off the Capes of the Delaware. Here, in consequence of information that the enemy had taken means that would render the navigation of the Delaware extremely dangerous, the commander-in-chief altered his plans, and proceeded to the Chesapeake, where he arrived about the middle of August: on the 25th, the Royal Welsh Fusiliers disembarked at Elk Ferry, in Pennsylvania. The army marched for Philadelphia, the enemy retiring, and taking up a position on the opposite side of the Brandywine, of which he determined to dispute the passage.

The able disposition of the British general, and the valour of his troops, however, prevailed, and on the 11th of September, after a sharp contest, the Americans were driven into the woods in their rear, where they took up a second position, from which they were also dislodged and completely routed. The Americans suffered severely in this action, having three hundred killed, six hundred wounded, and four hundred taken prisoners; the British loss was one hundred killed and three hundred wounded. Captain Thomas Mecan, of the regiment, was wounded in this action.

On the 20th of September another body of the Americans, under General Wayne, was completely routed by a detachment, commanded by MajorGeneral Charles (afterwards Earl) Grey, who, in pursuance of a system which he afterwards strongly inculcated on his army in the West Indies, commanded that not a shot should be fired, but the bayonet only should be used; the surprise was, in consequence of this precaution, most complete, and the slaughter of the enemy dreadful, at the expense to the English of one officer killed, and seven men killed and wounded.

On the 26th of September, Lieut.-General Sir William Howe advanced to Germantown, and, on the following day, Lieut.-General Earl Cornwallis took possession of Philadelphia The first object of the British Commander, after the occupation of the town, was to open a communication with the fleet, by removing the obstructions which the enemy had contrived to the navigation of the Delaware; large detachments were made for this and other services, which considerably reduced the main body of the army stationed at Germantown, an important post about seven miles from Philadelphia. General Washington, who was apprised of this circumstance, conceived the moment favourable for an attack on Germantown.

He accordingly moved from his encampment on the evening of the 3rd of October, and on the morning of the 4th, under cover of a dense fog, commenced a vigorous assault on the British outposts, which were driven into, the, village, while the Americans advanced in separate columns, with the view of at once penetrating the centre of the position, and attacking it on both flanks. Their designs were, however, frustrated by the gallantry of the fortieth regiment, which occupied a large stone house, in which it maintained itself, and checked the advance of the enemy till the whole of the British line had formed.

The action was kept up with considerable obstinacy for some time, but the thickness of the fog preventing the combination of the several attacks of the enemy, he was repulsed, and, under cover of the fog, withdrew, with all his artillery. The regiment was not engaged in any

A Soldier of the Royal Welsh Fuzileers c1750-1776

other operations during this winter, which it passed in Philadelphia, but it shared in some very severe duty at the reduction of the forts on the Delaware below the city.

In the spring of 1778, Lieut.-General the Honourable Sir William Howe returned to England, and resigned the command of the army to Lieut.-General Sir Henry Clinton, who decided on evacuating Philadelphia, and returning with the army to New York. The evacuation was effected on the 18th of June, when the army was transported, with its baggage, provisions, and stores, to the Jerseys, in the boats of the fleet. General Washington having received intelligence of the design, had despatched messengers to various points, with orders to collect all the troops that could be assembled, to harass and obstruct the British army on its march.

After a variety of movements on both sides, Sir Henry Clinton arrived on the 27th of June, at a place called Freehold, where, judging from the appearance of more numerous parties of the enemy, that a serious attack was meditated, he encamped in a very strong position.

The night passed without any hostile movement on the part of the enemy, and in the morning Sir Henry Clinton conceiving that the vast convoy of baggage, with which he was encumbered, would be the object of attack, despatched it at an early hour, escorted by General Knyphausen's division, himself following at some distance with the rest of the army. The rear-guard, composed of the flank companies, understood Lieut.-General the Earl Cornwallis had not proceeded, for when near Monmouth Court-House, a vastly superior body of the Americans made its appearance under Generals Lee and the Marquis Lafayette.

The British immediately commenced their dispositions for attacking them, but ere these were completed, the Americans retired to a rising ground in their rear. Sir Henry Clinton still resolved to engage, with the view of compelling the enemy to recall some parties that were advancing on the flanks of the army in pursuit of the baggage. The attack was made with such vigour, notwithstanding the exhausted condition of the men from the severe heat of the weather, that the Provincials were forced to give way, and were only saved from a total rout by the arrival of General Washington with the main body of his army.

The flank companies of the Royal Welsh Fusiliers distinguished themselves on this occasion; particularly the right flank company, which received the warmest thanks of Brigadier-General Sir William

Medows, who commanded the grenadier brigade; that company had one-third of its officers and men killed and wounded: among the latter was Captain Thomas Wills, who had his thigh carried away by a cannon shot, of which he died a few days after; he was assisted off the field by his subaltern, Lieutenant Saumarez. After this affair the army continued its march unmolested to Sandy Hook, from whence it was conveyed to New York on the 5th of July.

About this period the French King having taken part in the contest, a powerful fleet under the Count D'Estaing arrived on the coast of America, and appeared off the harbour of New York. The British Admiral, Lord Howe, though inferior in force, made such preparations for their reception, that the French thought it prudent to withdraw to Rhode Island, whither His Lordship resolved to go in pursuit of them. On this occasion, the Fifty-Second Regiment was ordered to serve on board the fleet as marines, but the Royal Welsh Fusiliers, desirous of paying a compliment to the brother of their colonel, volunteered their services, which were accepted, and the regiment embarked on the 2nd of August

The fleet was prevented, by contrary winds, from sailing before the 6th, and on the 9th, it arrived off Rhode Island, where a part of the hostile fleet was discovered at anchor, the remainder had gone up a river. Lord Howe immediately made the signal to prepare for action, and bore down to the attack; unfortunately, however, when almost within gun-shot of the enemy, the wind all at once became contrary, and the admiral was obliged to put back. On the following day, the French fleet was observed coming out of the harbour, and forming in line of battle; Lord Howe having manoeuvred unsuccessfully to gain the weather gage, at length resolved to attack the enemy without that advantage. But just as the fleets were nearing each other, so furious a tempest arose, that both were so completely dispersed, that, on the following morning, no two ships were in sight of each other.

A general engagement was thus prevented, but three encounters afterwards took place between single ships of the hostile fleet, which terminated most honourably to the British arms. On the evening of the 15th, the *Renown,* of fifty guns, fell in with the *Languedoc,* of ninety guns, Count D'Estaing's flagship, and attacked her so vigorously, that the French Admiral was every moment expected to strike his colours, when, unfortunately, six of the enemy's ships hove in sight, and compelled the gallant Captain Dawson to desist. On the same evening, Captain Hotham, in the *Preston,* also of fifty guns, engaged the *Tennant,* of eighty guns, with every prospect of success, when night put an end to the contest, which he was prevented from renewing in the morning by the appearance of the French fleet.

On the 16th, Captain Raynor, of the *Isis*, another fifty-gun ship, fell in with the *Caesar*, seventy-four, and engaged her in so spirited a manner, and with so much advantage, that she put before the wind, and sailed away, leaving the *Isis* so disabled in her masts and rigging, as to be unable to pursue. The loss of the *Isis* was only one man killed, and fifteen wounded, while that of the *Caesar* amounted to fifty, and her keel was so much damaged, that she was obliged to put into Boston harbour to refit.

The regiment disembarked at New York on the 4th of September, when Admiral Lord Howe was pleased to present:

> His most particular thanks to the officers and soldiers of the three companies of the Royal Welsh Fusiliers for their spirited and gallant behaviour on board the ships that had engaged the enemy, and to the whole regiment for its conduct during the time it served on board the fleet.

On the 27th of May, 1779, the regiment embarked with a part of the army, and sailed up the River Hudson to East Chester and Vereplanks, when it assisted at the taking of Fort Lafayette, and other fortified places, which the Americans had constructed there and at Stony Point. Soon after it proceeded on another expedition, under Major-General Tryon, to Newhaven, in Connecticut, a great rendezvous for American privateers. The troops landed, and having demolished the batteries that had been erected to oppose them, destroyed several ships, and a vast quantity of naval stores.

From Newhaven they proceeded to Fairfield, where they destroyed the stores, and reduced the town itself to ashes; Norfolk also shared the same fate, as did also Greenfield, a small seaport in the neighbourhood. The detachment then returned to New York, having, during an absence of not more than nine days, occasioned prodigious losses to the Americans,

On the 20th of September, the regiment embarked, with a strong detachment of the army, under Lieut.-General the Earl Cornwallis, and sailed under convey of Admiral Arbuthnot's fleet, with the intention of invading the whole of the French West India Islands. In consequence, however, of information received from an English frigate, that a greatly superior French fleet was within a few days' sail, the British fleet put back, and made all sail for New York, where the troops disembarked.

Towards the end of this year, the Commander-in-Chief, Lieut.-General Sir Henry Clinton, having resolved to carry the war into the southern provinces, embarked with a great part of the army, in which were the Royal Welsh Fusiliers, and sailed for Charlestown, in South Carolina. After a tedious and tempestuous voyage, during which some of the transports were lost, the troops disembarked, on the 12th of February, 1780, at North Ediston, on St. Johns Island, about thirty miles from Charlestown. So great were the obstacles encountered by the army in its advance, that it was the 29th of March before the commander-in-chief, having established the necessary posts to preserve his communication with the sea, crossed the River Ashley, and established himself on Charlestown Neck. This interval had been diligently employed by the Americans in strengthening and improving the defences of the town, which were, however, too much extended for the numbers of the garrison.

On the 1st of April, the British Army broke ground within; eight hundred yards of the works, and, on the 8th, the guns were in battery; on the 10th, Sir Henry Clinton and Admiral Arbuthnot, who had passed the outer defences of the harbour, summoned the town to surrender to His Majesty's arms, but the Governor, General Lincoln, declaring it was his determination to defend it to the last extremity, the batteries opened, and the fire of the enemy's advanced works was soon observed to slacken.

General Lincoln had been expecting supplies and reinforcements; but these, by the activity of Lieut.-General the Earl Cornwallis and Lieut.-Colonel Tarleton, were intercepted. A considerable body of militia and cavalry, that was marching to the relief of the town, was totally routed by these officers, who now crossed the Cooper River, and completed the investment of the place. Meanwhile the second and third parallels had been completed, and a second summons had been answered by proposals which were deemed inadmissible.

The batteries of the third parallel now opened on the town; the works were pushed to the very edge of the ditch, and preparations for an assault were in progress, when the terrified inhabitants presented a petition to General Lincoln, praying him to accept the proffered conditions. A flag of truce was sent out, and the articles of capitulation, which had before been rejected, were agreed to on the 11th of May, a circumstance highly honourable to the humanity of Sir Henry Clinton, considering the extremities to which the place was reduced. Great quantities of ordnance and military stores were taken in Charlestown, and several French and American ships were captured, or destroyed. The loss of the British during the siege was seventy-six killed, and one hundred and eighty-nine wounded. Soon after the surrender of Charlestown, Sir Henry Clinton returned to New York, leaving Lieut.-General Earl Cornwallis with four thousand men in South Carolina; to this part of the army the Royal Welsh Fusiliers were attached. As the season was unfavourable for active operations, the little army was distributed in cantonments, securing the frontiers of the province, the Welsh Fusiliers at Camden, with some others corps under Lord Rawdon. The Americans, however, were not disposed to leave the British in quiet possession of South Carolina; and, during the month of July, various parties, moving from different points, assembled under the command of General Gates, and entered the province. The British outposts were also called in, and united at Camden.

On the 15th of August, General Gates being at Rugeley's Mills, about twelve miles distant, Earl Cornwallis, who had arrived at Camden from Charlestown two days before, got his little band under arms about midnight, and marched with the intention of surprising and attacking him. At the same hour the American general moved from his ground with similar intentions, and about three o'clock in the morning of the 16th the advanced guards met. Some shots were exchanged, but the firing soon ceased, as if by mutual consent, and both armies lay on their arms till daylight. The ground, on which they had thus accidentally met, was a small sandy plain, with some straggling trees; some swampy ground on the flanks of the British narrowed the field of action, and made the numerical superiority of the enemy of less consequence.

Each army was drawn up in two lines; the right division of the first line of the English was composed of a small corps of light infantry, the Twenty-Third, and Thirty-Third Regiments, commanded by Lieut.-Colonel James Webster of the Thirty-Third. Observing a movement on the enemy's left, which appeared to be with the intention of making some alteration in their order, Earl Cornwallis directed Lieut.-Colonel Webster to begin the attack, which was done with great vigour, and in a few minutes the action became general along the whole front.

The enemy's left, which was composed of Virginia militia, soon gave way, thus leaving that flank of their army uncovered; on this, the Royal Welsh Fusiliers and light infantry, instead of pursuing the fugitives, wheeled up to their left, and falling on the exposed flank, materially contributed to the success of the day. Lieut.-General Earl Cornwallis re marked:

> Our line continued to advance with the cool intrepidity of experienced British soldiers, keeping up a fire, or making use of the bayonet, as opportunities offered.

After an obstinate resistance of three-quarters of an hour, the Americans were thrown into complete disorder, and forced to fly from the field in the utmost confusion. The cavalry pursued, and made about one thousand prisoners.

The army by which this victory was achieved did not exceed two thousand men, of whom not more than fifteen hundred were British or regulars, the remainder were militia or refugees; the American force was computed at six thousand, of whom eight or nine hundred were killed or wounded; the loss of the British was two hundred and thirteen. The Twenty-Third Regiment had six rank and file killed; Captain James Drury, and seventeen rank and file wounded. Seven pieces of artillery, all the enemy had, one hundred and fifty waggons, laden with ammunition, provisions, &c., and several stands of colours, fell into the hands of the victors.

Earl Cornwallis having awaited at Camden the arrival of some necessary supplies from Charlestown, set out on the 8th of September on an expedition, which he had long meditated, for the reduction of the province of North Carolina. Towards the end of the month His Lordship removed to Charlotte, where he halted and established a post. As the army depended entirely for subsistence on the country through which it marched, several mills in the neighbourhood of Charlotte were occupied by detachments in order to be preserved for the purpose of grinding corn for the troops. At one of these (Polk's Mill) a small detachment was posted, commanded by Lieutenant Guyon, of the regiment, a very young man. The Americans made an attack upon the mill with a very superior force, but were repulsed. Lieutenant Guyon's conduct was highly applauded. (Stedman's *History of the American War*, vol. ii.)

Here Earl Cornwallis received the intelligence of the defeat and destruction of the detachment of Major Ferguson; and as this disaster left the western frontiers of South Carolina exposed to the incursions of the enemy, His Lordship found himself under the necessity of returning to protect the loyal inhabitants of that province. On this march the army was exposed to the greatest privations, being frequently two days at a time without sustenance.

> For five days they were supported on Indian corn, which was collected as it stood in the fields—five ears was the allowance for two soldiers for twenty-four hours. (*Ibid.* The author was Commissary to the army.)

At this period, and for several months after, the army was without tents, bivouacking in the woods, under torrents of rain, while at every step the soldier sunk over the shoes in mud.

On the 29th of October, the troops arrived at Wynesborough, a convenient station for supporting two of the most important posts, Camden and Ninety-Six, where Earl Cornwallis halted to await the junction of reinforcements from New York, with whose assistance His Lordship would be able to resume his operations in North Carolina.

On the 17th of January, 1781, the British cause in North America suffered a severe blow in the defeat of a detachment under Lieut.-Colonel Tarleton, at Cowpens.

Earl Cornwallis, hoping to retrieve in some measure the disaster, by recovering the numerous prisoners made by the enemy on this unfortunate occasion, commenced the most vigorous pursuit of General Morgan, by whom the blow had been struck. To expedite the movements of the army, orders were issued for the destruction of all superfluous baggage; these were obeyed with the most rigid exactness: the soldiers, emulating the example of their Commander, destroyed even the spirits without a murmur. By extraordinary exertions the army reached the Fords of Catawba on the 29th of January, only two hours after the passage of General Morgan, having on this march suffered even greater hardships than on that from Charlotte to Wynesborough.

> The troops had to ford one or more rivers or creeks daily or nightly, and had to march generally all night, without any wine or spirits to drink, having destroyed all they had, and that without having ever been recompensed for so doing.

A heavy fall of rain during the night rendered the Catawba impassable for the next two days, and enabled General Morgan to disencumber himself of his prisoners, whom he despatched under an escort of militia, by a different route from that which he proposed to follow himself. On the 1st of February, the river having so far subsided as to be fordable, Earl Cornwallis made his dispositions for crossing during the night. A portion of his small force was detached to make a feint at a public ford called Beakies, while His Lordship marched with the remainder to a private one, called McGowans. The fires on the opposite side soon made it evident that this ford had not escaped the vigilance of the enemy; it was, nevertheless, determined to proceed with the enterprise, and the column entered the river, which was five hundred yards wide, and reached to the men's middles. The head of the column had not got half way over when the enemy's piquets were alarmed, and commenced firing. Sir Thomas Saumarez says:

> The current was so strong, that the officers and men were obliged to fasten to each other, otherwise they must have been carried down the river and perished. The bottom was rocky and uneven, and the enemy firing from the opposite bank all the time the troops were crossing. Notwithstanding all these difficulties, they made good their landing, and immediately attacked and dispersed the Americans. General Davidson was killed, and several of the enemy bayoneted.

Captain James, of the Royal Welsh Fusiliers, was wounded.

The enemy now fled with a precipitation that again baffled the most active pursuit, and crossed the Yadkin, where the British were again detained by a sudden rising of the river. Earl Cornwallis now endeavoured, by a circuitous route, to cut off the enemy's communication with Virginia; but in this design His Lordship was also frustrated by the excessive rains and the swollen state of the rivers.

The Americans were, however, driven from North Carolina, and Earl Cornwallis retired to Hillsborough, in that province, where he hoisted the Royal Standard, and invited the people to join him; but provisions becoming scarce in the neighbourhood, His Lordship was under the necessity of making a retrograde movement, and the enemy re-entered the province. Earl Cornwallis advanced to meet them, but General Green, who now commanded the American Army, declined a battle, till, being joined by strong reinforcements, he at length made a stand at Guildford Court-House. The British General seeing, with much satisfaction, that the long-wished-for opportunity of bringing his antagonist into action had arrived, put his little army in motion early on the morning of the 15th of March.

Sir Thomas Saumarez says:

About one o'clock, the action commenced. The Royal Welsh Fusiliers had to attack the enemy in front, under every disadvantage, having to march over a field lately ploughed, which was wet and muddy from the rains which had recently fallen. The enemy, greatly superior in numbers, were most advantageously posted on a rising ground, and behind rails. The regiment marched to the attack under a most galling and destructive fire, which it could only return by an occasional volley. No troops could behave better than the regiment and the little army did at this, period, as they never returned the enemy's fire but by word of command, and marched on. with the most undaunted courage.

When at length they got within a few yards of the Americans' first line, they gave a volley, and charged with such impetuosity, as to cause them to retreat, which they did to the right and left flanks, leaving the front of the British troops exposed to the fire, of a second line of the enemy, which was formed behind brushwood. Not being able to attack in front, the fusiliers were: obliged to take ground to their left to get clear of the brushwood. They then attacked the enemy with the bayonet in so cool and deliberate a manner, as to throw the Americans into the greatest confusion, and disperse them.

After this the Royal Welsh attacked and captured, two brass six-pounders, having assisted in the attack and defeat of the third line and reserve of the Americans. Such men of the Fusiliers and Seventy-First as had strength remaining were ordered to pursue the dispersed enemy. This they did in so persevering a manner, that they killed or wounded as many as they could overtake, until, being completely exhausted, they were obliged to halt, after which they returned as they could to rejoin the army at Guildford Court-House,

This action was unquestionably the hardest, and best-contested, fought during the American war. The Royal Welsh Fusiliers had about one-third of the officers and soldiers killed or wounded.

Earl Cornwallis, in his official account of the battle, thus characterises his troops:

The conduct and actions of the officers and soldiers that compose this little army, will do more justice to their minds than I can by words. Their persevering intrepidity in action, their invincible patience under the hardships and, fatigues of a march of above six hundred miles, in which they have forded several large rivers, and numberless creeks, many of which would be considered large rivers in any other country in the world, without tents or covering from the climate, and often without provisions, will sufficiently manifest their ardent zeal for the honour and interests of their sovereign and their country.

The victory at Guildford was gained by one thousand four hundred and forty-seven men over an army computed at seven thousand; the loss of the victors was ninety-three killed, and four hundred and thirteen wounded, a large deduction from so small a force. Unfortunately, too, many of the wounded perished on the night that succeeded the, action, as the great extent of ground on which it was fought, rendered it impossible to collect them all under shelter from the torrents of rain which continued to fall.

This brilliant and dearly-purchased success was followed by no beneficial results; the army could not be subsisted in that part of the country, and Earl Cornwallis was under the necessity of retiring to Wilmington. General Green now penetrated into South Carolina, and caused so much apprehension for the detached posts in that province, that Earl Cornwallis, with the view of drawing him off, marched into Virginia. At Petersburgh His Lordship; was joined, by a detachment from New York under General Arnold. From Petersburgh the army marched to Richmond and Williamsburgh, destroying everywhere vast quantities of tobacco and other produce, in which the wealth of the colonists consisted.

At this period seventy men of the Royal Welsh Fusiliers, under the command of Captain Forbes Champagne, were mounted, and detached with Colonel Tarleton to surprise the General Assembly of the State of Virginia, which was sitting at Charlotteville. This novel service they performed very efficiently, for they charged through a river into the town, took prisoners seven members of the Assembly, and destroyed one thousand stand of arms, and a great quantity of gunpowder, tobacco, &c.

While at Williamsburgh, Earl Cornwallis received instructions from Lieut.-General Sir Henry Clinton to detach a considerable portion of his force to New York, where Sir Henry expected to be attacked by General Washington. Earl Cornwallis, conceiving that he should not be able to maintain himself at Williamsburgh with the remainder of his army, resolved to march the whole to Portsmouth, where the detachment was to embark for New York. For this purpose, it was necessary to pass the River James, and while the army was thus engaged in doing so, on the 6th of July, the Marquis de la Fayette, who served as a volunteer in the American Army, came up, expecting to cut off the rear-guard after the main body should have crossed.

Earl Cornwallis, aware of his intention, made his dispositions such, that the *marquis* supposing that there was only a small body opposed to him, advanced briskly, driving in the piquets, which had been instructed to draw him on. The whole line was, however, under arms, and gave the enemy so warm a reception, that night alone saved them from total destruction; as it was, they lost three hundred in killed, wounded, and prisoners.

It soon became evident that the preparations of General Washington, which had caused so much apprehension for New York, were in reality directed against the army in Virginia. Earl Cornwallis's situation was indeed becoming most hazardous; General Washington, with eight thousand American troops, and the Count de Rochambeau, with an equal number of French, were rapidly approaching to surround him by land, while the French fleet was preparing to blockade him by sea. His Lordship selected York Town, at the mouth of the River York, as the best post for at once securing his own troops, and the ships by which he was attended. The army arrived at York Town in the month of August, and immediately commenced fortifying the place. The Royal Welsh Fusiliers were directed to construct a redoubt on the right flank, and in advance, having a ravine between it and the town, and were informed by Earl Cornwallis, that this post was to be entrusted to them to defend.

On the 28th of September, the combined French and American Army made its appearance, and Earl Cornwallis having the same evening received assurance of speedy succour from Sir Henry Clinton, withdrew his troops from the outer works, which were, on the following day, occupied by the enemy, and the place completely invested.

On the 6th of October the enemy opened the first parallel, and on the 9th, their batteries commenced firing on the British left; other batteries, fired at the same time against a redoubt, advanced over the creek upon the British right, and defended by one hundred and twenty men of the Twenty-Third Regiment and marines, who maintained that post with uncommon gallantry, (Lord Cornwallis's despatch); soon after three thousand French grenadiers, all volunteers, made a vigorous attempt to storm the right advanced redoubt, and were repulsed by only one hundred and thirty officers and soldiers of the Royal Welsh Fusiliers, and forty marines; two other attempts were also made by the French to storm the redoubt, which were also unsuccessful. (Sir Thomas Saumarez.)

On the night of the 14th October the enemy established the second parallel, and as it was evident that the half-ruined works of the town could not stand many hours against its fire, a sortie was determined on. This was made on the morning of the 16th, by a party of three hundred and fifty men, who gallantly forced their way into two of the batteries that were in the greatest state of forwardness, spiked the guns, and killed about one hundred of the enemy. This success was, however, of little avail, the guns having been hastily and imperfectly spiked, were soon restored, and before evening were fit for service. Not a gun could be shown on the works of the town, and the shells were nearly all expended; no alternative, therefore, remained, but to surrender, or attempt to draw off the garrison by the Gloucester side of the river, on which there was only a small French force, which could be easily overpowered.

The latter alternative was decided on, and some large boats were, on other pretences, ordered to be in readiness at night. In these a detachment of the army, including a part of the Royal Welsh Fusiliers, embarked, some reached the opposite side, but at this critical moment, the weather, from being calm and moderate, changed to a most violent storm of wind and rain, and drove all the boats, some with troops on board, down the river. Fortunately, they were all enabled to return in the course of the forenoon, but the design of drawing off the garrison was completely frustrated. Meanwhile the enemy's batteries had opened at daybreak; the defences were crumbling into ruins, and were already assailable in more than one point.

Under these circumstances, Earl Cornwallis, unwilling to expose his men to the carnage of an assault, which could not fail of success, made proposals for a capitulation on the 17th. The terms were adjusted on the following day, and on the 19th the articles were signed; and so, terminated the services of the Royal Welsh Fusiliers in the American war, though not ingloriously. Earl Cornwallis, in his official account of the siege, observed:

> The detachment of the Twenty-Third Regiment and marines, in the redoubt of the right, commanded by Captain Althorpe

(Twenty-Third), and the subsequent detachments commanded by Lieutenant-Colonel Johnstone, deserve particular commendation.

Sir Thomas Saumarez adds:

> For the gallant defence made by the troops which defended the right redoubt, they received the particular thanks of Earl Cornwallis, and also the most flattering testimonies of approbation from the general officers of the army, for their persevering and intrepid conduct during the siege, and on all former occasions.

Even the French general officers, after the termination of the siege, gave the Royal Welsh Fusiliers their unqualified approbation and praise, for their intrepidity and firmness in repulsing the three attacks made by such vastly superior numbers on the redoubt, and could not easily believe that so few men had defended it.

The combined army, including militia, amounted to twenty thousand men, while the garrison, on the day previous to the surrender, mustered five thousand nine hundred and fifty rank and file, of whom, however, only four thousand and seventeen were reported fit for duty. Lieutenants Mair and Guyon, of the Royal Welsh Fusiliers, were killed during the siege.

By the terms of the capitulation, the garrison surrendered prisoners of war, but the officers were permitted to return to Europe on parole, and to retain their private property; the colours of the regiment were thus saved, by Captain Peter and another officer wrapping them round their bodies. (The late Lieutenant-General Peter. Captain Julian's *Journal*.)

On the 29th of October, 1781, Captain Saumarez, who was appointed to attend the regiment during its captivity, marched from York Town with half the garrison, and on the 15th of November arrived at Winchester, in the back settlements of Virginia, where the soldiers were confined in barracks, surrounded by a stockade.

On the 12th of January, 1782, the regiment marched from Winchester, through the state of Maryland to Lancaster in Pennsylvania, a long and severe march, during which several of the soldiers were frost-bitten. Here, on the 2nd of June, 1782, Captain Saumarez was one of the thirteen British captains who were compelled to draw lots for their lives.

At this period King George III., having been induced to concede the Independence of the United States, hostilities ceased, and on the 30th of November, 1782, the preliminary Articles of Peace were signed at Paris by the commissioners of the King of Great Britain, and those of the American Congress.

The preliminaries of the treaties between England, France, and Spain, were signed at Versailles on the 20th of January, 1783. St. Lucia was restored to France; also, the settlements on the River Senegal; and the city of Pondicherry in the East Indies. France relinquished all her West India conquests, with the exception of Tobago. Spain retained Minorca (which she had captured in the previous year), and also West Florida; and East Florida was ceded in exchange for the restitution of the Bahamas to Great Britain.

In May, 1783, the regiment quitted Lancaster, and 1783 joined the British Army in Staten Island, and in January, 1784, embarked for England, and was stationed in the United Kingdom during the ten following years.

LEONAUR

ALSO FROM LEONAUR

AVAILABLE IN SOFTCOVER OR HARDCOVER WITH DUST JACKET

THE FALL OF THE MOGHUL EMPIRE OF HINDUSTAN *by H. G. Keene*—By the beginning of the nineteenth century, as British and Indian armies under Lake and Wellesley dominated the scene, a little over half a century of conflict brought the Moghul Empire to its knees.

LADY SALE'S AFGHANISTAN *by Florentia Sale*—An Indomitable Victorian Lady's Account of the Retreat from Kabul During the First Afghan War.

THE CAMPAIGN OF MAGENTA AND SOLFERINO 1859 *by Harold Carmichael Wylly*—The Decisive Conflict for the Unification of Italy.

FRENCH'S CAVALRY CAMPAIGN *by J. G. Maydon*—A Special Correspondent's View of British Army Mounted Troops During the Boer War.

CAVALRY AT WATERLOO *by Sir Evelyn Wood*—British Mounted Troops During the Campaign of 1815.

THE SUBALTERN *by George Robert Gleig*—The Experiences of an Officer of the 85th Light Infantry During the Peninsular War.

NAPOLEON AT BAY, 1814 *by F. Loraine Petre*—The Campaigns to the Fall of the First Empire.

NAPOLEON AND THE CAMPAIGN OF 1806 *by Colonel Vachée*—The Napoleonic Method of Organisation and Command to the Battles of Jena & Auerstädt.

THE COMPLETE ADVENTURES IN THE CONNAUGHT RANGERS *by William Grattan*—The 88th Regiment during the Napoleonic Wars by a Serving Officer.

BUGLER AND OFFICER OF THE RIFLES *by William Green & Harry Smith*—With the 95th (Rifles) during the Peninsular & Waterloo Campaigns of the Napoleonic Wars.

NAPOLEONIC WAR STORIES *by Sir Arthur Quiller-Couch*—Tales of soldiers, spies, battles & sieges from the Peninsular & Waterloo campaigns.

CAPTAIN OF THE 95TH (RIFLES) *by Jonathan Leach*—An officer of Wellington's sharpshooters during the Peninsular, South of France and Waterloo campaigns of the Napoleonic wars.

RIFLEMAN COSTELLO *by Edward Costello*—The adventures of a soldier of the 95th (Rifles) in the Peninsular & Waterloo Campaigns of the Napoleonic wars.